# HEIDEGGER'S
# PHENOMENOLOGY
# OF PERCEPTION

# New Heidegger Research

## Series Editors

Gregory Fried, Professor of Philosophy, Boston College, USA
Richard Polt, Professor of Philosophy, Xavier University, USA

The *New Heidegger Research* series promotes informed and critical dialogue that breaks new philosophical ground by taking into account the full range of Heidegger's thought, as well as the enduring questions raised by his work.

## Titles in the Series:

# HEIDEGGER'S PHENOMENOLOGY OF PERCEPTION

## An Introduction, Volume I

DAVID KLEINBERG-LEVIN

ROWMAN & LITTLEFIELD
INTERNATIONAL
London • New York

Published by Rowman & Littlefield International Ltd
6 Tinworth Street, London, SE11 5AL, UK
www.rowmaninternational.com

Rowman & Littlefield International Ltd. is an affiliate of Rowman & Littlefield

4501 Forbes Boulevard, Suite 200, Lanham, Maryland 20706, USA
With additional offices in Boulder, New York, Toronto (Canada), and Plymouth
(UK)
www.rowman.com

**British Library Cataloguing in Publication Data**

A catalogue record for this book is available from the British Library

ISBN:   HB 978-1-78661-211-3
        PB 978-1-78661-212-0

Library of Congress Control Number: 2019949270

ISBN 978-1-78661-211-3 (cloth: alk. paper)
ISBN 978-1-78661-212-0 (pbk: alk. paper)
ISBN 978-1-78661-213-7 (electronic)

∞™ The paper used in this publication meets the minimum requirements of
American National Standard for Information Sciences—Permanence of Paper for
Printed Library Materials, ANSI/NISO Z39.48–1992.

# CONTENTS

# BIBLIOGRAPHICAL ABBREVIATIONS

Abbreviations for works by Heidegger cited or quoted

### Gesamtausgabe

GA 1       *Gesamtausgabe*, vol. 1. *Frühe Schriften* (1912–1916). Ed. Fried-rich-Wilhelm von Herrmann, 1978.

GA 2       *Gesamtausgabe*, vol. 2. *Sein und Zeit* (1927). Ed. Friedrich-Wilhelm von Herrmann, 1977. Also published separately by Max Niemeyer, Tübingen. First edition: 1927. The Seventh edition (1953) was used for the English translations.

GA 3       *Gesamtausgabe*, vol. 3. *Kant und das Problem der Metaphysik* (1929). Ed. Friedrich-Wilhelm von Herrmann, 1991. Second ed., 2010.

GA 4       *Gesamtausgabe*, vol. 4. *Erläuterungen zu Hölderlins Dichtung* (1936–1968). Ed. Friedrich-Wilhelm von Herrmann, 1981, 2012 (rev. ed.).

GA 5       *Gesamtausgabe*, vol. 5. *Holzwege* (1935–1946). Ed. Friedrich-Wilhelm von Hermann, 1977.

GA 6.1     *Gesamtausgabe*, vol. 6, Part 1. *Nietzsche* I (1936–1939). Ed. Brigitte Schillbach, 1996.

GA 6.2     *Gesamtausgabe*, vol. 6, Part 2. *Nietzsche* II (1939–1946). Ed. Brigitte Schillbach, 1997.

GA 7       *Gesamtausgabe*, vol. 7. *Vorträge und Aufsätze* (1936–1953). Ed. Friedrich-Wilhelm von Herrmann, 2000.

GA 8       *Gesamtausgabe*, vol. 8. *Was heißt Denken?* (1951–1952). Ed. Paola-Ludovika Coriando, 2002.

GA 9     *Gesamtausgabe*, vol. 9. *Wegmarken* (1919–1961). Ed. Friedrich-Wilhelm von Herrmann, 1976, 1996 (rev. ed.).

GA 10    *Gesamtausgabe*, vol. 10. *Der Satz vom Grund* (1955–1956). Ed. Petra Jaeger, 1997.

GA 11    *Gesamtausgabe*, vol. 11. *Identität und Differenz* (1955–1963). Ed. Friedrich-Wilhelm von Herrmann, 2006.

GA 12    *Gesamtausgabe*, vol. 12. *Unterwegs zur Sprache* (1950–1959). Ed. Friedrich-Wilhelm von Herrmann, 1985.

GA 13    *Gesamtausgabe*, vol. 13. *Aus der Erfahrung des Denkens* (1910–1976). Ed. Hermann Heidegger, 1983, 2002 (rev. ed.).

GA 14    *Gesamtausgabe*, vol. 14. *Zur Sache des Denkens* (1927–1968). Ed. Friedrich-Wilhelm von Herrmann, 2007.

GA 15    *Gesamtausgabe*, vol. 15. *Seminare* (1951–1973). Ed. Curd Ochwadt, 1986, 2005 (2nd rev. ed.).

GA 16    *Gesamtausgabe*, vol. 16. *Reden und andere Zeugnisse eines Lebensweges* (1910–1976). Ed. Hermann Heidegger, 2000.

GA 17    *Gesamtausgabe*, vol. 17. *Einführung in die phänomenologische Forschung* (1923–24). Ed. Friedrich-Wilhelm von Herrmann, 1994.

GA 19    *Gesamtausgabe*, vol. 19. *Platon: Sophistes* (1924–1925). Ed. Ingeborg Schüßler, 1992.

GA 20    *Gesamtausgabe*, vol. 20. *Prolegomena zur Geschichte des Zeitbegriffs* (1925). Ed. Petra Jaeger, 1979, 1988 (2nd rev. ed.), 1994 (3rd rev. ed.).

GA 21    *Gesamtausgabe*, vol. 21. *Logik. Die Frage nach der Wahrheit* (1925–1926). Ed. Walter Biemel, 1976, 1995 (rev. ed.).

GA 22    *Gesamtausgabe*, vol. 22. *Die Grundbegriffe der antiken Philosophie* (1926). Ed. Franz-Karl Blust, 1993.

GA 24    *Gesamtausgabe*, vol. 22. *Die Grundprobleme der Phänomenologie* (1927). Ed. Friedrich-Wilhelm von Herrmann, 1975.

GA 26    *Gesamtausgabe*, vol. 26. *Metaphysische Anfangsgründe der Logik im Ausgang von Leibniz* (1928). Ed. Klaus Held, 1978, 1990 (2nd rev. ed.), 2007 (3rd rev. ed.).

GA 27    *Gesamtausgabe*, vol. 27. *Einleitung in die Philosophie* (1928–1929). Ed. Otto Saame and Ina Saame-Speidel, 1996, 2001 (rev. ed.).

GA 28    *Gesamtausgabe*, vol. 28. *Der deutsche Idealismus (Fichte, Schelling, Hegel) und die philosophische Problemlage der Gegenwart* (1929). *Appendix*: "Einführung in das akademische Studium" (1929). Ed. Claudius Strube, 1997.

GA 29–30    *Gesamtausgabe*, vol. 29–30. *Die Grundbegriffe der Metaphysik. Welt—Endlichkeit—Einsamkeit* (1929–1930). Ed. Friedrich-Wilhelm von Herrmann, 1983.

GA 31    *Gesamtausgabe*, vol. 31. *Vom Wesen der menschlichen Freiheit. Einleitung in die Philosophie* (1930). Ed. Hartmut Tietjen, 1982, 1994 (rev. ed.).

GA 33    *Gesamtausgabe*, vol. 33. *Aristoteles, Metaphysik Θ 1–3. Von Wesen und Wirklichkeit der Kraft* (1931). Ed. Heinrich Hüni, 1981, 1990 (2nd rev. ed.), 2006 (3rd rev. ed.)

GA 34    *Gesamtausgabe*, vol. 34. *Vom Wesen der Wahrheit. Zu Platons Höhlengleichnis und Theätet* (1931–32). Ed. Hermann Mörchen, 1988, 1997 (rev. ed.).

GA 35    *Gesamtausgabe*, vol. 35. *Der Anfang der abendländischen Philosophie: Auslegung des Anaximander und Parmenides* (1932). Ed. Peter Trawny, 2011.

GA 36–37    *Gesamtausgabe*, vol. 36–37. *Sein und Wahrheit* (1933–1934). Ed. Hartmut Tietjen, 2001.

GA 39    *Gesamtausgabe*, vol. 39. *Hölderlins Hymnen "Germanien" und "Der Rhein"* (1934–1935). Ed. Susanne Ziegler, 1980, 1989 (rev. ed.).

GA 40    *Gesamtausgabe*, vol. 40. *Einführung in die Metaphysik* (1935). Ed. Petra Jaeger, 1983.

GA 41    *Gesamtausgabe*, vol. 41. *Die Frage nach dem Ding. Zu Kants Lehre von den transzendentalen Grundsätzen* (1935–1936). Ed. Petra Jaeger, 1984.

GA 42    *Gesamtausgabe*, vol. 42. *Schelling: Vom Wesen der menschlichen Freiheit* (1809) (1936). Ed. Ingrid Schüßler, 1988. Redacted version published separately by Max Niemeyer, Tübingen.

GA 43    *Gesamtausgabe*, vol. 43. *Nietzsche: Der Wille zur Macht als Kunst* (1936–1937). Ed. Bernd Heimbüchel, 1985.

GA 44    *Gesamtausgabe*, vol. 44. *Nietzsches metaphysische Grundstellung im abendländischen Denken: Die ewige Wiederkehr des Gleichen* (1937). Ed. Marion Heinz, 1986.

GA 45    *Gesamtausgabe*, vol. 45. *Grundfragen der Philosophie. Ausgewählte "Probleme" der "Logik"* (1937–38). Ed. Friedrich-Wilhelm von Herrmann, 1984.

GA 46    *Gesamtausgabe*, vol. 46. *Zur Auslegung von Nietzsches II. Unzeitgemäßer Betrachtung "Vom Nutzen und Nachteil der Historie für das Leben"* (1938–1939). Ed. Hans-Joachim Friedrich, 2003.

GA 47    *Gesamtausgabe*, vol. 47. *Nietzsches Lehre vom Willen zur Macht als Erkenntnis* (1939). Ed. Eberhard Hanser, 1989.

GA 48    *Gesamtausgabe*, vol. 48. *Nietzsche: Der europäische Nihilismus* (1940). Ed. Petra Jaeger, 1986.

GA 51    *Gesamtausgabe*, vol. 51. *Grundbegriffe* (1941). Ed. Petra Jaeger, 1981, 1991 (rev. ed.).

GA 52.    *Gesamtausgabe*, vol. 52. *Hölderlins Hymne "Andenken"* (1941–1942). Ed. Curd Ochwadt, 1982.

GA 53    *Gesamtausgabe*, vol. 53. *Hölderlins Hymne "Der Ister"* (1942). Ed. Walter Biemel, 1984.

GA 54    *Gesamtausgabe*, vol. 54. *Parmenides* (1942–1943). Ed. Manfred S. Frings, 1982.

GA 55    *Gesamtausgabe*, vol. 55. *Heraklit* (1943, 1944). Ed. Manfred S. Frings, 1979, 1987 (rev. ed.).

GA 58    *Gesamtausgabe*, vol. 58. *Grundprobleme der Phänomenologie* (1919–1920). Ed. Hans-Helmuth Gander, 1992.

GA 60    *Gesamtausgabe*, vol. 60. *Phänomenologie des religiösen Lebens* (1918–1921). Ed. Matthias Jung, Thomas Regehly, and Claudius Strube, 1995, 2011 (rev. ed.).

GA 61    *Gesamtausgabe*, vol. 61. *Phänomenologische Interpretationen zu Aristoteles. Einführung in die phänomenologische Forschung* (1921–1922). Ed. Walter Bröcker und Käte Bröcker-Oltmanns, 1985, 1994 (rev. ed.).

GA 63    *Gesamtausgabe*, vol. 63. *Ontologie. Hermeneutik der Faktizität* (1923). Ed. Käte Bröcker-Oltmanns, 1988.

GA 64    *Gesamtausgabe*, vol. 64. *Der Begriff der Zeit* (Vortrag 1924). Ed. Friedrich-Wilhelm von Herrmann, 2004.

GA 65    *Gesamtausgabe*, vol. 65. *Beiträge zur Philosophie (Vom Ereignis)* (1936–1938). Ed. Friedrich-Wilhelm von Herrmann, 1989, 1994 (rev. ed.).

GA 66    *Gesamtausgabe*, vol. 66. *Besinnung* (1938–1939). Ed. Friedrich-Wilhelm von Herrmann, 1997.

GA 67    *Gesamtausgabe*, vol. 67. *Metaphysik und Nihilismus* (1938–1939, 1946–1948). Ed. Hans-Joachim Friedrich, 1999.

GA 69    *Gesamtausgabe*, vol. 69. *Die Geschichte des Seyns* (1938–1940). Ed. Peter Trawny, 1998, 2012 (rev. ed.).

GA 70    *Gesamtausgabe*, vol. 70. *Über den Anfang* (1941). Ed. Paola-Ludovika Coriando, 2005.

GA 71    *Gesamtausgabe*, vol. 71. *Das Ereignis* (1941–1942). Ed. Friedrich-Wilhelm von Herrmann, 2009.

| | |
|---|---|
| GA 72 | *Gesamtausgabe,* vol. 72. *Die Stege des Anfangs* (1944). Ed. Friedrich-Wilhelm von Herrmann. |
| GA 73.1 | *Gesamtausgabe,* vol. 73.1. *Zum Ereignis-Denken* (1932–1970s). Ed. Peter Trawny, 2013. |
| GA 73.2 | *Gesamtausgabe,* vol. 73.2 *Zum Ereignis-Denken* (1932–1970s). Ed. Peter Trawny, 2013. |
| GA 77 | *Gesamtausgabe,* vol. 77. *Feldweg-Gespräche* (1944–1945). Ed. Ingrid Schüßler, 1995, 2007 (2nd rev. ed.). |
| GA 79 | *Gesamtausgabe,* vol. 79. *Bremer und Freiburger Vorträge. 1. Einblick in das was ist: Bremer Vorträge 1949. Das Ding—Das Ge-stell—Die Gefahr—Die Kehre. 2. Grundsätze des Denkens: Freiburger Vorträge 1957.* Ed. Petra Jaeger, 1994. |
| GA 81 | *Gesamtausgabe,* vol. 81. *Gedachtes* (1910–1970). Ed. Paola-Ludovika Coriando, 2007. |
| GA 82 | *Gesamtausgabe,* vol. 82. *Zu eigenen Veröffentlichungen.* Ed. Friedrich-Wilhelm von Herrmann, 2018. |
| GA 89 | *Gesamtausgabe,* vol. 89. *Zollikoner Seminare* (1959–1969). Ed. Peter Trawny, 2017. |
| GA 94 | *Gesamtausgabe,* vol. 94. *Überlegungen II–-VI (Schwarze Hefte 1931–1938).* Ed. Peter Trawny, 2014. |
| GA 95 | *Gesamtausgabe,* vol. 95. *Überlegungen VII–-XI (Schwarze Hefte 1938–1939).* Ed. Peter Trawny, 2014. |
| GA 96 | *Gesamtausgabe,* vol. 96. *Überlegungen XII–-XV (Schwarze Hefte 1939–1941).* Ed. Peter Trawny, 2014. |
| GA 97 | *Gesamtausgabe,* vol. 97. *Anmerkungen I–-V (Schwarze Hefte 1942–1948).* Ed. Peter Trawny, 2015. |

About the *Gesamtausgabe* volumes and their English translations consulted and abbreviations.

[Note 1]. Not all the volumes of the *Gesamtausgabe* have been translated into English. [Note 2]. In the translation of some GA volumes, texts appearing together there have been separated, so their translation will only be found scattered in more than one English publication. [Note 3]. Most of the published translations I have used have been modified after I consulted the original German texts. In presenting these altered translations, in some cases altered in major ways, I have not hesitated to exercise a freedom that some scholars will no doubt challenge. Communicating and sharing the meaning is more important than dogmatic devotion to all the words. Judgment is required. But I have attempted, as much as possible, to make the thought that the texts convey more easily accessible and more comprehensible, giving words to the philosopher's thought that might faithfully and adequately express it in more idiomatic English. At this moment in time, I consider that attempt to be more important than producing translations that reproduce with obsessive exactitude the awkward grammar and style that expresses and reflects Heidegger's struggles to say something profoundly new and difficult. [Note 4]. The German text will be referenced first, and the English translation will follow.

AM      *Aristotle's "Metaphysics" Θ 1–3: On the Essence and Actuality of Force.* Trans. Walter Brogan and Peter Warnek. Bloomington: Indiana University Press, 1995.

BaT     *Being and Truth.* Trans. Gregory Fried and Richard Polt. Bloomington: Indiana University Press, 2010.

BC      *Basic Concepts.* Trans. Gary E. Aylesworth. Bloomington: Indiana University Press, 1993.

BCAP    *Basic Concepts of Ancient Philosophy.* Trans. Richard Rojcewicz. Bloomington: Indiana University Press, 1997.

BF      *Bremen and Freiburg Lectures: Insight into That Which Is and Basic Principles of Thinking.* Trans. Andrew Mitchell. Bloomington: Indiana University Press, 2012.

BPP     *The Basic Problems of Phenomenology.* Trans. Albert Hofstadter. Bloomington: Indiana University Press, 1982.

BPPh    *Basic Problems of Phenomenology: Winter Semester 1919/1920.* Trans. Scott M. Campbell. London: Continuum, 2013.

BQP     *Basic Questions of Philosophy: Selected "Problems" of "Logic."* Trans. Richard Rojcewicz and André Schuwer. Bloomington: Indiana University Press, 1994.

BT      *Being and Time.* Trans. John Macquarrie and Edward Robinson. New York: Harper & Row, 1962.

BTS     *Being and Time.* Trans. Joan Stambaugh. Revised and with a foreword by Dennis J. Schmidt. Albany: State University of New York Press, 2010.

BWP     *The Beginning of Western Philosophy: Interpretation of Anaximander and Parmenides.* Trans. Richard Rojcewicz. Bloomington: Indiana University Press, 2015.

CP      *Contributions to Philosophy (Of the Event).* Trans. Richard Rojcewicz and Daniela Vallega-Neu. Bloomington: Indiana University Press, 2012.

CPC     *Country Path Conversations.* Trans. Bret Davis. Bloomington: Indiana University Press, 2010.

CPE    *Contributions to Philosophy (From Enowning)*. Trans. Parvis Emad and Kenneth Maly. Bloomington: Indiana University Press, 1999.

CT    *The Concept of Time. The First Draft of "Being and Time."* Trans. Ingo Farin. London: Continuum, 2011. Also see *The Concept of Time* (bilingual edition). Trans. William McNeill (Oxford: Blackwell, 1992) and "The Concept of Time" in *Becoming Heidegger: On the Trail of His Early Occasional Writings, 1910–1927.* Ed. Theodore Kisiel and Thomas Sheehan, 1st ed. (Evanston, IL: Northwestern University Press, 2007).

DT    *Discourse on Thinking*. Trans. John M. Anderson and E. Hans Freund. New York: Harper & Row, 1966.

E    *The Event*. Trans. Richard Rojcewicz. Bloomington: Indiana University Press, 2013.

EF    *Schelling's Treatise on the Essence of Human Freedom*. Translation of the Niemeyer edition. Trans. Joan Stambaugh. Athens: Ohio University Press, 1985.

EGT    *Early Greek Thinking*. Trans. David F. Krell and Frank A. Capuzzi. New York: Harper & Row, 1975.

EHF    *The Essence of Human Freedom: An Introduction to Philosophy*. Trans. Ted Sadler. London: Continuum, 2002.

EP    *The End of Philosophy*. Trans. Joan Stambaugh. New York: Harper & Row, 1973.

ET    *The Essence of Truth: On Plato's Cave Allegory and "Theaetetus."* Trans. Ted Sadler. London: Continuum, 2002.

FCM    *The Fundamental Concepts of Metaphysics: World, Finitude, Solitude*. Trans. William McNeill and Nicholas Walker. Bloomington: Indiana University Press, 1995.

FS    *Four Seminars*. Trans. Andrew Mitchell and François Raffoul. Bloomington: Indiana University Press, 2003.

GI    *German Idealism*. Trans. Peter Warnek. Bloomington: Indiana University Press.

H    *Heraclitus: The Inception of Occidental Thinking and Logic: Heraclitus' Doctrine of the Logos*. Trans. Julia Goesser Assaiante and Shane Ewegen. London: Bloomsbury, 2018.

HB    *The History of Beyng*. Trans. William McNeill and Jeffrey Powell. Bloomington: Indiana University Press, 2015.

HCT    *History of the Concept of Time: Prolegomena*. Trans. Theodore Kisiel. Bloomington: Indiana University Press, 1992.

HGR    *Hölderlin's Hymns "Germania" and "The Rhine."* Trans. William McNeill and Julia Ireland. Bloomington: Indiana University Press, 2014.

HI *Hölderlin's Hymn "The Ister."* Trans. William McNeill and Julia Davis. Bloomington: Indiana University Press, 1996.

HP *Elucidations of Hölderlin's Poetry.* Trans. Keith Hoeller. Amherst, NY: Humanity Books, 2000.

HR *Hölderlin's Hymn "Remembrance."* Trans. William McNeill and Julia Ireland. Bloomington: Indiana University Press, 2018.

HS *Martin Heidegger and Eugen Fink. Heraclitus Seminar 1966/67.* Trans. Charles Seibert. Tuscaloosa: University of Alabama Press, 1979. Reprint: Evanston, IL: Northwestern University Press, 1993.

ID *Identity and Difference.* Trans. Joan Stambaugh. New York: Harper & Row, 1969.

IM *Introduction to Metaphysics.* Trans. Gregory Fried and Richard Polt. New Haven, CT: Yale University Press, 2000.

IMM *An Introduction to Metaphysics.* Trans. Ralph Manheim. New Haven, CT: Yale University Press, 1959.

IP *Introduction to Philosophy.* Trans. William McNeill. Bloomington: Indiana University Press.

IPR *Introduction to Phenomenological Research.* Trans. Daniel O. Dahlstrom. Bloomington: Indiana University Press, 2005.

KPM *Kant and the Problem of Metaphysics.* Trans. Richard Taft. 5th enlarged ed. Bloomington: Indiana University Press, 1997.

LQT *Logic: The Question of Truth.* Trans. Thomas Sheehan. Bloomington: Indiana University Press, 2010.

M *Mindfulness.* Trans. Parvis Emad and Thomas Kalary. London: Continuum, 2006.

MFL *The Metaphysical Foundations of Logic.* Trans. Michael Heim. Bloomington: Indiana University Press, 1984.

N *Nietzsche.* Ed. and Trans. David Farrell Krell. 4 vols. New York: Harper and Row, 1979–1987. Translation includes revised versions of GA volumes 43, 44, 47, and 48.

N1 *Nietzsche, vol. I: The Will to Power as Art (1936–1937).* See GA 6.1 and GA 43

N2 *Nietzsche, vol. II: The Eternal Recurrence of the Same and the Will to Power (1937).* See GA 6.2 and GA 44.

N3 *Nietzsche, vol. III: The Will to Power as Knowledge and as Metaphysics (1940).* See GA 6.1 and GA 47.

N4 Nietzsche, *Nihilism (1939).* See GA 6.1 and GA 48.

NUM *Interpretation of Nietzsche's Second Untimely Meditation.* Trans. Ullrich Haase and Mark Sinclair. Bloomington: Indiana University Press, 2016.

OBT     *Off the Beaten Track*. Trans. Julian Young and Kenneth Haynes. Cambridge: Cambridge University Press, 2002.

OHF     *Ontology—The Hermeneutics of Facticity*. Trans. John Van Buren. Bloomington: Indiana University Press, 1999.

OTB     *On Time and Being*. Trans. Joan Stambaugh. New York: Harper & Row, 1972.

OWL     *On the Way to Language*. Trans. Peter D. Hertz and Joan Stambaugh. New York: Harper & Row, 1971.

P       *Parmenides*. Trans. André Schuwer and Richard Rojcewicz. Bloomington: Indiana University Press, 1992.

PIA     *Phenomenological Interpretations of Aristotle: Initiation into Phenomenological Research*. Trans. Richard Rojcewicz. Bloomington: Indiana University Press, 2008.

PLT     *Poetry, Language, Thought*. Trans. Albert Hofstadter. New York: Harper & Row, 1971.

PM      *Pathmarks*. Ed. William McNeill. Cambridge: Cambridge University Press, 1998.

PR      *The Principle of Reason*. Trans. Reginald Lilly. Bloomington: Indiana University Press, 1991.

PRL     *The Phenomenology of Religious Life*. Trans. Matthias Fritsch and Jennifer Anna Gosetti-Ferencei. Bloomington: Indiana University Press, 2004.

PS      *Plato's "Sophist."* Trans. Richard Rojcewicz and André Schuwer. Bloomington: Indiana University Press, 1997.

P2      *Ponderings II–VI: Black Notebooks 1931–1938*. Trans. Richard Rojcewicz. Bloomington: Indiana University Press, 2016.

P7      *Ponderings VII–XI: Black Notebooks 1938–1939*. Trans. Richard Rojcewicz. Bloomington: Indiana University Press, 2017.

P12     *Ponderings XII–XV: Black Notebooks 1939–1941*. Trans. Richard Rojcewicz. Bloomington: Indiana University Press, 2017.

QCT     *The Question Concerning Technology and Other Essays*. Trans. William Lovitt. New York: Harper & Row, 1977.

QT      *The Question Concerning the Thing*. Trans. James Reid and Benjamin Crowe. London: Rowman & Littlefield International. Translates GA 41.

RZL     *Reden und andere Zeugnisse eines Lebensweges* (1910–1976). Ed. Hermann Heidegger, 2000.

WIP     *What Is Philosophy?* Trans. Jean T. Wilde and William Kluback. New Haven, CT: College and University Press, 1958.

WCT    *What Is Called Thinking?* Trans. J. Glenn Gray. New York: Harper & Row, 1968.

WT     *What Is a Thing?* Trans. W. B. Barton and Vera Deutsch. Chicago: Henry Regnery Company, 1967. Translates GA 41.

ZSE    *Translation: Zollikon Seminars: Protocols—Conversations—Letters.* Trans. Franz Mayr and Richard Askay. Evanston, IL: Northwestern University Press, 2001. This is a translation only of *Zollikoner Seminare: Protokolle, Gespräche, Briefe.* Ed. Medard Boss. Frankfurt am Main: Klostermann, 1987.

ZSG    Not in the *Gesamtausgabe*: *Zollikoner Seminare: Protokolle, Gespräche, Briefe.* Ed. Medard Boss. Frankfurt am Main: Klostermann, 1987.

# ACKNOWLEDGMENTS

For their generous encouragement and support over the years, I want to thank Lawrence Berger, Richard Capobianco, Edward Casey, Françoise Dastur, Peter Fenves, Gregory Fried, Wayne Froman, Lawrence Hatab, David Krell, Reginald Lilly, Thomas McCarthy, Richard Polt, François Raffoul, Robert Scharff, Dennis Schmidt, Thomas Sheehan, and David C. Wood. They have been, for me, important interlocutors—although, of course, readers should not assume that they are necessarily acquainted with, and in any case would concur with, the interpretations and extrapolations in this volume. Plainly enough, on certain matters, some do not at all concur. But often, thoughtful disagreement proves to be more fruitful than happy consensus.

# EPIGRAMS

The question of existence can be brought to clarity only in the course of existing itself.

—Martin Heidegger, *Being and Time*

What is in question is a transformation in the human way of being.

—Heidegger, *Basic Questions of Philosophy*

Learning from living, become who you [already] are!
γένοι' οἶος ἐσσί μαθών

—Pindar, *Pythian Odes*

# PREFACE

## The Project and Its Key Words

> Today thinking must make itself alarming [*anstößig*] in order
> to jolt us into experiencing for the very first time the passion
> of thinking [*die Leidenschaft des Denkens*] and urge us to learn,
> and put into practice [*üben*] the difference [*Unterscheidung*]
> that such genuine, underlying thinking could make in every-
> day life.
>
> —Heidegger, *The Event* (GA 71: 252/E 217)

This is the first volume of a two-volume work. Whereas the *second* volume is an attempt to glean from Martin Heidegger's writings a timely
contribution to the hermeneutics and phenomenology of perception,
concentrating on the disclosive *capacities* and *capabilities* of two organs of
perception fundamental in our bodily engagement in the world—seeing
and hearing—in order to formulate a historically informed critique of the
Western world and its metaphysics, the *first* volume is an introduction to
Heidegger's project, proposing, in phenomenologically grounded terms, an
interpretation of what I consider to be the five key words in his project,
namely, (i) *Sein*, (ii) *Da-sein*, (iii) *Ereignis*, (iv) *Lichtung*, and (v) *Geschick*,
showing the complications confronting even reasonable assumptions about
what these words must mean, as the more we ponder them, the more their
meaning seems to be far from transparent, far from settled. In a correspondingly ordered but simplified and purely preliminary interpretation, these
key words might be translated as (i) being, (ii) the essential nature of human
existence, (iii) event of appropriation, (iv) clearing, and (v) destiny. These
translations need to be amended because as Heidegger worked with these
words, their common and familiar meanings gave way to the unfolding
and disclosing of strange new meanings, raising challenging questions, and

calling us to thought. The translation of these key words from Heidegger's German into comprehensible English consequently requires debatable interpretive decisions and intricate argument. In fact, as I shall argue, each of the key words unfolds into more than one meaning, not only making it necessary that we undertake the work of explication and interpretation but also compelling thoughtful ventures in the hermeneutics of translation.

The two volumes may be read independently. If read together, however, these two volumes set out to explore seeing and hearing as disclosive capacities, or capabilities, considered in terms of a hermeneutical phenomenology and in the light not only of Heidegger's searing critique of contemporary life and the historical character of its perception but also of his visionary projection of a transformed world.

The first volume concentrates on an interpretation of Heidegger's five key words, showing how they work together to introduce and unfold the logic of his great project. The second volume lays out the history-making significance of this project for the character of our seeing and hearing, working through in some detail Heidegger's twofold critique—a critique of our contemporary life and world and a critique of the history of metaphysics—exploring the purport of those critiques for a possible future in which the paradigmatic character of our ways of seeing and hearing could undergo a process of profound transformation. As Wordsworth expressed it, in question is the transformation "of all the mighty world/Of eye, and ear,—both what they half create,/And what perceive."[1]

In both volumes, it is argued that, for Heidegger, what is ultimately crucial is our assumption of responsibility, even in the realm of perception, for our embodied nature as sentient, percipient beings who are thrown open to experience, cast into a world where we are compelled for a time to sojourn in its inexhaustible dimensions, making the meaning of its opportunities our own as we venture our way.

Now, in this first volume, following Heidegger's own project and method, I shall engage a phenomenology of perception in the context of a comprehensive critique of the modern world and a corresponding critique of the history of Western metaphysics that shows how, even as it reflects theoretically and critically on that world, Western metaphysics remains a problematic reflection of it.

Summarized in a highly condensed form, but also showing something of the implicit "logic" in how the five key words are woven together to compose a compelling narrative, the argument I am making in this volume and further developing and demonstrating in the second volume, where I concentrate on our experience in seeing and hearing, is that the question of being (*Sein*), which organizes the entire enquiry in *Being and Time* as well as all Heidegger's subsequent works, summons us to recognize, understand, and acknowledge, or enown, our ownmost responsibility (our *Er-eignis*, *Er-eignung*) as *Da-sein*, grounders and guardians of the functioning of the clearings (*Lichtungen*) our existence involves, opening and laying down the conditions that make worlds of meaning possible. This calls us to a history-making task: (i) retrieving forgotten historical opportunities from the past we inherited and (ii) exploring the ontological possibilities and opportunities that appear in the givenness of the historical situations we find ourselves in. At stake in this project, as Heidegger conceives it, is a profound questioning of the very meaning of being, the conditions of intelligibility for the experiencing of what is an ontological task for the sake of our shared destiny (*Geschick*)—a profound transformation of humanity and the world. Ultimately, this means taking responsibility for our existence and our world, both as individuals and as members of various historical and cultural communities.

†

There are many ways of reading and interpreting Heidegger's project of thought. Their differences, even when conflicting and seeming to be irreconcilable, are not necessarily to be regretted. They can, on the contrary, be fruitful. I imagine that, drawing on the prevailing consensus, there will be arguments against my interpretation of Heidegger's thought. And I imagine that there will be objections appealing to specific passages in Heidegger's texts. Things could hardly be otherwise, considering that, as I read him, the five key words with which Heidegger was working his project are given multiple uses. But unless I am engaged merely in repeating with other words what Heidegger has already said, rather than trying to unfold what might be carried, unsaid, within his thinking, there cannot always be textual passages saying precisely what I am attempting to say. Often in the course of struggling to translate the philosopher's words into understandable English, I concluded that, for the sake of rendering a worthy interpretation, there were compelling grounds for preferring to formulate something closer to a paraphrase. So, I am not necessarily troubled, if certain features of the interpretation offered in this volume do not have unequivocal confirmation from certain passages in Heidegger's texts. I welcome such divergences as provocations for all of us to continue questioning and thinking. I intend this work to be suggestive, provocative, and polemical, even challenging Heidegger himself as well as the numerous scholars from whose interpretations, commentaries, and thoughtful engagements with Heidegger's texts I have been able to benefit.

†

I greatly respect, and wish to honor, much in Heidegger's words, but I am more concerned with what they might plausibly be taken to imply or suggest than I am with proposing an interpretation that claims an uncontroversial, strictly correct understanding—one that neatly fits everything he ever thought to say. In deference to the text, Heidegger's words, I will not claim to offer here the one and only true, or correct, reading, but only to take over, and work with, what his words might possibly open and expose for further thought. If my interpretation makes sense, and if the sense that it makes serves in some small measure to illuminate the world we are living in, then I shall be quite satisfied, feeling abundantly rewarded for my many years of inhabiting Heidegger's thought, years struggling to understand, make sense, and draw out from it what might be beneficial to think about, not only for the fulfillment of our most worthy hopes and intentions for the future of humanity but also for the future prosperity of the earth and sky and all the plants and animals dependent on their bounty.

Fidelity to a great philosopher's thought cannot be, indeed must not be, slavish repetition or parrot-like imitation. Nor, for that matter, praise and reverence. After all, Heidegger's own thinking underwent significant changes of mind, uncanny turns and twists. And there are, confided here and there in his writings, indications of hesitation and dissatisfaction regarding what he is saying. Occasionally, there are even what seem to be equivocations and inconsistencies—indications of uncertainties, traces of ambivalence, changes of mind, and experiments in thought, trying out different possibilities. And considering the estranging terminological innovations, terms with multiple meanings, it would not be entirely surprising if we should find what seem to be some unresolved and indeed unresolvable ambiguities in Heidegger's thinking—ambiguities he must not have been aware of or ambiguities he himself, despite great struggle, was not able to settle. Most troublesome are terms that are not recognized as merely formal indications and locutions, such as those using "*des Seins*," which express his thinking in a way that can all too easily tempt readers into hypostatizing being, or that even suggests his own lapse into hypostatization, as if "being" were the name of an independent entity. (Be it noted here that I take this dangerous temptation so seriously that I will not ever spell the word *being* using a capital letter—not even when quoting texts that do capitalize it.) However, these traces, vestiges of his enormous struggles as a path-breaking, ground-breaking thinker, in no way diminish the greatness of his project of thought.

Problems understanding what Heidegger is thinking are especially acute and challenging with regard to his history of metaphysics. Heidegger has a very important narrative to tell: a comprehensive, richly deep, and powerfully compelling history of philosophy, presented in the pursuit of the question of being. But the problem is that this narrative, in my judgment his most significant and most enduring contribution to philosophical thought, gets inextricably entangled in a philosophy of history and a history of the meaning of being that are deeply stressed and problematic: not only confusing and full of ambiguities that suggest changes of mind and struggles with unresolved, and perhaps unresolvable, tensions, even conflicting dispositions, within his own thinking but also freighted with terminology that seems at times, especially during the years of the Second World War, to bend his narrative in the direction of a dangerous ideology and an apocalyptic eschatology. Something of this orientation is already present in *Being and Time* (1927), notably in his discussion of the inheritance, in Germany, of its history and the nation's commitment to an exemplary mission and destiny. Every one of the terms in the constellation of terms that his history of being engages—but above all, *Ereignis* and *Geschick*—is problematic in at least two ways: first, because it is not at all clear or certain what the terms mean and what the philosopher is trying to say, and second, because they seem, in certain texts, to lend themselves to interpretations that not only perpetuate the very metaphysics he is determined to overcome but also encourage a theological, apocalyptic vision of history, informing, and shaping—or, as I would say, distorting—his narrative reading of the history of philosophy. What are we to make of such texts? There is at least one textual note, one that we shall consider, in which Heidegger seems to repudiate altogether, expressing himself in exceptionally vehement words, the very idea of an ontological history, a *Seinsgeschichte*, together with the constellation of terms that the notion engaged. What I think he renounces and wants to abandon, however, is not his comprehensive historical narrative regarding the course of philosophical representations of being but rather the onto-theological *metaphysics* of being. It is not difficult to understand why he would do that. But it is not entirely clear that he actually did abandon it, although in his later, post-War years, these ideas were, if not abandoned, at least left in the keeping of silence. Be that as it may, I shall work with his narrative, but attempt to give it, and the constellation of terms it involves, an interpretation that makes sense. I shall not claim, however, that it is an interpretation that, in all respects, he would have favored.

†

On July 25, 1934, while Heidegger was writing about the greatness of National Socialism, André Gide penned in his *Journals*: "Wherever my gaze turns, I see around me only distress. He who remains contemplative today demonstrates either an inhuman philosophy or a monstrous blindness."[2] Although written before he could have known of Heidegger's collaboration, these words serve well as a fitting indictment of the German philosopher and a contemplative cast of mind that, even as it reaches into the sublime, sometimes seems inhuman. The philosopher who speaks in such lofty and exalted terms of *das Kommende* could neither see nor hear the danger that others sensed to be coming. And now, today, all Heidegger's thought suffers suspicion and rejection because of his ill-conceived complicity in the genocidal politics of Hitler's Germany. But I submit that ultimately, and most importantly, what makes the recently published revelations contained in Heidegger's wartime "Black Notebooks" an event to be welcomed is not the shameful truth about his character that they belatedly confirm, and not the revisions and refinements of his earlier thought that he consigned to them, but rather that these revelations of character— his ignoble arrogance, his contemptible provincial small-mindedness, his mean-spirited, hate-filled prejudices, his mindless invocation of medieval folkish superstition, and his unforgivable participation in the Nazis' rise to power—and passages in the writings that reveal philosophically significant uncertainties, confusions, ambiguities, inconsistencies, and major changes of mind finally—finally—release us from too many years during which much scholarly endeavor worked in the compass of his thought as if under a spell, as if bewitched, unable to break away from a certain reverence, devotion, and loyalty—or, in a word, idolatry. So, I think that, thanks to these "Notebooks," we scholars are finally *free* to take from Heidegger whatever it is we have learned from him and to continue on our own, without any need for apologies, the forever-beckoning adventure of philosophical thought.

That said, it has not been easy for me, a Jew who lost family relatives in the Holocaust, to persevere in this project, working with the texts of Heidegger's philosophical thought. Why, then, have I not simply abandoned my project, ceasing to think with Heidegger? I am working with his thought because of what, in it, remains worthy of our engagement. In brief, I consider his most enduring contributions to be (1) an insightful and boldly challenging reading, comprehensive in its reach, of the history of Western philosophy and, above all, the Western discourse of metaphysics, from the pre-Socratics to and through the neo-Kantians and Husserl; (2) a very compelling critique of Western philosophy that is based on this reading and attempts to deconstruct, and move beyond, its metaphysical foundations and scaffolding; (3) corresponding to this critique of metaphysics, an equally compelling critique of the increasing technologization [*Machenschaft*] and dehumanization of life in the Western world; and finally (4) the sketch of a utopian vision, suggesting the character of a transformed humankind living in a poetically transformed relation to one another and to the whole of nature. These constitute a truly extraordinary contribution—not only to the discourse of philosophical thought but also to the understanding and very living of our lives in a time of momentous challenges, confusing and in some ways frightening.

Ultimately, for me at least, the question this volume should leave its readers with is whether or not my reading can, on its own, yield a coherent, compelling, and fruitful account that makes sense of our world, the world we have inherited and are obliged to try interpreting in a way that opens possibilities and opportunities for the future. What is accomplished must be worthy of thought, attempting, as far as possible, to take the discussion into what Heidegger calls "the open clearing," where, like a bolt of lightning, the new just might emerge. Only that is genuine fidelity to the matter—the *Sache*—with which Heidegger has entrusted us.

†

One of the ways of approaching and interpreting the matter of Heidegger's project concentrates on his critique of the modern world. This is a critique inspired in large measure by Nietzsche, which sees the world suffering under the increasing nihilism and dehumanization that the institutions and technologies we created in our reckless will to power are imposing.

Heidegger's project, however, is much more than a critique; it is also an attempt to imagine the possibility of a different, better world. As he says forcefully in *Being and Time*: "Higher than actuality stands possibility. We can understand phenomenology only by seizing upon it as concerned with possibility" (GA 2: 51–52/BT 63). Consequently, we shall also explore what his project implies for the transformation in the character of our seeing and hearing. In this regard, I want to propose, as rewarding for our own thinking, a reading of Heidegger that ultimately brings out for our consideration the significance of his project as a contribution to what Schiller called "the aesthetic education of man," a reading, therefore, that finds in the philosopher's thought his distinctly original inheritance of nineteenth-century German idealism and romanticism: inspiration from the philosophers and poets who, in one way or another, envisioned some kind of transformation in the consciousness and character of the human being, a more enlightened, more humane, and more poetic way of living. And they accordingly gave thought to the importance of encouraging processes and stages in the education and development of our senses and sensibilities as well as our power of imagination and our cognitive ability to construct new concepts for critical understanding, knowledge, and invention. Like this earlier generation of German poets and philosophers, Heidegger understood that in the philosophical project he was envisioning, such education and development would be essential. For first of all we need to recognize and understand ourselves: who we are and what we are capable of, both as individuals and as communities.

Transformation gets underway when, even in the most prosaic act of perception, its phenomenology as world disclosive is recognized: not only (i) the fact that perception is inherently the laying out of the conditions necessary for worlds of intelligibility and meaning but also (ii) the fact that everything meaningfully disclosed in those worlds takes place in the tension of an interplay between concealment and unconcealment and, moreover, (iii) the fact that we are in large measure responsible for protecting and preserving the conditions that make the disclosive phenomenology of that interplay possible. It is not sufficient that, simply by existing, we *are* (always already) world-disclosive; it is crucial that we *become reflectively mindful* of our role, our participation, hence responsibility, in sustaining the dynamics—the hermeneutical dimensions—of that phenomenology. That is the task enjoined by what Heidegger calls *Einkehr in das Ereignis*: entering into the event and process of our appropriation (GA 14: 49–50/OTB 40–41).

†

In "The Method of Nature," Ralph Waldo Emerson bids us to consider: What can be achieved "as the eyes of men open to their capabilities"?[3] In the modern world, Western metaphysics, reflecting the character of our quotidian lives, reduces the inherent openness of the perceptual field to a subject–object structure that forgets our preconceptually undifferentiated, interactive belonging together with being. Prereflectively, hence always *already*, before self-awareness and self-understanding, our seeing and hearing are ontologically attuned organs: organs intrinsically attuned by their given nature to the very *being* of the beings we see and hear. But they are also *not yet* ontologically attuned: that prereflective, preconceptual attunement only constitutes the first phase of their given potential. That potential, undergoing suppression in the prevailing nihilism of our time, is the granting of a promise, a *Versprechung*, that requires of us a difficult process of transformation.[4] The potential needs to be recognized, understood, enowned, and finally enacted; it needs to be actualized. Our appropriation is the task. And the "promise" that, significantly, the philosopher emphatically invokes in his critical commentary on Nietzsche abides in the claim of our appropriation.

†

For me, *die Leidenschaft des Denkens* carries a doubled meaning in this regard, at once affirming a passionate, binding commitment to thinking while also recognizing the sympathy and sorrow that responsible thinking must learn to carry today for the sake of understanding and resisting all that is oppressive, and offering hope in preparing for a transformation of the world worthy of our still-to-be-achieved humanity. This *Leidenschaft* is what the ancient Greek philosophers and tragedians called "pathos." We shall discuss the importance of *pathos* in the chapter on appropriation (*Er-eignung*).

The two-volume work I am offering, wrought from many years of thought, years during which my thinking has been intensively engaged with Heidegger's texts, is about learning to see and hear—see and hear better, see and hear differently, see and hear more attentively, more caringly, and perhaps more wisely. At stake is the retrieving and developing of a potential intrinsic to our perception such that it would be more in touch with our ethical and moral sensibilities. This is surely of the greatest importance, insofar as Heidegger's project is intended to be, uniquely and at once, both ontological and historical, arguing for a revolutionary, history-making transformation in our way of being human and, correspondingly, in the world we live in, where how, in all our engagements with this world, we are understanding the very meaning of being determines the fate of all entities, all beings—everything that in any way is, including ourselves.

This requires our appropriation (*Ereignis*), the process in which, after getting lost in the self-estrangement that we undergo in entering the social-cultural world, we "come back" to ourselves: recognizing, understanding, taking up and making one's own, or enowning, the *claim* of appropriation, our responsibilities for what takes place in the formation of meaning within the realm of perception: a claim appropriating us, first and foremost, to acknowledge and assume responsibility for the *character* of our response abilities, our capabilities in response to all that we encounter in the clearings we, as *Da-sein*, essentially *are*—and consequently appropriating us to enown and assume responsibility for the character of the worlds of meaning that our existence clears, the *Spiel-Räume* within the dimensions of which entities meaningfully emerge, stay for a while, and vanish in the interplay of concealment and unconcealment. Thus, engaged by, and in, this appropriation, our care taking role in the clearings, the various worlds of our projects, we make it possible for whatever things (entities, beings) we encounter in those worlds, those clearings, to be present and absent *as they are*, disclosed in their phenomenological truth.

†

In *Being and Time*, Heidegger, recalling the Socratic thought, says that the human being is that being for whom its being is—and should be—always in question. Always being in question, and always putting ourselves in question, are what define our humanity. We cannot get to know ourselves and live up to the humanity constitutive of our potential, without that questioning, even questioning our most fundamental assumptions about what constitutes our ideal of humanity. In fact, all that we encounter in the world addresses us with the following questions: Who are we, we beings who call ourselves human? What does our way of seeing and hearing tell us about ourselves—about our way of being human and our understanding of what it means to be human? What can we learn from the things we are seeing and hearing about the corresponding *character* of our seeing and hearing? These questions make a claim on our responsibility—a responsibility that engages our ability, in perception, to be appropriately responsive to what it is that we encounter in our journey through the world.

To think of perception—seeing and hearing—as disclosive capacities or capabilities is to question them not only in regard to what and how they are but also in regard to their potential, their promise, hence their development. Do we know what these modes of perception, these perceptual capacities are capable of? If our ways of seeing and hearing, our ways of receiving what is given to be perceived affect how the world presents itself, or how the world is, then changes in the character of our seeing and hearing might correspondingly change the world in ways that might resist, or even overcome, the forces of nihilism that Heidegger sees increasingly devastating our world and threatening our very existence as human beings. Consequently, the argument proposed in this volume and in the volume that follows bears on the historical conditions of the Western world and on the history of a metaphysics indebted to a paradigm of knowledge, truth, and reality generated by certain experiences with vision—a vision the character of which needs to be subjected to interrogation. There is much that we can learn about perception from thinking with—and after—Heidegger.

What I am interested in doing, after Heidegger (in both senses of that word "after"), is (i) spelling out the *development* of our modes of perception based on (ii) the recognition that these modes of perception (seeing, hearing) are *capacities* and *capabilities* and on (iii) the recognition that *capacities and capabilities are such that they can undergo learning and development*. In this regard, I want to argue that (1) Heidegger's thought implicitly recognizes these three points and that indeed (2) perception requires such learning and development, but that, unfortunately, (3) Heidegger does not explicitly attend to learning and development as such. However, (4) these capacities and capabilities *need* to be—and *can* be—developed, realizing and fulfilling their potential, *if* the form of life he envisions in his later, more poetic evocations of life, ending the malevolence of our time, is to be actualized as more than mere daydreams. As Michel Foucault once argued: "There are times in life when the question of knowing if one can think differently than one thinks, and perceive differently than one sees, is absolutely necessary if one is to go on looking and reflecting at all."[5] After Heidegger, we have work to be done: not only philosophical work regarding the nature of our perceptual capacities, their historical role, and the cultural development of their potential but also concomitant work on ourselves. Rainer Maria Rilke called it "heart-work"—*Herzwerk*.[6]

†

Recognizing that perception is a matter of capacities and capabilities is not at all something new in philosophical thought. Nor is there anything new in recognizing that, as such, our perceptual faculties, our organs of perception are capable of cultivation and guided development. What *is* new, however, is attempting, first of all, to think of this cultivation, this development, in the context of Heidegger's critique of Western metaphysics and of the lifeworld within which that metaphysics emerged and maintained its sway, and, second, to think the education and cultivation of our perceptual faculties in the context of his philosophy of history—which is to say, in the context of an interpretation of history that imagines and projects, in the inheritance of Western history, the possibility of a revolutionary transformation, achieving the potential to which, as to our destiny, it summons us. Thus, inherent in this project is the envisioning of a singular ontological responsibility in regard to our perceptual abilities.

†

In a letter to a friend, Rilke wrote: "It is certain that the divinest consolation is contained within humanity itself—we would not be able to do much with the consolation of a god; only that our eyes have to be a trace more seeing, our ears more receptive, the taste of a fruit would have to penetrate us more completely, we would have to endure more odor, and in touching and being touched be more aware and less forgetful—in order promptly to absorb out of our immediate experiences consolations more convincing, more preponderant, more true than all the suffering that can ever shake us to our very depths."[7] In 1910, five years earlier, the eponymous character in his short work of prose fiction *The Notebooks of Malte Laurids Brigge* had penned this reflection:

> I am learning to see. I don't know why, but everything penetrates more deeply into me and does not stop where until now it always used to finish. I have an inner self of which I was not aware. Everything goes thither now. What happens there I do not know.[8]

Like the character in his story, the poet sought to make his perception more receptive, more susceptible to learning from what it is given to see and hear.

In his lecture on "The End of Philosophy and the Task of Thinking" (1964), Heidegger suggested that "thinking must first learn what remains reserved, remains in store for further thought to engage." And he said, "It is in such learning, that it prepares for its own transformation."[9] The two-volume book I am offering here is essentially about learning: learning to see and hear—see and hear more carefully, more attentively, more mindfully, and perhaps even more wisely.

†

The Greek etymology of the word "phenomenology," as well as the pre-Socratic notion of *aletheia*, translated as "unconcealment," reminded Heidegger that his work in phenomenology must learn to respect the hidden, the inapparent, an inherent dimension of all phenomena. The phenomenology of perception must accordingly be a hermeneutical project. And that means, as I shall be arguing, that, in its encounter with whatever matter is in question, the appropriate phenomenological attitude needs to be hermeneutically disclosive in an ontological attitude that he called *Gelassenheit*: letting the phenomenon be what and as it is, granted an openness to show itself in its own way. Only our perception initially adopting this attitude enables us to let what we encounter present itself in its truth. When, however, yielding to the pressures of our historical time, we lose touch with this *ontological* dimension, the dimension of being, then an appropriate *ontic* relation to the truth of what we encounter can become exceedingly difficult. The stakes are high.

How we understand being, whether in reflection or without reflection, makes a real difference in how we live our lives. Consequently, our own being, namely, our being human, is called upon to account for itself. Such being-put-in-question constitutes, and calls for, the taking on of a certain responsibility for self-examination. But our being also embodies the claim on another responsibility: the responsibility, above all, to protect and preserve the hermeneutical character of the ontological dimension of our perception—what Heidegger will call "the truth of being"—in the way we live our individual and social-cultural lives. It is a question of protecting the interplay of concealment and unconcealment: a task especially needed, but also especially difficult, in a time—our time—when nihilism constantly threatens reification and its ontological closure. Heraclitus said that nature loves to hide. In today's world, when nature is under siege, we must say that nature *needs* to hide.

The recognition and understanding of the fundamental claim on our existence, a claim potentially awakened or bestirred within us by every encounter we have in the world is an *event*—an *Ereignis*—that, when it occurs, can have momentous consequences for our historical life. Some of the early Greek philosophers—especially Heraclitus—experienced entities as presencing in the dimension of that interplay, but they did not make the self-reflective phenomenological "reduction" to recognize and understand what in the modern era that commenced with Descartes would be called the "subjective" pole of that experience. Hence they did not recognize and understand their experience of being as something *appropriating* them, making a claim on their appropriation, their recognition, and acknowledgment— their enowning—of its phenomenological character. The phenomenology in this event, constituting a process of appropriation (*Ereignung*), together with its historical significance, only came fully into light for the first time in the context of Heidegger's thought, coalescing in the key word *Ereignis* and its related terms. (This phenomenological appropriation is illuminated with singular lucidity in Heidegger's "The Principle of Identity.") For Heidegger, what is given (*geschickt*) in such a momentous event always bears within it the potential for a historical revolution; that *event* of appropriation could lead into a *process* preparing the ground for a reception of our history that could enable us to approach our *Geschick*—the destiny we make of our lives—in a leap (*Sprung*) that might take us into a new beginning, indeed another origin (*Ur-sprung*) for Western life.

†

Heidegger's history of Western metaphysics is somewhat like Hegel's, though without the latter's system of teleological determinism, a contribution to the history of the human spirit, guided by a philosophy of history, remarking the different stages in passing through which the spirit brings to light possibilities for progressively understanding and achieving itself in taking responsibility for its world. His history of philosophy is thus in the service of a project summoning us in the West to a responsibility for transforming ourselves and our world—a project inspired and guided by a philosophy of history grounded in the idea of a singular destiny, a singular *Geschick*, which the philosopher can only project in hope, for the future depends on our wise use of freedom. Consequently, in regard to its historical purport, and even its very intelligibility, this idea of destiny, the potential destination of our humanity, must itself be kept in question. The history of human suffering—the *Leidenschaft* that is the element in which thinking must find its voice—demands nothing less.

## NOTES

1. William Wordsworth, "Lines Composed a Few Miles above Tintern Abbey, On Revisiting the Banks of the Wye during a Tour. July 13, 1798."

2. André Gide, *Journals 1928–1939*, trans. Justin O'Brian (Urbana and Chicago: University of Illinois Press, 1987), entry for July 25, 1934, vol. III, 306.

3. Ralph Waldo Emerson, "The Method of Nature," *Essays and Lectures*, ed. Joel Porte (New York: Library of America, 1983), 116.

4. See Martin Heidegger, "Die seinsgeschichtliche Bestimmung des Nihilismus," *Nietzsche*, GA 6. 2: 368–69; "The Onto-Historical Determination of Nihilism," *Nietzsche*, vol. 4, 226. My translation: "Insofar as being is the unconcealment of beings as such, being has already addressed itself [*zugesprochen*] to the essence of humanity. Being itself has already spoken out for, and laid claim to [*vor- und sich dahin eingesprochen*], the essence of humanity, insofar as it has withheld and reserved itself [*sich selbst vorenthält and spart*] [even] in the unconcealment of its essence. Addressing [us] in this way, . . . being is the promise of itself [*Sein ist das Versprechen seiner selbst*]. Thoughtfully encountering being itself in its staying-away [*Ausbleiben*, i.e., its resistance to the nihilism increasingly taking over our historically given present] means: to become aware of this promise [*dieses Versprechens innewerden*], the promise as which being itself 'is'."

5. Michel Foucault, *The Use of Pleasure* (New York: Pantheon, 1985), 8.

6. Rainer Maria Rilke, "Wendung," *Gesammelte Werke, Gedichte* (Leipzig: Insel-Verlag, 1927), Bd. III, 460–62; "Turning-Point," *Rainer Maria Rilke. Poems 1912–1926*, trans. Michael Hamburger (Redding Ridge, CT: Black Swan Books, 1981), bilingual ed., 46–49.

7. Rilke, *Letters of Rainer Maria Rilke 1910–1926*, trans. Jane Bannard Greene and M. D. Herter Norton (New York: W. W. Norton, 1947, 1972), 139–40.

8. Rilke, *The Notebooks of Malte Laurids Brigge*, trans. M. D. Herter Norton (New York: W. W. Norton, 1949, 1964), 14–15. My translation.

9. Heidegger, "Das Ende der Philosophie und die Aufgabe des Denkens," *Zur Sache des Denkens*, 66–67; GA 14: 75; "The end of philosophy and the task of thinking," *The End of Philosophy*, 60: "Was dem Denken vor-und aufbehalten bleibt, darauf sich einzulassen, muß das Denken erst lernen, in welchem lernen es seine eigene Wandlung vorbereitet."

# INTRODUCTION

## PRELUDE AND PROMISE

Our guardianship [*Wächterschaft*] of the truth of being [i.e., the openness of the clearing that makes presencing possible in the interplay of concealment and unconcealment] is the ground for another history.

—Heidegger, *Contributions to Philosophy: Of the Event*
(GA 65: 240–41/CP 190)

*Er-eignen* [the appropriation laying claim to the essence—the fundamental dis-position—of the human being in its experiencing of its interactive relation to the being of beings] originally meant: *er-äugen*, i.e., look, see [*blicken*], catch sight of [*im Blicken zu sich rufen*], and lay claim to [*an-eignen*].

—Heidegger, "The Principle of Identity"
(*Identität und Differenz*, GA 11: 45/ID 136)

In *Of the Power of the Intellect, or, On Human Freedom*, the final part of his *Ethics*, Spinoza says: "The mind can cause all the modifications of the body, or the images of things, to be related to the idea of God" (Proposition XIV).[1] Moreover, he also argues that "in God, there exists an idea which expresses the essence of this or that human body under the form of eternity" (Proposition XXII).[2] Arguing that "it is the nature of reason to conceive things under the form of eternity," he explains what this proposition means, saying: "Everything that the mind understands under the form of eternity

1

it understands . . . because it conceives the essence of the body under the form of eternity" (Proposition XXIX).[3] These propositions, together with others, lead him to the proposition that, as he puts it, "he who possesses a body fit for many things possesses a mind of which the greater part is eternal." (Proposition XXXIX)[4] Elaborating the significance of this proposition, he explains that "in this life, it is our chief endeavour to change the body of infancy, so far as its nature permits and is conducive thereto, into another body which is fitted for many things, and which is related to a mind conscious as much as possible of itself, of God, and of objects." Developing the mind, one correspondingly develops the body, hence its perceptivity; developing the body, hence its perceptivity, one correspondingly develops the mind. In this regard, what is most important for Spinoza is the cultivation of what he calls the "intellectual love of God."

Arguing for a certain idealism and rationalism that later, in Schelling, would give substance to romanticism, Spinoza also identifies this "love of God" with the assumption, or rather adoption, of the viewpoint of eternity (Proposition XXIX): "It is the nature of Reason," he says, "to conceive things under the form of eternity [*sub specie aeternitatis*]."[5] In other words, it is important for us to imagine what we think would be the ideal world, a morally perfect world—"things as they would present themselves if contemplated from the standpoint of redemption [*wie vom Standpunkt der Erlösung*]," as Adorno phrased it in *Minima Moralia*—because that speculative vision, that projection, would both encourage and guide us to work for the moral improvement of the actual world.[6] That, he argues, is "the only philosophy that can be responsibly practised in the face of despair." Heidegger calls that standpoint as one of the *Geschick*—the destiny that would befit our humanity. However, it is not easy to determine what world his vision of destiny imagines. What would be the character of a redeemed perception in such a world? There are hints in numerous texts, such as "Building, Dwelling, Thinking," "Poetically Man Dwells," "The Thing," and "The Origin of the Work of Art."

The *Ethics* may be read as Spinoza's answer to the question, what is the *character* of the perceptivity that must correspond to this "intellectual love of God"? In "Of human bondage" (Proposition XXVII), Spinoza brazenly overturns the epistemological priority of the mind in the entire history of idealism from Plato to Descartes. With thinking steeped in Aristotle's *Metaphysics* and *De Anima*, he says: "The more capable the body is of being affected in many ways, and affecting external bodies in many ways, the more capable of thinking is the mind."[7]

What embodiment, what perceptual capabilities, would correspond to the mind's intellectual love of God? What transformations in the historical character of perception are needed? These questions constitute a responsibility engaging the potential inherent in our perception. They represent a claim carried by, and in, the disposition of our embodied nature. That claim calls and appropriates us, demanding that we consciously appropriate it, taking it up to realize and fulfill it as befits our propriation, our ownmost "essential nature."

In the chapter on Heidegger's conception of *Ereignis*, I shall argue that this key word refers to an event of the greatest historical importance: an event of appropriation, in which a potentiality, or potency (*dunamis*) borne by, and in, our embodiment as the most fundamental disposition and law of our nature is recognized, released, and brought into actualization (*energeia*)—for instance, in our perceptual capabilities.

In this volume, I want to think about what it would mean for the capability of our two most developed modes of perception—seeing and hearing—to serve as *ontologically attuned* organs. Considered "under the form of eternity"—that is to say, from the standpoint of an inner-worldly redemption, what might the *character* of our perception become?

†

In 1784, Kant stirred European thought with two major contributions to the philosophy of history: "What Is Enlightenment?" and "Idea for a Universal History with a Cosmopolitan Purpose." In the latter, he wrote, as the eighth proposition: "The history of the human race as a whole can be regarded as the realization of a hidden plan of nature to bring about . . . a perfect political constitution as the only possible state within which all natural capacities of mankind can be developed completely."[8] Heidegger, too, formulated a philosophy of history, eventually giving it considerable weight in his thinking, especially during the late 1920s, the 1930s, and the 1940s. And, like Kant, he gave thought to the development of our natural capacities—in particular, and above all, our seeing and hearing but also our gestures. Also like Kant, his reflections on such development and his hopes for the future emerged from a critique and diagnosis of our "natural" capacities and capabilities. But, diverging from Kant, he decisively relinquished any hint of teleology, historical determinism, the inevitability of progress, and the idea of perfection—a completed process of development. He also left Kant behind by situating his philosophy of history in a temporality that challenges history itself as a succession of discrete, irrecoverable events taking place in an irreversible, one-dimensional, linear order.

†

It has not been common, nor customary, to consider Heidegger's phenomenology to be a contribution to processes of learning and, in the

broadest sense, education; however, John Dewey once wrote, provoca-
tively, that "if we are willing to conceive education as the process of forming fundamental dispositions, toward nature and fellow-men, philosophy
may even be defined as *the general theory of education.*"⁹ It has been in the
spirit of this abiding sense and purpose of philosophical thought that I have
undertaken the project in this present work, which is very much about the
recognition, understanding, and enowning of our most fundamental disposition—and the capacities, capabilities, and response abilities it underlies and
claims. So what I would like to do here is propose in that light a reading of
Heidegger's phenomenology of perception.

†

In his 1962 lecture on "Time and Being," Heidegger adumbrates the
hope behind his project that, in "perceiving and receiving" (*Vernehmen
und Übernehmen*) all that is given to us in presence, we might attain "the
distinction of human being": *das Auszeichnende des Menschseins* (GA 14: 28/
OTB 23). What is the character of the perceiving and receiving that would
correspond to this distinction? What is it that Heidegger thinks we need
to learn? Is it not strange to be told that, in our way of being, we have not
yet attained our humanity?

In an afterword to the edition presenting the *Zollikon Seminars*, the
Swiss psychiatrist Medard Boss summarized, in homage to Heidegger, what
he had learned from the philosopher:

> Being human [*Mensch-Sein*] fundamentally means to be needed as
> the preserve of a capacity that, opening the world and remaining
> open to it, can receive-perceive [*weltweit offenständige Bereich eines
> Vernehmen-Könnens*], so that the things given us in perception [*die
> Gegebenheiten*], making up the world by their significance and refer-
> ential relationships [*Bedeutsamkeiten und Verweisungszusammenhängen*],
> can emerge in it, show themselves, and come to their presencing
> and to their being [*in ihn hinein aufgehen, zum Vorschein, zu ihrem
> Anwesen, ihrem Sein gelangen können*]. If there were not something
> [*gäbe es kein Wesen*] like open-standing being-human [*offenständigen
> Mensch-Seins*], then how, and into what, should something come
> into presence at all [*anwesen*] and disclose itself [*sich entbergen*], that
> is, come to be [*sein können*]?¹⁰

In this volume and the next, I would like to draw on Heidegger's texts in
order to provide further substance for the claim and the question articulated
here so lucidly by Medard Boss.

†

In *On the Vocation of Philosophy*, a collection of his early Freiburg lectures (1919–1923), lectures preceding the writing and publication of *Being and Time* and including thoughts concerning the role (*Bestimmung*) of philosophy in university education, Heidegger referred his project to teachings that encourage us, as in the words of Pindar and Goethe, to develop the inherent, latent virtues constitutive of our nature (GA 56/57: 5). I would like to approach Heidegger's project—the project that is the substance of my two volumes—by interpreting his thought from the congenial perspective of learning: learning about the character of our capacities and capabilities, learning of what we are capable, and learning how we might develop them, becoming who, as human beings, we are called to be.

Many years later, in his lecture on "The End of Philosophy and the Task of Thinking" (1964), Heidegger, still, as always, concerned about education and the most favorable conditions for learning, suggested that "thinking must first learn what remains reserved, remains in store for further thought to engage." And he said: "It is in such learning, that it prepares for its own transformation" (GA 14:75/EP 60). Learning—in particular, learning to see and hear—is what the present work is all about.

†

Perception is qualified in many ways: a clear view, a sharp look, a knowing glance, a faint visibility, a soft gaze, a quick look, an intense listening, a gracious hearing, and defective hearing. What significance is there in the fact that we can look into a room and notice the fragments of a bowl on the floor but somehow not really see it, not see it with a recognition and understanding of what it means about our friend's marriage? We can see immediately that there are tracks of an animal in the snow, but we need to look more closely in order to see and identify the species that made them. Likewise, we can hear the sound of distant footsteps but not listen, not give it our attention, in order to determine whether or not it is coming closer. We can also listen to someone's story but not really hear the pain or the shame it is conveying. Are many of these distinctions not ways of indicating the falling short of an achievement? Do they not tell us that the grammar of perception recognizes positive and negative degrees and qualities of attention, learning, attainment, and fulfillment?[11]

Our eyes are the organs of sight, but they can also weep. What is the significance of this fact, this uncanny affinity, that the very same organ that is endowed with vision, a capability appropriated by its very nature for objective clarity, should also be capable of tears, indeed susceptible to weeping precisely because of what has been seen or not seen? Should we not recognize that *pathos*, weeping as an expression of sympathy, affective connection, or as a final acknowledgment of some painful truth intensely resisted is actually the *root* of seeing? Should we not recognize that our eyes can be moved to tears by what they see or do not see because their sight is essentially rooted, preconceptually, in *pathos*, a synesthetic, *sympathetic relation* to the world—a relation to which, of course, the circumstances of life in the historical world can all too easily do enduring or permanent damage? If always subject to the historical conditions that shape their world, of what attainment and fulfillment, what historical destiny in skillfulness—what *Geschick* in *Schicklichkeit*—are our eyes and ears capable?

In T. S. Eliot's "The Love Song of J. Alfred Prufrock," the poet laments the prevailing character of our capacity for vision, recognizing at the same time what has happened to our sense of history and our sense of ourselves as human beings dwelling in a world reduced to the dimensions of the visible and knowable: "eyes that fix you in a formulated phrase."[12] How might we interrupt and break the historical continuum, the endless repetition of the same oppressive institutions, the same violent gestures, the same types of blindness and deafness, the same old horizons delimiting sensibility, *pathos*, and intelligibility?

†

For Heidegger, what he calls "the history of being"—the history, that is, of ontology, the Western world's shared understanding of what *is* and what matters—can be differentiated into a succession of ontological epochs, the essence and character of each epoch defined by its distinctive conditions of intelligibility; its distinctive paradigm of knowledge, truth, and reality; and its understanding of the meaning of being. Heidegger uses the word "epoch" in keeping with the sense belonging to its Greek derivation because each epoch of ontology is inherently a *hermeneutical* constellation, not only a form of life disclosive of the meaning of being but also a time defined by a withdrawing *of* meaning, even a withdrawing *from* meaning— a concealing or suspending of possibilities for meaning. Each ontological epoch conceals more than it reveals regarding being. We need to take this dimension of concealment into account in thinking about the history of "the truth of being."

In the twentieth century, the century of Heidegger's life, and the twenty-first into which we have recently entered and which I am designating as late modern or postmodern, we have not only witnessed the most appalling genocides, but we have seen, driven by technologies absolutely unimaginable only a century before, the most comprehensive, most deeply engaging, most spectacular, and also most frightening transformations in our way of life. In this extreme break with the past, of our time and our age, Heidegger discerned the nearness of that extreme consummation of nihilism about which Nietzsche had warned us. Today, the *truth* of being is frightening.

†

When Rilke's main character in *The Notebooks of Malte Laurids Brigge* reflects on the fact that he is "learning to see," what does he feel a need to learn? Most people suppose that all they need do is open their corporeal eyes in order to see what is given to be seen. But the poet knows that what is given is much more than what eyes of that character see. As he learns to see, he discovers that, as he expressed it, "everything penetrates more deeply into me and does not stop at the place where until now it always used to finish."[13] For Heidegger, there is more to seeing than what is visible and more to hearing than what is audible. Beyond the ontic presence and absence of beings, there is an ontological dimension belonging to the ground of the interplay of the visible and the invisible; and similarly, there is ontological dimension belonging to the ground of the interplay of the audible and the inaudible. This dimension, the transcendental, cannot be seen and heard—is not visible and audible—in the way one sees visible beings and hears audible beings. But it is not a merely theoretical construct; it is not metaphysically transcendent. Rather, it is immanent in the phenomenology of our experience. It is the sensible preserve of being. Using the word *Lichtung* to name this transcendental, Heidegger retrieved the old meaning it had among the country folk: clearing. The word does not invoke the light, but instead recollects—recalls—the lighting and the fact that it is our openness to the world, laying out the conditions of our visionary existence, that gives us the possibility of light. And, in our enjoyment of it, we might call the giving and givenness of this fact a "gift" (GA 14: 16, 24–29/OTB 16, 19–23).

Even much of what is in plain sight is, in effect, neglected, overlooked, and unappreciated. Even the most ordinary things have a fascinating uncanny presence—if only one gives them some attention, responsive to their silent appeal. In closing his miniature story, "A Little Ramble," Robert Walser urges us to recognize the importance of all the little things we ignore: "We don't need to see anything out of the ordinary. We already can see so much [*Man braucht nicht viel Besonderes zu sehen. Man sieht so schon viel*]."[14] Just seeing rightly what is right before our eyes—seeing in particular the presence of all the little things, the shy things that do not attract attention: that is very much a part of what we need to learn. To see such things requires serenity, a peaceful vision moved by its *pathos*, its attunement, not by the urgings of the will. We need to see things in a dimensionality that belongs to, and respects, their concealment, their withdrawing from presence. But this way of seeing—Heidegger called it *Gelassenheit*—is easier said than done. As Maurice Blanchot observed: "The everyday is what we never see a first time, but only see again."[15] This is an exaggeration, to be sure, but it marks a certain truth. The arts, including literature, invite us to look and see again but really always for the first time. Heidegger's ceaseless questioning in the realm of thought invites that same endeavor, to retrieve missed opportunities.

But I would add, letting Nietzsche's spirit provoke me, that we also need to see what we do not want to see—what we resist seeing: the things that challenge our shibboleths, the things that accuse our prejudice and indifference, the things that cause our institutions to tremble. We shut our eyes to the poverty visible in the city; we do not want to see it and consequently, in a way, actually do not really see it. And we turn our eyes away as we pass a homeless beggar on the sidewalk. We know as if instinctively that, if we were really to look, what we should see would demand, because of the intrinsically empathic rootedness of perception, an appropriately ethical response that we are not prepared, or not willing, to give.

†

Everything in our world has a history. For the most part, this historicity remains unnoticed. It has no role in forming our perception, no bearing on the way we live with things. Without a sense of the presence of history, we live in a world bereft of a sense of fate, the impermanence of all beings. And, more fatefully, we lose our connection to the immanence of transcendence. In "The Turning," Heidegger gives voice to a lament: philosophical thought has failed so far to "bring us into the proper relation to destining [*schicklichen Bezug zum Geschick*]":

> No merely historiographical representation of history as happening [*kein historisches Vorstellen der Geschichte als Geschehen*] brings us into the proper relation to destining [*in den schicklichen Bezug zum Geschick*], let alone into the essential origin of destining [*zu dessen Wesensherkunft*] in the disclosing coming-to-pass of the truth of being, that is, the disclosiveness of the clearing that makes it possible for everything to come into its own [*im Ereignis der Wahrheit des Seins*]. (GA 11: 123, GA 79: 77/ BF 72, QCT 48)

Heidegger's indictment is grave. Philosophical thought has not only failed to guide us toward the proper relation to our essence, our ownmost potential, so that we might realize more fully what we are capable of; it has also failed, correspondingly, to guide us toward creating, given what is possible, the conditions of a common world in which its spiritual richness and potential for enlightenment might be redeemed. And, reflecting critically on our time, he tells us: "We do not yet hear, we whose hearing and seeing are perishing through radio and film under the rule of technology."[16] Explaining the significance of this diagnosis, he argues that our loss of *pathos*—loss of an ontological dimension of felt attunement in perception—is causing an "injurious neglect of the thing." What he is lamenting is an ever-spreading, ever-deepening nihilism, leaving us empty of spirit, lost in a meaningless world, a world in which the things we have made, the things we have brought forth in the world, are now turning against us, imperiling our way of life, in part because of the violent way we see and envision things—a way Heidegger has described as an assault, the expression of what Nietzsche called our will to power. Might learning to see and hear differently make a significant difference in our world? Could such learning redeem the promise bestowed in our perceptual faculties?

As the German translator of Heidegger's seminars in Le Thor comments, explaining the philosopher's interpretation of *Da-sein*:

> It is important to experience *Da-sein* [i.e., the *Da-sein* of the human being, of *Menschsein*] in the sense that man himself *is* the *Da*, i.e., the openness of being for him, in that he undertakes [*übernimmt*] to preserve this and in preserving it, to unfold it [*sie zu bewahren und bewahrend zu enfalten*]. (GA 15: 415/FS 88)

For Heidegger, this response ability—preserving and developing the openness, the receptivity of the *Da* that we are—constitutes our first and last responsibility.

†

In this volume, I want to begin the process of questioning the historical character of our habits of perception, concentrating on exploring the potential that abides in seeing and hearing. This requires that I lay out (i) my understanding of Heidegger's narrative about the history of being, a narrative belonging to the history of philosophy and, more particularly, to the history of metaphysics. This is, as I shall argue, a history of philosophy that is under the influence of a certain *philosophy of history*, and it accordingly follows the neglect of being, being itself and as such, in the texts of metaphysics down through the ages, bringing that neglect to light in a compelling form of critique, centered on the "propriation" or "enowning" of our human potential to realize, achieve, and become the kind of being we by disposition most essentially, most deeply, already are: a task that is more difficult than it might at first seem, as it demands that we constantly struggle against forgetting and betraying it. This struggle is also a struggle against the oppressive weight of history, a weight all the more oppressive for not being recognized and understood. Thus, I want to connect the historical narrative with (ii) what I suggest is a corresponding twofold critique of perception: a Heidegger-inspired critique of what Husserl called "the natural attitude," our habitual, insufficiently mindful quotidian ways of seeing and hearing and a critique showing that, and how, the philosophical representation of these ways has figured in the history of metaphysics, rendering its discourse neglectful of the very thing it strives to understand.

At stake in these critiques is also, therefore, (iii) the possibility of a profound transformation in our typical way of seeing and hearing: a transformation retrieving and perhaps redeeming their deepest, ownmost potential in relation to being, the ontological dimension of the world. And as this redeeming transformation would take place in our historical life, it might well be accompanied by correspondingly significant revisions taking place in relation to the history of metaphysics: revisions that might shatter all the inherited concepts and even originate and inaugurate what might be called another beginning for philosophical thought.

†

In *Being and Time*, and subsequently in texts such as his "Letter on Humanism," Heidegger distinguishes and separates the human being (*Mensch-sein*) as in their everydayness from their essential nature, which is *Da-sein*, nature's "design," bearing our ownmost, (still) unrealized, most authentic potential and claiming each of us for the possible actualization of that potential in the historical achievement of a new humanity and destiny truly worthy of our endowment. The distinction he draws between *Mensch-sein* and *Da-sein* is crucial. How can we become in actuality the *Da-sein* that, as *Mensch-sein*, we already in essence are—but so far, only in potential? Heidegger leaves much to be thought concerning the *way* to our achievement, the actualization of our potential, our essence, in an awareness that protects and preserves it.

Nevertheless, what we know is that the promising force of that potential calls upon, and calls into question, the modalities of our awareness, our attentiveness in relation to being. So I want to ask, what would the achievement of such awareness, such mindfulness involve in regard to our capacity for perception—our potential as beings endowed by nature with the "gift" of seeing and hearing? I want to show that, in his writings both early and late, Heidegger's thought actually offers much more in this regard than has heretofore been recognized.

†

In "The Fundamental Concepts of Metaphysics" (1929), staking out his sharp divergence from Husserl's phenomenological method, Heidegger argues that "the task assigned to philosophy" is "not to describe the consciousness of the human being [*Mensch*], but to evoke and educe the *Da-sein* [i.e., the essential nature and disposition of our existence] in the human" (GA 29–30: 258/FCM 172). By this, he meant what is needed today is an *existential* task, namely, to evoke and educe our *a priori*, already operative "assignment," our "appropriation," namely, to live our lives together in a way that measures up to the humanity in our human nature, a humanity that silently calls us to be true to ourselves, becoming more fully—with more awareness and greater resoluteness—the human beings we already are in essence, hence in our potential, taking up the challenge to realize the humanity that is already inherent even in our bodily disposition as human beings. We are, each one of us, summoned, says Heidegger, "to undertake a transformation [*Verwandlung*] of ourselves into being-a-*Da-sein*" (GA 29–30: 430/FCM 297)—becoming what, by virtue of that inherent disposition, we, to a certain extent, always already are and yet also, in some ways, have yet to become: a thrown-open existence, beings fully exposed, cast like dice, into the givenness of a historical world we did not make, but for the future of which, as our inheritance and our legacy, we are nevertheless responsible. "Thus," as Heidegger says in his *Contributions to Philosophy*: "The human being is originarily . . . claimed by the truth of being—that is, by the allotted clearing. Through this claim of being itself, the human being is assigned as the guardian of the truth of being: being human, understood as 'care,' grounded in *Da-sein* [i.e., grounded in our nature as thrown-open ex-istence, projected outside ourselves]" (GA 65: 240/CP 189).

Accordingly, "our fundamental task now consists in awakening a fundamental ontological attunement [*in der Weckung einer Grundstimmung*] in our philosophizing" (GA 29–30: 89–93/FCM 59–63). Heidegger believes that, in experiencing this awakening, we will find ourselves in need of "a complete transformation of our conception of the human [*einer völligen Umstellung unserer Auffassung vom Menschen*]." In other words,

"to question concerning this fundamental attunement does not mean to further justify and continue the contemporary human traits of mankind, but to *liberate* the humanity *in* mankind [*die Menschheit im Menschen befreien*], to liberate the humanity *of* mankind, i.e., the *essence* of mankind, *letting the Dasein in us become essential* [*das Dasein in ihm wesentlich werden lassen*]. It is *the liberation of the Dasein* [*die Befreiung des Daseins*] *in the human being* that is at issue here. And this liberation of the *Dasein* in mankind is something that we human beings can accomplish only by retrieving the very ground of our essence" (GA 29–30: 248/FCM 166).

As we shall discuss in the chapters to follow, this means entering into our appropriation and retrieving for real awareness and self-understanding, as our ownmost responsibility, the *fact* that, in our propriation, our becoming, we are dispositioned as thrown-open clearings. And it is the self-reflective turn in phenomenology—what we might, if with requisite caution, characterize as new form of subjectivity—that makes this appropriation possible. I shall argue that it is in making that turn that we can get in touch with our most fundamental bodily disposition, our most fundamental ontological attunement, the grounding *pathos* in which our seeing and hearing, our modes of perception, are deeply rooted. Getting in touch with the "origin" of our humanity, we can learn the way to our destination as mortal, earth-bound beings dwelling on this planet.

This task *does* require careful phenomenological description. Heidegger is wrong to deny that such description has an essential role to play in educing the potential in perception. He fails to recognize that, when description is genuinely phenomenological, its reflective character makes it inherently performative or metaphorical in the sense of carrying us into a different experience. A phenomenology such as Heidegger practices it can significantly change our perception. In 1963, Heidegger reflected on his way into phenomenology, casting light on what its method meant to him and on how he practiced it.

The age of phenomenological philosophy appears to be over. It is already taken as

> something past, recorded in history along with other schools of philosophy. But in what is most its own, phenomenology is not a school. It is the possibility of thinking, at times changing and only thus persisting, of corresponding to the claim of what is to be thought. If phenomenology is thus experienced and retained, it can disappear as a designation in favor of the matter of thinking. (GA 14: 101–102/OTB 82)

I think it is clear that Heidegger was attempting to move beyond the metaphysics he inherited, but I dispute the interpretation that he attempted to get entirely beyond phenomenology. What he attempted in that regard, and succeeded in accomplishing, was to take phenomenology out of Husserl's transcendental idealism, returning it to the world we live in. He remained a phenomenological thinker to the end of his life.

Looking back on the course of his thinking in his 1969 "Supplement" to this text, a brief text written many years after *Being and Time*, Heidegger lets us understand that he still considered his project to be phenomenological, but he defined his understanding of the phenomenological method in decisively new terms: "The understanding of phenomenology consists," he said, "solely in realizing it as possibility [*liegt einzig im Ergreifen ihrer als Möglichkeit*]." Possibility is what this volume is about: what we might learn from Heidegger regarding the fundamental nature and of perception—and its character in our time so that we might venture our possibilities for transformation and more fully embody the meaning of our humanity in the character of our perception and in new forms of sensibility. We are right to emphasize possibility, but we also need to appreciate that the *Ergreifen* is a call to enactment, putting the method into performative practice.

In this way, Heidegger very succinctly differentiates his phenomenological approach from Husserl's, asking: What is it that phenomenology is concerned with? What is *die Sache selbst*? His answer, phrased as a question, gives us the fundamental task: "Is it consciousness and its objects [*Bewußtsein und seine Gegenständlichkeit*] or is it the being of beings in their unconcealment and protective hiddenness [*das Sein des Seienden in seiner Unverborgenheit und Verbergung*]?" (GA 14: 99/OTB 79). Phenomenology teaches us how to notice, see, and hear—even in what is visible and audible—that which remains unnoticed, unrecognized, and hidden. It instructs us in this, even as it also teaches us to protect and preserve the dimension that withdraws from our apprehension.

†

Heidegger's little word, his invention *Zu-sein* ("to-be" or "toward-being"), is telling us that our existence, our way-of-being as human beings, is radically different from everything else in the world as we know it: that is, radically different from nonliving things (the being of a stone, for instance); the being of something in nature that grows (an acorn, for instance); and the being of the other animals.[17] Our being, our existence, is not like a stone, a tree, or a cup, something that simply is what it is (*Was-sein*), nor is it the being of something that is simply present-at-hand (*Vorhandensein*), but it is rather something given to us as a task, an *Aufgegebenes*: we are always to-be, *Zu-sein*, always a potential-to-be-enacted, always in a condition, or process, of becoming, always called upon to take up our being human as a task, indeed, as the task of our lifetime: always evolving, always emerging from our essential nature, taking responsibility for the "redeeming" of an essence that is never finished.

Following Heidegger's exemplary critical observations where I think they lead us, we shall accordingly interrogate perception itself and, more specifically, the prevailing *character* of our seeing and hearing as *ontological organs of receptivity*, organs responsive to the *givenness* of sensible beings in the given conditions of our present world order. This enquiry should be recognized as necessary, inasmuch as Heidegger's *Geschichte des Seins*, his lifetime reflections on being as it figures in the history of metaphysics, never really ceases to engage a certain philosophy of history (explicitly in the late 1930s and 1940s, implicitly and silently in the post-War years) that speculatively conjectures another beginning, another founding of our "destiny": at stake in this philosophy of history is a profound transformation in our relation to being as that which makes encounters possible in the perceptual field. This is lucidly argued in his extremely important 1957 lecture on "The Principle of Identity" (GA 11: 38–47/ID 29–38). And surely, if there were ever to be another inception, it would require, as Heidegger says, for instance, in *The History of Beyng*, "an essential transformation of the human"—hence, among other matters, fundamental changes in the *character* of our sensibility, our perception, our way of receiving and responding to being—that which is given to us in our fields of perception: "If the ground of the human essence [*Wesensgrund des Menschen*] is the draw of connection to being [*Bezug zum Sein*], then the transformation of the human being [*der Wandel des Menschen*] can come only from the transformation of this draw into connection [*nur aus dem Wandel dieses Bezuges kommen*]." Tentatively, Heidegger imagines another humanity: *Ein anderes Menschentum—veilleicht* (GA 69: 99, 139/HB 84, 119–120). That Heidegger's project envisions the possibility of a profound transformation in how we live understandingly, standing on this earth under the sky, is a theme that appears in his lectures and writings again and again, spanning his lifetime. Nothing could be clearer—and yet nothing could be more difficult for us actually to achieve or even know *how* to achieve. In any case, as the philosopher argues in "The Principle of Identity" (GA 11: 38–47/ID 29–38), this would surely depend on "a more originary appropriation" (*ein anfänglicheres Ereignen*), that is, a deeper sense of our role and responsibility, hence "a more originary experience of being," than what has eventually become feasible and typical because of our abandonment of the ontological dimension, a fact that prevails in disguise, unrecognized, in this, the age of total reification that Heidegger calls the *Ge-stell*. In such an "originary appropriation," our response ability in relation to being would have to be recognized, understood, enowned, and taken up in acknowledgment of the task. As a beginning, the prevailing *character* of our experience—for instance in seeing and hearing—would have to be questioned.

†

It is accordingly to provide a context for understanding the possibility and character of such changes that this study introduces this problematic in terms of Heidegger's history of philosophy (more specifically a history of metaphysics) and attempts to read this history in its refraction through a philosophy of history oriented—but not teleologically—toward the possibility of "another beginning," a new beginning, not only for a philosophical thought that would overcome or convert the reign of metaphysics but also for a Western *world* that would finally be released from the nihilism that corresponds to that metaphysics. Throughout his life, Heidegger argued that nihilism, the attitude that regards *being* as *nothing* of any importance, must be recognized as the greatest danger we human beings need to confront. And we alone are responsible for the consequences of this attitude: consequences that are not at all abstract but very real, manifest, and felt, whether we understand them or not, even in the smallest and seemingly most inconsequential matters of our everyday life. For, as the being of beings, being concerns everything, present and absent, that in any way *is*.

At stake in this project, therefore, is a history and destiny (*Geschick*) that draws us in our mindfulness to reflect critically on the appropriate skillfulness (*Schicklichkeit*) needed in our perception of the given (that which, to it, is *geschickt*), with due consideration of its deeper, hidden, more elusive dimensions in order to make a decisive and fundamental difference in the disposition and character of our perception, the conduct of our lives, and the conditions in our world—a difference, that is, of destiny, conditions promising a secular redemption of our potential as human beings. And it is for the sake of recognizing the prospect of another beginning, one that would serve the promise envisioned as our destiny, that Heidegger will emphatically differentiate (i) the rhythms and measures of serial time and history that we commonly live by (*Zeitlichkeit*) from (ii) the ecstatic dimension of temporality (*Temporalität*) that is the underlying ground of its possibility, a temporality of freedom belonging to the destiny of what is given (the *Geschick*) in the event of our phenomenological appropriation, whereby we can finally take appropriate responsibility for the way that our world is. But entering into this dimension, "the realm of the clearing for being," would represent a challenge to our *Zeitlichkeit*—the time that belongs to our clocks, our watches, the times, and dates in our calendars.[18] For, in the transformed world that Heidegger envisions, the serial order of time would no longer reign, no longer determine the course of historical existence; predominance would belong to the phenomenology of an underlying temporality, in which both the past and the future, as what we bring into question, are gathered into the life of the present.

Heidegger interprets the history of philosophy in a critique that is intended to overcome the prevailing metaphysics. But this overcoming requires a philosophy of history that is committed to a way of thinking that recognizes and understands the underlying dimension of temporality without which there can be no retrieval of the missed opportunities that were available in the past.

†

In "Time and Being," another extremely important lecture, delivered in 1962, thirty-five years after the publication of *Being and Time*, Heidegger showed that he continued, despite major disagreements with Husserl, to affirm the commitment of his project to the phenomenological method (GA 14: 53–54/OTB 44–45). He still believed that self-knowledge and self-understanding are of the utmost importance—are, indeed, constitutive of our highest responsibility and that phenomenology is uniquely qualified to guide our thinking in that project. And it is this responsibility that accounts for why Heidegger's use of the word *Ereignis* emerged as the guiding word—the *Leitwort*—for his thinking after *Being and Time*, not only to designate (i) historically significant ontological *events* in which the prevailing meaning of being is called into question or even profoundly altered but also to call attention to (ii) the most fundamental disposition of our bodily nature, the disposition, namely, that summons human *Dasein*, human existence, to its essential task of enownment and fulfillment, making an existential claim on the potential in our capacities. But, as I shall argue in the chapter devoted to this word, *Ereignis* can serve in this way only when its functioning is understood in phenomenological terms, hence not only as a word referring to a history-making event but also as a word referring to our appropriation, a process in which the most fundamental disposition of human nature is recognized, understood, enowned, and actualized.

†

In "Time and Being," Heidegger suggests that we consider the giving and givenness constitutive of our experience as a "gift" and uses a constellation of cognate and associated words (*schicken, Schickung, Gabe, Geben, Gegebenheit*), words gathered around the term *Geschick*, commonly translated as "destiny," to illuminate the nature of experience. His reliance on this constellation is, however, unfortunate, as *Geschick* and the associated words it gathers almost inevitably draw thinking into the discourse of metaphysics. Without disconnecting that term from its metaphysically freighted, onto-historical (*seynsgeschichtlich*) sense of destiny, Heidegger wants, nevertheless, to have this constellation serve to convey a much humbler, more ordinary and familiar experience: for instance, the giving and givenness that "merely" describes what takes place all the time in the phenomenology of perception—the given facts of the situation. But for Heidegger, there is also the possibility of a certain benefit in retaining that key term and its constellation despite the metaphysical baggage, namely, that, insofar as we understand and absorb the phenomenological explication he articulates regarding the *Ereignis* (appropriation) operative in the perceptual relationship between *Mensch* and *Sein*, and do so in such a way that the explication actively guides and attunes the mindfulness with which we enter into that relationship, then our future—in sum, the gift of our destiny—could possibly be determined by what is most promising in the givenness of the perceptual situation we find ourselves having been given. In other words, Heidegger wants us to seek and discern, in the givenness of what we are given to see and hear, something much deeper than what everyday perception recognizes: the possibility, in the belonging together of being and our being, of something promising in, and as, our destiny. Perhaps even intimations of the possibility of our breaking through and beyond the nihilism that prevails in the present epoch, determined as it is by a technological and technocratic rationality that requires the total imposition of its ontologically destructive order.

"Our thinking," said Emerson, "is a pious reception."[19] If perception is our endowment, our gift, then it must be in and as perception that we remember to give thanks. Likewise, if what we are given is given in perception, given to be perceived, then, again, thanksgiving must belong to the essential character of perception. And would that not be performed or expressed most appropriately by virtue of the thoughtful character of our reception? Heidegger wants us to understand that perception is not the one-sided subjective bestowal of meaning, as in Husserl's *Sinngebung*, but also that perception involves a reception of the meaningfully given that is not merely passive submission to what is already given. Properly experienced, perception is a *reception* of the given that becomes our sheltering of the conditions of possibility—conditions of perceptual intelligibility—necessary for the truth to emerge, and moreover be *shown* to emerge, from the time–space interplay of concealment and unconcealment.

Although we need to think of perception—and of course experience it—in terms of potentiality and realization, terms reminiscent of Aristotle, there is no completely fixed, determinate "design," no teleology in the Aristotelian sense, structuring our capacities. In fact, if we let ourselves be truly appropriated by the inherent openness of the perceptual field, we are drawn into self-estrangement, where the very terms of our identity—our *Zu-sein*—might be radically called into question because the openness is ultimately abyssal. As Heidegger says in *The Event*:

> To see the human being merely humanly (humanistically, humanely, anthropologically) and even all-too-humanly ("psychologically") means to experience nothing of the human being. (GA 71: 93/E 78)

Heidegger's thinking does not explicitly discuss, as such, the existentially appropriate, ontologically appropriated, development and cultivation of our perceptual capacities. However, he does nevertheless give us phenomenological descriptions that, in stark terms, reveal the presently prevailing character of our seeing and hearing, and these descriptions generate, as in the writings of Nietzsche, a critique of our time, a kind of ontologically inspired "diagnosis" of our habitual way of seeing and hearing, bringing to light their unmistakable ontical shortcomings and failings—and, too, going beyond Nietzsche's account of nihilism, showing their ways of falling into ontologically significant errancy, destructiveness, and violence. This critique, moreover, is not only (i) contextualized in relation to the history of being, but it is also (ii) formulated in relation to a philosophy of history that is (iii) oriented toward preparing for the future possibility of a radical overcoming and transformation of our historical experience of being—a transformation inaugurating another inception, beginning the redeeming of the great, still unfulfilled, promise already granted in the meaning of the earliest of the great ontological discourses. However, Heidegger differs from Hegel—or perhaps rather, from a common reading of Hegel, in that the transformation he has in mind can never actually be achieved, never completed, never fully realized, and that is because its nature, its character, inherently remains incessantly, endlessly questionable, open to the conditions of the world, open in the exercise of our freedom.

So, using the word "metaphorical" in the sense it derives from the Greek language, namely as referring to a shift, or movement, in experience, bearing us elsewhere, I shall attempt to show that, and how, Heidegger's critique prepares the way for poetical, metaphorical thinking to venture imagining the development of a potential in our perceptual capacities—our capacities for receiving in seeing and hearing what manifests in sensible experience—that would profoundly alter their currently prevailing character, thereby preparing for the possibility of another momentous, history-shattering *Er-eignis*, a situation—probably a crisis—urgently appropriating us for an experience of the meaning of being and setting in motion the conditions for a very different world: a world, namely, that would be grounded in a new understanding and new relation to the meaning of being, hence to presencing as such. As I read Heidegger, there is in his writings, early to late, an implicit, unacknowledged representation of the ontological fulfillment, or destination, of our self-development as human beings endowed with an ability to see and hear. This representation, implicitly operative in his never adequately acknowledged philosophy of history, urgently needs to be made an object of philosophical thought.

It is my hope that, by interpreting Heidegger's thought in terms of a hermeneutical phenomenology of perceptivity oriented toward the unfolding of the potential for an ontologically disclosive, ontologically grounding form of self-development inherent in our perceptive capacities, the stakes in his critical history of philosophy as a history of being, and the stakes in his philosophy of history as a time of preparation for another originating event of appropriation, might be further illuminated when considered in their most concrete form. For surely, if we are to prepare ourselves for the inception of another ontological order in emergence, much depends on the character of our receptivity in perception. This, however, is an angle, a perspective, that has so far been woefully neglected.

†

In the long history of philosophical thought in the Western world, the nature of perception has been subjected to one hostile narrative after another. There is, consequently, an important truth in what T. S. Eliot observed in "The Dry Salvages," but it is a truth that need not be burdened with any theological doctrine: that our embodiment—our "incarnation"—is a "gift"—our blessing, not our curse. Our corporeality is what, in the course of natural history, we human beings have, in a certain manner of speaking, been "granted." And for each one of us, it is, in a sense, a gift we never asked for, something bestowed—in terms of a worldly causality—by, of course, our parents and bestowed with a question attached: what shall we make of the capacities the body possesses? As perception is obviously fundamental in the way we live on the earth as embodied mortal creatures, this question calls into question the character of our perception, our perceptivity, marking something of its difference from the merely physical nature of perception. Can we think of perception as a refuge for the being of beings—a refuge for the conditions that enable the very possibility of such presencing?

Although for too long a neglected dimension of Heidegger's hermeneutical phenomenology and his "Daseinsanalytic," perception assumes, as it must, a crucial role in the formation of what I shall call the emerging body of ontological understanding. It is this body of understanding, standing under the sky and on the earth, ruled by the law of mortality but free as a god to imagine ideals worth sacrificing for, a body at once intimately familiar and yet also strange, suspended between nature and culture, disposition and transformation, the potential and the actual, forgetfulness and recollection, the known and the unknown/unknowable, to which, despite only the most perfunctory of acknowledgments, he dedicated his entire lifetime of thought, and not only his early work, exploring its historical context and bringing out its philosophical significance. Our response ability—as in perception—holds an essential, indispensable key to the hidden promise—the hidden gift—in this venturesome project of enquiry. In his major work on Nietzsche, Heidegger speaks of this promise, this *Versprechung*, requiring our responsibility in confronting the ever-increasing dangers in nihilism:

> Insofar as being is the unconcealment of beings as such, being has already addressed itself [*zugesprochen*] to the essence of humanity. Being itself has already spoken out for, and laid claim to [*vor- und sich dahin eingesprochen*], the essence of humanity, insofar as it has withheld and reserved itself [*sich selbst vorenthält and spart*] [even] in the unconcealment of its essence. Addressing [us] in this way, . . . being is the promise of itself [*Sein ist das Versprechen seiner selbst*]. Thoughtfully encountering being itself in its staying-away [*Ausbleiben*, i.e., its resistance to the nihilism taking over our historically given present] means: to become aware of this promise [*dieses Versprechens innewerden*], the promise as which being itself "is." (GA 6.2: 368–69/N4: 226)

This "promise" governs, as a gentle law, the ontological attunement of our perceptual faculties. Among the perceptual capacities we have been granted by nature, seeing and hearing are, precisely as capacities, dispositions capable of being developed, appropriated in mindfulness: as in the painter's art of seeing and the poet's ear for reverberations of meaning, these capacities are potentialities that can be disciplined, educated, refined, sharpened, deepened, and extended, and they are favored by nature with some inherent measure of skillfulness, a certain fitting attunement or *Schicklichkeit*, bearing in the depths of their reserve a love for the emergence of truth—and, too, therefore, intimations of a way of life befitting our humanity, the redeeming of the promising possibilities constitutive of our *Geschick*. These two faculties, seeing and hearing, are for that very reason the most historical, the most consequential, of our perceptive senses.

In this present work, we shall engage as our project the potential in perception: a project that despite his formidable contributions to its undertaking, Heidegger himself never adequately formulated and pursued as such. Carrying forward Heidegger's thinking, taking it beyond where he was prepared to go, we shall concentrate on seeing and hearing, questioning and drawing out, first, the ontological potential—the *Seinkönnen*—inherent in our capacity as visionary beings, beings granted the power of vision, and then second, the potential inherent in our capacity as auditory beings, beings enriched by the receptivity in hearing.[20] As human beings, we are stretched out in time, oriented toward the future by existing in the in-between: between potentiality and actuality, between the disposition of our capacities and the fulfillment of their ownmost ontical and ontological appropriation.

The phenomenology of perception that we shall elaborate here is set out, therefore, within a framework profoundly indebted to the Aristotelian concepts of potentiality and actuality, concepts that Hegel appropriated in charting the itinerary we read in his phenomenology of spirit and that, in a very Hegelian way, Merleau-Ponty exploited in working out his own phenomenological project, making way, in the critical and analytical arguments he formulated in *The Structure of Comportment*, for his subsequent contributions to the phenomenology of perception.[21] These subsequent contributions, making a compelling argument for the method of phenomenology after the dialectical destruction of both rationalism and empiricism, were profoundly influenced by Schelling and by what he learned, especially in the later years of his life, from a rereading of Heidegger that finally enabled him to complete his release from Cartesianism.

In *Being and Time*, Heidegger drew on Aristotle's concepts to emphasize that, in nature's *a priori*-like "design," *Da-sein* represents our ontological potential, that self-questioning existence in relation to the question of being, by which our being as human is to be measured. Our capacities are dispositions always stretched between actuality and potentiality: that is, between natural development, or development according to nature, and possibilities for development according to skills and arts acquired by cultural learning. The given potentiality puts us in question, questioning our ability to take it up as a challenge, a responsibility, making it actual in our historical existence. Thus, in that early major work, Heidegger suggests important criticisms of the *character* of our prevailing ways of seeing and hearing. But he leaves these criticisms without considering how the character of those ways might be developed, changed for the better, and how such changes might in turn affect our historical existence—an existence he considers to be in the grip of nihilism—in relation to the question of being. In his later thought, when he formulates his critique of our technology-driven world, he once again registers criticisms of the prevailing character of perception but again leaves essentially unthought, or at the least only implicit, the question of a potential for development and cultivation—processes of learning. Nevertheless, when he contemplates the fragments that remain with us of pre-Socratic thought, his rigorous interpretation brings out modalities of perception—modalities of seeing and hearing—that show us a very different way, a very different character: what I think we would all agree represents a more appealing, more desirable, more poetic character. And although he lucidly delineates the difference between that pre-Socratic character and the character that prevails in the modern epoch, implicitly expressing admiration for the ancient ways, he does not sufficiently explore how *retrieving* the pre-Socratic provenance, the historical *Herkunft* of our perceptual ways in a bodily processed work of recollection could alter the prevailing modalities of perception and sensibility, transforming them in ways that might be of great consequence for our historical existence.

Heidegger's attempt to retrieve the pre-Socratic experience is not undertaken out of a misguided romanticism, a nostalgia for a lost past; it is rather his way of deepening his conceptual understanding of the contemporary world—deepening it enough to illuminate something of our potential today as human beings. His retrieval of the past is therefore to show us that things could be otherwise. What we take as inevitable, as irreversible, as fate are in fact contingencies of a history that has many times been interrupted and altered—a history that, we may suppose, always still can be transformed by our assumption of responsibility for the way things are—and above all, for the way *we* are.

†

Embracing our given nature as percipient, a nature that, contrary to what cultural conventions, habits, and the natural sciences induce us to believe, is in its deepest truth unfathomable, we can grow into our responsibility as human beings by attending with care to the immeasurability of the dimensions opened up by our appropriated, appropriately attuned response ability. This response ability, freeing all beings from presentification and reification (*Vergegenständlichung*), is concisely characterized in this beautiful passage on the term *Eignung* (claim of appropriation) published in *The Event* (1941–1942):

> To the unique claim of beyng [*Anspruch des Seyns*], namely, *that it is*, there pertains . . . the gathering of all capacities [*die Versammlung aller Vermögen*] into the unity of the preservation of the truth of beyng [*die Wahrung der Wahrheit des Seyns*, i.e., the clearing for the interplay of concealment and unconcealment]. (GA 71: 162/E 139)

Consequently, in their disposition, assigned and committed to their preservation of the in-between (*angeeignet zur Wahrung seines Inzwischen*), human beings can move toward what is most proper to their existence only insofar as they are, in appropriation, "steadfastly responsible [*inständlich verantwortet*] for the pure enowning eventuation of beings, i.e., bringing beings into the time-space of their inceptual truth [*die reine Eignung des Seienden in den*

*Zeit-Raum seiner anfänglichen Wahrheit*]." This extremely dense but crucial formulation of Heidegger's claim will, I hope, be satisfyingly interpreted in the course of our work in this volume and the next.

†

Now, it is crucial to recognize that Heidegger presents his project in a historical context, meaning not only that he understands that the matters with which he is concerned cannot be properly thought outside of their historical context but also that his critique of our time is intended to constitute an *intervention* in the course of history—an intervention that has history-breaking and history-making consequences. That is because his history of philosophy is, unusually, as he says, the history that we are, and because, too, his history of philosophy is inspired and guided by a philosophy of history, a vision of what inheritance and destiny can mean for a community (GA 47: 1–46/N3: 3–31).

According to Heidegger, metaphysics, understood not as an esoteric discourse taking place among philosophers but as naming a form of life, a way of living in the world, "grounds an age [*begründet ein Zeitalter*], in that, through a specific interpretation of what *is* [*auf eine bestimmte Auffasung der Wahrheit*], it gives the age the ground of its essential form [*Wesensgestalt*]." In our time, what Heidegger calls "the time of the world as picture," this purports nihilism, the reification and reduction, or even worse, the absolute negation of being (GA 5: 75/QCT 115). Metaphysics, as understood in this "existential" way, shapes our very sense of what it means for something—anything at all—to *be*. Thus, as Heidegger argues in his 1935 *Introduction to Metaphysics*, Western humanity, in all its comportment toward entities, including itself, is in every way sustained and guided by metaphysics—by our historically shaped and shared ways of making sense of the world we live in.

But, as we know, over time, the conditions of living change, and this eventually means that, to some degree, our sense of reality will also undergo change, so that what we take to be "real"—*das Wirkliche*— is always "something that comes about [*seiend*] on the basis of the essential history of being itself [*aus der Wesensgeschichte des Seins selbst*]" (GA 6.2: 376/N4: 232). Contemplated from the point of view of this history of being, such changes appear to constitute a hermeneutical succession of epochs, each epoch defined in terms of a distinctive unconcealment of being, a coherent, shared sense of what is and what matters. The epochs are thus constructs of interpretation unified and informed by different constellations of meaningfulness (*Bedeutsamkeit*), that is, in terms of *what* entities, or *kinds* of entities, are recognized as meaningful and in what distinctively different shared ways those entities that are recognized as being meaningful are experienced and understood.

†

The history of metaphysics that Heidegger tells enables him to demonstrate the truth in his critique. However, the neglect, distortion, or denial of being—being as such—in the discourse of metaphysics that his telling of its history reveals, gives rise in Heidegger's thought to speculative conjectures belonging to a *philosophy of history* that imagines the possibility of another, very different relation to the meaning of being—that is, the manifestation of being in thought, hence what might be called "another beginning," setting in motion another ontological order—both for the lifeworld and for the philosophical thought it encourages. We can thus discern the way in which the history of philosophy that Heidegger tells and, in particular, his history of metaphysics, as the discourse concerned with being, represents the subtle influence over his thinking of a certain highly abstract, speculative philosophy of history, envisioning, for the sake of its "redemptive" possibility, an entirely new relation to the existential and philosophical meaning of the manifestation of being.

In much later writings, Heidegger no longer invokes his speculative—and in some respects problematic and justifiably controversial—philosophy of history; but his silence in that regard does not necessarily mean that he has entirely abandoned it. Instead, he opposes the world and the metaphysics he has accused by turning to poetic evocations of a different way of building and dwelling—living mindfully on the earth of this planet, living mindfully, too, under the vastness of the sky.

In his *Überlegungen II–IV* (1931–1938), private notebooks registering his "ponderings" during the 1930s, Heidegger wrote that we need to "learn to find the great joy in little things [*die große Freude an den kleinen Dingen lernen*]" (GA 94: 321/P 2: 233). This thought, undoubtedly a way of reminding himself as well as us, tells us that there were times when, perhaps in the spirit of a mood inspired by words from the poet Rilke, he put aside for a moment his highly abstract speculations regarding the *Geschick des Seins*, the promising possibility of destiny that might be carried, unnoticed, hence hidden, in the unfolding of the grand "history of being," and permitted himself to feel, and understand, that in our learning this joy, a redeeming "transformation in our way of being present here in the world [*Verwandlung des Da-seins*]" just might already be happening.

We can also discern this sentiment reading Heidegger's 1962 wedding wish for Peter Rees, son of Theophil Rees, a close friend: "[May] you remain awake for the saving power [*das Rettende*], ready and able to savor everywhere the secret sense of things [*wach bleibt für das Rettende, bereit und tätig, überall den geheimen Sinn der Dinge zu kosten*]" (GA 16: 585–866). We cannot read the invocation of *das Rettende* without recognizing Heidegger's reference to Hölderlin's verse, in which the poet expressed his faith that a "saving power" would emerge where the greatest danger lies.[22] But in this wedding wish, this prayer, Heidegger suggests, or implies, that the redemption of our world, our lives—messianicity—is not to be found in something to come, something redemptive transcending the world and breaking into its historical continuum. Rather, it is to be found in every moment and in every situation, even in the seemingly most insignificant events and things of everyday life. It is a question of our openness, our ability to be mindfully present, awake to the "secret sense of things." The "saving power," he suggests, is to be found within us.[23]

In his "Theses on the Philosophy of History," perhaps also thinking of Hölderlin's verse, Walter Benjamin tries to remind us that what is ultimately crucial is that we recognize, as a gift kept within ourselves, our appropriation by a "weak messianic power."[24] We are appropriated to the exercise of this "power." Heidegger, however, in the very next entry in his notebook of "ponderings," and in fact on the very same page, shifts back to the grander, loftier onto-historical discourse of the *Geschick* and challenges the simplicity and naïvety of this reliance only on mindfulness and the feelings it brings forth: "Richer than all fulfillment is the ripening of anticipation and preparedness [*Reicher denn alle Erfüllung fruchtet die Bereitschaft und Erwartung*]." Although this is a concession to hope, it should also serve as a warning to restrain premature and false claims:

> The present task for thought is only preparatory, not founding. It is content with awakening a readiness [*Erweckung einer Bereitschaft*] in human beings for a possibility the contour of which remains obscure, and the coming of which remains uncertain. Thinking must first learn what remains reserved and in store for thinking to get involved in. It prepares its own transformation [*seine eigene Wandlung*] in this learning. (GA 14: 75/OTB 60)

The engagement of historically informed consciousness in thinking toward the future is of course necessary. But philosophical thought must find a way to reconcile and join together the two equally compelling versions of the redeeming transformation, namely the onto-historical and the personal-existential. Heidegger has set the process in motion. It needs to be continued.

## NOTES

1. Benedict Spinoza, *Ethics*, Preceded by *On the Improvement of the Understanding*, ed. James Gutmann (New York: Hafner Publishing Co., 1960), 263.

2. Ibid., 268.

3. Ibid., 271.

4. Ibid., 277ff.

5. Ibid., 271.

6. Theodor Adorno, *Minima Moralia: Reflexionen aus dem beschädigten Leben* (Frankfurt am Main: Suhrkamp Verlag, 1951, 1969), 333; *Minima Moralia: Reflections from Damaged Life*, trans. E. F. N. Jephcott, (London: Verso NLB, 1978), 247.

7. Ibid., 249.

8. Immanuel Kant, "Idea for a Universal History with a Cosmopolitan Purpose," in Hans Reiss, ed., *Kant's Political Writings* (Cambridge: Cambridge University Press, 1970), 50.

9. John Dewey, *Democracy and Education*, in *John Dewey: The Middle Works*, vol. 9 (Carbondale: University of Southern Illinois Press, 1985), 338. Italics in the original.

10. Medard Boss, "Schlusswort," *Zollikoner Seminare*, GA 89: 366; "Afterword," *Zollikon Seminars*, 295. Translation revised.

11. A similar grammar in languaging our sensory experience is manifest in tasting, touching, and the olefactory sense: We speak of a tasting that shifts into savoring; a touching and handling that shifts into a sensitive feeling, an appreciatively caressing touch; an involuntary experience of smelling something that shifts into a deliberate, focused sniffing, and then into an even more deliberate, more intense, more concentrated engagement of smelling.

12. T. S. Eliot, "The Love Song of J. Alfred Prufrock," *The Wasteland and Other Poems*, 5.

13. Rainer Maria Rilke, *The Notebooks of Malte Laurids Brigge*, trans. M. D. Herter Norton (New York: W. W. Norton, 1949, 1964), 14–15.

14. Robert Walser, *Kleine Wanderung* (Frankfurt am Main: Reclam, 1967).

15. Maurice Blanchot, "La parole quotidienne," *L'Entretien infini* (Paris: Gallimard, 1959), 355–66; "Everyday Speech," *Yale French Studies*, no. 73 (1987), 14.

16. "Die Kehre," *Identität und Differenz*, GA 11: 123. For two English translations, see "The Turning," *The Question of Technology and Other Essays*, 48, and Andrew Mitchell's newer translation of "Die Kehre", GA 79: 77, "The Turn," in *Bremen and Freiburg Lectures*, 72. See Samuel Taylor Coleridge's reflections on William Wordsworth's claim to use the power of the poetic word to "give the charm of novelty to things of every day . . . by awakening the mind's attention from the lethargy of custom, and directing it to the loveliness and the wonders of the world before us—an inexhaustible treasure, but for which in consequence of the film of familiarity and selfish solicitude we have eyes, yet see not, ears that hear not, and hearts that neither feel nor understand." *Biographia Literaria*, ed. James Engell and W. Jackson Bate, vol. 2 (Princeton, NJ: Princeton University Press,1983), 7.

17. Martin Heidegger, *Sein und Zeit*, 41–45, but especially 42; *Being and Time*, 67–71, but esp. 67–68. See also Heidegger's 1925 *Prolegomena zur Geschichte des Zeitbegriffs*, GA 20: 205–6, 220, 325, and 340 and his 1925 *Logik: Die Frage nach der Wahrheit*, GA 21: 414.

18. See Heidegger's reference on *Temporalität* in regard to a "transcendental temporality" that is fundamentally different from *Zeitlichkeit*, in *Das Ereignis*, GA 71: 213/E 182. And see *Die Geschichte des Seyns*, GA 69: 95/HB 80: "Temporalität" refers to "the realm of the clearing for being." Also see the important statement in "Recollection in Metaphysics," GA 6.2: 490/EP 83, where Heidegger lays out the difference between ontic *Zeitlichkeit* ("historically calculative time") and the *Temporalität* belonging to the process of recollection (*Erinnerung*) in the history of being.

19. Ralph Waldo Emerson, "Intellect," in Joel Porte, ed., *Essays and Lectures* (New York: The Library of America, 1983), 418–19.

20. My two volumes are the culmination of a project that began in the 1970s regarding Heidegger's phenomenology of perception and his contributions to an emerging body of ontological understanding.

21. I have long been drawn to the possibility of a very fruitful dialectic between Heidegger and Merleau-Ponty with regard to embodiment, or say incarnation, and, more specifically, with regard to perception. What Merleau-Ponty could give to Heidegger is a much richer phenomenology of embodiment, concretely fleshing out his analytic of *Dasein*, which, in its finitude, its vulnerability, and its cast of moods and dispositions, is very much in need of a more elaborated representation and philosophical analysis of its incarnation. Thus, for example, Heidegger attributes to *Dasein* a pre-ontological understanding of being, but he fails to explicate the nature of its embodiment, without which his conception of that understanding risks remaining within the metaphysical dualism of a Cartesian or Kantian theory of mind. Merleau-Ponty significantly illuminates this dimension of our bodily experience. And correspondingly, what Heidegger could give to Merleau-Ponty's early phenomenology of perception is the ontological dimension, which disrupts the subject–object structure—and indeed the other persistent metaphysical assumptions—that his phenomenology inherited from Cartesianism, Husserl, and the systems of German idealism.

22. Friedrich Hölderlin, "Patmos," *Sämtliche Werke*, ed. Paul Stapf (Berlin and Darmstadt: Der Tempel-Verlag), 328, 334. And see the argument that Heidegger makes around these lines of the poet's verse, GA 7: 29, 35 /QCT 28, 34.

23. In that same poem, "Patmos," the poet states that divine work is like our own: "Denn göttliches Werk auch gleichet dem unsern."

24. See Walter Benjamin, "Über den Begriff der Geschichte," *Gesammelte Schriften* (Frankfurt am Main: Suhrkamp Verlag, 1974), vol. I.2, 693–94; "Theses on the Philosophy of History," *Illuminations*, trans. Harry Zohn (New York: Schocken, 1969), 253–54. In addition to recalling Hölderlin's lines in "Patmos," Benjamin's thought of a "weak messianic power" (*schwache messianische Kraft*) recalls the "weak ray of hope" (*schwache Strahl der Hoffnung*) that Kant invoked in §80 of his *Critique of Judgement* and also Apostle Paul's words in 2 *Corinthians* 12: 9–10: "My grace is sufficient for you, since my power is made perfect in weakness."

# PART I

# ANOTHER HUMANISM?

The human is something that will be overcome. Man is like
a rope, stretched between the animal and a superior form of
human—a rope over an abyss. What is great in the human is
that it is a bridge and not an end.

—Friedrich Nietzsche, *Thus Spoke Zarathustra*[1]

In his "Letter on Humanism," a letter written in December 1946 to the
French philosopher Jean Beaufret in response to his questions, Heidegger
formulated a searing critique of Western humanism. Although the critique
is justified, it ignores how this humanism encouraged the flourishing of the
arts and the sciences and laid the groundwork for the social and political
progress represented by the Enlightenment. Heidegger ventures his critique
in the name of, and for the sake of, *another* humanism. Although this other
humanism can for the most part be gleaned only by carefully considering
the substance of the critique and its far-reaching implications, I submit that,
in at least one crucial respect, it takes over and reaffirms the humanism it
inherited, making us take responsibility for the world we have created.

Formulated in a preliminary way for the purposes of this introductory
chapter, I think it is fair to say that, for Heidegger, we of the Western world
are enthralled and captivated by our enormous powers, above all, our technological powers. The humanism that Heidegger fears, criticizes, and warns
against is an ideology that justifies and encourages us, we human beings,
especially those belonging to the Western world, to make ourselves—and
our happiness, a happiness he regards as tragically corrupted—the absolute
measure of all things. It is a humanism that, as Heidegger represents it, glo-
rifies human power—a Nietzschean will to power—that today is primarily
technological and technocratic. With this unprecedented power, we rule

29

over earth and sky. But we are not willing to acknowledge the responsibilities that this rule makes imperative.

†

The Lacandon Mayans, a tribe struggling to survive the loss of its forest and all the life it sustained, used to regard the gigantic ancient trees of their forest as the "lords of the earth." In that attitude, which we dismiss as childlike, there is awe, wonder, humility, reverence, and respect. They did not destroy the forest to exploit its lumber for commerce and profit. Their religion kept them in harmony with the exigencies of their environment, the earth, the waters, the sky. They made use of nature to serve their fundamental needs; they did not destroy it in greed; and they, in turn, served nature as its guardians. We, however, are making *ourselves* the lords of the earth, leaving nothing untouched by our avarice, our endless lust for material pleasures, our arrogant authority, imposing our will, our measure, on all things:

> What the people of the city do not realize . . . is that the roots of all living things are tied together. When a mighty tree is felled, a star falls from the sky. . . . I know that soon we must all die. There is too much coldness in the world now; it has worked its way into the hearts of all living creatures, and down into the roots of the grass and the trees.[2]

†

As we are incapable of infinite extension, infinite power, we reduce the immeasurable to something within our limited powers to measure. In that way, we lose for moral guidance the perspective of the immeasurable. Our hands are no longer guided, as Heidegger says, by gestures "befitting the measure": "*Gebärden die dem Maß entsprechen.*" Can we learn how to "dwell poetically": on the earth and under the sky? Thinking of Hölderlin's verse, "*dichterisch wohnet der Mensch,*" that is Heidegger's question (GA 7: 202/ PLT 223).

The humanism that emerged in the Renaissance was a revolution revolting against the God-centered world of the medieval age and joyously affirming celebrating the importance and merit of this human, earth-bound world. Instead of submitting every nook and cranny of this jumbled world to God's omnipotent, all-encompassing, all-seeing gaze and judgment, Renaissance humanism recognized that its world could be seen from many different points of view: although acknowledging a vanishing point, a point beyond which the power of the human eye cannot venture, it ordered the world according to the geometric law of perspective. This was a rationalizing order imposed on a disorderly world; but it was also an order that expressed a new self-confidence, a new faith in our capacity, as human beings, to create a world for ourselves worthy of our moral aspirations. However, according to the narrative Heidegger wants to tell, in the centuries that followed the Renaissance, this measured humanism, still earth-bound, still conscious of its limits, its finitude, became increasingly arrogant, increasingly narcissistic, increasingly drunk on its power. Humanism became a doctrine encouraging and justifying a will to power that knows no limits. And in order to defend and maintain this power, it reduced the immeasurable to what human power could measure and reduced the ontology of being to an ontology that can only recognize beings.

†

In "The Age of the World Picture," Heidegger claims that "humanism first arises when the world becomes picture" (GA 5: 92–93/QCT 133). He leaves more indeterminate than one might wish the factual history defining this momentous event. Nevertheless, it would be reasonable to hold that the connection between humanism and the worldview that enframed the world as a picture first arose in the European Renaissance, when there were great ventures in maritime commerce and navigation, significant projects mapping the oceans and continents, and, in the art of painting, not only the first depictions of perspective but also a revolutionary paradigm reversal of the power-relation between God and human beings, such that, instead of God beholding us, we could now for the first time claim the power to behold God. In any case, whatever historical date we assign to the emergence of humanism and its worldview, Heidegger wants to argue that the historically prevailing form of humanism is "nothing but a moral-aesthetic anthropology," in the sense that it is "the philosophical interpretation of being human that explains and evaluates whatever is, in its entirety, from the standpoint of man and in relation to man" (GA 5: 93/QCT 133). It is a worldview (*Weltanschauung*) in which, for the first time, "man brought his life as *subjectum* into precedence over other centres of relationship. This means whatever is, is considered to be in being only to the degree and to the extent that it is taken into and referred back to this life [*Dies bedeutet: Das Seiende gilt erst als seiend, sofern es und soweit es in dieses Leben ein- und zurückbezogen, d.h. er-lebt und Erlebnis wird*]." Thus, he argues: "The fundamental event of the modern age [*Grundvorgang der Neuzeit*] is the conquest of the world as picture" (GA 5: 94/QCT 134). To represent the world as a picture is to enframe it, suggesting a mastery of the whole as a totality. And that transformation of the world into picture, into objecthood, was inseparable from the emergence of man into the philosophical position of subject—a position that reflected the emergence of individualism in the economic and political life of the Western world. (GA 5: 92–94/132–33)

In *Being and Truth*, containing lectures delivered during the Winter Semester 1933–1934, Heidegger comments that philosophical thought "is a fundamental happening [*Grundgeschehen*] in the history of humanity . . . , which has the character [*Charakter*] of a quite distinctive questioning, a questioning in which and through which it is possible for the essence of humanity to transform itself [*sich verwandelt*]" (GA 36/37: 208/BaT:159). He continues, declaring, without his customary restraint, that "the question of man must be *revolutionized* [*revolutioniert*]. Historicity is a fundamental dimension of our being. This revolution demands of us a completely new relationship to history and to the question of the being of the human being" (GA 36/37: 215/BaT 163). Similar thought also appears in many other texts—*The History of Beyng*, for instance, written during the years 1938–1940, in which Heidegger describes his philosophical project as calling for "eine wesentliche Verwandlung des Menschen": "an essential transformation of the human"—"an other humankind" (GA 69: 90, 139/ HB 76, 119–20).[3] This is not sufficient as a *description* of what he thinks is needed; but it is, much more, a *summons*, an impassioned *calling* to thought. The philosopher here is not merely a neutral observer. But his summons is without the serenity we ascribe to the philosopher. On the contrary, in these years of political tumult, that summons is sometimes followed by words of a prophetic nature, bearing an apocalyptic tone: "Possible," he says next, "only after the most extreme and extensive shatterings": "*Nur möglich nach den äußersten und längsten Erschütterungen.*" This thought also figures in his *Contributions to Philosophy* (*Of the Event*): We should expect that the transformation bringing about a new ontological epoch, a new paradigm of knowledge, truth, and reality could take place "only by way of great breakdowns and upheavals in beings" (GA 65: 241/CP 190).

Like Nietzsche's idea of the *Übermensch*, which obviously inspired him, even though he never entirely agreed with it, Heidegger's projection in thought of a great transformation in our humanity, our being human, provides little detail, hardly enough even for a sketch—although perhaps we might attempt to imagine it, drawing out some implications—conjectures and speculations—from the details in his critique of our postindustrial, technologized world, with its imposition of a reifying totality. But would it be a total transformation all the way down to our very essence? Would it involve a total change in the very essence, the very structure of our existence, our being? It is conceivable that it is just such a transformation that Nietzsche, and perhaps for a while—say, during the 1930s and early 1940s—Heidegger too had in mind. Both invoked the idea of an originary "leap" (GA 11: 48–49/ID 39).[4] But even our fulfillment as human beings, recognizing and understanding ourselves, and comporting ourselves accordingly, would not necessarily involve the most radical change we can imagine, namely, a total transformation in our very *essence*, our fundamental *nature*—but only perhaps a mindfulness that retrieves and maintains what, in "Recollection in Metaphysics," Heidegger described as "the essential structure of human being in relation to being [*die Fügung des Menschenwesens in den Bezug zum Sein*]" (GA 6.2: 485/EP 78–79). It would already be a great accomplishment for us to be appropriated by that given essence, enowning and actualizing it. What is at stake, then, is rather the *fulfillment*—he thinks of it as a releasing, a *Freigebung*—of the "true worthiness" of the human nature we have been already been given and, so to speak, entrusted with.

My project in this book will not assume that, even if a certain originary "leap" is necessary for the transformation to occur, what Heidegger had in mind involves such an extremely radical apocalyptic event. What I think the "leap" suggests is that this transformation cannot be achieved by steps that maintain continuity with the past. This should not be understood, however, to mean that I consider the human essence—our "human nature"—to be immutable, totally determined and totally determinate. It is an essence, a "nature," in ceaseless interaction with the conditions operative in our world: an essence-in-process, rather than an essence in the familiar, traditional metaphysical sense. And there is certainly much in the character and disposition of what we consider to be "human nature" that we can and, I think, should change: change by learning and developing new habits, new skills, and new abilities; change, too, by altering the various conditions— socio economic, geopolitical, environmental, and genetic—that are determinative of the way we are living. As Heidegger says in his "Letter on Humanism," for human beings it is ever a question of "finding what is fitting in their essence [*in das Schickliche seines Wesens*], finding what corresponds [*entspricht*] in our lives to the meaningful granting of being [*Geschick des Seins*]" (GA 9: 331–32/PM 252–53). And, as the text makes clear, what corresponds is our mindfully taking care, as much as possible, of the world-historical conditions in terms of which beings can come into meaningful presence. For we are the grounders and preservers, the guardians, of being.

†

So who are we, we human beings? What, in our becoming-in-essence as human beings, are we? What does it mean to be a human being? What meaning, what destiny, if any, is constitutive of our existence? And how are we different from other beings—indeed, from *all* other beings? In *Being and Time* (1927), Heidegger states that what most distinguishes us as human beings is the fact that our being, our existence, is such that it is necessarily always in question for us. Among all the living beings, we are the only ones for whom our existence is, and has to be, in question. Needless to say, that also distinguishes us from inanimate things such as books, desks, trees, and clouds.

We are, moreover, the only beings endowed with a self-consciousness that compels recognition of our finitude, our mortality—our being-unto-death. Authentic existence is living with this intimate sense of our nature, our condition, and the shadow of death that walks with us, making vividly meaningful all the moments of our time on this earth. As Heidegger formulates this understanding in "Building Dwelling Thinking," setting it out in sharpest opposition to the humanism still prevailing in our time: "To be a human being means to be on the earth as a mortal. It means to dwell" (GA 7: 149/PLT 147). But "on the earth" already means "under the sky." And both of these also mean "remaining before the divinities," that is, being judged by the highest values and ideals we profess; and they include "being with one another" (GA 7: 151/PLT 149). Thus, "mortals dwell in that they initiate [hence bear responsibility for] their own nature" (GA 7: 152/PLT 151). This text marks a significant enrichment in Heidegger's own thinking about the being of the human. But its representation of the human, written in 1951, twenty-four years after the publication of *Being and Time*, is manifestly very much at odds with the humanism Heidegger attributes to our time—although there are, and in fact have been for many years, philosophers such as John Dewey and theologians such as Paul Tillich for whom what "humanism" means is not the narcissism of the will to power but an ethical commitment to the moral humanitarian enlightenment of humanity. Heidegger's critique is nevertheless of great value because what prevails today is nothing but a hollowed-out perversion and subversion of the original conception of humanism, nothing but a doctrine that attempts to disguise and justify the madness of an ideology that celebrates the ruthless pursuit of self-interest.

†

In *Being and Time*, Heidegger declared that the most urgent, most important question not only for philosophers and their discourse but also for all of us human beings is the question of being—the *Seinsfrage*. Yet of all the most exigent existential questions, this question, this most uncanny, most unsettling question is, he argued, the most forgotten, most ignored, most neglected. So Heidegger accordingly set out, in *Being and*

*Time*, to give the *Seinsfrage* the careful reflective attention it demands. However, one cannot read this work without noticing that, at the same time that "being" is brought into thought, so too is the existence—the *Da-sein*—of the human being. This is because, as we shall see, being and human being—*Sein* and *Mensch*, or *Sein* and *Da-sein*, to use Heidegger's words—are inseparably intertwined. There can be, and have been, beings, entities, things, without us; in the pre-Cambrian period, long before any human beings walked the earth, there already were, as we know, plants and animals. Beings do not need us human beings to be conscious of them in order to exist, to be. Heidegger defends realism in this sense. But he also defends phenomenology: there can be no unfolding of the *meaning, essence*, and *history* of being without us. Consequently, although Heidegger's ontological enquiry evolves in various ways, undergoing certain turns and twists, it is throughout—from its earliest beginnings into its very last formulations—not only hermeneutical, as befits its ontological dimension, but also, necessarily, a project in existential phenomenology.[5] And, as we have discovered, it was not long after he gave the manuscript of *Being and Time* to be published that he was struck by the insight that, for the next stage in his project, the phenomenological explication of our existential appropriation (*Ereignis, Ereignung*) actually works better than reflecting directly on the question of being.

†

It should thus not be at all surprising, however, that Heidegger would at some point recognize that he needed to take up for critical thought how the being of the human is conceptualized in the discourse he calls "humanism." In his "Letter on Humanism," first published in 1949 but presenting thoughts that were already beginning to take shape in the early 1920s, Heidegger ventured an argument against the figure of "the human" that emerged to hold sway in a certain prevalent interpretation of humanism (GA 9: 313–64/PM 239–76). The argument proposed in that letter is frustratingly sketchy, abstract, and obscure, and because of these weaknesses, these deficiencies, the substance of the argument has—understandably—been misunderstood. What Heidegger's critique rejects is, as he phrases it, that "the highest determinations of the essence of the human being in humanism still do not realize the proper dignity [*eigentliche Würde*] of the human being. . . . Humanism is [to be] opposed because it does not set the *humanitas* of the human being high enough" (GA 9: 330/PM 251). It is thus a question of "bringing the human being back to his essence" so that man can become truly human (GA 9: 319/PM 243). It is, he says (in the 1949 edition), a question of our "propriation"—our *Eignung*. According to Heidegger, by conceptualizing humanism in terms of metaphysics, philosophical thought lost sight of that essence, that is, with what we as human beings are capable of becoming in fulfilling our humanity, our proper dignity.

We should note here that there is, implicit in his rethinking of the human in the discourse of humanism, the adumbration of an ontologically attuned ethics, an "originary ethics," the substance of which Heidegger has persisted in illuminating in his lifetime of contributions to an existential phenomenology. This ethics is unequivocally suggested when he says, for instance: "The human being is not the lord of beings. The human being is the shepherd of being." Living according to this understanding, human beings "gain the essential poverty of the shepherd, whose dignity consists in being called by being itself into the preservation of the truth of being," that is, the interplay of concealment and unconcealment within which unconcealment takes place (GA 9: 342/PM 260). An ethics for guiding life is also suggested there when he says, venturing to characterize his new version of humanism:

> *Humanitas* really does remain the concern of such thinking. For this is
> humanism: meditating and caring, that human beings be human and not
> inhumane, "inhuman," that is, outside their essence.

"But," he then asks, "in what does the humanity of the human being consist?" And he answers: "It lies in his essence."

This is still exceedingly abstract. So what more, with more phenomenological concreteness, can be said about that essence? That question cannot be answered without first considering Heidegger's problematization of that essence as it figures in metaphysical thought, because every humanism "is either grounded in a metaphysics or is itself made to be the ground of one. Every determination of the essence of the human being that already presupposes an interpretation of beings without asking about the truth of being . . . is metaphysical" (GA 9: 321/PM 245). As metaphysical, "humanism fails to ask about the relation of being to the essence of human being." This is undoubtedly, despite its seeming beside the point, Heidegger's most fundamental objection to humanism. What he means, I think, is that we do not take responsibility for being—for the being of meaning and, above all, the meaning of being, and this is because we do not recognize ourselves—do not recognize our role—in the meaningful presence of being. We human beings are alone responsible for taking into our care, our thought, what is and what is not, and how things are as they are in our world. That ontological responsibility—that "appropriation"—is what I think he is calling our "true, proper dignity": a dignity he thinks metaphysics does not recognize.

So Heidegger does not argue that the metaphysical definition of the human being in humanism is false. Rather, he argues that it is conditioned by a metaphysics that "does indeed represent beings in their being, and so it also thinks the being of beings. But it does not think being as such [i.e., it does not think about what makes meaningful encounter possible as such], does not think the [ontological] difference between beings and being [i.e., the phenomenology of the clearing, as that which makes possible the meaningful presence of those beings]" (GA 9: 322/PM 246). Hence, it "does not ask about the truth of being itself [i.e., it does not enquire about our thrown-openness, the clearing itself, as that which is necessary for the phenomenology of meaningful presence]. Nor does it therefore ask in what way the essence of the human being *belongs* to the truth of being." This "belonging," however, is the crucial point: precisely what humanism, bound as it has been to a problematic metaphysics, has failed to recognize and interpret. As we shall see, Heidegger very effectively uses the term *Ereignis*, and a constellation of kindred terms, to interpret this relation of belonging that binds us human beings to being in our capacity, our disposition, as *Da-sein* (GA 9: 316/PM 241).[6] Emphasizing the inherently ontological nature of our responsibility in this belonging, Heidegger tells us that

> only so far as the human being, ek-sisting in the truth of being [i.e., existing in the world its existence opens up], belongs [*gehört*] to being can there come from being itself the assignment of those directives that must become law and rule for human beings. (GA 9: 360–61/PM 274)

We *belong* to being in the sense that we are *responsible* for being—that is, for the meaning of being and the truth of being, that is, the conditions in our world according to which beings can enter into meaningful presence and depart from that presence within the interplay of concealment and unconcealment. In sum, Heidegger's criticism of humanism is that it perpetuates a metaphysics that fails to recognize the phenomenology constitutive of human existence. Hence, it fails to recognize crucial dimensions of our responsibility for the way the world is.

Moreover, traditional humanism cannot understand—cannot even begin to think—how this responsibility might prepare for the possibility of an ontologically grounded ethics, an ethics arising not from abstract principles of reason but inherently from the very nature of our phenomenological relation to being, that is, in our relation to the fundamental existential conditions of meaning and intelligibility. As Heidegger phrases it, what is at issue is "the assignment contained in the dispensation of being." Because "only such [inherently generated] enjoining," he says, "is capable of the supporting and obligating [of an originary ethics]. Otherwise, all law remains merely something fabricated by human reason" (GA 9: 361/ PM 274). What Heidegger means by "the assignment contained in the dispensation of being" refers us to what our relation to being demands of us when we attend to its calling. We might condense the entire argument against humanism and the metaphysics Heidegger takes to be behind it in just one key word: humanism fails to think of the human from out of the ontological claim on our appropriation—*aus der Ereignung*. That is to say, in all our encounters with the beings in our world, we have a role we need to acknowledge in regard to their being: the bond constitutive of our belonging in togetherness with those beings makes a claim on our responsibility in regard to their being. When Heidegger accuses traditional humanism of not recognizing the true dignity of "mankind" and not giving thought to the essence of our humanity, our being, in relation to the question of being, what I take him to be arguing for is this ontological responsibility—our appropriation.

This interpretation is supported by a note published in *The Event*, where Heidegger asserted that the "nobility" (*Adel*) of our historical existence and essence consists in our "appropriation to the truth of being." In other words, our distinction is to be found in our recognition that the conditions for the way things can be present and absent, bearing in mind the meaning that they have for us, are essentially matters calling for the exercise of our responsibility: a responsibility, in fact, that requires a certain response ability (GA 71: 212–13/E 181–82). And years later, in the lecture "Time and Being" (1962), he again articulates the distinction and dignity of the human being in terms of the appropriation (*Er-eignung*) of perception, hence in a way that is especially relevant for the project undertaken in this present volume:

> In being as presence [*Sein als Anwesen*], there is manifest the concern [*bekundet sich der Angang*] that concerns us humans in such a way that, in perceiving and receiving it [*im Vernehmen und Übernehmen dieses Angangs*], we have attained the distinction of human being [*das Auszeichnende des Menschseins erlangt haben*]. (GA 14:28/OTB 23)

Our distinction as human beings is that, in perceiving and receiving what presences, we have been endowed and favored with the ability—the intelligence—to recognize and understand what is always already operative in being as presence, namely, our role in the phenomenology of the truth of being, a role involving our *appropriation* to bear the most awesome onto-logical responsibility, which Heidegger has characterized as "guardianship" (*Wächterschaft*) of the truth of being. We alone are capable of protecting and preserving the interplay of concealment and unconcealment taking place in the clearings our existence, our very presence, inevitably, necessarily makes.

Further explaining this claim regarding our distinction, Heidegger makes a connection between our appropriation (*Ereignis*), our becoming who we are most authentically as human beings and the fact that our per-ception is determined by its taking place in time: "appropriation has the peculiar property [*das Eigentümliche*] of bringing man into his own [*in sein Eigenes bringt*] as the being who perceives being [*als den, der Sein vernimmt*] by standing within authentic time [*indem er innesteht in der eigentlichen Zeit*]" (GA 14:28/OTB 23). Our being-in-time, hence our mortality, is once again emphasized as a crucial feature, a crucial appropriation of the human condition that the discourse of humanism neglects. In its representation of human nature and human existence, philosophical humanism completely ignores temporality and historicity.

†

Perhaps the clearest, sharpest formulation of the distinction, the dig-nity Heidegger attributes to humanity, is to be read in "The Question Concerning Technology" (1954, 1962):

> The granting [*Das Gewährende*] that sends in one way or another into the unconcealment of presencing [*in die Entbergung schickt*] is as such the saving power [*das Rettende*]. For the saving power lets man see and enter [*schauen und einkehren*] into the highest dignity of his essence [*die höchste Würde seines Wesens*]. This dignity lies in keeping watch over the unconcealment—and with it, from the first, the concealment—of all coming-to-presence [*alles Wesens*] on this earth [*auf dieser Erde zu hüten*]. (GA 7: 33/QCT 32)

We are claimed, appropriated, "needed by being," so to speak, "to preserve and keep safe the coming-to-presence of being into its truth [*das Wesen des Seins in seiner Wahrheit zu wahren*]." In the version of humanism that Hei-degger envisions, the responsibility in this role of immense and incalculable historical consequence is what should summon our attention and call for philosophical thinking. This is the *Einkehr in das Ereignis*: our entering into our appropriation, the claim on our responsibility, our "saving power"—weak though it inherently is.

Addressing the question "what is the human?"—or the question that is not quite the same thing, namely, "what is it to be human?"—in the very midst of the War years 1941–1942, Heidegger declared, in *The Event*, the intent of his project: "To experience [and bring to light] the clearing for beyng [i.e., for presencing] in humanity [i.e., as operative appropriation in the very being, or existence, of the human] and to ground the open realm for beings" (GA 71: 242–43/E 209). Stated in extremely condensed form, Heidegger is arguing that the essence of our humanity is (to be) "grounded in *Da-seyn*," grounded in our recognition, understanding, and enownment of our responsibility, as thrown open to being, in regard to the historical conditions that make the meaningful presencing of beings possible. *We* are appropriated and accordingly grounded—grounded to be the grounders, the guardians, of beyng, the conditions necessary for meaningful engagement with the world—regardless of whether we are able to recognize ourselves in that uncanny capacity.

This is a far cry from the humanism that engaged philosophical thought from the time of the Renaissance through the time of the Enlightenment. And yet, when the implications in Heidegger's interpretation of humanism are unfolded in terms of its phenomenology, its representation of the human is not entirely unrecognizable, although the humanism it is urging would certainly take us into a future very distant, very far from our current understanding of ourselves. It is a representation that, in our present moment of time, can probably be felt only as estranging and unsettling. But *Da-sein* is not monstrous, whatever disquieting truth acknowledging it might happen to show us. In any event, we should not miss the opportunity to let this representation engage and challenge us—especially if we believe that Heidegger is right in seeing a deep connection between the nihilism of our time and the self-understanding that has been, and still is, reflected in the discourse of humanism.

†

Besides challenging the arrogance—the *hubris*—in humanism, its ignoring or even defying our finitude, our mortality, the measure proper and appropriate to our condition, Heidegger sees other grave problems in how the metaphysics of humanism has understood the being of the human. According to Heidegger's critique, after Aristotle, humanism has somehow consistently assumed that the essence of the human being is to be "a rational animal" without critically reflecting on, or compellingly explaining, the two terms involved in this interpretation of the essence (GA 9: 321/ PM 245). In what sense and way are we animals? And how can rationality be embodied in an animal nature? Cartesian mind–body dualism and its numerous alternatives in idealism and empiricism are not satisfying answers to these questions. Not even the human body—the embodiment of the human being, which Heidegger considers to be in itself an extremely challenging matter, gets, from his point of view, a compelling representation in the historical versions of idealism and empiricism he inherited. For the human body (*der Leib des Menschen*), as he thinks it, "is something essentially other than an animal organism" (GA 9: 324/PM 247).

Moreover, in all these philosophical ventures, what Heidegger finds equally problematic—and ultimately, in fact, alarming—is the positioning of the human being in a subject–object structure, in which the human being is abstracted from temporality, reduced to an encapsulated subjectivity or to a complex, intricately functioning neurophysiological animal organism, and placed in opposition to the things of the world, which are correspondingly reduced to readily available objects.

After all the metaphysical humanisms of the past, Heidegger proposes another humanism, a different humanism—a humanism of ontological responsibility that, recognizing the significance of our constitutive role in the truth of being, hence our role in the being—the meaningful happening—of beings, holds open in perception the open of the world.

In this revolutionary humanism, we are responsible for history and destiny: responsible not only for the world of beings and the world itself but also, *a fortiori*, for the *meaning* of beings, for what they mean in the contexts of our living. In this humanism, our greatness consists in our existence as sole guardians and caretakers of being—the existential *meaning* of all that is, was, and will be. In his "Letter on Humanism," Heidegger argues with metaphoric eloquence that the human being is not "the lord of beings." The human being is rather "the shepherd of being," whose dignity consists in "being called into the preservation of the truth of being" (GA 9:342/PM 260).

†

We cannot predict where the historical conditions that are granted us, making possible the meaningful presencing of beings, might lead us. However, in a Supplement to "The Age of the World Picture," Heidegger reminds us, lest we fall into fatalism regarding "the given historical conditions shaping mankind's contemporary life [*dieses Geschick seines neuzeitlichen Wesens*], that "man can, as he thinks ahead, ponder this: Our humanity, understood in terms of our being-a-subject, has not always been the sole possibility belonging to the essence of historical man, . . . nor will it always be [*noch je sein wird*]" (GA 5: 111/QCT 153). We may think of this argument as evoking the prospect of another humanism, another epoch in the history of our self-understanding as human beings. But in this refutation of fatalism there can be something else no less unsettling, as it throws us in our freedom and responsibility into the unknown. Heidegger will only counsel a difficult courage, invoking an almost forgotten past and arguing, in his "Letter on Humanism," that "if the human being is ever to find his way once again into the nearness of being, he must first learn to exist in the nameless" (GA 9: 319/WM 243). As Heidegger uses the word *Geschick* (meaning *destiny*) and its cognate terms, he is telling us that the sense of our existence as human beings is to be found in our release from the powers of fate, cast open into the openness of this world and sent (*geschickt*) on our way to engage the given—whatever our life in the world should happen to send us.

In Heidegger's project, we are called, in the name of *Da-sein*, to take responsibility for another humanism. How does the responsibility in that project engage the question of being, the question that in the 1920s, and in particular, in *Being and Time*, published in 1927, Heidegger thought was the most important, most urgent, of all questions—not only for philosophical reflection but also for the very living of our lives? And how does that responsibility engage our capacities and capabilities in perception? These questions impose themselves because the meaning of being cannot be separated from the *character* of our perception. So who are we, and who do we want to become, we who call ourselves human beings? And what character is befitting our answer to that question?

We can change much in the world by changing ourselves. And we can change much in ourselves when we recognize and understand our capabilities, our so-called powers, and the conditions for the possibility of meaningful experience operative in perception, recollection, imagination, and conception.

Without denying or diminishing the enormity of the changes that would be called for, both in ourselves and in the world itself, I think that what Heidegger envisioned in his historically new humanism is something very much like what Hölderlin imagined when he evoked a poetic, *dichterisch* way of dwelling here, standing on this earth and under this sky, taking all that lives into our care and protecting and preserving the elements of nature, earth and sky, on which the fate of all life depends. In fact, as a preponderance of evidence is warning us, the fate of nature itself depends on our ability to transform our will to power into a more sensitively attentive, more sympathetic way of engaging the world we share with nature and all the forms of life it bears. The new humanism Heidegger envisioned grounds us in the hermeneutics of our phenomenology and makes us the humble guardians of being—an awesome and sacred responsibility. We must assume that responsibility, that care—because otherwise, the being of everything in our world, and ultimately even our own being, will suffer the consequences of indifference.

## NOTES

1. Friedrich Nietzsche, *Thus Spoke Zarathustra*, trans. Walter Kaufman (London and New York: Viking Penguin, 1954, 1966), 12, 14–15.

2. Victor Perera and Robert D. Bruce, *The Last Lords of Palenque: The Lacandon Mayas of the Mexican Rain Forest* (Boston: Little, Brown and Co., 1982), 86.

3. See Martin Heidegger, *Die Geschichte des Seyns*, GA 69: §71, 90 and §119, 139; *The History of Beyng*, 76 and 119–20. And see an indication of his Nazi-era apocalypticism in these words at the very beginning of his 1939–1941 *Überlegungen XII–XV*, GA 96:5 (a) "Zerstörung ist der Vorbote eines verborgenen Anfangs, Verwüstung aber ist der Nachschlag des bereits entschiedenen Endes. Steht das Zeitalter schon vor der Entscheidung zwischen Zerstörung und Verwüstung? Aber wir wissen den anderen Anfang, wissen ihn fragend— (vgl. S. 76–79)." "Destruction is the herald of a hidden beginning; devastation however is the final blow in the already determined ending. Does our age already stand before the decision between destruction and devastation? We know the other beginning—know it, that is, only in our questioning." My translation.

4. See Heidegger's discussion of a "leap" (*Sprung, Satz*) and a "step back" (*Schritt zurück*) in "Der Satz der Identität," *Identität und Differenz*, GA 11: 48–49; "The Principle of Identity," *Identity and Difference*, 39: The principle of identity, he says there, has become "a principle [*Satz*] bearing the characteristics of a spring [*Sprung*] that departs from being as the ground of beings, and thus springs into the abyss." But then he warns against misunderstanding this point: "But this abyss is neither empty nothingness nor murky confusion, but rather: the event of appropriation [*Ereignis*]. The event of appropriation vibrates the active nature of what speaks as language, which at one time was called the house of being. 'Principle of identity' means now a spring demanded by the essence of identity because it needs that spring if the *belonging together* of man and being is to attain the essential light of the appropriation." This is far from being a mad Empedoclean leap into some volcanic abyss. But it is a very different way of experiencing our relation to the being of the beings that we are engaged with.

5. In his introduction to *Being and Time*, Heidegger stated: "Phenomenology is our way of access [*Zugangsart*] to . . . ontology. *Only as phenomenology is ontology possible.*" GA 2: 48; *Sein und Zeit*, 35; *Being and Time*, 60. Moreover, Heidegger declared (GA 2: 49–50; *Sein und Zeit*, 37; *Being and Time*, 61–62): "This phenomenology is, and must be, hermeneutical, because its grounding is hidden in pre-reflective life."

6. In the first, 1949 edition, Heidegger says that *Ereignis* "has been the guiding word [*Leitwort*] of my thinking since 1936." However, in the later edition, this remark is dropped without explanation.

*PART II*

# 1

## *SEIN*

## What Is Being?

In his *Introduction to Metaphysics*, a text originally drafted in the mid-1930s, Heidegger argued that the fundamental question of metaphysics is "why is there anything at all rather than nothing?" Or, cast in other words, "why are there beings, rather than nothing?" Perhaps, once we are no longer captivated by theological stories, there is ultimately no possible answer, because science, that other great source of cosmological stories, cannot provide the answer, nor can it be expected to, as the question inherently takes us beyond the logic of causal explanation.

What, then, is being (*Sein*), antithesis of nothingness? A strange question—and a daunting one, if taken seriously. However, as it never arises in the course of ordinary life, why should we care? In *Being and Time*, Heidegger sought to convince us that for philosophical thought, and indeed for everyone else, too, no question is actually more important, more fundamental, and more urgent than the question of being. However, despite his endeavor that text left the question of being still haunting us as a question. That is because, before we can even begin to ponder the importance Heidegger claims, we need to achieve clarity in regard to the very *meaning* of the word.

The word "being" (*Sein*) looks like a noun. But its grammatical form is peculiar: it does not seem to function like any of the nouns we are commonly familiar with. What entity does it designate? We are told that that question is faulty; it already misunderstands what is in question. *Being* is not a thing, not an entity: the word "being" names nothing, designates no thing, concerns nothing thing-like. Much ado about nothing? Some philosophers have certainly thought so, arguing that bewilderment is inevitable when philosophers construct a metaphysical abstraction completely disconnected from the familiar situations of life: a word the functioning of which is not "geared in." But Heidegger argues that the nothingness of being is not to be ignored, and moreover that, paradoxically, it is precisely the ignoring or denying of being, simply because it *is* nothing—which is to say, nothing thing-like—that has led us into a culture of nihilism, the greatest of all threats, not only to human existence but to the earth itself.

In an attempt to bring the meaning of "being," hence the philosophical questioning of being, down to earth, Heidegger called our attention to certain moods—for instance, depression, dread, despair, loneliness, and boredom—ways of being attuned to the world in which, he believes, we can find ourselves vulnerable and susceptible to experiencing nothingness, emptiness, meaninglessness, or the loss of any sense of purpose. Thus, beginning in 1929, just two years after the publication of *Being and Time*, he gave a course of lectures eventually published as *The Fundamental Concepts of Metaphysics: World, Finitude, Solitude*. In these lectures, he made rigorous use of the phenomenological method in order to show that, and how, our moods can be engaged by the question of being. Nevertheless, the meaning of "being," construed as a philosophical question, somehow remained an intractable problem for thought.

Would it be less mysterious, less inaccessible, and perhaps less difficult to ponder if the question were rephrased: What does it mean for something—anything—to be? Or, in a phrasing perhaps even farther from metaphysical abstraction: What do we mean when we predicate of something that it *is*? In "On the Grammar and Etymology of the Word 'Being'," the second chapter in his *Introduction to Metaphysics* (1935), Heidegger tried out another approach, shifting from metaphysical reflections to reflections on the grammar of the words we use to invoke what metaphysics calls "being." The chapter begins with this humble introduction:

If being has become no more for us than an empty word and an evanescent significance, we must try at least to capture this remaining vestige of significance. With this in mind, we ask first of all:

1. In regard to its grammatical form, what kind of word is "being"?
2. What does the science of linguistics tell us about the original meaning of this word?

Noting, significantly, that the abstract noun—the substantive—was derived from the verb, language in its ordinary, everyday practical use, appropriating the infinitive and transposing it into the substantive form, Heidegger begins, in the third chapter, to reflect on the multitude of ways in which we use the little word "is" in everyday speech, beginning with a line of verse from Goethe: "Over all the summits/is rest." And he proceeds to the consideration of other sentences also using the word "is": "The lecture is in the auditorium," "The earth is a sphere," "The cup is of silver," "The peasant is to the fields," "The book is mine," "Red is the port side," "There is famine in Russia," "The enemy is in retreat," "The dog is in the garden" (GA 40: 95–98/IMM 74–77). One can easily multiply examples: "It is likely to snow tonight," "That is a heartwarming welcome," and "That is impossible!" And there is the "is" in my question: "What is being?" Only a few philosophers may be able to answer that question, but everyone who knows English recognizes the grammar and understands intuitively how the "is" is functioning. After these examples, making it, as he says there, "difficult, perhaps impossible," to discern a common meaning, a universal generic concept, under which, despite all these different contexts, the "is" might be classified, what Heidegger finds compelling as well as astonishing and perplexing is that they all somehow are meant to indicate *what is*, namely what is called *being*—the abstraction to which Heidegger leaps, convinced that that substantive is absolutely necessary for comprehending something of the greatest importance about our world and the ways we experience it. Through the profusion of instances, he can see a "determinate horizon," a certain "delimitation" of the meaning of "being": it "remains within the sphere of actuality and presence, permanence and duration, abiding and occurrence [*im Umkreis von Gegenwärtigkeit und Anwesenheit, von Bestehen und Bestand, Aufenthalt und Vorkommen*]" (GA 40: 98/IMM 77).

Pondering this fascinating abundance of sentences using "is" and its cognate grammatical forms (including the tenses imperfect, past, future, future past, conditional, subjective) is not only bewildering but also very instructive. Why should we not be satisfied with the exhibition of such richness? What is it that provokes and compels philosophers to concentrate on the infinitive and substantive form, challenging us with its abstractness? As far as Heidegger is concerned, the answer lies in what all these tenses exhibit, namely, the absolutely inseparable connection between being and time. There can be no grammatical form of being without situating it in a dimension of temporality. Only the mathematician's statements and the philosopher's invocation of being, an abstraction from the grammar in everyday use, can appear to be released from that fatality. Whence the metaphysician's dream of overcoming the sentence of death that the tenses bound to time impose. Heidegger, however, does not let us forget that even being itself belongs to time—indeed, in a certain sense, it *is* time, or is how time manifests.

†

Considering these different phrasings of the ontological question, we are confronted by a puzzling fact, itself worth pondering: that, when we give thought to "being," we find ourselves contemplating an isolated abstraction with only one meaning, whereas, when we give thought to the "is," we find ourselves confronting a multitude of different meanings. Heidegger explores the ways we use the "is" and touches on this fact. Perhaps the inaccessibility of the matter when phrased in terms of a metaphysical abstraction is indicative of some kind of philosophical confusion and error. A warning? Heidegger wants to say that *being* discloses itself in all the different ways in which we experience and understand the being of *entities*—the being of all that in any way *is* (GA 6. 2: 368–69/N4 226). But even saying this is problematic, because, as Heidegger insists, there is an ontological difference between being and beings.

For getting at the deepest understanding of what Heidegger wants to say about "being," and about the four other key words—*Stichwörter*—in the constellation we shall here be considering, namely, *Ereignis, Da-sein, Lichtung,* and *Geschick,* perhaps no texts could be more useful, more consequential, than the 1957 lecture on "The Principle of Identity" (GA 11: 29–50/ID 85–106) and the text on "The Onto-Theo-Logical Conception of Metaphysics" (GA 11: 51–79/ID 107–43), together with the 1962 lecture "Time and Being," the "Summary" of that lecture produced in a seminar that took place soon after (GA 14: 3–64/OTB 1–54), and the 1964 lecture text on "The End of Philosophy and the Task of Thinking" (GA 14: 67–90/OTB 55–73). These texts, representing as lucidly as seems possible his most mature thinking, confirm the commitment of his project to the phenomenological approach while at the same time dismantling in the boldest, most fundamental way its transcendental idealism. This release of phenomenology from the metaphysics of idealism enabled Heidegger to challenge the philosophical representation of worldly human existence in terms of a correlation between subject and object. And it made it possible for him to interpret in a compelling way the meaning of being in its relation to our experience.

†

Metaphysical interpretations of *Sein* that inflate it and cut it loose from experience, the realm proper to phenomenology, nevertheless persist, along with contrary interpretations that, taking "being" to be nothing (no-thing) but the projection of a meaning, reduce it to our subjectivity. For Heidegger, both positions are mistaken. In this regard, it might be useful to consider the assertion by Parmenides that mind (Greek *nous, noein*) and being are "the same." In his lectures on Parmenides (1942–1943),

Heidegger says: "Being and the truth of being are essentially beyond all human beings and every historical humanity [*alle Menschen und Menschentümer*]" (GA 54: 249/P 166). What he means by "beyond" in this proposition must be carefully thought through. Understood as referring to beings (entities), *Sein* is indeed "beyond": not reducible to subjectivity. (GA 9: 373–74/PM 283) Even the unicorn of my imagination is *in a sense* irreducible, although, so far as I know, no unicorns actually exist in the real world, grazing in fertile valleys and meadows. As Heidegger interpretively appropriates the thought of Parmenides that being and cognition are "the same," what he wants to argue is the *phenomenological truth* that "only so long as *Da-sein is* [i.e., only so long as we human beings exist, beings endowed with minds], is there [*gibt es*] being" (GA 9: 336–37/PM 256). This does not mean that nothing could possibly exist *prior* to the existence of human beings. Rather, it only means the self-evident truth that, before there were any human beings, the *existence* of beings (entities)—that is to say, the *fact* of their being—could not be have been known about, could not be the object of cognitive acts—acts of perception, memory, imagination, and intentional action. The existence of entities (beings) is independent of our experience, independent of our own existence (GA 2: 224/ BT 228). But insofar as "being" refers to the *meaningfulness* of things, refers to the way our consciousness (the "nous" of Parmenides) relates to the *fact* that things are, or are in a certain way, "being" is *not independent* of human existence.[1] Even so, however, that does not make the phenomenology of being *reducible* to our subjectivity: intrinsic to the phenomenology of meaningfulness, there is still a bonding of intentionality, an opening and stretching out to *something experienced as other*. Even as meaning, being is not reducible to my subjectivity—though it is necessarily dependent upon my consciousness, my cognition.

Heidegger is always bringing to our attention the intertwining of our life and our metaphysics, deconstructing thereby this persistent metaphysics. Thus, he argues that *Da-sein* and *Sein* (sometimes written as *Seyn*) are not two separate items, because *Sein*, unlike entities, cannot stand independently, on its own, apart from *Da-sein*. As Heidegger observes: "The connection [his word here is *Bezug*, not *Verhältnis*] is not to be thought as spanning a distance [*eingespannt*] between two distinct things, being [*das Seyn*] and human beings [*Menschen*]. . . . Rather, the *Bezug* is *das Seyn selbst*, and human life [*das Menschenwesen*] *just is* that very connection [*der selbe Bezug*]" (GA 73: 790). So, what seem to be two distinct terms brought into relation are really, phenomenologically considered, nothing but two aspects of the *same* event—two terms for the *same* event. In his 1957 "The Principle of Identity," Heidegger boldly attempts to deconstruct this relation, the subject–object structure posited by metaphysics, and he accordingly characterizes this encounter between us as human beings and something in our world by speaking, instead, of an appropriating belonging together ("das Zusammengehören von Mensch und Sein"), a correspondence (*Entsprechung*) in reciprocity or reversibility appropriating *Mensch* and *Sein* to one another, *an-eignet* and *zu-eignet* in the realm, or dimension, of a *wechselweise*, mutual back-and-forth vibration: *ein in sich schwingende Bereich, ein in sich schwebende Bau* (GA 11: 30–48, 75/ID 29–39, 69). In this reciprocal appropriation, the "truth of being," that is, the clearing for the meaningful presencing of things, is "grounded" in a thrown openness that makes us *Da-sein*: emphatically grounded in our experience as *Da-sein*, and that means, not in *Mensch*, and not in subjectivity (GA 65: 26/CP 22–23).

†

In *Being and Time* (1927), Heidegger already attempted to explain both (i) the ontological *belonging together* of the human being (as *Da-sein*) and being and (ii) the ontological *difference* between being and beings. Thus, for example:

1. GA 2: 244/BT 228: "Being 'is' . . . only in the understanding of beings" (*Sein 'ist' . . . nur im Verstehen des Seienden*).
2. GA 2: 281/BT 244: "Only as long as *Da-sein is*, i.e., only as long as there is the ontic possibility of an understanding of being, is there being" (*Allerdings nur solange Dasein ist, das heißt die ontische Möglichkeit von Seinsverständnis, 'gibt es' Sein*).
3. GA 2: 281/BT 245: "Dependence of being . . . on the understanding of being" (*Abhängigkeit des Seins . . . von Seinsverständnis*).

And see also:

4. *Metaphysische Anfangsgründe der Logik im Ausgang von Leibniz,* GA 26: 194/MFL153: "There is being only as long as *Dasein* exists" (*Sein gibt es nur, sofern Dasein existiert*).
5. GA 66: 139/M 118: "Beyng is dependent on human beings" (*Das Seyn ist vom Menschen abhängig*).

But there are contexts where, it seems, the *des Seins* would best be left untranslated as such, *provided* the ontological sense or dimension of the referent is recognized. Thus, "the truth of being" (*die Wahrheit des Seins*) refers to the ontological dimension that *grounds* what we commonly understand to be truth, namely, the dimension of the clearing, making time–space for (the being of) beings in the interplay of concealment and unconcealment. There is no separate "being" in a special, singular relation to truth. The same interpretation holds for the logic, or grammar, in other key phrases, such as *Lichtung des Seins*, which simply tells us that *Lichtung* ("clearing") is to be understood as an ontological phenomenon, hence not a reference to the phenomenon of light, and *Geschick des Seins* or *Seinsgeschick*, which tells us that destiny concerns beings in their ontological dimension and belongs to the ontological dimension of our historical existence: in question is the historical unfolding of paradigms of being, not something ontic, some specific, particular entity or congregation of entities. In any case, the grammatical form *"des Seins"* inevitably makes trouble for interpretation, because it tempts one to think of being as some kind of independent agency, source of truth, lighting, and destiny. Metaphysical inflation. The *des Seins* should be treated as if it were often just an *adjective*, signifying that thinking has moved from the realm of the ontic into the realm of the ontological. (The quotation marks that will be used, in discussing the meanings of *Geschick*, I will put around "giving" and "sending," "given" and "sent" are meant to warn against the assumption, here and in all the chapters to follow, of a metaphysical agency—call it "Being" or "Destiny"—operating in silence behind the perceptual situation. These words—as well as the unnecessarily grandiose word "dispensation," vestige of a metaphysical theology from which Heidegger struggled to escape, at times translating *Geschick* and at times *Schickung*—simply refer to what happens to be occurring, what is taking place, in the clearing; and perhaps they also refer to the occurring of the clearing itself, that is, the taking place of some particular clearing.)

†

Clearly, Heidegger spent many years struggling to understand what this term—"being"—means and what is at stake in any such understanding. Thus, for many years, despite reluctantly leaving the term in a certain ambiguity, indeterminacy, or enigmatic confusion, he considered the question of being (*die Seinsfrage*) to be the most important matter for philosophical thought to address.[2] As he said in "The Onto-theological Constitution of Metaphysics" (Seminar 1957):

> The little word "is," which speaks everywhere in our language, even where it does not appear expressly, contains the whole destiny of being [*das ganze Geschick des Seins*]—from the *estin gar einei* of Parmenides to the "is" of Hegel's speculative sentence, and to the dissolution of the "is" in the positing of the will to power with Nietzsche. (GA 11: 79/ID 73)

Now, as we have noted, *Sein* ("being") is a constructed term, obtained by means of a certain abstraction from, and generalization of, the grammatical forms in daily use: "is," "are," "was," "were," "will be," "would be," "should be," "will have been," and so on. As Heidegger compels us, in his *Introduction to Metaphysics* (1935), to recognize, the (English) "is" lends itself to a surprisingly diverse array of meanings, which philosophical thought has gathered and collected into the abstraction to which it gives the name "being." This procedure, however, is not philosophically innocent. As the history of philosophical thought shows, the word "being," to all appearances a noun, readily encourages thinking of what it designates as some kind of entity, an unruly, uncanny presence in our world. For some metaphysicians, it even functions like an omnipotent agency, operating outside the gravity of the world. Nevertheless, although Heidegger unequivocally repudiated that metaphysical transgression, his prolonged and intense meditations on the question of being, and the different ways in which his phenomenology used the word, have encouraged the metaphysical spirit. Heidegger shows us, however, that we cannot, and must not, abandon the thinking that the word "being" makes possible—and formally protects.

We cannot avoid reflecting on metaphysics despite the danger. We must continue to ask: What is being? What is it for something—anything—to be? As Heidegger points out, no matter how we phrase the question, it is necessary that we presuppose an understanding of the "is"—the "to be." Even in asking the question, we had to make use of "is," thereby presupposing an already advanced understanding of the word. So, it is a matter of making explicit what we have somehow always already understood—understood well enough to be able to use the grammatical forms of "being" correctly. This is something that seems as if it should be very easy to do. But the presupposition is so fundamental that it turns out to be not merely difficult, but inherently problematic, as every attempt to define the matter is an interpretation that presupposes it. We find ourselves trapped in the circularity of the hermeneutical method. Our thinking is threatened by an abyss.

Might we avoid metaphysical temptations by following Wittgenstein's recommendation in his *Philosophical Investigations*, limiting our reflection to usage—the grammar of "is"? In this situation, simply observing how we actually use our words, fascinating and revealing though it can be, is of no avail here. That kind of approach would be the proper concern of linguistics and the human sciences, not philosophy. But if we supplement such observation by considering in a phenomenological way the *situations* in which we are using the words that speak of being, of what *is* in its various moods and modalities, then perhaps we could at least get an inkling of the fundamental conditions that make it possible to use those words appropriately. And ultimately, I believe, that is where Heidegger's enquiry takes us. Later in this chapter, four interpretations will be proposed to explicate the meaning of "being." But let us proceed to those interpretations by steps that will take us away from linguistic phenomenology into the realm that is more congenial to the metaphysically tempered mind.

†

In *Being and Time*, Heidegger argues for what he calls the ontological difference: the difference, namely, between (i) beings (in the realm of the ontic) and (ii) "being" as referring to the ontological, the being of beings (*das Sein des Seienden*). That should immediately make intuitive sense. *Beings* (e.g., trees, chairs, ants, and people) are not reducible to the status of cognitive objects, the percepts that appear in our experience; *being*, however, "is" only in the human understanding of beings. "Being" is not the name of anything that could ever be found among the beings in the world: therefore, it is, in this sense, nothing. Such is, we might say, its logic, its grammar. Without recognizing this difference, we could not even begin to engage in philosophical thought; we would simply belong to the world, living entirely immersed among things—beings animate and inanimate, living without the word we seem to need in order to rise above these things and reflect deeply on them as a whole and as such. So, as Heidegger argues, in the Le Thor Seminar (1968), we must recognize "that all metaphysics moves in the dimension of the [ontological] difference" (GA 15: 310/FS 24).

The ontological difference, separating beings from being, is not itself reducible, however, to a philosophical abstraction. Nor is metaphysics merely a conceptual construction, product of philosophical discourse. The ontological difference is the formal indication that points toward the primordial phenomenological event that takes place in all manifestations of human life: calling attention to this primordial event—*das Ereignis des Unter-Schiedes*. This is another way of recognizing that the existential structure of our experience, clearing a context of intelligibility and meaning for everything encountered, necessarily and inherently involves the metaphysical *transcending* of things, of beings—which is, after all, what the Greek origin of the word "meta physical," μετὰ τὰ φυσικά, is saying, meaning going beyond, or behind, the physical, the sensible, the visible. As disposed and appropriated to be, to exist, as situated, as *Da-sein*, by our bodily nature, the human being is inherently metaphysical, inherently thrown open, hence into the ontological difference. Before being an abstract philosophical concept, "being" refers to a distinction that occurs primordially in the structuring of all worldly experience: a difference, or rather, a differentiation (*Scheidung*), that is necessarily presupposed, hence underlying, all our worldly experience and all our discourse. Exceptionally useful in this regard are Heidegger's ruminations on the emergence of being in the ontological difference that run through the texts collected in *On Thinking Through Appropriation* (*Zum Ereignis-Denken*, GA 73.2).

But the failure to recognize and understand the generation of the substantive form has encouraged metaphysical thought to posit being as some special kind of entity. Nevertheless, recognition of the ontological difference at once lifts thinking out of its immersion in the lifeworld, lifts *us* above all worldly beings, all things, so that we can regard them for the first time from a metaphysical perspective—that perspective, namely, in accordance with which we can contemplate all beings, all things that in any way are, in their being, that is, in terms of that principle which constitutes their most fundamental unity—and finally think being itself, the facticity of being as such. Thus, being is of the greatest importance, and yet, as it is no-thing, it is, in the context of everyday life, nothing, nothing at all. Despite this, however, it is not something we can simply ignore or neglect. Without at least prereflectively experiencing being, we would be experiencing things *without* their world—without their past and future, without their situation, their context. Thus, in fact, we could not experience even one being, much less a world.

Whereas this nothingness has inspired important reflections by philosophers such as Nietzsche and Sartre—and Heidegger, too, with regard to our moods, it has also aroused scorn and derision from philosophers who belong to other schools of thought. With regard to the latter, I am thinking, for instance, of philosophers committed to a narrowly pragmatic, instrumental empiricism.

However, even though the recognition of the difference between being and beings constitutes a crucial moment or stage for philosophical thinking, setting the discourse of metaphysics in motion, Heidegger reached a moment in his ruminations when he realized that philosophical thought, if committed to the phenomenological method, must ultimately overcome, and indeed *could* overcome, the "natural way of thinking" in order to think appropriately about the meta physical difference (GA 7: 68–98/ EP 84–110). The problem is that the formulation of that difference is still a *projection* of being from the viewpoint of beings; hence being itself will necessarily appear as something *other* than beings, instead of showing itself to be "merely" a way of referring to the *dimensionality* of their appearing.

In other words, the ontological difference between being and beings appears in thought with the projection, in a comprehensive metaphysical abstraction, of the figure–ground differentiation that initially takes place in the dynamics of the perceptual *Gestalt*.

So, what "being" refers to is the dimension of differentiation within which beings can appear in their meaningfulness. Being—the manifestation of being—is never given by itself; it is given *only* in our experience of the presencing of beings, beings from which it is differentiated in accordance with the phenomenological structuring of experience, and serving to protect beings—entities—from reduction and reification within a field of disclosiveness—being—that sets the terms of intelligibility. This is the crucial historical role that the recognition of "being" must assume. Whenever we witness an assault on some being or type of being, whenever we witness reification or reductionism, as when everything must be regarded and judged solely in terms of its practical usefulness and availability, it can be an audacious act of philosophical courage to invoke "being" and insist, in the name of "being," and for the sake of the being of those things, that things subjected to such violence—reification, commodification, standing reserve—must be released. "Being" is like a battle cry, defending beings from violations threatening their very being. Recollecting being, the very *being* of beings, we can begin to, or attempt to, rescue things—beings—from the destructive forces of our time. Insisting on recognition of the being of all things, the being of all entities, is the beginning of their "redemption." That is the decisive historical difference that what Heidegger calls "being" can make.

As Heidegger says, in thinking about Nietzsche, being concerns the unconcealment of entities as such. But unconcealment is possible only in relation to concealment: just as the figure in the perceptual *Gestalt* can appear as figure against a ground—a ground that withdraws, receding into the being, the dimensionality, of concealment. We always at least implicitly experience and understand the being of entities in terms of being as such. So, although being is not a thing, and in that sense, it *is* nothing, it nevertheless plays an absolutely crucial role in our relation to entities, our experience and knowledge—and in that sense, it is not unimportant, not nothing.

In our time, beings are under siege. We are living in an epoch of nihilism that Heidegger defines in terms of the *Gestell*. This nihilism is the total reification of beings, subjecting them to the imposition of our will to power. So, we see that the importance of "being" lies in its reminding us that entities are necessarily such that they *exceed* what we (can) know of them, and indeed that they are always intrinsically richer in meaning than we are capable of recognizing in our concepts. Thus, insofar as we keep "being" in mind, we can, at least to some extent, *protect* entities, *protect* beings, from the nihilism of the *Gestell*—the reductionism, instrumentalism, and reification imposed on entities by the will to power in all its operations and institutions. "Being" thus works in Heidegger's meta-narrative as a term useful in his attempt, through critique, to overcome (*verwinden*) the history of metaphysics, which has been taken over, he believes, by a dangerous nihilism.

†

Confronted with this danger, Heidegger returned for inspiration and guidance to the words of the earliest philosophers in the Western world. In Heidegger's reading of the fragments of the early Greek thinkers, there are a manifold of "names" for being itself (*Sein selbst*). Among these, he found *kosmos* (the glorious, ultimately harmonious whole), *hen* (the one), *physis* (the realm of nature as the forever emerging and setting), *alētheia* (the realm of an interplay between concealing and unconcealing), *moira* (the realm of allotting and imparting), *apeiron* (the boundless), *diké* (the order in cosmological justice), and the primordial *logos* (the ordering of beings that articulates and lays out its governing law). For Heidegger, each of these Greek words named the earliest and most fundamental Western understanding of "being," as the temporally conditioned unfolding of all things. However, according to Heidegger's history of metaphysics, this originary understanding of being, deeply rooted in myth, was later neglected and forgotten—lost, as Western thinking, influenced in part by Platonism, conceived of being in terms of the timeless and changeless. He consequently believed that the most urgent task for thinking in our time was to recollect and retrieve for the possible redeeming of the promise still summoning our time something of the earliest Greek experience and thought of being.

†

Drawing inspiration from this early, pre-Platonic Greek thought, Heidegger recognized the need to recover, even for perception, their dynamic sense of the ways of the *cosmos*, and, in particular, our world: not only its *Aufgehen* and *Untergehen*, its emerging and setting, its coming forth into presence and its withdrawing into absence, but, more fundamentally, its boundless energy and creativity, its ceaseless flow of changing formations. Thus, he recognized the need to reconsider the fate, in our time, of the perceptual *Gestalt*, compelled to fit into the subject–object structure and forced into a reification of figure and ground.

In the figure–ground *Gestalt* that forms in perception, "being" designates the ground of intelligibility and meaningfulness. In the age of the

*Gestell*, however, there is an inveterate tendency operating in perception to (i) impose on experience a rigid structure of subject and object that conceals a prior more fluid, more undifferentiated dimension underneath it, and to (ii) reduce the ground into a manipulatable figure. This is a reification of the ground that, in turn, reifies and reduces the entity that appears in the *Gestalt*. The properties attributed to the entity, and even its very identity, are thus as if frozen in time: there is no more fluency between entity and ground, no openness receptive to other properties, another interpretation of meaning, a different perspective, a different perception of the entity's identity. The projection of "being," field of intelligibility, protects the entity, even though being ultimately depends, in turn, on our capacity for world-disclosiveness and on our assumption of a guardian responsibility for the openness of that field, that clearing of a ground. In our age, the age of nihilism, the age of reducing "being" to nothingness, it is not only entities (beings, things) that are under siege, but it is also "being" itself that is cast in this hostile light. And this is why Heidegger considers the question of being to be of such historically immense significance, determining the very fate of the planet. If we heed Heidegger's prophetic warnings, and carry out the recollection of being he calls for, perhaps it will have been (future past tense) precisely our worldwide recollection of being that made the difference: not only the difference between beings and being but the difference between a world of catastrophic destitution and a world of poetic redemption.

†

Now, as indicated earlier, I am convinced that, in the case of "being," there are four different but connected meanings for Heidegger's uses of the word. The first is the level of sheer facticity; the three others are at different levels in the formation of meaningful experience.[3]

i. *First sense.* The first sense, understood as emerging in an extraordinary event (*Ereignis* used in the familiar sense of "event") is succinctly expressed in a statement that appears in *The Event*: "In the pure 'fact that being is' [*Im reinen 'Daß'*] is the inceptual event [*das anfängliche Ereignis*, the event that put in motion the discourse of metaphysics]" (GA 71: 68/E 55) Philosophical thought in the Western world began in experiences—events—of wonder and awe, and perhaps dread as well, when freely enquiring minds found themselves profoundly struck, and challenged, by the thought that there are beings—that there is anything at all, instead of there being absolutely nothing at all: being instead of nothing. *Es gibt Sein*: "There is being," or "being is given [to us]." In his introduction to *Being and Time*, Heidegger recognizes this sense of "being" when he argues that the most important question for philosophical thought is "the question of being." For Heraclitus, *physis* and *logos* seem to have served as terms signifying what Heidegger thought of as *Sein*, namely, that which lets-be everything that in any way is. So *Sein* can be used, as in a poetic gesture, to evoke in a "grand" way the sheer facticity of life, existence, world, cosmos, the "All": a facticity for which we can find no *ultimate* explanation, no reason—a wonderful enigma the sheer givenness of which it seems we simply must accept without ever understanding it.

This sense of "being" as sheer existence, something wonderful to be experiencing, is evoked, for instance, in Goethe's fictional work *The Sorrows of Young Werther*, where the eponymous character, rebelling against what he feels to be the excessive rationalism of the Enlightenment, declares: "I am so happy, dear friend, so completely sunk in the sensation of sheer being."[4] Heidegger himself used the word in a somewhat similar way in a letter to his brother Fritz written in 1946 in the aftermath of the Second World War.[5] He began his sentence with the words "Oft danke ich dem Seyn, daß," using *Seyn* merely to express a sentiment without actually referring to anything in particular. In this usage, *Seyn is* meaningful but, without any *object* as referent, its function is merely emphatic. In what I am defining as its first sense, *Sein* simply expresses what, recalling the Greek philosophers' word *thaumazein*, Heidegger describes as "the wonder of all wonders: the fact *that* beings simply *are* [*daß Seiendes ist*]" (GA 9: 307, 309–10/PM 234, 236). And, he explains, this experience in relation (*im Bezug*) to being is an *Ereignis* (event) that lays on us a claim (*Anspruch*), a claim that calls for our responsibility, our care—a response (*Antwort*), namely, in regard to our abilities: responsible thinking "responds to the claim of being [*antwortet dem Anspruch des Seins*]," by maintaining the conditions it requires (GA 9: 307/PM 234).

This interpretation of the first sense of "being" is very abstract; but it can be made simple and clear. On a bench in Central Park, I noticed a small plaque the children had given in remembrance of their deceased father: "Sometimes, we need to pause, sit down, and take it all in." The "it all" is another way of invoking this first sense of being—the *hen kai pan*.

According to the history of philosophical thought that Heidegger tells in the text published as *Contributions to Philosophy (Of the Event)*, "the basic disposition [*Grundstimmung*] constitutive of the beginning of metaphysical thought [hence our first experience of being, an experience that is also our most fundamental claim of appropriation] is wonder [*Er-staunen*]." "Wonder that beings *are*, and that humans themselves *are*, and *are* in the midst of that which *they* are not" (GA 65: 46/CP 37). As Wittgenstein once phrased it, "the aesthetic wonder is that the world exists."[6] Later, he unfolded this thought: "Not *how* the world is, is the mystical, but rather *that* it is."[7] In a 1943 text, Heidegger refers to this sense of *Sein* when he describes what he calls "originary thinking": "Originary thinking [*Das anfängliche Denken*] is the echo of being's favour, a favour in which a singular event is cleared and lets come to pass [*sich ereignen*] the fact that beings are" (GA 9: 310/ PM 236). This experience of wonder and awe, and perhaps dread, in the contemplation of being—the sheer fact that beings are, or, in other words, the fact that there is anything—has not only been a decisive *event* (*Ereignis*) at the intersection of personal life and historical life, setting Western philosophical thought in motion, but it has also been, for Heidegger, an encounter with the world—with being—that makes a claim, a summons, and a calling: in other words, it was, and still is, an event of appropriation— an *Ereignis* (event) in the distinctive sense of being an experience that laid claim, and continues to lay claim, to our humanity, a claim that we take the sheer facticity of being, and what that inexplicable gift—the *Es gibt*—means for us, into the care of our thought. The early Greek philosophers saw this wonder, this mystery, illuminated in their understanding of Ἀλήθεια (*aletheia*), unconcealment in the interplay of concealment and unconcealment: what Heidegger sometimes refers to as "the truth of being"—*die Wahrheit des Seins*. Since the beginning of the modern epoch, however, philosophers have neglected this experience, until Heidegger recollected and retrieved it (GA 71: 67–68/E 54–55).

In the winter of 1962, Heidegger gave a lecture in Freiburg on "Time and Being." In a summary or protocol of that lecture, Heidegger is said to have described the experience of being in this first sense as a sudden "awakening." And, moreover, an awakening that involves a process somewhat like Plato's "recollection," without, however, his reincarnations:

> [Thinking is] on the one hand an awakening [*Erwachen*] from the oblivion of being [*Seinsvergessenheit*], an awakening that must be understood as a recollection [*ein Sicherinnern*] of something that has never been thought—but on the other hand, as this awakening, it is not an extinguishing [*kein Tilgen*] of the oblivion of being, but rather placing oneself in it and standing within it. (GA 14: 37–38/OTB 29–30)

And he explained further that this experience of being is an *Erwachen in das Ereignis*—an "awakening into appropriation." I take this to mean that our being struck by the sheer facticity of being is an experience, an event, that awakens us and reminds us of our role, hence our responsibility, in relation to being: not only in regard to the meaning and character that things have in our world but even—and indeed first and foremost — in regard to the conditions enabling their very presencing or absencing. To experience the being of beings is to experience our appropriation. This experience suddenly awakens us and reminds us of the *claim* (*Anspruch, Aneignung*) that being in the other three senses (the second, third, and fourth) makes on us: in contemplating being, pondering, like Pascal, what it means that there is something rather than nothing, we find ourselves as having been, without knowing it, *always already claimed*, appropriated and disposed—indeed "seized"—by our being in the reciprocity and draw of a binding interaction (*Bezug*) with the very being of beings, responsible not only for conceiving the essence of things but also for our openness to the presencing of things as they are and for maintaining the clearing as that which makes presencing and absencing, concealment and unconcealment, possible: "Beyng as event of appropriation [*Seyn als Ereignis*] attunes and appropriates [*stimmt und ereignet sich*] 'thinking' to itself. The latter is opened and seized by beyng [*vom Seyn ergriffen*]" (GA 69: 146/HB 125).

ii.   *Second sense.* In the history of metaphysics, *Sein* has always been understood in the sense of essence (*Wesen*), as in the being of beings (*das Wesen des Seienden*), or in the beingness of beings (*die Seiendheit des Seienden*). "Being" in this sense figures, albeit with variations in the way it was to be understood, in the thought of Plato, Aristotle, Aquinas, and the medieval Christian and Jewish philosophers. It characterizes or defines the whatness and the howness of things in terms of a distinction between their necessary and contingent properties or features. In terms of the metaphysical tradition that has long held sway, *Sein* in this second sense is thought to correspond to the Greek words *einai, ousia,* and *eidos.* This claim is, however, extremely problematic, because, in the metaphysical discourse from the Roman period into our contemporary times, "essence" has undergone a reification and instrumentalization absent from Greek thought, when its meaning as essence was influenced in its originality by the vitality it experienced in *physis* and the concealment it experienced in *aletheia.*

From medieval times on, the notion of "essence" has been the subject of considerable controversy. The polemics are not without significance and consequence. It is a notion introduced for the sake of intelligibility; but does it in fact work to disclose and illuminate, or is it instead an obscurantism—or worse, an obstruction? Is it even an intelligible notion? Readers of a certain postmodern cast of mind want to do away with all permutations of meaning attached to the word, regarding all of them as hostile to interactional openness, contingency, possibility: for such readers, the notion of "essence" can seem to be nothing but an indefensible reification, a structure of properties or attributes totally determinate and immutable, a definition that is absolutely settled, hence irrevocably closed to challenges, the contingencies of time and circumstance, possibilities still unimaginable. But readers steeped in the history of metaphysics might find, rather, that Heidegger's notion radically deconstructs the traditional notion, which, by way of Roman thought and medieval Christian scholasticism, the modern cast of mind inherited from the ancient Greeks—notably Plato and Aristotle, each of these two proposing a fundamentally different notion of essence—the former originating idealism, the latter originating a pragmatic realism. Heidegger does not relinquish or simply abandon the notion, ceasing to give it a philosophical function; however, his notion conforms to neither pattern. In *Wesen*, Heidegger hears the very antithesis of reification. And that is because he draws inspiration from the pre-Socratics, especially Heraclitus. Thus, he envisions *Wesen* in terms of, or in the light of, *physis*, meaning that "essence" is better understood as a verb, essencing, something taking place in the dynamics and hermeneutics of emerging and withdrawing, concealment and unconcealment.

It is well known that Gertrude Stein once wrote that a rose is a rose is a rose. One could take her words to be deflationary and reductive, saying that the identity of anything claimed to be a rose is absolutely settled. We all know what a rose *is*. There is no controversy surrounding its identity and identification. So, there is really nothing to say about it. The rose is just a rose, a matter of the strictest logical identity. No poeticizing. However, that is surely not at all what Stein was saying. She was urging us to linger and tarry, undistracted, in order to concentrate our mindfulness, letting the rose simply be, be vividly present. And when we attend to a rose in that way, then, she believes, we might understand—ironically, paradoxically—that what this rose before our eyes actually *is* is anything but irrevocably determinate. There is, after all, so much that could be seen—and said—regarding what it is: more, indeed, than we can currently imagine. The *being* of the rose—*this* rose—cannot be reduced to an identity, a *state* of being; its being, its essence, is intrinsically excessive. I take it that this is also part of the point that René Magritte was making in his ironic and paradoxical painting "This is not a pipe," a canvas simply showing us a pipe—or rather, only a *picture* of a pipe. All things considered, what *is* a pipe?

Heidegger's *Wesen* is an essence that protects and maintains this indeterminacy, this excess of being—an excess *in* being; an excess of meaning that the idea of "being" is alone able to vouchsafe. To insist on recognizing the "being," or *Wesen*, of the rose or the pipe is precisely to refuse their reduction to a fixed, forever-settled identity; it is to repudiate their reification.

It is to reclaim them for their role and their truth in the life of a world. Things have cultural histories. The "properties" or "attributes" regarded as "of the essence" of some entity in fourteenth-century Casablanca might be quite different from what is today regarded as the "essence" of that very same thing in Halifax. But what today makes the idea of essence not merely important but crucial is that remembering and invoking the being or essence of a thing can be a desperately needed way of rescuing the thing from its reification in a time when things are increasingly reduced to their utility or commercial value.

   iii.   *Third sense.* The third sense—*Sein* as signifying the *presencing* of beings, *das Anwesen* [i.e., *das Sein*] *des Seienden*, and *das Anwesen des Anwesenden*—is, unlike the first sense, properly phenomenological, but in a way, or sense, that originates in Heidegger's thinking. Whereas the first sense "merely" refers to the realization of a wondrous fact—that there is (*es gibt*) a world rather than nothing—the third sense takes us *into* the experience as such. As phenomenological, this sense of being *connects* what is encountered to the experience, constituting an *understanding* of the thing *as something experienced*. In his 1962 Freiburg lecture, Heidegger observed: "From the early years of Western European thinking until today, 'being' has meant the same as presencing [*Anwesen*]. . . . Being was determined in terms of time as presence [*Anwesenheit*]" (GA 14: 6/OTB 2). He offers this interpretation of the history of Western thought as a way of reminding us of the fact— in a time when being is increasingly reified in constant availability—that the recognition of the importance of time in forming the experience and understanding of being has a very ancient and long history supporting it. The determination of being as presencing keeps being open to change in time and history.

   Although indebted to Husserl, his teacher, the illumination of this sense represents his distinctive contribution, his uniquely insightful way of defining "being" in terms of the phenomenological method. In *Being and Time*, bringing out, by way of justification, the hermeneutical character of his approach, Heidegger says that the question of being "is nothing other than the radicalization [*Radikalisierung*] of an essential disposition of being [*wesenhaften Seinstendenz*] belonging to *Dasein* itself" (GA 2: 20/BT 35). It is a radicalization in the literal sense because it retrieves the rootedness of the question of "being" in *Dasein*'s forgotten "pre-ontological understanding of being [*vorontologischen Seinsverständnisses*]." This radicalization works by way of a hermeneutically revealing step back (*Schritt zurück*) from our everyday forms of engagement with beings—a step back from what Husserl called "the natural attitude"—into the phenomenological attitude, getting at the virtually forgotten pre-conceptual, *pre-ontological roots* of the ontological understanding Heidegger ultimately wants to attain.[8] Disclosing our preconceptual, *pre-ontological* understanding of being—"first nature," we might say—not only shows where our experience and understanding of being comes from, bringing to awareness an *experience* in relation to being that we have always already been living, yet without recognizing and knowing it as such; it also gives an authoritative hermeneutical grounding to the ontological enquiry itself, bringing us back to our most fundamental *disposition* in relation (*im Bezug*) to being, namely, to be in oscillation (*Gegenschwung*)—or perhaps rather, as Merleau-Ponty argued in *The Visible and the Invisible*, in a certain dynamic reversibility of interaction—with the beings we encounter in their meaningful presence in the world, hence to be claimed and appropriated for response ability in relation to that which is presencing.

In the phenomenological attitude, we must suspend questions regarding reality for the sake of concentrating awareness and attention on our experience as such: in this instance, the *meaningful presencing* of what presences. That is, in regard to what is present, we attend only to *its meaningful presencing*, and we do this by *letting* it show itself just as it is. (In repeating Husserl's formulation of the phenomenological method, Heidegger actually profoundly revised it, returning to the Greek sense of the word, namely *phainesthai*, to bring out the importance of the middle voice approach for understanding the phenomenon itself and understanding, correspondingly, the most fitting, most appropriate discipline in the method.) From within the phenomenological approach, or *Einstellung*, *Sein* indicates the meaning or meaningfulness (*Bedeutung* or *Bedeutsamkeit*) of something's current appearing to the human being (*Dasein*), always appearing as this-or-that within a given context of meaning, a given world of meaning that shows itself, moreover, as having been conditioned by various historical and socio cultural factors and forces. *Sein* in this third sense, calling attention to the phenomenology of presencing, obviously cannot obtain apart from *Da-sein*, that to whom, and in the openness of whom, something meaningful presences—presences, that is, either as something present (e.g., the desk I am using now to write this chapter) or as something absent (e.g., the performance of Monteverdi's *L'Incoronnazione di Poppea* that I heard last night).

As Heidegger shows in his *Introduction to Metaphysics*, the little, often-inconspicuous word "is" can have many different meanings, depending on the context: meanings that indicate the multiplicity of ways in which beings can be present and absent. First of all, beings can *be* either as ready-to-hand (in *Zuhandensein*) or as present-at-hand (in *Vorhandensein*). But, second, although kept within these modalities of presence, the "is" can bring forth, thanks to the gift of language—its declensions, inflections, and other characteristics—numbers, moods, temporalities, voices, identities, and nonidentities: the vast, inexhaustible, intricately rich texture of human experience.[9] This richness of presence is constitutive of its essence.

In "The Principle of Identity," Heidegger makes it clear that *Sein* is to be understood in strictly phenomenological terms, arguing that we need a new understanding, free from metaphysics, of the "belonging together of man and being" (GA 11: 39/ID 30–31). This belonging, he says, "prevails [*waltet*] within us, a belonging that listens to being because it is appropriated [*übereignet*] to being." Thus, as regards what I am differentiating as a third sense of "being," he argues that we should keep in mind "its originary sense [*anfänglichen Sinne*] as presence [*Anwesen*]." This means "being is present and abides [*west und währt*] only as it concerns [*an-geht*] man through the claim [*Anspruch*] it makes on him. For it is man, open toward being, who alone lets being arrive *as* presence [*als Anwesen*]." "Such becoming present," he says, "needs the openness of a clearing [*das Offene einer Lichtung*], and by this need remains appropriated [*übereignet*] to human being" (GA 11: 40/ID 31). In other words, the presencing of beings is a *belonging together* of man and the beings encountered: more than a mere coordination through intentionality, and more than a mere intertwining (*Verflechtung*), but rather a dynamic bonding (*Bezug*) that involves their *interactive, reciprocating appropriating*, each affecting the other (*sind einander übereignet*) (GA 11: 39–41/ID 32–33).[10] In this *Bezug* of *Mensch* and *Sein*, each is drawn *to* the other and drawn *by* the other: in this belonging together, there is no relation—*kein Verhältnis* in the normal sense, which requires two distinct entities. I take this to be an unequivocal affirmation of the phenomenological method but with important and consequential revisions of the intentional relation as it is represented in Husserl's transcendental phenomenology.

iv. *Fourth sense.* The fourth sense, still to be understood in the context of phenomenology, concerns what it is that makes meaningful presencing possible. This fourth sense of being opens up the ontological dimension but in a way that connects it to the appropriation (*Ereignung*) of *Da-sein* as that which is disposed to embody openness (*Da-sein* as *Lichtung*).

So, our interpretation of the fourth sense of being will be completed only by the chapters that follow, taking up, in turn, the key words *Da-sein*, *Ereignis*, and *Lichtung*. What Heidegger means by being cannot be understood apart from understanding these other key words. This is also true for the key word *Geschick*, because, without understanding how Heidegger is working with the four other key words, we cannot understand the significance of his project insofar as it pertains to his philosophy of history—and his hopes for "another inception." The five key words mutually imply or engage one another.

After the publication of *Being and Time*, wherein "the question of being" was declared to be the paramount concern of his project, Heidegger came around to recognizing that his project was ultimately not about *being* as such but rather about the phenomenology of *presencing*. And this, he realized, should keep our attention concentrated on *Da-sein* as the realm appropriated (*ereignet*) to the phenomenology of the field in which being as presencing is experienced: *der Entwurfbereich des Seins* (GA 73: 82ff.). The fourth sense of "being" thus concerns the deeper dimension of the phenomenon, a deeper dimension of presencing, namely, what it is that makes the presencing of things possible, indicated by the terms "the essence [*Wesen*] of the presencing of presencing" or "essence of the being-of-beings" (*Wesen des Seins des Seienden*). In the 1942 lectures on Parmenides, Heidegger declared: "The Open . . . is being itself": *Das Offene . . . ist Sein selbst* (GA 54: 224/P 150). And a few years later, in his 1946 "Letter on Humanism," he stated: "The clearing itself is being" (GA 9: 331–32/PM 252–53). Heidegger was not satisfied with the phenomenological illumination of *Sein* in the third sense: "being" understood as designating *Anwesen*, or rather, *das Anwesen des Anwesenden*, the meaningful presencing of that which presences. He needed to understand what makes *Sein*, understood as meaningful presencing, possible. This question led him to the clearing, the openness of a field of experience, a matrix or context for meaningful presencing: *Sein selbst*, being itself, that which enables beings to presence, that within which beings can come into meaningful presence.

In "Time and Being" (1962), Heidegger noted that, in "the beginning of Western thinking, 'being' [that which is 'given,' i.e., that-which-is] was indeed thought, but not 'the giving' as such [*das 'Es gibt' als solches*]." In other words, the Greeks did not—and apparently could not—make the phenomenological turn, to reflect on what makes such givenness possible. The text continues: "The latter—that which enables beings to presence—withdraws [*entzieht sich*] in favor of what is given [*zugunsten der Gabe, die Es gibt*]. That gift [i.e., that giving, or making possible] is thought and conceptualized from then on exclusively as being with regard to beings [*auf das Seiende gedacht*]" (GA 14: 12/OTB 8). But what about *Sein* as the *Es gibt*—that which gives—that which enables—as such? This is ultimately what Heidegger's thought was attempting to bring into recognition and understanding. And what his thought brought forth was *Sein* in its fourth sense, namely, as the clearing, the *ereignendes* "*Es gibt*" to which *Dasein*'s existence is appropriated.

And once he attained this deeper understanding, he found it necessary to rethink in its entirety the phenomenological analytic of *Dasein* worked out in *Being and Time* because what accounts for being in the sense of the that-there-is, namely, the fact of presencing, is really nothing other than the essence of *Da-sein*'s experience itself: *Dasein* as appropriated (*ereignet*) and thrown open to be clearings. It is the clearings that the very nature of *Dasein*'s existence is intrinsically capable of forming, forming, initially, always involuntarily, that account for (*gibt, schickt, ermöglicht*) the meaningful presencing of being (GA 73: 642, 644).[11]

Although the phenomenology of *Dasein*'s appropriation (*Ereignis, Ereignung*) is not given a crucial role in *Being and Time*, Heidegger's subsequent endeavor to account for presencing and his eventual insight into its phenomenology brought his thinking back to the nature of the *Dasein* whose existence he had explored in *Being and Time*; but in this return to *Dasein*, what concerned him was a fundamental dimension of *Dasein*'s thrown openness that had not been adequately recognized before, namely, *Dasein*'s appropriation, *Dasein*'s being (*-sein*) the site (the *Da-*) for clearings, shapings of openness—perceptual fields, worlds of memory and imagination, universes of thought and discourse—making possible what can meaningfully presence.

In explicating the structural role of the clearing, Heidegger deepened the phenomenological "analytic" of *Da-sein* that he laid out in *Being and Time*, assigning to "being" an interpretation that was not yet manifest. It also made it possible for him to think more rigorously about *Da-sein*'s inherent responsibility in the history of ontological paradigms and ontological epochs.

Using exceedingly misleading terminology, Heidegger asks: What gives (*gibt*), lets (*läßt*), or sends (*schickt*) such presencing? What is the *essence* (*Wesen*) of this phenomenon presencing? Those are the deeper questions, yielding the fourth sense of *Sein*. Shifting in a further step back to bring to our attention this deeper, more recessive dimension of the phenomenon, which he sometimes designated using the archaic spelling of *Sein*, namely *Seyn*, Heidegger eventually realized that, while the words *Sein* and *Seyn* brought him into this deep dimension, they were actually no longer needed for this work, and indeed no longer helpful: in getting at the *Urphänomen*, he says, "*ist sogar für den Namen Sein kein Raum mehr*" (GA 15: 365/FS 60). This surprising twist in his thought occurred in a 1969 seminar. Thinking in terms of our appropriation—the appropriation (*Er-eignung, Zu-eignung*) of our existence to being, *Da-* (i.e., our appropriation to *Da-sein*),works much better in disclosing the phenomenology of presencing, illuminating the appropriation of *Da-sein* to be the clearings that make presencing possible. *Seyn* refers us to the *Da* of existence, the ownmost *essence* of the human being, namely our to-be-the-t/here-site of clearings—*Da-sein*. And it is in terms of our appropriation (*Er-eignung*) in this structural dimension of clearings that the phenomenology of beings—that is, of their presencing in meaningful relations to *us*— must be illuminated.

Thus, even during the War years (1938–1939), and with even more confidence and commitment in the years after the War, what Heidegger wanted to bring to our attention was "the clearing, which is *being* itself": "*die Lichtung, die Seyn selbst ist*" (GA 95: 302–309). He reiterated this extremely important point again and again. "The clearing itself," he declared, arguing that key thought in his "Letter on Humanism," *ist das Sein* (GA 9: 325, 331/PM 248, 253). The clearing occurs as, and is, the *Da*, where all presencing takes place: it is that site or situation (*Ort, Ortschaft, Aufenthalt, Stätte, Herdestätte*) that lets presencing happen (*Anwesen-lassen*), enabling beings in their various configurations to come into presence in its openness (GA 11: 74–75/ID 136–37).[12] Thinking in terms of the *Es gibt*, Heidegger unfortunately uses "sending" and "giving," and words associated with them, to refer to the fact that it is the openness of the clearing that makes presencing possible. These constellations of terms are misleading because they are susceptible to interpretations that suggest metaphysical agencies at work—as if the clearing were, perhaps, the operation of Destiny.

Following Heidegger's lecture "Time and Being," there was a seminar on the lecture, and in a summary, or protocol, of that seminar we can find some important clarifications. Concerning the fourth sense of "being," the summary states: "With regard to beings, being is that which shows, makes something visible without showing itself"—"*Das Sein ist hinsichtlich des Seienden dasjenige, was zeigt, sichtbar macht, ohne sich selber zu zeigen*" (GA 14: 45/OTB 36). Significantly, the seminar recognized in this interaction between the visible and the invisible (the *sichtbar* and the *unsichtbar*) the same dynamics, the same *energeia*, that intrinsically operates in the formation of every perceptual figure–ground structure (*Gestalt*). And it recognized in the inapparent that which *exceeds* the structure of comprehension: an excess that phenomenology nevertheless scrupulously compels us to acknowledge in its exceeding. Like the ground in the figure–ground *Gestalt*, the clearing— for instance, the open field of meaningful visibility—yields to that which presences, receding from attention and awareness, at times almost as if it were invisible, hidden. But the clearing is actually hidden in quite another sense: "intrinsically hidden" because there is no explanation for why human experiencing functions by way of clearings, as this ultimately returns us to the fact that there is no explanation for why we human beings exist in the form that we do. Also, as openness, the clearing goes beyond visibility.

Articulating the fourth sense of being in still other words, the summary report on the seminar says: "Thought with regard to what presences [i.e., beings], [being as] presencing shows itself as the letting-presence of that which is presencing"—"*Im Hinblick auf das Anwesende gedacht, zeigt sich Anwesen als Anwesenlassen des Anwesenden*" (GA 14: 9/OTB 5). This leads to a clear recognition of the two dimensions of being—and the corresponding two senses of being—the third and the fourth, that Heidegger's phenomenology was attempting to articulate:

α. Letting-*presence* (*Anwesen-lassen*): Letting-*presence* what is present. This phrase concentrates attention on "being" in the third sense, namely, on the fact that something is presencing: *Es gibt ein Seiendes*. There is a being, an entity, meaningfully presencing. Something is presencing to a human being.

β. *Letting*-presence (*Anwesen-lassen*). This phrase concentrates attention on that which makes presencing possible, namely, our *Da-sein* as the clearing. *Es gibt Sein*. Literally, it means that there is being. But what that means is that there is a clearing, that which lets meaningful presencing happen, that which makes meaningful presencing possible, that which, so to speak, "gives" or "sends" being. *Sein*, here, understood to designate the clearing, is making such presencing possible: its letting or making possible is, moreover, in Heidegger's somewhat misleading formulations, a "giving" (*Geben, Gabe*) or "sending" (*Schicken, Schickung, Geschick*). Letting-presence thus characterizes the fourth sense of "being": *Sein* (at times, especially in the 1930s, written in its archaic spelling, *Seyn*) as the appropriated, thrown-open clearing (*ereignete Lichtung*), the experiential field that, in its openness, makes possible (*läßt*) the presencing of what presences, letting that presencing happen (GA 14: 45–46/OTB 37). Letting-presence, by contrast, characterizes the third sense of *Sein*, namely, the fact of presencing itself. According to Heidegger, "Only insofar as there is a giving, sending, or enabling of presencing is there a possibility for beings to meaningfully presence"—*Nur insofern es das Lassen von Anwesen gibt, ist das Anwesenlassen von Anwesendem möglich*. Here, then, we are thinking in another way the ontological difference between being (as in *Es gibt Sein*) as the dimension of the letting, or what used to be called the necessary transcendental condition of possibility, and beings (as in *Es gibt Seiendes*) as belonging to the dimension of what is enabled to presence—what is "given" and "sent" (GA 14: 48–49/OTB 40–41). And, according to the protocol, Heidegger explained that this "letting" (*Lassen*) should be understood to mean "to set free into the open" (*freigeben ins Offene*) (GA 14: 45–46/ OTB 37). But there are other words that Heidegger will draw upon to think about this letting. They include to give (*geben*), to extend (*reichen*), to send (*schicken*), and to let-belong (*gehören-lassen*) (ibid.). However illuminating these terms may be, they, and other associated terms—above all, the term *Geschick*, which commonly means "destiny"—can easily be misunderstood, giving rise to egregiously inflated metaphysical claims—the worst sort of metaphysical speculations.

We might call being as understood in what I am calling its fourth sense (*Sein*, sometimes written in its archaic form, *Seyn*) the "transcendental dimension." However, *being* is very different from the transcendental that figures in Kant and Husserl and must not be confused with it, as *Da-sein*, the deep essential nature of the human being, is not a Kantian or Husserlian transcendental ego. In fact, as appropriated to be the site of clearings, the Open, human *Da-sein* is not any kind of subjectivity. Nor is the clearing, being itself, any kind of objectivity. The clearing that is *Da-sein* simply cannot be understood in terms of subjectivity and objectivity.

After commenting, in his 1946 "Letter on Humanism," on *Mögen* (favoring) as "the proper essence of enabling" (*Das Ver-mögen*), meaning what "not only can achieve something, but also can let something essentially unfold in its provenance, that is, let it be," Heidegger uses these words to define what I call the fourth sense of "being":

> Being is the favouring-enabling, the may-be [*das Mögliche*]. As the element, being is "the quiet power of the favouring-enabling, that is, of the possible." (GA 9: 148–49/PM 241–42)

I suggest that this is a beautiful evocation of the fourth sense of "being," describing its operation—its "favouring enabling"—as the clearing, the silently opened field of meaningfulness, cleared for the presencing of whatever presences within its expanse, for example its field of visibility and audibility, encompassed by dimensions of the invisible and the inaudible.

In the lecture on "Time and Being," written years later in 1962, Heidegger offered a useful illumination of this "favouring-enabling," but without explicitly mentioning the earlier text, arguing:

> Being [i.e., in what I call the third sense] means presencing. However, thought with regard to *what enables* this presencing, what shows itself is a *letting-presence* [*Anwesen-lassen*]. So now we must try to think this *letting-presence* itself [*eigens*], insofar as presencing is admitted [*zugelassen*]. *Letting-presence* [*Anwesen-lassen*] shows its distinctive character [*sein Eigenes*] in bringing forth into unconcealment [*das Unverborgene*]. To let presence means: to unconceal [*Entbergen*], to bring into openness [*ins Offene bringen*]. [Considered phenomenologically,] there operates [*spielt*] in unconcealing a giving [*ein Geben*], namely, the giving that gives presencing, gives being, in *letting*-presence [*jenes, nämlich, das im Anwesenlassen das Anwesen, d.h., Sein gibt*]. (GA 14: 9/OTB 5)

So, in a phrase the wordplay of which is perspicuous in German but not in English, as the *Es gibt* ("there is") literally means "it gives," Heidegger states that "being"—"being" in what I am referring to as the fourth sense— is "*die Gabe dieses 'Es gibt'*": "the gift of this 'there is'.'" So being is the clearing, that which makes possible—"gives" or "sends—the "gift" that is the presencing of beings. "Being belongs to the giving": "*Sein gehört zum Geben*" (GA 14: 10/ OTB 6). Further explicating the phenomenology that is involved, Heidegger tells us:

> To think being itself properly [*eigens*] requires disregarding being to the extent that it is only grounded and interpreted in terms of beings [*aus dem Seienden her*] and for beings as their ground, as in all metaphysics. To think being properly [*eigens*] requires us to relinquish being as the ground of beings in favour of the giving [*das Geben*], the operating of which is concealed in unconcealment, that is, we must relinquish being [in the old metaphysical sense] in favour of that which gives [the *Es gibt*]. As the gift of this "It gives," being belongs to giving. (GA 14: 10/ OTB 6)

In other words, we should turn from questioning in terms of "being" to thinking in terms of the clearing as that which *ver-möglicht*, that is, makes presencing possible. He also states:

> A giving [*Ein Geben*] that gives only its gift [*seine Gabe*], but in the giving holds itself back and withdraws [*sich selbst jedoch dabei zurückhält und entzieht*], such a giving [*ein solches Geben*] we call sending [*das Schicken*]. (GA 14: 12–13/OTB 8–9)

Although derived from the prose of philosophical treatises, Heidegger's terminology is no longer prosaic, no longer familiar and easily recognizable, but one should not be misled by its strangely poetic, metaphorical character. What is at issue is still something the understanding of which can be approached by way of a *phenomenological description* of the intrinsically dynamic nature—the Greek philosopher's *energeia*—operative in the figure–ground *Gestalt* formed in perception: a dynamics in which the ground, the open spatio temporal field or clearing, that which brings forth, "sends" or "gives," the "gift" of the figure (object, entity) upon which attention is concentrated. Thus, in the *Gestalt*, the ground yields, letting the figure emerge into attention in the unconcealment of meaningful presence, while it necessarily and spontaneously holds itself back and withdraws from attention, ultimately receding beyond the horizon of encounter into the dimension of concealment, which accordingly tends, in consequence, to be forgotten or ignored, both in the course of everyday living and in the history of metaphysics (GA 14: 11–12/OTB 7). What is given, or dispatched, to our perception—what appears or presences as the "gift" that is "sent" and "given" in the *Es gibt*—enters as a meaningful presence, a meaningful phenomenon, into the field of intelligibility and meaning that the very existence of the human *Da-sein*, as *Da-sein*, clears. And what is "given" enters the *relationality* of an entire field of meaning, a context, that, correspondingly, *gives* or *lends* meaning to everything that appears in its embrace, its layout—that is to say, if I may borrow a word from Heraclitus, its *legein*.

It is essential to understand, here, that the fourth sense of *Sein* is what Heidegger invokes by the phrase "the truth of being" (*die Wahrheit des Seins*), where "truth" is understood not as correctness but as *aletheia*, the dimension *underlying* and *always presupposed* by truth-as-correctness: that dimension in which all that in any way *is* necessarily appears in an interplay of unconcealment and concealment. The phrase thus refers to the clearing, but, as befits the phenomenology of *aletheia*, we must think this clearing, this openness, as a field or region (*Gegend*) for the presencing of beings *in the hermeneutical interplay of unconcealment and concealment*. That interplay in the inherent openness of the field of presencing, which the ancient Greek philosophers named *aletheia*, is what Heidegger's phrase "the truth of being" attempts to remind us of.

The "truth of being" cannot be adequately understood, therefore, apart from the phenomenology of *Da-sein*'s clearing. In his *Contributions to Philosophy* (1936–1938), Heidegger takes pains to illuminate this problematic. "Accordingly," he says,

To speak in the strict sense of the relation of *Da-sein* to beyng is misleading, inasmuch as it implies that beyng essentially occurs "for itself" and
that *Da-sein* only subsequently takes up a relation to beyng.

This would amount to abandoning phenomenology. Continuing the explication, he argues that

> the bond [*Bezug*] that draws *Da-sein to* beyng pertains [*gehört*] intrinsi-
> cally to the essential occurrence of beyng itself [*Wesung des Seins selbst*],
> which could also be conveyed by saying that beyng needs [*braucht*]
> *Da-sein* and does not at all essentially occur without this appropriation
> [*Ereignung*]. (GA 65: 254/CP 200)

This means that the draw in the bond is reciprocal: being is correspondingly
drawn to *Da-sein*. We must, however, recognize, as Heidegger points out
here, that

> to speak of a relation to *Da-sein* makes beyng ambiguous: It makes
> beyng into something over and against, which it is not—inasmuch as it
> itself first appropriates [*selbst erst er-eignet*] precisely *that which* it is sup-
> posed to be over against.

"Therefore," he concludes, "this relation is also utterly incomparable to
the subject-object relation" (ibid.). In other words, understood in its fourth
sense, "being" does not designate an object but instead refers to the clearing
as that which makes possible our experience of objects. This analysis also
figures in the important reflections from Heidegger's so-called *middle period*
on the connection, or rather the inseparable bond intertwining *beyng* and
man that he calls *der Bezug*:

> The bond [*Bezug*] is however not stretched [*eingespannt*] between beyng
> and man. . . . The bond is beyng itself, and the essence of man [i.e.,
> *Da-sein*] is that same bond. (GA 73.1: 790)

If *beyng* (the fourth sense of being) is Heidegger's name for the appropriated
clearing, then *we are* the clearings (*beyng*): clearings are constitutive of our
very existence and our "appropriation," our "coming home" to ourselves,
our being true to ourselves. The role of *Da-sein* is further illuminated in this
same text, although it is difficult to translate Heidegger's innovative double
meaning of *es gibt*, namely, (i) according to ordinary usage, to refer to the
sheer fact of being, as in "there is" and "there are," and (ii) more literally,
but in a strange usage peculiar to Heidegger's project, as "it gives," referring

to a making possible or enabling. "*Welt 'gibt' Sein*," he says, assuming this thought to be understood as phenomenological: "World makes possible the presencing of beings." Working with the double meaning of *es gibt*, he leaves no uncertainty regarding the status of being, illuminating the role of *Da-sein* in opening worlds of meaning, in which we can meaningfully experience the *being* of what is and what is not:

> *Das Dasein* is the ever-individuated "it" [*das je vereinzelte "es"*] that gives [*das gibt*], that makes possible and *is* the t/here is [*das "es gibt,"* the that-there-is]. (GA 73.1: 642)

It is the human being (*Dasein*), in its essential functioning as *Da-sein*, that is, as what forms, or gives (*gibt*), the structure that makes it possible for there to be experience of what is and what is not. The sentence lucidly explicates the structure and operation of the clearing that is *Da-sein*, namely, its making possible the meaningful presencing, the *being*—the *es gibt*—of things. It is only in that functioning of *Da-sein*, namely, in its projecting of a meaningful field of experience for beings, that *being* is possible. In *Contributions to Philosophy*, Heidegger states: "Only on the ground of *Da-sein* does beyng enter into truth" (GA 65: 293/CP 231). In other words, only through *Da-sein* does *aletheia* (the clearing, dimension of the interplay of concealment and unconcealment) enable us to enter into (i.e., makes statements concerning) truth—truth as correctness.

†

Before we move on to give further thought to *Da-sein* and what is involved in the *Ereignis*, that is, *Dasein*'s coming-to-its-true-self (i.e., its appropriation), I would like to argue, in preparation for the next chapter (chapter 2), that a certain responsibility corresponds, for Heidegger, to each of the four senses of *Sein* we have considered. I submit that, for each of the four senses, there is, in Heidegger's project, a corresponding claim on us that calls us to our appropriation, calls us to measure up to a certain responsibility:

i. In *Sein* as in the experience of the sheer facticity that there is—*daß es gibt*—anything at all, instead of nothing, we are summoned to a responsibility to dwell in the world with awe, wonder, and an appropriate humility and gratitude.

ii. In *Sein* as essence, we are summoned to a responsibility to avoid violating the *essence* of things—the reduction, reification, and commodification of beings. A thing is not merely an object of use. A tree is not lumber. A mountain, as Cézanne sought to demonstrate, is more than its definition, ever exceeding its category. And Monet shows us the transformations that haystacks can undergo in their illumination at different times of day. Bringing things into presence, the painter seeks to reveal this dynamic sense of the essence of things.

iii. In *Sein* as referring to presencing, we are summoned to the responsibility to *let things initially simply be*, and show themselves as, what and how they are—as in the *preliminary* openness of *Gelassenheit* as an *ontological* attitude.

iv. In *Sein* as referring to the clearing, that is, that which makes presencing possible, we are summoned to a responsibility for opening the clearing, and for safeguarding and maintaining its *openness*, that which enables—lets happen—such presencing; and we are summoned, too, to take responsibility for our response ability, the way we greet and receive what, in that clearing, we are given to experience.

This summoning is our appropriation (*Ereignis, Ereignung*). Though normally its claim on us remains unrecognized, we can find ourselves stirred and awakened to the awareness, recognition, and understanding of this claim, this summons, in the course of our interactions, our engagements, in and with the world: summoned to enown the responsibility and enact it in care. What we encounter in the world always addresses us with questions. This can help us become true to ourselves because, as Heidegger tells us, we tend to be farthest from what is nearest: most unaware of that which is most fundamental to the character of our life.

Heidegger himself was still far from a deep philosophical understanding of *Da-sein* when he wrote *Being and Time* and centered that work on "the question of being." And yet, he somehow intuited, even then, that the secret of being and time is to be found by venturing deeper into the phenomenology of *Da-sein*.

So, in preparation for the following chapters, it might also be useful now to summarize in abbreviated form some of the moves in the history of Heidegger's thinking after *Being and Time*, as he reinterpreted *Sein* (*Seyn*), or *Sein selbst* (*Seyn selbst*), recognizing that the way to think it phenomenologically needs to be in terms of *Ereignis*, the appropriation of the human being (*Da-sein*) to be the *Da* of the clearing. In other words, *Sein* now implicates *Da-sein*, *Ereignis*, and *Lichtung*:

1. 1936–1938: "*Beyng* presences eventfully as claim of appropriation" (GA 65: 30/CP 25).

2. 1938–1939: "*Beyng* is the eventful claim of appropriation." ("*Das Seyn ist Ereignis*") (GA 66: 101/M 84)

3. 1962: In his lecture on "Time and Being," Heidegger argued that "the sole purpose of the lecture" (*des Vortrags einzige Absicht*) was "to bring 'being itself' into view as appropriation" ('*Sein selbst*' *in den Blick zu bringen*) (GA 14: 52/OTB 43).

4. 1962: "When being comes into view as appropriation [*als das Ereignis in den Blick kommt*], it disappears as being" [*es als Sein verschwindet*]" (ibid.).

5. 1962: According to Heidegger in the "Letter on Humanism," the term "being itself" (*Sein selbst*) "was already naming appropriation [*bereits das Ereignis nennt*]" (ibid.).

Thus, it was not long after publishing *Being and Time*, a work Heidegger never completed, that the philosopher realized that his project would be better served by shifting his thought from the metaphysical question of being to the phenomenology of our distinctive human existence as *Da-sein*, human existence as appropriated to the structural formations of meaning he called "clearings."

†

Phenomenology will always guide us to turn back, in our thinking and questioning, from being to *Da-sein*. Actually, as this chapter on being has made abundantly evident, we cannot properly think about being without also thinking about the themes of the chapters that follow: *Da-sein* and its appropriation (*Ereignis*) to be the site of clearings. Five of Heidegger's key terms, the constellation of terms we are critically interpreting, are absolutely inseparable from one another, each one understandable only in relation to the others. So it is impossible to introduce any one of them without presupposing or considering all the others. This is the way that a hermeneutical circle works. The terms defy introduction and definition in the logically pure order of seriality. In the following chapters, therefore, a certain amount of repetition is unavoidable—but it is to be hoped that, with each of the repetitions, the differences in the contexts will supplement and deepen the earlier expositions. The circularity that is produced by the interdependencies, interactions, and implications among these terms also means that the order of the exposition is to a certain extent arbitrary. Bearing that in mind, we will now move from a focus on being to a focus on the nature (essence) of *Da-sein*—human existence as thrown open in its clearings.

## NOTES

1. See Martin Heidegger, *Aristoteles: Metaphysik IX*, GA 33: 202: *"Das Ansich-sein der Dinge wird nicht nur etwa unerklärbar, sondern völlig sinnlos ohne die Existenz des Menschen; was* nicht *heißt, daß die Dinge selbst vom Menschen abhängig seien"* (Italics added).

2. See Heidegger's exchange of thought regarding the meaning of "being" with Tezuka Tosiro in the 1950s. In that exchange, he acknowledged that he was aware of the indeterminacies and ambiguities but was still struggling with the concept and the word. See *Aus einem Gespräch von der Sprache: Zwischen einem Japaner und einem Fragenden*, GA 12: especially 103–8; *Unterwegs zur Sprache*, 108–13; "A Dialogue on Language," *On the Way to Language*, esp. 19–23.

3. I am grateful to Thomas Sheehan for his insights and illuminations regarding these senses of *Sein*. One should read his book, *Making Sense of Heidegger* (Lanham, MD: Rowman & Littlefield, 2015), for more textual detail and argumentation. He does not seem to recognize, however, what I take to be the first, most indeterminate but also most common of these senses, although I cannot imagine that he would not be willing to grant it. It is, indeed, to be found in Heidegger's words and thought.

4. Johann Wolfgang von Goethe, *The Sorrows of Young Werther*, trans. David Constantine (Oxford: Oxford University Press, 2012), 6.

5. Walter Homolka and Arnulf Heidegger, ed., *Ausgewählte Briefe von Martin und Fritz Heidegger* (Freiburg im Breisgau: Verlag Herder, 2016), §267, 134. The letter is dated February 21, 1946.

6. Ludwig Wittgenstein, *Tagebücher 1914–1916*, in *Werkausgabe* (Frankfurt am Main: Suhrkamp Verlag, 1984), vol. I, 181.

7. Wittgenstein, Proposition 6.44, *Tractatus Logico-Philosophicus*, trans. David F. Pears and B. F. McGuiness (London: Routledge and Kegan Paul, 1961), 84.

8. In his *Beiträge zur Philosophie* (GA 65: 321), Heidegger asserts that *Da-sein* can be understood only hermeneutically. (For the English, see *Contributions to Philosophy*, 254.) On Heidegger's use of the hermeneutical approach, see Thomas Sheehan, "Sense, Meaning, and Hermeneutics: From Aristotle to Heidegger," in Niall Keane and Chris Lawn, eds., *The Blackwell Companion to Hermeneutics* (Hoboken, NJ: Wiley-Blackwell, 2016).

9. See Heidegger, *Einführung in die Metaphysik*, GA 40: 56–79, *An Introduction to Metaphysics*, trans. Ralph Mannheim (New York: Doubleday, 1961), chapters 2–3, 43–77. And see Gregory Fried, "What's in a Word?", in Richard Polt and Gregory Fried, ed., *A Companion to Heidegger's Introduction to Metaphysics* (New Haven, CT: Yale University Press, 2001), 124–42.

10. Also see the explication of *Bezug* in Heidegger's "Wozu Dichter?" GA 5: 282–84; *Holzwege*, 260–62; "What Are Poets For?" in *Poetry, Language, Thought*, 105.

11. Heidegger, *Zum Ereignis-Denken*, GA 73: 642: *das Dasein ist das je vereinzelte 'es,' das gibt; das ermöglicht und* ist *das 'es gibt.'* And two pages later, on 644, he says *Das Da-sein schickt vor* a clearing, with its horizon.

12. For Heidegger's emphasis on *Anwesen-lassen*, inspired by the *Legein* of which Heraclitus speaks, see Heidegger, "Die Onto-theo-logische Verfassung der Metaphysik," GA 11: 74–75. Or see *Identity and Difference*, 136–37. This 1956–1957 text is interesting because, in it, Heidegger explicates presencing using the Heraclitean word *Legein*, which he interprets as laying-out or letting-lie-before. "Being shows itself in the unconcealing overwhelming [*entbergenden Überkommnis*] as that which allows whatever arrives to lie before us [*als das Vorliegenlassen des Ankommenden*], as the grounding of the manifold ways in which beings are brought about before us." And "Being becomes present [*west*] as *Logos* in the sense of ground, as allowing to let lie before us [*im Sinne . . . des Vorliegenlassens*]. The same *Logos*, as the gathering of what unifies [*das Einende*], is the *Hen*."

# 2

## DASEIN

### From *Menschsein* to *Da-sein*

*Dasein* [is] a not-yet that every *Dasein*, as the being that it is, has to become.

—Heidegger, *Being and Time* (GA 2: 324/BT 288)

In *Basic Concepts of Ancient Philosophy* (1926), Heidegger discusses self-development in the context of Aristotle: the highest *bios*, the highest possibility of existence, he argues, is one that satisfies to the highest degree the proper human potentiality for being. In *Being and Time*, deeply influenced by Aristotle and Augustine, Heidegger argues that this authenticity means one takes responsibility for oneself—responsibility for one's ownmost potentiality-for-being. From the moment we enter this world, we begin adapting to its social and cultural conventions. And we forget ourselves, lost in the everydayness of a life that fits into expected roles. Overcoming that estrangement from ourselves—that is, from our *given essential nature*, we would become free to become what, without knowing it, we always already have been—but so far, only in our potential. As, however, our appropriation (*Er-eignung*), the process in which we come back to and actualize our true nature, takes us *away* from our familiar, comfortable, but still unfulfilled selves, Heidegger notes that appropriation is also our *ex*-propriation (*Ent-eignung*): it can feel like an estrangement, casting us in a strange relation to the once familiar world. But, of course, we are also free, indeed as a matter of essence, to ignore or neglect—or twist out of shape—our essential appropriation and the claim it makes on us.

In *Being and Time* (1927), Heidegger quotes Augustine's question: *Quid autem propinquius meipso mihi?* "What could be closer to me than myself?" This is a strange question. But Heidegger's answer is even more unsettling because he reverses the references of "near" and "far," arguing that we are actually farthest from what is nearest, farthest, that is, from our true selves; there is nothing of which we are more ignorant, or more afraid to recognize, than the truth about our innermost, ownmost nature—what philosophical thought traditionally called our "essence." For Heidegger, this means that we are not in touch with the ontological dimension of our being, our existence. What is *ontically* near to us in the everydayness of our lives, hence what we readily know about ourselves and readily acknowledge, is actually farthest from the essence, farthest from that which is nearest in the sense of being the deepest *ontological* truth about our existence as human beings. In fact, we do not recognize ourselves, and do not understand ourselves, in regard to the *truly* near—the ontological dimension of our existence. And because we have not yet recognized our true selves, have not yet deeply understood our true selves, and consequently have not yet achieved our true selves, Heidegger argues that we have yet to *become* who we *are*. But *who* are we? What *is* our "essential nature"?

In *Thus Spake Zarathustra*, Nietzsche argued that "*soul* is only a word for something about the body."[1] There is truth in this observation; but it cries out for further explication. I consider Heidegger's interpretation of the human *Da-sein* to be an elaboration of that insight, and I shall accordingly argue that appropriation is a claim and summons carried, in the form of our most fundamental disposition, by the very nature of our embodiment. In *Being and Time*, Heidegger argues that "the 'essence' of *Da-sein* lies in its existence." And he explains how this "essence" he calls "existence" is to be understood:

> The characteristics of this being are accordingly not the present-at-hand "properties" [*vorhandene "Eigenschaften"*] of some entity that is itself present-at-hand, but rather in each case possible ways for it to be and no more than that. All the being-as-it-is [*Sosein*] that this being possesses is primarily being. Therefore, when we designate an entity using the term Dasein, we are not referring to its "what"—as if it were a table, house, or tree—but to its being. (GA 2: 56/BT 67)

What Heidegger means by "essence" is different from what it has meant in the history of metaphysics: different, in that, whereas in metaphysics, the essence is something immutable and enduring, in Heidegger's thought the essence is temporal, not eternal; moreover, it is a formation that is always stretched between potentiality and actuality; and even in its relative stability, it is in incessant interaction with the world, never complete, never perfect, never final. The essence of our existence is thrown openness.

Some twelve years after the publication of *Being and Time* (1939), thinking about *Da-sein* in the context of his critical commentary on Nietzsche, Heidegger stated:

> For us the word *Dasein* [i.e., *Da-sein*, with the hyphen, indicating its essence as a thrown-open clearing] definitively names [*vollends benennt*] something that is by no means coterminous [*deckt mit*] with human being, and also something entirely distinct [*vollends ganz verschieden*] from what Nietzsche and the tradition prior to him understand by "existence." What we designate with the word *Dasein* [i.e., the hyphenated *Da-sein*] does not appear in the preceding history of philosophy. (GA 44: 26/ N2: 26–27)

Considered from the standpoint Heidegger is proposing, all preceding representations of *Da-sein*, that is, *Menschsein*, even those that claim to be transcendental, are ultimately, in one way or another, anthropological— anthropocentric. They do not get at the ontological dimension of our existence. In a passage published in *The Event* (1941–1942), Heidegger attempted to understand how his thinking evolved after *Being and Time*. This evolution involved a deeper understanding of the human being (*Mensch*) as *Da-sein*, appropriated ground of the clearing, and correspondingly, a new insight into how being needs to be thought. In *The Event*, he explains:

> All beyng is *Da-seyn* [*Alles Seyn ist Da-seyn*]. Yet *Da-sein* is not a being [*das Seiende*] called the human being, but instead is, in terms of the history of beyng, the ground [*der seynsgeschichtliche Grund*] of the essence of the human being, . . . and is determined expressly and exclusively out of the relation to being [*eigens aus dem Bezug zum Sein bestimmt*], i.e., according to *Being and Time*: out of the "understanding of being." The appropriation of the "there," the appropriative event of the clearing, is *Da-sein*, and that is the essential occurrence of the truth of beyng, i.e., beyng itself [*Das Da-ereignen, das Er-eignis der Lichtung, ist das Da-sein und dies ist die Wesung der Wahrheit des Seyns, d. h. dieses selbst*]. *Da-sein*, experienced in accord with the history of beyng [*seynsgeschichtlich erfahren*], is the first name for beyng, which is thought out of the essential occurrence of truth [*aus der Wesung seiner Wahrheit gedacht wird*]. (In *Being and Time*, *Da-sein* is surmised [*geahnt*] and in that way decisively brought to consciousness, but it could not yet be adequately thought.) (GA 71:140–41/E 120)

Not yet "adequately thought," because being had not yet been thought in terms of the *Ereignis*.

In one of his post-War *Notes* (*Anmerkungen* II) written during the years 1945–1946, Heidegger again reflects on what he was attempting to think some twenty years earlier in *Being and Time*:

> What is thought in *Being and Time*? *Being and Time* is thinking the truth of being [*die Wahrheit des Seins*], whereas previously the attempt was to think this truth [solely] in its essence as *Da-sein*. This word names neither the human "subject" and human beings as "subjectivity," nor does it name in general humans [*Menschen*] as ontically distinguished beings [*ontisch gesondertes Seiendes*]. The word [*Da-sein*] names the essential element [*das Wesende*] in which the being of the human [*Menschsein*] abides [*beruht*]; and this essential element [*dieses Wesende*], this "being" ["*Sein*"] as *Da-sein*, "is" in itself the essential element of being as such [*das Wesende des Seins als solchen*], i.e., the truth of being [*die Wahrheit des Seins*, the openness of being, the clearing]. (GA 97: 175)

The text continues, explaining how *Da-sein* opens out in clearings for meaningful experiencing:

> This being [*Wesende*], *Da-sein*, does not "make" ["*macht*"] and "posit" ["*setzt*"] being, neither "subjectively" nor "objectively," but rather projects [*entwurft*], i.e., it opens up the clearing and holds it open [*es lichtet und hält die Lichtung des Seins aus*], which is something that *Da-sein* can do [*vermag*] only insofar as it takes place [*west*] as the clearing of being [*als Lichtung, Da, des Seins west*] and thus "is" "the *Da*", i.e., *Da-sein*. Therein lies the fact that *Da-sein* does not make itself; it was also not made by another, but rather is to be thought out of the essence of being itself [*aus dem Wesen des Seins selbst, i.e., it is to be thought in terms of the clearing*], since it belongs to this. *Being and Time* calls this thrownness [*Geworfenheit*]. (GA 97: 175–76)

The character of the clearing that, as *Da-sein*, we are, being here, present-in-our-openness, lays out the terms of intelligibility according to which things (entities, beings) can be encountered; it determines *what* can be disclosed and *in what ways* they can be disclosed. Or, as Heidegger is wont to say, the clearing that, we are, in our being here, is what determines *what* entities can be "given" (*geschickt*) to us, and *how* they can be "given." But as a clearing is what we *are*, opening up a world, then whether or not we recognize and understand ourselves *as* such, and whether or not that self-recognition and self-understanding stirs us to be more vigilant, more mindful, and more responsible can make a huge difference in the unconcealment of being—hence in our preparation for the possibility of a future epoch in the hermeneutics of being.

As the character of the world that takes place in the perceptual clearing—whether and how it is open, receptive, and responsive—determines the meaning of being, that is, *what* can be and *how* it can be, the question of our responsibility is fundamental. This is why the concept of *Ereignis* as event and process of appropriation plays such an important function in Heidegger's phenomenology of perception and his philosophy of history.

†

Perhaps nothing moves Heidegger farther from anthropocentrism, even anthropocentrism in its transcendental version, than his insistence on "essence" (*Wesen*). In *The Metaphysical Foundations of Logic* (1928), Heidegger defends his attribution of a human essence by arguing against any positing of a *telos* in connection with that essence:

> It must become clear from the metaphysics of *Dasein* why, in conforming to the essence of its being, *Dasein* must itself take over the question and answer concerning the final purpose [i.e., of human existence], why searching for an objective answer is in itself *a* or *the* misunderstanding of human experience in general. (GA 26: 239/MFL 185)

He believes that we do have a certain nature or essence; but it does not inscribe and prescribe any determinate *telos*. There might not even be any final purpose at all. But if there is any, it could only come from individual, personal commitments. Our essence, or nature, does, however, make a claim that calls and summons us to its recognition: we are responsible for whatever ultimate meaning our lives and our world might have. But that responsibility, calling, summoning, and importuning though it is, can always be ignored, neglected, refused, denied, or remain simply without awareness. Another difference from the conception of essence in metaphysics is that the human essence, *Da-sein*, is not encapsulated or isolated; nor is it immutable and eternal; it exists in interaction with the world. The nature, or essence, that Heidegger attributes to *Da-sein* is consequently very different from human nature described in the Aristotelian teleology. But the human being is not at birth just an empty, shapeless cabinet or jug waiting to be filled by social forms. Both as individuals and as members of a species, we are born endowed with certain predispositions, capacities, and abilities. But whether, and if so, how the given potential in these capacities and capabilities is taken up and developed depends both on the individual and on the social culture.

†

In Heidegger's introduction to *What Is Metaphysics?* (1943, revised in 1949), there is useful elaboration of these matters:

> To characterize with a single term both the relation of being [*Sein*] to
> the essence of man and the essential relation of man to the openness
> [the *Da-*] of being as such, the name *Da-sein* was chosen to characterize
> the essential dimension [of human existence] in relation to which the
> human being becomes human. (GA 9: 372/PM 283)

Thus, as he says: *Da-sein* designates "that which is first of all to be experienced, and subsequently thought, as the locality [*Ortschaft*] of the truth
of being [i.e., the locality where a clearing for the experiencing of being
opens and takes place]." In our thrown openness, we become, wherever we
are, the *Einbruch*, the eruption, of an opening, a unique clearing, a singular
world within the historical world that, in our being-with-others (*Mitsein*),
we belong to, share, and keep open together.

We can express this point in a condensed form: in the truth of our
being, we *Dasein* are *Da-sein*. Clearings. And, as I shall argue, primarily in
chapter 4, it is in regard to this clearing that we are "appropriated" (*ereignet*) to an essential responsibility, claimed for an ontological responsibility,
claimed by the clearing itself. The "clearing"—*Lichtung*—is one of Heidegger's key themes. There are some important questions about it which
will be considered in detail in the fourth chapter. For our present purposes,
however, I think it should suffice for me to say that, for Heidegger, each
one of us is essentially, right where we are, wherever that might be, a clearing. Simply by virtue of existing, of being bodily present somewhere in the
world, we are the opening up, right there, of a certain unique, distinctly
individuated openness: our presence in the midst of things is, as Heidegger
says, cherishing the simile, like a clearing in the midst of a forest. Another
image comes to mind: we are like the pebble that falls into a pond, producing ripples that, confirming the event, appear on the surface of the water,
serenely encircling the place where the pebble fell while moving steadily
outward, away from that place, but with ever-diminishing force and visibility. We live in the clearings our presence makes. Such is our sojourn
on this earth. What the philosopher is hoping for is that we dwell in these
clearings with mindfulness—as much attentiveness and responsibility as we
can muster.

†

Now, *Dasein* is the common German word to designate or acknowledge the *existence* of some being in the world. It could refer to an animal,
though perhaps most often it refers to a human being. In that sense, each of
us human beings is, quite simply, but in our own personal way, a *Dasein*.
However, there is promising *design* in our capacities. So, according to Heidegger, we human beings are actually not yet, as such, *Da-sein*, ones who

are mindfully aware of our inherent openness and exposure to the world (*Ausgesetztheit*)—a thrown openness that the hyphen emphatically signifies, although, inconsistently, Heidegger only sometimes used it. Nevertheless, there is a crucial distinction between what is named by the word *Dasein*, referring to us as *Menschen*, human beings, and what he means when, interpolating a disruptive hyphen, he speaks of *Da-sein*. I shall try to be more consistent in my use of the hyphen. In any case, to the extent that we move toward our most proper, most appropriate, most authentic existence, to that extent we become what we always already have been assigned and disposed by nature to be, namely, *Da-sein,* beings who are cast into the world in openness to it, cast *a priori* to be (*-sein*) situated here (*Da-*) where we are. Thus, according to Heidegger, because this ontological dimension of thrown openness is neither experienced with awareness nor properly understood, the human being—*Mensch, Dasein* without the hyphen—both is already, and yet also, is not yet, *Da-sein*. We can fulfill ourselves individually—and fulfill our historical destiny as Western civilization—only insofar as we realize this essential nature with which, at birth, we are endowed, not only in our individual lives but also in our collective historical existence, belonging to, and inheriting, the Western world. As Heidegger repeatedly and unequivocally tells us, the very essence of our humanity is (to be) "grounded in *Da-sein*" (GA 71: 247/E 213). *Becoming* grounded in *Da-sein*, hence *becoming* the grounding of the openness inherent in the *Da-* where we are, is the ownmost, most essential, most properly fulfilling task for us as *Da-sein*. And, as we noted in the introduction, Heidegger argues, in *The Event* (1941–1942):

> To the unique claim of beyng, namely that it *is*, there pertains—as stemming from the arrogation [*Zu-eignung*] of man to become *Da-sein*—the gathering of all *capacities* and capabilities [*Versammlung aller Vermögen*] into the unity of the preservation of the truth of beyng [i.e., the preservation of the opened clearing, the field of experience that makes possible our unconcealment and concealment of beings]. (GA 71: 162/E 139)

In awakening to, recognizing, and taking responsibility for the presencing of beings in the time–space clearing of their truth, *all our capacities* are gathered into the redemption of their inherent potential. These capacities and capabilities are, first of all, constitutive of human perception—a perception always already appropriated, summoned, to actualize its potential: that is, always already, even if not consciously experienced as such, neither recognized nor understood, and always already, even if ignored, neglected, or denied.

†

In a text for lectures delivered in 1951–1952 and subsequently assembled under the title *What Is Called Thinking?*, Heidegger made a comment that is crucial to both his project and mine:

> The things for which we owe thanks are not the things we have from ourselves. They are given to us. We receive many gifts, of many kinds. But the highest and really most lasting gift given to us is always our essential nature, with which we are gifted in such a way that we are what we are only through it. That is why we owe thanks for this endowment, first and unceasingly. (GA 8: 94/WCT 142)

This at once suggests some questions: How might we, or how should we, most appropriately enact and express our thankfulness? As that gift of a human nature is the gift of a potential, would we not consider the most appropriate way for us to express our appreciation to be, quite simply, the practicing, hence actualizing, of that gift of nature? That seems right. But what would that actualization be? What would its fulfillment look like? In the two volumes belonging to this project, I shall show, in regard to our perception, in particular our seeing and hearing, that there is in fact much that can be said to answer these questions in a useful and satisfying way.

†

In the years following the publication of *Being and Time*, Heidegger strengthened his commitment to an existential phenomenology, emphasizing the importance of our recognizing and understanding ourselves in our essential being and accordingly taking on, as our most fundamental task, the corresponding responsibility. As we shall see, that responsibility requires attentiveness in preserving and protecting the openness of our perceptual fields. This is an openness we *are* by nature; but we are nevertheless capable of narrowing and closing it or subjecting it to various conditions and restrictions.

In our thinking further about this responsibility, it would be useful to retain a terminology that Heidegger introduced in *Being and Time*. I am referring to the terms "existential" and "existentiell." The first term designates what pertains to the structure of our essential nature, the *ontological* dimension of our existence, which, for Heidegger, means our thrown openness, our being-as-clearings; the second term, by contrast, designates the personal, individual way of living in relation to that given essence or nature. This is a terminology that, for some reason, he did not continue to use in his later thinking, although I want to argue that the distinction that that terminology brought to our attention is something that permanently remained in his thinking. Indeed, I am convinced that neither Heidegger's critique of the Western world nor the transformation at the heart of his philosophy of history, and crucial for his project as a whole, can be thought without somehow drawing that distinction.

There is a related terminological distinction, also introduced in *Being and Time*, that we need to bear in mind: the phenomenological distinction, namely, that between (i) ontical and (ii) ontological. Whereas the ontical is concerned with the realm of facts about entities (beings), the ontological is concerned with the meaning of being, hence we can say that it is concerned with what, in the context of post-Kantian thought, would be called the transcendental *a priori* conditions of meaning, or intelligibility, that make possible, and define, our experience, not only of entities but also categories or types of entities. Thus, our thrown openness, as *Da-sein*, is ontological, but in the ontical facticity of our lives, that dimensionality of openness, that clearing, could be ignored, neglected, denied, somehow narrowed. And so, when Heidegger summons us to a guardian responsibility—a *Wächterschaft*—for the clearing, the "truth of being," what is in question is our awareness, understanding, and protecting of the ontological dimension, the ontological structure, of our experience. He is not urging us to hold ourselves open to terrorism; he is not counseling that we maintain an open mind about witchcraft. These are ontical matters. However, maintaining, with awareness and understanding, the existential, structural openness of the ontological dimension can be of great benefit in the ontical realm, in that it enables and encourages us to discern more carefully, more astutely, even perhaps more safely, the nature or disposition of whatever it may be that we encounter.

A similar argument pertains to the attitude of *Gelassenheit* that Heidegger praises. The "letting-be" that he urges must be understood to be the attitude of an *ontological* disposition. He is not urging that we "let be" a drowning stranger or "let be" an assault on a homeless man. But getting in touch with the ontological dimension of our experience can make possible more appropriate, more effective *ontical* responses to such events. In order to assess and determine what *ontical* comportment a situation requires of us, nothing can be more appropriate than an initial moment of neutral openness. That is the moment of ontological *Gelassenheit*.

†

*Wer sind wir?*—"Who are we," we who call ourselves human beings? What is it that makes us essentially, distinctively human? With these questions, Heidegger asks us to begin questioning and exploring the shibboleths we cling to and the assumptions we never challenge: what it is we believe and think we know about ourselves, our bodies, and how we inhabit and dwell in our perceptions, our communities, the realm of nature, and the world. Proposing for consideration his own ontological conception of the human being, Heidegger takes us far beyond our familiar boundaries into a phenomenology and hermeneutics of existence that can, perhaps for the first time, make our life, our being, seem very strange, showing us to ourselves in an uncanny, even perhaps disquieting, and certainly demanding light.

In *Kant and the Problem of Metaphysics* (1929), Heidegger observed that "man is the *Da* with whose being the opening eruption into the midst of beings takes place [*mit dessen Sein der eröffnende Einbruch in das Seiende geschieht*]" (GA 3: 229/KPM 156). That opening eruption, that breaching, the constitution of a world, happening wherever human existence, *Dasein*, appears, is indicated by writing *Dasein* with a hyphen: *Da-sein*. The *essence* of human *Dasein* is thus *Da-sein*, to be (*sein*) the clearing (*Da*): "The human being [*Dasein*] is that being [*dasjenige Seiende*] that is such that it can be the site and layout of an opening [*ein Da*]. The '*Da*': a sphere of openness [*Offenbarkeit*]."[2] This 1929 determination is given further definition in his 1946 "Letter on Humanism," where Heidegger says: "Man happens in such a way that he is the '*Da*', that means, the clearing of being [*die Lichtung des Seins*]."[3] What are we to make of the thought that to exist as a human being *means*, as he says in this "Letter," "standing out in the clearing of being [*Stehen in der Lichtung*]" (GA 9: 323–24/PM 247)? As the philosopher maintains that we are not yet what in essence we are, what does this strange attribution—"thrown openness"—still require of us? What does it mean that each of us is a *Da-sein*? What does it purport that each of us is, hence, exists as, a clearing?

One of the unfortunate matters in this regard is that, in laying out the phenomenology of our fundamental nature as the thrown openness, a nature for which he uses the hyphenated word *Da-sein*, emphasizing the breaking open that word is actually conveying, Heidegger seldom acknowledges our embodiment. In *Culture and Value*, Wittgenstein said, as if commenting on Heidegger's way of thinking about *Da-sein*: "The purely corporeal can be uncanny [*Das rein Körperliche kann unheimlich sein*]."[4] But, as Heidegger interprets it, it is our human *Da-sein* as thrown openness—a *Leib*, not a *Körper*—that is likely to seem more uncanny. We have to learn to be more "in our bodies" in that thrown-open way. We need to be more aware of our role in the opening out of our time–space fields and more aware of our role and responsibility in sustaining their ontological dimension of openness.

How do we human beings *become* who we already—and yet also, not yet—essentially are? Although this question can at first seem paradoxical, in truth it simply is a recognition of the fact that, like all living beings, albeit in an essentially distinctive way, we human beings are capable of learning and growing, given by nature the possibility of developing and realizing our given potential—a potential that is not fully developed at the beginning of our lives. Aristotle understood this matter well. But all one needs for confirmation of this fact is manifest at once when one compares the experiential openness of an infant to the experiential openness of an adult. Growing up, the child learns, for better and for worse, the need to relinquish that degree of openness. The adult's openness is a world enclosed by many protective defenses, most of which operate without awareness and recognition. So, it would be reasonable to suggest that we should, at the very least, become more aware of our thrown openness and learn to recognize the conditions we impose. The other animals on this planet also *live* in clearings, *are* themselves also clearings, each species in its own biologically predetermined way; but we are the only ones capable of self-awareness and self-recognition and with an ability to shape and develop our clearings accordingly.

†

Heidegger did not complete the project he designed in 1927 for *Being and Time*. But he did not cease thinking about being, time, and *Da-sein*. Thus, in "The Origin of the Work of Art" (1935–1936), Heidegger further elaborated his understanding of the phenomenology of the human being as *Da-sein*, exploring the significance of the semantic composition—the *Da-* and the *-sein* of that key word: "In the midst of beings as a whole an open place occurs [*Inmitten des Seienden im Ganzen west eine offene Stelle*]. And it is there that a clearing [*Lichtung*] occurs" (GA 5: 39–40/PLT 53). This clearing *is*—is nothing other than—*Da-sein*; it occurs, it takes place *as Da-sein*; so it *is Da*, nowhere but *here*, situated where the human being, as existing in thrown openness, that is, as *Da-sein*, *is*. We human beings exist in the freedom and vulnerability of a fated condition of thrown openness. This thrownness (*Geworfenheit*) is our most fundamental *disposition*; it is the situatedness (*Befindlichkeit*), the facticity, in which we find ourselves: we *are*, quite simply, the opening and clearing of certain worlds: worlds of perception, of memory, of imagination, of theoretical conception; worlds we share; worlds of solitude in which we dwell unto death. It is where we exist, namely right here (*Da-*) where we *are* (*-sein*), that the opening and clearing of a world occurs. We are the grounding *center* of every clearing. Nevertheless, even though we are "in the midst" of beings, and consequently, in that sense, can be said to find ourselves *surrounded* by beings, when our fundamental function is taken into consideration, we will realize that we are rather what *encircles* all the beings in our world because it is within our clearings that the beings meaningful to us appear in their presence and absence. And of course, we dwell in the world we open; we are ourselves present in it.

This is an extraordinary representation of the essence of our existence. But what does it mean for us to become aware of ourselves, recognizing and understanding ourselves, in this way? How does our coming to this awareness, this self-recognition and self-understanding engage us, or change us? What do we make of it? These questions are implied by Heidegger's phenomenology; but for the most, they remain, in the framework of his project, without guiding answers.

†

Reading *Being and Time* today, one cannot overlook the fact that, despite his assertion that being—or the question of being—must be the most important, most urgent thing for us to give our thought to, Heidegger's project *always* worked within the precincts of the phenomenology of *Da-sein*, showing how *being*, whether understood as essence, as the meaning of beings, as meaningful presencing, or as the clearing that makes such presencing possible, is inherently *dependent* on *Da-sein* as the "layout" of a field of meaning. And this insight, already operative in "The Principle of Identity" and "Identity and Difference" (1955–1957), brought him, by 1962, in a seminar called "Time and Being," to an astonishing conclusion:

> Wenn das Ereignis nicht eine neue seinsgeschichtliche Prägung des Seins ist, sondern umgekehrt das Sein in das Ereignis gehört und dahin zurückgenommen wird (auf welche Weise auch immer), dann ist für das Denken im Ereignis, d.h., für das Denken, das in das Ereignis einkehrt—sofern dadurch das Sein, das im Geschick beruht, nicht mehr das eigens zu Denkende ist—die Seinsgeschichte zu Ende. Das Denken steht dann in und vor Jenem, das die verschiedenen Gestalten des epochalen Seins zugeschickt hat. Dieses aber, das Schickende als das Ereignis, ist selbst ungeschichtlich, besser geschicklos. (GA 14: 49–50/ OTB 40–41)

In my interpretive paraphrase, this says:

> If the *Ereignis* [the event in which a claim on our appropriation to be *Da-sein* occurs, as it always does whenever we encounter anything in our world] is not the emergence of a new onto-historical formation of being, but on the contrary being is recognized as belonging to, and belonging in, that *Ereignis*, and thus is drawn back into it (absorbed in whatever way), then the history of being is at an end for a thinking that operates in terms of *Ereignis* [the appropriation of *Menschsein* to be *Da-sein*], that

is to say, for a thinking that enters into the *Ereignis*—in the sense that the destiny of *being*, which [*im Geschick beruht*] lies in the layout of a field that makes the meaningful presencing of beings possible, is no longer primarily to be thought. Thinking then stands in and before that [namely, *Da-sein*, our appropriated thrown-openness] which has made possible [*zugeschickt*] the various epochal formations of being in the layouts, or clearings, that its existence, its presence in the world, has opened. However, that [i.e., *das Schickende*] which is making those formations possible, namely our thrown-openness [i.e., *Da-sein*] as *appropriated* to be the clearings in which the meaningful presencing of beings takes place, is itself unhistorical, or more precisely, without determination by something metaphysical, called "destiny." (GA 14: 49/50/OTB 40–41)

In a unique sense of "event," being is "the highest, most significant event of all" (GA 14: 26/OTB 21). But what matters is the philosophical recognition and understanding of *that which makes possible* the *Es gibt*, the *sheer fact* of being, the sheer giving and givenness of being. And that turns out to demand of Heidegger's project an enduring commitment to exploring *Da-sein*'s phenomenology. *Das Schickende*—what is doing the "sending" and "giving" of being, that is, making possible that which presences in the fields of our perceptual experience—is the appropriated clearing that the very nature of our existence, our presence as *Da-sein*, has opened up. Drawing inspiration from Parmenides, for whom being (*einai*) and cognition (*noiein*, *nous*) are "the same," Heidegger suggests that the *Es gibt* ultimately involves the *appropriation* of *Da-sein*—*Ereignis* in this other, second sense: that is, not understood just as "event" but rather as a *claim* on *Da-sein*'s responsibility, properly taking into its care its being the layout of and for the *Es gibt*, the open clearing that makes possible, which enables and lets-be, the presence and absence of all meaningful beings. As Heidegger will also say, drawing the phrase *Es gibt* into its more phenomenological sense: it is nothing other than *Da-sein* that, *as the layout of a clearing*, is the *Es* (i.e., *Da-sein* is the "it") that *gibt* (i.e., it is *Da-sein* that, in its very existence, intrinsically lays out, "gives" or "sends"—or forms—the clearing for the presencing of entities) (GA 73.1: 642, 644). This is why *Da-sein* is the appropriated clearing: *Das Schickende*—*geschicklos*. It is *Da-sein* that "sends," not Destiny.

This passage from *Time and Being* that we just paraphrased presents every translator with a number of difficulties for interpretation. The sentences all require interpretative decisions in order to resolve them. Heidegger's use of *zugeschickt*, like his use of *das Geschick* and *das Schickende*, creates echoes of metaphysics, ambiguities, and puzzlements that could, I think, have been avoided. Despite the metaphysical reverberations,

Heidegger was slow to relinquish the semantic constellation surrounding *Geschick*. I believe that my rendering not only makes sense on its own but also catches what is important in Heidegger's text, namely, that what ultimately matters in addressing the question of being is the appropriation of *Da-sein* as (and for) that which opens and lays out clearings for the meaningful presencing of things. Being depends on *Da-sein*. And once we attain a deep understanding of this dependency, we no longer need to concentrate thought on being. Illuminating the nature of the appropriating claim in relation to the various historical epochs of being, the 1962 seminar on "Time and Being" reached the conclusion that "thinking stands in and before that which has sent the different epochal formations of being," that is, thinking stands in and before the *appropriation* of human existence to that openness, that clearing, which makes possible the meaningful presence of these different historical formations of being. Our appropriation to *Da-sein* is the ontological dimension Heidegger wants us to retrieve. Thus, if we want to understand the "logic" in the unfolding of the different formations—different historical paradigms—of being, we need to interrogate the appropriation of *Da-sein* in its historical world orders.

In *Zum Ereignis-Denken*, there is a textual passage that, although working with the two different meanings of *es gibt*, namely the literal "it gives" and the idiomatic "there is," quite clearly resolves many of the questions raised by the texts we have been examining. In my paraphrase, it says:

> "World" names the realm of intelligibility and meaning that provides a clearing that is open for the meaningful being of beings in their presence and absence; it is where what is experienced in its meaningfulness can happen; *Da-sein* is the ever-individuated "it" that gives, that makes possible and [hence] *is* the "it gives" in regard to what there is in the world": "*Welt 'gibt' Sein; das Dasein ist das je vereinzelte 'es,' das gibt; das ermöglicht und ist das 'es gibt'.*" (GA 73.1: 642, 644)[5]

*Dasein*, or rather, the human being understood in terms of its essential structure and function *as Da-sein*, is the *es* (it) responsible for the attribution, or giving, of meaningfulness to beings. Because of our very nature, the structure and function of our bodily existence, we human beings are thrown-open layouts of clearings (*Da-sein*); and as such, *Da-sein* is the *es* that *gibt*: we are what makes possible (what lets, what enables) the *Es gibt*, that is, the fact that there is a world of meaningfully presencing things.

We, each of us a *Dasein*, are appropriated, or claimed, through our inherent, essential bodily nature, hence claimed *a priori*, to *be* thrown open as *clearings*, fields of meaning, and intelligibility: *Da-sein*. And it is those fields that, in their layouts, make it possible for us to experience what there is—what *es gibt*—in its presencing and absencing, unconcealment and concealment. Our clearings form worlds in which it is possible for beings to be present and absent: "*Welt gibt Sein.*" *Welt*, here, is to be understood as also signifying the clearing: a "world" is a time–space field, fictional or real, a layout of conditions for intelligibility and meaning which lets-be, enabling beings to be meaningful.

"On the Question of Being" (1955) not only supports this interpretation, but, going beyond the phenomenological analysis in the texts we have been considering so far, it unequivocally brings out, without actually mentioning it, the claim of appropriation (*Er-eignis, Er-eignung*) that is inherently operative in the interaction of *Mensch* and *Sein*—operative, that is, in the relation that is really not a relation, because of the inseparable belonging togetherness of *Mensch* and *Sein*:

> Presencing ("being") [*Anwesen* ("*Sein*")], as presencing, on each and every occasion [*je und je*] a presencing directed toward the human essence [i.e., *Da-sein*, our being situated here], insofar as presencing is a call [*Geheiß*] that, on each occasion [*jeweils*] calls upon the human essence [*des Menschenwesen ruft*]. The human essence as such is a hearing [*ist als solches hörend*], because the essence of human beings belongs to the calling of this call [*weil es ins rufende Geheiß ins An-wesen gehört*] in the approach of this presencing. (GA 9: 408–9/PM 308–9)

Using two distinct senses of "appropriation," I am arguing that every perceptual encounter addresses us, summons us, calls us, appropriating us (i.e., taking hold of us) for our appropriation (i.e., for the actualizing of our ontological potential) as disposed in responsibility for the character of our role in the encounter. Every encounter summons us to awaken to our ontological responsibility in regard both to *what* is presencing in the encounter and *how* that which we encounter happens to be presencing. The call may be experienced as coming from what we encounter in the world; but in any event, because of the intertwining of the "subjective" and "objective" aspects, or poles, of the situation, the call demands to be heard, and felt, to resonate "inside" us with the claim of appropriation that is constitutive of the disposition of our ownmost nature.

"Appropriation" and clearings will be the topics of the following two chapters. But the first thing to consider must be how *Menschsein* comes into its essence—into its own—as *Da-sein*. This, of course, is the *process* that Heidegger will call *Er-eignung*—that is to say, appropriation.

†

It is now possible to read Heidegger's rethinking, in 1936, of his 1927 book, *Being and Time*. In *Running Notes on "Being and Time"* (*Laufende Anmerkungen zu "Sein und Zeit"*), he is unequivocal in emphasizing (1) that human existence, the human being (*Dasein*), is not to be identified with *Da-sein*; (2) that *Da-sein* is something that has to be achieved; (3) that such achievement is an ongoing, never-completed process; and (4) that entering into this process requires a certain leap because it is not simply the continuation of human existence as we have lived and known it: it is not just more of the same. In the *Laufende Anmerkungen*, Heidegger says: "*Da-sein* is what must originally be gained—what 'is' only in the happening of a leap and its development. [In *Being and Time*] *Da-sein* is taken [erroneously] as the being of man, and [consequently] being-human is not grasped as the springing-open [*Ersprung*] of *Dasein* [*from* out of the human]" (GA 82: 22). And he goes on to say: "The question of the being of *Dasein* is not [i.e., as it is in Husserlian phenomenology] the search for an adequate *description* of *Dasein* (as if it 'were' already 'present at hand'), but rather the *working out of the beyng* [*Seyn*] *of the t/here* [i.e., the working out of the *being* of the *Da*, our situating situatedness]!" (GA 82: 51; see also GA 82: 53). The phenomenological enquiry into the human *Da-sein* is a hermeneutical process, retrieving what is operative even in its hiddenness. Thus, the being of the "t/here" (the *Da*) must be "carried out (achieved)" through a "gathering into steadfastness [*Inständigkeit*] in the 't/here,' [so that] through persistent commitment [*Inständigkeit*], the 't/here' is sustained in its always historical essence" (ibid., 39). This involves a resolute "leap" into an ongoing, never completable *process*. Being-in-the-world is no "structure-in-itself," an essential nature already "there," as in the traditional notion of "essence," fully formed and unchanging, but is rather an *ongoing process, structurally organized* in relation to our disposition in a given historical situation (*geschichtet*): the *fact* of existence is only the *basis* for a persistent commitment (*Inständigkeit*) to ongoing transformation (ibid., 56–57). Hence, *Da-sein* is *both* event and process: as awakening and leap, it is an event, but as a disposition bearing a potential to be enacted and achieved, it is a process. Serving two needs in one thought, *Ereignis* therefore requires an interpretation that recognizes both meanings. More on this in the next chapter (chapter 3).

†

As should already be apparent from the preceding discussion, Heidegger's vision of a new "humanism" differs in many significant ways from the humanism he inherited. In question is not so much—any more—the question of *being* in the history of metaphysics, and of course Heidegger's critique of that historically dominant understanding, but much more the question of our self-recognition and self-understanding, eventuating in the transformation of *Menschsein* into a consciously appropriated exposed existence as *Da-sein*, that is, as layout of, and for, world-openings, clearings that, while possible only through us, nevertheless exceed, or transcend, our presence as human beings. But transformation is possible only insofar as we begin by acknowledging the fundamental difference, a difference in essence, between our existence as *Menschsein* and our existence as *Da-sein*, and take responsibility for ourselves: for the character of our ways of engaging the world and for achieving what we in potential already are.

However, we have yet to understand in phenomenologically meaningful, practical terms, just what our being thrown-open clearings purports. We shall explore this matter further in the next chapter, wherein the *existential*, ontological claim on *Da-sein*—*Da-sein*'s appropriation (*Ereignis*)—is taken up for consideration. But for now, let us continue pondering some of Heidegger's illuminating statements regarding the nature of our being, our existence, as *Da-sein*.

†

In *The Event*, Heidegger's increasing recognition of the importance of working out the phenomenology of *Da-sein*, hence the phenomenology of the clearing, leads him to formulate a crucial argument regarding the relation between *Mensch* and *Sein*, a relation that, for too many centuries, has been represented in metaphysics as the subject–object structure:

> A *being* is a *possible* object, something standing over and against, only because it stands in the open domain of beyng [i.e., stands in the clearing]. Precisely where there is an "over and against" [*Gegenüber*], something more originary occurs essentially [namely], the clearing constitutive of the "in-between." (GA 71: 17/E 10)

And in that clearing, the being that appears, in perception, as "object" over and against a human "subject" *belongs together with* that percipient subject in the togetherness and belongingness of a certain back-and-forth dance (*Schweben*) of address and claim. So I would like to follow this by suggesting that what Heidegger is bringing to our attention is the fact that there is, *preceding* the formation of the subject–object structure, and normally remaining hidden underneath it, a more originary preconceptual dimension in which a certain oscillation (*Gegenschwung*) prevails, a dynamic, two-way (*wechselweise*)[6] interactive flow, bringing together what eventuates, from metaphysical reflection on the relation between *Mensch* and *Sein*, as subject and object. Walter Benjamin articulates the preconceptual, affective dimension of perception, that dimension which precedes and underlies the subject–object structure, when, in a fictitious dialogue, he has Margarethe report on her experience: "I was not a seer, I was only seeing [*Ich war keine Sehende, ich war nur Sehen*]."[7] She is completely immersed in seeing. This affectively constituted, more originary dimension, in which what we recognize as subject and object interact in a belonging together, is experienced preconceptually in what the ancient Greek philosophers called "pathos." With the remarkable exception of Schelling's system of metaphysics, which was no doubt a significant influence on Heidegger's phenomenological explication of the *Mensch-Sein* interaction, and in which the earlier philosopher called attention to the "thrust" (*Schwung*) of primordial energy operating beneath conceptual experience,[8] metaphysics does not see this dimension of *pathos*, because of its prejudice against feeling and the felt and its favoring of abstract thinking and the speculative thought. Metaphysics, settled in abstract concepts of the understanding, takes as primary and fundamental what is actually secondary. In *pathos*, however, we experience and recognize a certain unity and undifferentiated wholeness that comes before the emergence of any subject–object dualism. *Pathos* is an engagement with the world that takes place in the *pre-ontological* dimension of the clearing; it precedes and underlies the ontic, everyday experience of the structure of perception.

Unfortunately, after his introduction to *Being and Time*, Heidegger abandoned the notion of a "pre-ontological understanding of being." However, his project requires our recognition of this pre-ontological dimension. Thus, it should not be surprising that, in "The Principle of Identity," Heidegger's thinking recognizes this dimension of experience, although no longer retaining the earlier terminology.

Can we discover ourselves—our role in setting out the conditions of intelligibility and meaning—in apprehending what we encounter? To experience this role would be to recognize the belonging together (*Zusammen-gehörigkeit*) of what metaphysics posits as the opposition structure (*Gegenüber*) of subject and object (GA 11: 39/ID 30–31).[9] It would be, moreover, the beginning of a recognition of the *Ereignis*, the claim on our responsibility, that the world we have opened, cleared, and inhabited inherently makes: instead of opposition, belonging togetherness.

In this belonging together, our being as *Da-sein* is always much more in question than is the being of that "object" with which we find ourselves concerned. Our essential nature is not a sealed fate but rather an opportunity—to continue learning and unfolding. Who we are is always an open question, closing only with our death.

†

In common usage, as we noted, *Da-sein* refers in general to the *existence* (*Existenz*) of beings. However, as he so often did, Heidegger appropriated these two key terms for use in his project bringing out a meaningfulness hidden in them. The word "existence" is derived from the Greek; it is composed of "*ex-*," meaning outside, exterior, and external, and "*-istence*," deriving from the Greek word for standing, staying, or being. "Ecstatic," also derived from the Greek, carries the same fundamental sense: expanding out, standing out, being outside, reaching out: in Merleau-Ponty's French, we exist in *écart*—not, as Descartes argued, enclosed in a substance body. Husserl called this ecstatic phenomenon "intentionality." Heidegger pointed out a similar meaningfulness hidden in the word *Da-sein*, namely, a reference to being (*sein*) and a reference to situatedness (*Da*), the latter more literally meaning simply "here" and also "there." Together, these meanings yield Heidegger's conception of the essence of the human being as an embodied, situated thrown openness—*Geworfensein*.

In *Being and Time*, Heidegger lays out the fundamental existential structures (*Existentialen*) that constitute (*konstituieren*) the being of our existence as *Da-sein* (*das Sein des Da*). We find ourselves in our situatedness (*Befindlichkeit*) cast into the openness (*Erschlossenheit*) of a world; we are *given* a world already opened, a world we did not make, a world we shall share with others on our sojourn through life. Within this shared world, however, we do inherently open and make a distinctive world of our own. It is our own uniquely personal (*existentiell*) perspective on this common world. When we die, this latter world, our *Eigenwelt*—ceases. Our window, our unique perspective on the world in common, closes. Forever.

†

Heidegger seems to have become increasingly convinced that the word *Ereignis* provides the best way to think about the significance of our thrown openness—our ownmost essential disposition—in relation to being. Indeed, he realized that the appropriation of our existence that his insightful use of that word "*Ereignis*" revealed made it possible to shift his attention *from* the question of being *onto* the appropriation operative in *Dasein's relation* to being. An extremely dense and paradoxically formulated statement in *Zum Ereignis-Denken* regarding the "relation" between the human being as *Da-sein* and being brings the shift into sharply thought-provoking relief:

> The bond [*Bezug*] between beyng [*Seyn*] and man [*Menschen*] is not a fixed span [*eingespannt*]. . . . The bond is beyng itself, and the essence of the human being [*das Menschenwesen*, i.e., *Da-sein*] just *is* that same bond, each drawing the other to it. (GA 73.1: 790)

In other words, the apparent "relation" is *not* really a relation, because there are not *two distinctly separate things* to be related, one to the other; rather, despite what the wording suggests, we are actually merely contemplating the *same* situation from two different angles. If *Seyn selbst* is the clearing, it cannot be something metaphysically independent of *Dasein*, because, as it so happens, the human being *is* always, in its deepest truth, a clearing. This is where we can see the significance of recognizing the pre-ontological dimension: the preconceptual dimension of *pathos*, a certain dance or oscillation, a *Schwingen* and *Schweben*, in which *Mensch* and *Sein* come together in meaningful dynamic interaction.

Everything that in any way *is* is only as appearing in its relationality—a network of relations: that is how *Da-sein* experiences the meaningfulness of its world. This network of relations is a field, a ground, a clearing, a world—it is the necessary condition of meaningful appearance, inherently open. It is imperative that we let the clearing *be* clearing, let the ground *be* ground; and that means that, as the figure emerges into salience, we preserve and protect the sheer *energeia*, the play of the ground or field in its natural propensity for *yielding and withdrawing* into self-concealment. In the forming of a meaningful *Gestalt*, the ground *yields* in both of its two possible senses: (i) it retreats, or recedes, but in that dynamic, (ii) it also at the same time brings forth, or lets come forth, a figure.

However, Heidegger believes that what is distinctive of the modern age is the way that the withdrawing and self-concealment of the ground are either neglected or actively defied. Although the yielding of the ground, as ground, inherently resists totalization, making absolute control of the perceptual situation impossible, in the present world, where the nihilism of the will to power increasingly prevails, the being of the ground is constantly subjected to processes of reification and, frequently, processes that bind it in obedience to the economic demands of control and commodification, reduced to the finitude of a figure by the will to power in the perceptual grasp.

The more powerful the subject becomes, the more that which it experiences in perceptual interaction is reified, immobilized in the state of objecthood. Can we discover and recognize ourselves in our way of apprehending as objects what we encounter in the world? Guiding us to this self-recognition and self-understanding, Heidegger hopes to release the subject–object structure from its reification—a situation that is as stultifying for the human being reduced to a subject as it is destructive for whatever is reduced to the being of an object.

The above passage on the *Bezug* connects nicely with another passage, this one from what Sheehan characterizes as Heidegger's "middle period" (mostly the 1940s): *"[Das] Wo als das Da der Bleibe gehört zum Sein selbst, 'ist' Sein selbst und heißt darum das Da-sein"* (GA 6.2: 358/N4: 217–18). This beautifully defines the phenomenology of the human *Da-sein*—and does this, moreover, in a way that explains the deeper, hidden meaning Heidegger draws out of the word. In English, the sentence says: "The 'where' as the *Da* that situates the human being belongs to being itself, 'is' being itself and thereby is called *Da-sein*." We human beings—we, each one of us a *Dasein*, an existent being, are sites and layouts where the meaningfulness of things in their presencing (*Bedeutsamkeit*) is to be experienced: "The *Da* in *Da-sein*," says Heidegger, is ontological, not ontic: it "does not designate some actual, determinable positions *here* and *there*, but refers, rather, to the *clearing* of beyng itself [*die Lichtung des Seyns selbst*]" (GA 65: 298/CP 235). The "It" that "sends" and "gives" the beings that we encounter in their presencing is not other than the time-space field—the clearing that we, in the very nature of our existence, have opened.

In his 1957 "The Principle of Identity," Heidegger boldly attempted to deconstruct the metaphysically constructed relation between *Mensch* and *Sein*, basis for the subject–object structure posited by metaphysics; and he accordingly characterized this event, this encounter between us as human beings and something in our world, by speaking, instead, of an appropriating belonging together ("*das Zusammengehören von Mensch und Sein*"), a correspondence (*Entsprechung*) in reciprocity or reversibility appropriating *Mensch* and *Sein* to one another, *an-eignet* and *zu-eignet* in a *wechselweise*, mutual back-and-forth vibration: "*ein in sich schwingende Bereich,*" "*ein in sich schwebende Bau*" (GA 11: 39–48/ID 29–39).[10] In this reciprocal appropriation, the "truth of being," that is, the clearing for the meaningful presencing of things, is "grounded" in *Da-sein*: emphatically in *Da-sein*, and that means, not in *Mensch*, and not in subjectivity (GA 65: 26/CP 22–23).

In Heidegger's "later period" (the 1950s, 1960s, and early 1970s), the philosopher concentrated on thinking the intrinsic nature of the human being as laying out clearings of meaningfulness. Here is a beautifully lucid statement taken from a 1973 seminar: "*Dasein muß als die-Lichtung-sein verstanden werden. Das Da ist nämlich das Wort für die offene Weite*" (GA 15: 380/ FS 69). In English: "*Dasein* must be understood as being-the-clearing. The *Da* is thus the word for the open expanse." *Dasein* makes the presencing of beings possible by *being*-the-clearing, *being*-the-*Da*, sustaining, simply by existing, the open layout that lets things have their particular meaning or significance. The *Da*, opening and sustaining the clearing, a world, is the "it" (the *es*) that makes being possible (*ermöglicht*). In other words, words that might mischievously tempt one to think onto-theologically: the clearing formed by and in the *Da* is a layout that "gives" or "sends" being (*gibt, schenkt* or *schickt, Sein*).

†

I suggest that the intent of Heidegger's phenomenological project is beautifully expressed in "The Origin of the Work of Art," when he speaks of "the opening up of the human being, out of its captivity in that-which-is, i.e., in the being of the world, to the openness of being": *"Die Eröffnung des Daseins aus der Befangenheit im Seienden zur Offenheit des Seins"* (GA 5: 55/PLT 67). This captivity deeply, essentially involves our self-recognition and self-understanding as *Da-sein*—that living being which is responsible for its clearings: What it means to be human, what it means to exist—hence, what it means, or what is implied, when we think to call ourselves *Da-sein*.

It is Heidegger's conviction that we have lost touch with—or say forgotten—what it is that the word *Da-sein*, used to refer to ourselves, is calling us to, namely the clearing. Making phenomenology hermeneutical, as it needs to be, Heidegger attempts to retrieve our pre-ontological understanding of being, a prereflective, prepropositional understanding, borne by the intrinsic nature of our embodiment, of our role in the clearing—and the claim (*Er-eignung*) on us that that role makes. This retrieval (*Erinnerung*) resembles to a certain extent Plato's *anamnesis*, a work of recollection. Understood as mindfulness, however, *Erinnerung* can give us a more immediate experience than what "recollection" suggests. But this does not mean that we can easily break out of the cultural self-understanding in which, since the beginning of the modern age, we have determined ourselves and which, at the same time, the discourse of metaphysics has reinforced in its various representations of the human being. What Heidegger hoped for was more than merely a different self-understanding; he was manifestly hoping for an enownment and enactment of this self-understanding that might bring about a profound transformation of our historically conditioned lives.

†

Sheehan considers our thrown openness, our *Geworfenheit*, to be *a priori*, constitutive of our nature, our essence, prior to all experience: our *Befindlichkeit* consists in finding ourselves *always already* thrown open, *already* having opened, or cleared, a world—the world, namely, in which we find ourselves situated. This reading of *Geworfenheit* as being *a priori* seems to conflict with Heidegger's vehement arguments against the *a priori*, even while he continues to support some notion of an essence, a human nature.[11] But I think we must assume that, in Heidegger's phenomenology, the notion of the *a priori* would differ hugely from the versions of the *a priori* that figure in all the earlier texts in metaphysics: first of all, in the context of his thought, the *a priori* must be embodied, borne or carried by our nature as embodied beings. And, second, it cannot be eternal, free of temporality. Nor can it be isolated from our interactions with the world.

The *a priori* givens constitutive of our nature *interact* in intricate and complicated ways with our natural environment and with our social-cultural practices and institutions, giving rise to new ways of living, new social-cultural forms, and sometimes important new abilities, new habits, and new dispositions. But whatever we as individuals happen to be granted by nature is potential grist for our *existentiell* (personal, individual) appropriation: we can resist, reject, ignore, neglect, fail to recognize, fail to appreciate, feel ashamed or embarrassed, and try to repress; or, alternatively, we can recognize, understand, embrace, and feel pride, adopting and adapting and developing the *a priori* potential in that essence.

In our paradoxical-seeming being called, or claimed—appropriated, *ereignet*—to become who we are, we human *Da-sein* find ourselves thrown open, stretched by the nature of our *a priori* between an always already (*schon immer*) and a not yet (*noch nicht*). Granted existence as human beings, we are not yet (fully) ourselves, not yet all that we could be. Such is the phenomenology—the grammar—of our most fundamental disposition: what Aristotle would have called *dunamis*. We need to bear in mind, here, that the notions of *Ereignis* and *Ereignung* originate in *Eignung*, the German word that interprets Aristotle's word, *dunamis*, meaning *Zu-sein*, the potential constitutive of a disposition, the condition of something still always coming into its own, being appropriated by and toward its proper *telos*—but not as an acorn is drawn unto its proper completeness in the form of an oak tree.[12] In some ways, of course, our maturing is like that of the acorn. But in other ways, we in our maturing are radically different from the acorn. That is because, in the human being, incompleteness reaches all the way down—down into our very essence. We human beings do not simply *emerge* from the fixed givenness, the facticity of our essence; rather, in our emergence, we *interact* with, and alter, the very essence from which we emerged. And that is because we are living in ceaseless interaction with the world. Human existence is a perpetual hermeneutical spiral. For Heidegger, the "essence" of the human being, its *Da-sein*, exists, or is, *only* in its becoming. It is never final, never complete, never totally determinate. This interpretation of "essence" could not be more at odds with the teleological concept of "essence" that has persisted throughout the history of philosophy, no less in Aristotle than in Plato, despite the enormous differences between these two Greek philosophers. As Heidegger conceives it, the human essence is always something of our own making—always what, in the living of our life, we make of what we have been given.

For this reason, our next chapter (chapter 3) must be on the appropriation that, inherent in this existential essence, lays claim to our ontological responsibility. The key word *Ereignis* and its constellation of cognate terms will draw us into the question of this responsibility: How should we take over the fact of our thrownness? How should we take up the claim on our appropriation? What responsibility does Heidegger have in mind when he attempts to contemplate the human *Da-sein* in its uncanny role as "vigilant guardian of the truth of being"—"*Wächter der Wahrheit des Seyns*"?

†

Time to begin our summation. According to Thomas Sheehan, it can be useful to differentiate three periods or phases in the unfolding of Heidegger's phenomenological understanding of *Da-sein*. The distinguishing of these periods or phases is useful because it can show, I believe, an understanding that becomes progressively deeper and more dimensional. Thus, although it seems possible to demarcate an "early Heidegger," a "middle period Heidegger," and a "later Heidegger," I think it is crucial to recognize that there is remarkable continuity and coherence in the *logic* according to which these three phases or periods unfold. I am using here the three propositions that Sheehan has proposed for marking the three periods:

i. *The early years*: The emphasis is on thinking *Dasein* as *Da-sein*. "*[Dasein] ist* in der Weise, sein Da zu sein.": "*[Dasein] is* in such a way that its essence is to be its *Da*" (GA 2: 177/BT 171). Here Heidegger is bringing to light the essence of human existence: to *be* the *Da*.

ii. *The middle years*: In the middle period, he is engaged in further explicating the essence of this existence (*Da-sein*) by showing the *Da* in relation to the claim of being. The emphasis shifts to thinking "being," "being itself," *in relation to* the *Da* in this *Da-sein*. "*[Das Da] gehört zum Sein selbst, 'ist' Sein selbst und heißt darum das Da-sein.*" "[The *Da*] belongs to being, 'is' being itself and is accordingly called *Da-sein*" (GA 6.2: 358/N4: 217–18). In these years, he is concerned to bring out the distinctive phenomenological nature of the *relation* between *Da-sein* and *Sein*, demonstrating the fact that *Da-sein* and *Sein*—*Sein selbst* are really just two ways of thinking about "the same" phenomenon: two "angles" of approach to their dynamic, interactive belonging together. Here the philosopher is reinterpreting the phenomenology of the relation *Mensch-Sein*, completing his break with metaphysics.

iii. *The later years*: In interpretive readings of Heidegger's invocations of *Da-sein* in *Being and Time*, the *Da* was typically translated as "here-being," "being here," "being there," or "the there," different ways of indicating the concrete situatedness of human existence. But, in the later years, the emphasis shifts, this time to thinking more fully what it means for *Da-sein* to be a layout, a field of meaning, the openness of a clearing: "*Dasein muß als die-Lichtung-sein verstanden werden. Das Da ist nämlich das Wort für die offene Weite.*" "*Dasein* must be understood as being-the-clearing. The *Da* [i.e., *Sein selbst*] is accordingly the word for the open expanse" (GA 15: 380/FS 69). In its existing, its being as the *Da*, *Da-sein* is that [*das "es"*] which "belongs to being" in the sense that it is what opens up [*erlichtet*], lays out, and sustains [*aussteht*] the clearing, the open expanse of the world (GA 73.1: 642). That opening up and sustaining is the functioning that Heidegger attempts to think about using the key word "appropriation"—*Ereignis*. According to Heidegger, it is in "entering into the *Ereignis*" that we will understand how it is that we find ourselves appropriated—and summoned to our highest responsibility—in the actual and potential layout of clearings that our very existence has made possible for us.

In this third textual passage, Heidegger brings together, as "the same," the principal terms in the phenomenology: (i) the *Da* of *Da-sein*, (ii) *being itself*, (iii) the clearing, and (iv) our appropriation to the clearing. This, in effect, completes the drawing of a circle, a constellation of concepts, central to his project. The only other key concept his project requires *Geschick*. But it is already implicitly at work in this constellation, in that, once we understand how *Ereignis* is the key that illuminates *Da-sein*'s engagement—*Dasein*'s appropriation—to *be* the site, the layout—or, in Heraclitean terms, the *legein*—of clearings, we can think of *Geschick* as the key that illuminates the functioning of the clearing, that is, its *Schicken*, the making possible of presencing, and the fact that, always bearing possibilities for our appropriation of destiny, there are different historically conditioned formations of being— "*die verschiedenen Gestalten des epochalen Seins*"—that we are given (*geschickt*) to work with; so *Geschick* is the key that also illuminates, at the same time, our critical role in these formations and our historically appropriated responsibility for them (GA 14: 49–50/OTB 40–41). It should be understood, in this context, that the historical factors influencing and shaping the layout of the clearings—being itself—inevitably condition the intelligibility or meaningfulness (*Bedeutsamkeit*) of what presences, determining to a considerable extent, in fact, not only *how* beings can appear within its horizon but also even *what* beings, or what types of beings, can appear, coming into the light of unconcealment.

†

It is, I think, noteworthy that, even in his 1925 *History of the Concept of Time*, Heidegger already clearly understood the history-making significance of his phenomenological explication of human existence as *Da-sein*:

> The disclosive capability of *Dasein*, in particular, its disposition, can be made manifest by means of words in such a way that certain new [history-making] possibilities in *Dasein*'s being are set free. Thus, discourse, especially poetry, can even bring about the release of such new possibilities for the being of *Dasein*. (GA 20: 375–76/HCT 272)

Our disclosive capacity as fated to be thrown-open clearings is both determined by history and determinative of what hitherto unrecognized possibilities for the future the inheritance of history might have borne. Heidegger's hope for a history-transforming future abides in *Da-sein*'s disclosive capabilities—or rather, in *Dasein*'s assumption of responsibility for the mindful exercise of those capacities.

Consequently, by way of continuing Heidegger's project, our task, in this volume and the next, is to interpret the *Mensch-Sein* dynamic as one that intrinsically summons us to our highest responsibilities in the engagement of our ontological response abilities.

†

*Wer sind wir?*—"Who are we, we who call ourselves human beings?" As a beginning, we might say that to think of ourselves as *Da-sein* is to endeavor to be truly *here* in the world, truly being present, here where we are, truly vigilant and attentive, mindful of the way in which we are here, present in a certain world, as we are. Although we, as open clearings, as *Da-sein*, *are* what makes perception possible, hence *are* the *Es gibt*, *are* the layout that is letting-presence (*Sein-lassen*, *Anwesen-lassen*) by virtue of our being an open field of perception (*Vernehmen*), in "Time and Being" (1962), Heidegger asks us, as he did a decade earlier in *What Is Called Thinking?*, to make of perception a profoundly different kind of experience.

Might we learn to experience perception as if we were *receiving* what is "given" "as a gift"—*als Gabe*—something "given" in and through the clearing that our existence has laid out, something that addresses us with questions and challenges?[13] Heidegger would like our perception to be informed by the ontological understanding he has retrieved. And since, as he knows, perception is always also a question of reception, the *character* of our reception is also of great importance for him. In his *Critique of Pure Reason*, Kant discusses perception in great detail, concentrating critical thought on the nature of the sensory given and on the epistemic processes engaged in its reception. But, surprisingly, he never gives thought to the *character*, the *ethos*, of our receptivity in perception. I think Heidegger would like us to receive the givenness of what is given mindful always of the ontological dimension. Perhaps it is in learning to see and hear with thanksgiving for our abilities and opportunities that we may find our greatest and highest response ability.

## NOTES

1. Friedrich Nietzsche, *Thus Spake Zarathustra*, trans. Walter Kaufmann (New York: Viking Press, 1966), 34.

2. Martin Heidegger, *Einleitung in die Philosophie*, GA 27: 136–37. My translation. This is a text from 1927, written therefore around the same time as *Being and Time*.

3. Heidegger, "Brief über den Humanismus," *Wegmarken*, GA 9: 325; "Letter on Humanism," *Pathmarks*, 248. And see "Seminar in Zähringen 1973," *Vier Seminare*, GA 15: 380; "Seminar in Zähringen 1973," in *Four Seminars*, 69: "*Dasein* must be understood as being-the-clearing [*die Lichtung-sein*]. The *Da* is thus the word for the open expanse [*die offene Weite*]."

4. Ludwig Wittgenstein, *Culture and Value*, bilingual ed., trans. Peter Winch (Chicago: University of Chicago Press, 1984), 50.

5. Heidegger, *Zum Ereignis-Denken*, GA 73.1: 642. It is *Da-sein* that "sends" or "gives" by clearing a time–space for presencing: "*Das Da-sein schickt*": Op. cit., 644. In its thrown openness, *Da-sein* is thus the "*Entwurfsbereich des Seyns*." In other words: *Da-sein* "sends" and "gives"—"*schickt*"—as a clearing, by being-the-clearing.

6. On the *wechselweise Bezug* binding *Mensch* and *Sein*, see Heidegger, "Die Gefahr," *Bremer und Freiburger Vorträge*, GA 79: 64; "The Danger," *Bremen and Freiburg Lectures*, 60 and see "Der Satz der Identität," *Bremer und Freiburger Vorträge*, GA 79: 124–25; "The Principle of Identity," *Bremen and Freiburg Lectures*, 116–17.

7. Walter Benjamin, "Der Regenbogen: Gespräch über die Phantasie," *Gesammelte Schriften*, vol. VII, 20.

8. See Friedrich Wilhelm Joseph von Schelling, *Sämtliche Werke*, ed. Karl Friedrich August Schelling (Stuttgart-Augsburg: J. G. Cotta, 1856–1861), vol. I, 292, 394, 400.

9. See that same point in *Besinnung*, GA 66: 313; *Mindfulness*, 279.

10. See also Heidegger's "Die onto-theo-logische Verfassung der Metaphysik," GA 11: 75/ID 69.

11. See, for example, the *Beiträge zur Philosophie*, GA 65: 58 and 222–23; *Contributions to Philosophy*, 47 and 174.

12. See *Platon: Sophistes*, GA 19: 265 and *Wegmarken*, GA 9: 285. I am indebted to Tom Sheehan for these references.

13. Heidegger, GA 14: 16. Or see *Zur Sache des Denkens*, 12; "Time and Being," *On Time and Being*, 12. My own translation, objecting to the interpretation that Joan Stambaugh's translation encourages. She has Heidegger's clause, *daß er das Anwesen, das Es gibt, als Gabe empfängt* saying "man standing within the approach of presence, but in such a way that he receives as a gift the presencing that It gives by perceiving what appears in letting-presence." I read the *das Es gibt* as simply *another way of saying das Anwesen*—or as simply acknowledging the fact that something is given, something comes into meaningful presence in the clearing of human experience. Her translation posits an *Es gibt* that, *as other*, accounts for the possibility of presencing. This translation is unnecessarily misleading in that it suggests the operation of a metaphysical agency.

# 3

## EREIGNIS

## Da-sein in Appropriation, Gentlest of All Laws

What is learning? We human beings learn when we dispose everything we do so that it answers to [*in die Entsprechung bringt*] whatever essential matters [*an Wesenhaftem*] are addressed to us [*zugesprochen*] in any given moment [*jeweils*].

—*What Is Called Thinking?* (GA 8: 5–6/WCT 4)

The disclosive capacity [*die Entdecktheit*] of *Dasein*—in particular its situated disposition [*Befindlichkeit*]—can be made manifest by means of words, and in such a way that certain new [history-making] possibilities [*Seinsmöglichkeiten*] in *Dasein's* being are set free.

—*The History of the Concept of Time* (GA 20: 375–76/HCT 272)

The human being [*Der Mensch*] is the one appropriated for the steadfastness of its situated thrown-openness [*der in die Inständichkeit im Da-sein Ereignete*].

—*The Event* (GA 71:196/E 167)

In a comment published not long ago in the *New York Times*, the French philosopher Bernard-Henri Lévy argued that "our humanity is a *process* that begins with negation. . . . We are not born human; we become it. Humanity is not a form of being; it is a destiny. It is not an immutable essence, delivered once and for all, but a process."[1] This process of self-recognition and self-understanding—becoming who we essentially are in coming into our ownmost nature—is what Heidegger calls *Er-eignen*. It is the appropriating, or enowning, of that process, our propriation. And he insists that we

109

must think about it in phenomenological terms, the language of our experience: "The awakening to our appropriation must be experienced; it cannot be proven [*Das Entwachen in das Ereignis muß erfahren; es kann nicht bewiesen werden*]" (GA 14: 63/OTB 53).

In this chapter, we shall give thought to this process—a process of "appropriation" into which Heidegger's polysemic word *Ereignis* will be taking us. This word, meaning "becoming true to our essential nature as human beings," hence "becoming what is proper to us" ("propriation"), is crucial to the comprehension of Heidegger's entire project: so crucial, in fact, that eventually, he even wanted it to dislodge "being" as the most important of his conceptual artifacts. In the midst of his lecture on "Time and Being," Heidegger pauses to tell us, in case we should be slow to appreciate the significance of the argument he is venturing, that "the sole purpose of this lecture is to bring before our eyes being itself as the appropriation" (GA 14: 26/OTB 21). Explaining this statement, he says:

> Being proves to be destiny's gift of presence [*die von Zeit gewährte Gabe des Geschickes der Anwesenheit*], the gift granted in accordance with time. The gift of presence is the property of appropriation [*Die Gabe von Anwesen ist Eigentum des Ereignens*]. Being vanishes in appropriation [*Sein verschwindet im Ereignis*]. In the phrase "being as appropriation," the word "as" now means: being, letting-presence, sent in appropriating [*Sein, Anwesenlassen, geschickt im Ereignen*], time extended in appropriating [*Zeit gereicht im Ereignen*]. (GA 14: 27/OTB 22)

"Appropriating," he says, "has the peculiar property of bringing human beings into their own as the beings who perceive being by standing within [*innesteht*] true time" (GA 14: 28/OTB 23). I will at times use the word "enowning" to designate this complex process of appropriation.

Despite this explication, "*Ereignis*" continues to be, perhaps, the most difficult to grasp of all his key words. There is probably no key word in Heidegger's thought that has generated more controversy than *Ereignis*. Is it to be understood, as the word in everyday German usage suggests, as referring to an event? Thomas Sheehan has argued that Heidegger's conception of the *Ereignung* can be traced back to his reading of Aristotle. The "clue" is to be found, he thinks, in Heidegger's 1928 summer semester seminar on Aristotle's *Physics* III (GA 83), in which Heidegger begins to recognize in δύναμις, and its being-appropriate for and being-appropriated to its τέλος, a way to think about *Da-sein*'s *propriation*, actualizing the essence constitutive of its being. But how can *Ereignis* be interpreted in this way when it seems so far from the interpretation that contextualizes it in Heidegger's history of metaphysics and accordingly understands it as an extraordinary inceptive event? This question generates many more questions. I shall, nevertheless, propose interpretive resolutions, attempting to address the critical problems they raise.

However, before we work our way through them, I would like to acknowledge that it is not at all apparent what Heidegger would think of the interpretation I am suggesting in this chapter, especially my contention that the appropriation lays down a claim that needs to be understood as carried by our most fundamental bodily disposition. I can find no textual formulations that explicitly assert or confirm it. Nevertheless, I am convinced, not only that it makes good sound sense of the matter, and that there is nothing in Heidegger's texts that would necessarily contradict it, or even be in some other way incompatible, but that, moreover, this interpretation, recognizing the role of embodiment, is actually necessary. Indeed, the many texts that I quote seem strongly to lead us into its proximity. In any case, I am offering this interpretation, with texts and arguments, in the hope that it might serve well as a useful working hypothesis for further enquiry.

Not merely making sense of the *Ereignis* by explicating it in phenomenological terms but making it thereby instructive for the conduct of our lives—that, coming *after* Heidegger, is for me good enough.

†

When, in his 1951–1952 winter semester lectures *What Is Called Thinking?*, Heidegger defines "learning" as responding to what essential matters are addressing us, he is, without saying so, thinking of the *Ereignis* and our corresponding task: the taking up and taking over, that is, the appropriating, of our appropriation, the claim that summons us for the task of propriation. This responding to the essential that summons us is, in effect, a correspondence: it is, in fact, what Heraclitus, using a word that Heidegger rejuvenates, called "*homologein*."

In the years that followed the publication of *Being and Time* (1927), Heidegger, posing the question of our propriation as *Da-sein*, substituted the phenomenology of the *Ereignis* for the phenomenological explication of *Sein* in a way that somewhat resembles the Hegelian sublation (*Aufhebung*), thereby making *Ereignis* the crucial, key matter for thought in his project. In fact, by the 1960s, he had come to the conclusion that, "when the 'letting' ['*lassen*'] in 'letting-presence' ['*Anwesen lassen*'] is audibly emphasized [*Wenn die Betonung lautet: Anwesen lassen*], there is no longer any need even for the word 'being'": "*kein Raum mehr*" (GA 15: 365/FS 60). All the necessary work could henceforth be accomplished—and accomplished better— by *Ereignis*. "*Sein*," he said in "Time and Being" (1962), disappears into

*Ereignis: Sein verschwindet im Ereignis* (GA 14: 27/OTB 22). It also vanishes, that is, becomes unnecessary, once phenomenological thinking begins working with the clearing. As he said as early as 1943, in his introduction to *What Is Metaphysics?*: "*Sein entschwindet in der Wahrheit*" (GA 9: 366, n. "a"/*Pathmarks*, 278, n. "a"). It is not that *Ereignis* carries exactly the same *meaning*; nor does it designate the same *thing*. Rather, the word is deemed to be *better* than *Sein* for getting at what needs to be brought into thought.

Our appropriation is also already prefigured in Heidegger's 1949 text on "The Turning," in which Heidegger reflects on the prospects for breaking out of the *Gestell*, the total imposition of an order of ontological reductionism and reification:

> In the coming to presence [*Im Wesen*] of the danger [i.e., in the ever-increasing dominion of the *Gestell*], there is *concealed* [*verbirgt sich*] the possibility of a turning in which the forgetfulness belonging to the coming to presence of being will be turned in such a way that, through this turning, the truth of the coming to presence of being will [at last] properly enter into beings [*in das Seiende eigens einkehrt*]. (GA 11: 118, BFL 67/QCT 41)

Heidegger explains the argument:

> The essence of technology [today] is the *Gestell*. The entrance [into this epoch of the *Gestell*], as the event of the turn into ontological forgetfulness [*Die Einkehr als Ereignis der Kehre der Vergessenheit*], enters into [*kehrt in das ein*] what is now [*jetzt*] the epoch of being. That which genuinely [*eigentlich*] is, is in no way this or that particular being. What genuinely is [*eigentlich ist*], i.e., what properly dwells and endures as present in the "is" [*d.h. eigens im Ist wohnt und west*] is solely being [*einzig das Sein*]. (GA 11: 120, BFL 70/QCT 44)

This *Ereignis* seems to be what Heidegger was ultimately concerned with in *Being and Time*. However, thinking of our experience of being in terms of *Ereignis* ultimately represents a truly dramatic departure from the entire historical inheritance of Western philosophical thought. And Heidegger emphasizes just how significant this move is when he tells us, in unusual bluntness: "With '*Ereignis*' we will no longer be thinking within the Greek inheritance": "*Mit Ereignis wird überhaupt nicht mehr griechisch gedacht*" (GA 15: 366–67/FS 60–61).[2] "No more," because, given their historical world, the Greeks were not able to *step back* from the immediacy of their experience to engage and reflect on it *phenomenologically*, recognizing and enowning the belonging together of *Mensch* and *Sein*, and the human participation in the phenomenon of presencing. In other words, he put *Sein* aside but only because, like Wittgenstein's ladder, it had completed its task, calling attention to our role—hence our responsibility—in the meaningful presencing of beings: a role of responsibility for which he eventually wanted to use the word *Ereignis*, referring to the event—the experience—in which a fundamental ontological claim *appropriates* us.

In light of the argument for the question of being that he made in *Being and Time*, this sublation of being seems at first to represent a truly shocking shift. But, though this might seem puzzling, what it recognizes is in fact a powerful vindication of the phenomenological approach. What matters, after the significance of being (the *Es gibt*, the sheer fact of being) has been recognized, is the appropriation of *Da-sein* to—and for—its intrinsic, structurally constitutive role: *Da-sein*'s very existence is, as such, the laying out of a field of conditions that make such a fact as being, that is, the meaningful presencing of beings, at all possible. What I hope to demonstrate here is that this ontological function, once articulated solely in terms of our relation to being, but subsequently articulated more insightfully in terms of the key word, *Ereignis*, designates not only an event of experience but also our appropriation and, accordingly, our responsibility, in regard to the achieving of our proper, ownmost, essential being—our propriation—as *Da-sein*. And at the same time that this appropriation makes a claim that constitutes a responsibility to and for ourselves, that is, ultimately, a responsibility to and for the developing of our ownmost potential as a human being, it also constitutes a corresponding responsibility intrinsic to that very process, to sustain the conditions that make meaningful presencing (being) possible. In other words, because appropriation concerns us human beings in our relation to being, it also has potentially enormous historical significance.

†

Before proceeding further, we need to recognize that *Ereignis* and its constellation of cognate words (*Eignis*, *Er-eignung*, *An-eignung*, *Ver-eignung*, *Zu-eignung*) present us with some exceedingly difficult problems and questions—matters involving both interpretation and translation—that must be settled. However, even the recognition of these problems and questions immediately throws us into substantive determinations. First of all, we need to make sense of the fact that, while Heidegger uses the word *Ereignis* in a way that seems to require understanding it to signify an event, which is what the ordinary, common understanding of that word takes it to signify, he nevertheless insists that, as he is using it, it does not mean an event or occurrence as commonly understood. In ordinary German usage, *Ereignis* signifies an event, an occurrence, a happening—a *Vorkommnis*, a *Geschehen*.

But Heidegger unequivocally warns against interpreting his key term *Ereignis* as an ordinary event in ordinary historical time. Thus, at the same time that he shifted away from *Sein* to unfold his thinking in terms of *Ereignis*, he also introduced into his project a profoundly altered meaning of *Ereignis*:

- "What the term *Ereignis* names can no longer be represented by way of the current meaning of the word, for in that meaning *Ereignis* is understood as an event and a happening." (GA 14: 25–26/OTB 20)
- "In the *Ereignis*, nothing happens. Here there is no more happening; no destiny, either. In the *Ereignis*, the essence of history is abandoned. All talk of the history of beyng is an embarrassment and a euphemism." [*Im Ereignis geschieht nichts. Hier ist kein Geschehen mehr; auch kein Geschick; denn auch Schickung west noch aus dem Gegenüber. Im Ereignis ist das Wesen der Geschichte verlassen. Die Rede von der Seynsgeschichte ist eine Verlegenheit und ein Euphemismus*]. (GA 97: 382)

Unfortunately, however, Heidegger is far from clear about the concrete phenomenology of the *Ereignis*. How does it actually function or operate? Nor is it obvious that, after he wrote down these ruminations, he actually abandoned thinking of the *Ereignis* as a historical event. On the contrary, he seems to have regarded it as pointing to the possibility of an event that breaks up the historical continuum for the sake of a new beginning, one in which the promising potential belonging to the Western world would be retrieved from its past for the achievement of this new beginning. Since, as I want to argue, Heidegger's project essentially engages a substantive philosophy of history, he needs *Ereignis* to mean "event." Even his history of philosophy—his narrative regarding this history—requires this interpretation and translation of *Ereignis*.

How, though, does this event differ from an event that is fittingly described as a *Vorkommnis*, a *Geschehen*? What is the difference? Does the difference consist in its belonging, as an event, to the dimension of temporality underlying and grounding the events in the historical time series, hence in its release from the linear time series of historical events? Does the difference essentially consist in its singular role in history?

The most difficult problem, though, is not that the term as Heidegger uses it does not designate an ordinary kind of event, but that, in contexts of decisive significance, it seems no longer to be used to mean an event at all. What conveys the sense of *Ereignis* operative in these other contexts is "appropriation," the sense of which, I suggest, would be better expressed by the words *Ereignen* and *Ereignung*, words more suggestive of a process. (Perhaps Heidegger himself eventually began to think so too. See GA 12:

248–49/OWL 128–29; GA 14: 27, 53–55/OTB 22, 44–45; and GA 65: 34, 322/CP 29, 254.) Might we not, then, for the sake of an easy reconciliation, simply bring the two readings together, translating the word as *"event* of appropriation"? The answer is complicated. If we translate *Ereignis* in that way, we still need to understand what is meant by "appropriation." And that, by itself, as I shall argue, poses further questions for interpretation, hence, too, for translation, because, as I shall argue, appropriation is not only an event; it is also a *claim*, and moreover, a claim that summons us, calling for a *task* that requires a *process*. Appropriation involves a process, not, or not only, an event.

As I understand him, Heidegger is suggesting that, in our existence, we are summoned—called—to the task of appropriation, a task he describes as "entering into the *Ereignis*" (*Einkehr in das Ereignis*), by interpreting certain *events* in the world as making a *claim* on us, a challenge that calls *us* into question, summoning us to attend to the phenomenology of our engagement, our interaction, with the world. Thus, the summons to enter into this appropriation, taking up this claim of appropriation as a task—a task, I suggest, requiring our recognizing, understanding, enowning, and enacting, or actualizing, the appropriation that the claim calls for—does originate in an *event*, an experience with what we encounter in the world. But the *event* that draws us into the task of appropriation sets in motion a certain *process*: a process that engages our most fundamental bodily disposition and that culminates in our propriation as *Da-sein*, appropriated to be clearings. All of these matters need to be interpreted: argued, explained, clarified. In particular, we need to interpret the dizzying multiplicity of ways in which the English term "appropriation" will be used to interpret and translate Heidegger's key word.

†

At this point, so that we do not lose our way as we attempt in this chapter to address the problems of interpretation and translation that *Ereignis* poses, I want to set out the logical structure of the argument I am going to venture. I propose, first of all, that we begin by drawing a distinction between the two basic *meanings* of *Ereignis*: (1) event and (2) appropriation. I will argue that this *Ereignis* is not only an event but also a bodily disposition that calls for a process of appropriation. However, considered solely as meaning "event," it recognizes three instantiations, the second and third of which are of special historical significance. Thus:

1.  Its first basic meaning (*Sinn*): *Event*
    Interpreted as event, *Ereignis* has *three* instantiations, three referents (*Bedeutungen*). All are events involving a distinctly *ontological*

experience and interpretation. An ontological event is an encounter experienced with reflection on the *being* of the beings that are encountered: the sheer *fact* of being and the question, what it means for something—anything—to be. It is an event such as, for example, what the Greek philosophers experienced when, lifting up their eyes from the various things captivating their attention in order to survey and contemplate the whole world of beings, they found themselves pondering—as we might express it—being as such, being itself, being as being, suddenly struck, as if by a bolt of lightning, by the wonder and strangeness of it all. Many are the questions that eventually came to mind. What these earliest Greek philosophers experienced, finding themselves compelled to contemplate abstract theoretical questions in regard to being—that is, the being of beings—were *events in the world* but events of an extraordinary character: I shall call them, in abbreviation, *ontological events*, that is, events that are taken to concern being, rather than beings, at once illuminating and challenging in the most fundamental ways their understanding of the world. We can accordingly distinguish *three* different event-experiences of an ontological nature. As events involving an experience of the meaning of being, they bear on the history of metaphysics and, too, on the present and future of the lifeworld, hence on the question of destiny as it figures in Heidegger's philosophy of history.

i.    *Ereignis* refers to events in which, emerging from a singularly surprising, puzzling, or unsettling encounter with what is, one has a certain insight or epiphany regarding the meaning of being. Such events typically involve an ontological experience of wonder and awe—that there is a world of beings rather than absolutely nothing, raising the question regarding what it means for something—anything—to be. This kind of event is not necessarily limited to the experience of philosophers. It is something that can engage anyone at any time. It apparently engaged some pre-Socratic philosophers, whose ruminations continued to unfold, generating the discourse that represents the history of metaphysics in the Western world from its origin in archaic times right into the configurations of contemporary thought, not only in Heidegger and Derrida but also in Dewey, Carnap, and Quine. As Sartre's *Nausea* suggests, however, this metaphysical moment is not always, and not necessarily, experienced, as it was for Heidegger, in relation to Western history and philosophical thought; nor is it necessarily experienced with phenomenological understanding, although, in modern and contemporary times, it might be.

ii. *Ereignis* also refers to that same kind of ontological experience, but as history-making, not only setting in motion and informing what Heidegger calls "the archaic first beginning," or "first inception," in ancient Greece, of the discourse of metaphysics but also informing the culture of the entire Western world, shaping its understanding of the being of entities—what it means for something to be in regard to all that is in any way present and all that is in any way absent. Heidegger argues, however, that the ancient Greek philosophers did not undergo this experience in phenomenological terms. Judged from the perspective of a later metaphysics grounded in subjectivity, their thinking, their metaphysics, was, in that regard, naïve, preceding by more than 2,000 years of history the momentous reflexive turn into subjectivity that eventually made possible the turn into appropriation. Appropriation is only recognized, and consequently only becomes possible, in modern times, by virtue of the phenomenological turn that eventually emerged, in revolt, from the much earlier turn into forms of subjectivity, as represented in Descartes and his philosophical heirs—especially, perhaps, the representatives of German idealism, the last of whom was Husserl.

iii. *Ereignis* refers to that same basic ontological experience but with a phenomenological reflexivity that makes it singularly history-breaking and history-remaking, informing the possibility of what Heidegger calls "the other beginning" or "the second inception," not only involving the "circumventing" and "sublation" (*Überwindung*) of the metaphysics we in the contemporary world have inherited from the past but also involving profound transformations in our present world, somehow "overcoming" the fateful dangers we now confront—above all, the dangers in nihilism. According to Heidegger, this experiential event, an encounter with what *is* that bestirs and awakens uncanny thought, has the capacity to interrupt and reconstruct history, inaugurating the task of a second beginning, with its corresponding responsibilities, because it is mindfully grounded in the processes constitutive of our appropriation—our propriation to, and as, *Da-sein*.

2. Its second, derivative meaning (*Sinn*): Appropriation

Interpreted in the English language as "appropriation," *Ereignis* refers, as I shall argue, to a bodily disposition that calls for a process of appropriation that has three distinct moments or phases, which I shall for convenience call three referents (*Bedeutungen*). Although appropriation *originates* as an *event* in which we are bestirred to ontological thought, it is ultimately not a matter of events but rather of *processes* that are called for by the task that is claiming us, namely, to recognize, understand, enown and enact, or actualize, the *disposition* that is constitutive of our *a priori* given (*voraugeschickt*) essential nature as *Da-sein*, our being as thrown-open, situated beings. These are processes that involve "propriation," the awakening, enowning, retrieving, and activating of our "forgotten" essential nature, the nature with which we have been endowed, together with its preconceptual, pre-ontological understanding of being. The awakening and retrieving involves a process of *Erinnerung* (a form of recollection different from the Platonic but similar in that it is a process of going "down" *into* one's essential nature, the depths of oneself, to retrieve as a task its neglected, "forgotten" claim on us) and *Gedächtnis* (a gathering of our experience into a thoughtful remembering of its forgotten dispensation, its origin in the endowment of a fundamental disposition of nature). There are, accordingly, three phases or moments in the *Ereignis*—better called *Ereignung* or *Ereignen*—as a process of appropriation engaging this bodily carried disposition. Unlike the German word *Ereignis*, the English word "appropriation" enables us to think in a more differentiated way what Heidegger's inventive use of the German word, retrieving its forgotten, hidden sense of *eigen* (i.e., own) involves. In the English language, the three distinct meanings of "appropriation" enable us to think the *Ereignis* in terms of a *process* involving three moments or three phases:

i. The *Ereignis* in its first moment or phase: appropriation$_1$, interpreted as meaning, or denoting, an exigent claim and call, or summons, seizing our attention—in sum, the *Ereignis* interpreted as denoting (a) that which is appropriating us, claiming, calling, and summoning us, namely, the disposition of our ownmost nature, and (b) the appropriating itself, that is, the claiming, calling, and summoning itself. This claim and its call abide in and as a *vorausgeschickt*, *a priori* disposition—our most fundamental disposition, a bodily carried disposition, in fact a gentle "law" of nature, always already operative, already appropriating us, claiming and calling us to and for a task of appropriation—as in (ii) and (iii) below—even before, and even without, our having any adequate awareness of it, any recognition, and any enownment of it. This claim with its call *come* from the *disposition* "within" us; *but they are bestirred* by what we encounter "outside" ourselves in the world, that is, events addressing us and calling us into question.

ii. The *Ereignis* in its second moment or phase: appropriation$_2$, interpreted as meaning, or denoting, our *response* to this claim, this call and summons, in a *process* that involves taking it up, taking it over, making it our most fundamental task—in sum, the

*Ereignis* as denoting our appropriating of the claim, undertaking
it as a task.

iii. The *Ereignis* in its third moment or phase: appropriation$_3$, interpreted as meaning, or denoting, the *process* of our "propriation,"
our "enowning," our becoming who we as human beings
essentially are, hence our "owning" of ourselves, or "owning
up"—measuring up—to the kind of being we already are in our
potential but also are not yet in our achievement of actuality. In
sum, appropriation is seen as dwelling in a certain "inner" poetry
of homecoming after we have been losing our way, losing ourselves, in the "distractions" of the everyday ontic world (GA 9:
337–38/PM 257). What this involves is a task and process of recognizing, retrieving, understanding, enowning, and actualizing,
with mindfulness of our essential nature as *Da-sein*, our thrown
openness (our *Befindlichkeit* as *Geworfenheit*), to become, and be,
the situated open clearings for being—for presencing—that we
in our essential nature (already) are.

As must be evident by now, many of the interpretive problems surrounding Heidegger's deployment of the term *Ereignis* are caused by the fact that
some of his texts seem to require understanding *Ereignis* as referring to an
*event*, while some of his other texts seem to call for a reading that unfolds
its hidden meaning as *appropriation*. This causes considerable confusion.[3] Is
this appropriation properly speaking an event? That interpretation seems
especially difficult to sustain because there are contexts where Heidegger's
usage of that word as "appropriation" suggests that the word bears *three*
distinct but intrinsically interrelated meanings, or referents, that cannot
be adequately understood if regarded simply as belonging to the category
of events. In order to interpret what Heidegger wants us to think about
in regard to the phenomenology of the *Ereignis*, we need to heed the
three distinct meanings of the English word and unfold the three different
moments or phases of "appropriation." However, as I must say with a certain irresistible glee, the differentiation of these three moments or phases in
a process is available only in the English language, which, in this instance,
bears a gift not offered by German.

In this chapter, I shall accordingly argue, *first*, that *Ereignis* basically
has two distinct but interconnected senses, namely, (i) event and (ii) appropriation. *Second*, I shall argue that, in Heidegger's project, appropriation is
*both* event and process, not only connected to a history-breaking, history-
making *ontological event*, such as the early Greek philosophers experienced,
and such as we too could perhaps experience but also connected to a *claim*,

*task, and process* that the experience of the ontological event brings to our attention. *Third,* I shall argue, bearing in mind the three different senses, in English, of the word "appropriate," (i) that, as individual *Dasein,* we are called—appropriated$_1$—to undertake a process of appropriation$_2$, called to the task and process in this claim, (ii) that this claim that appropriates$_1$ us (i.e., takes hold of us) and that we in response should take up and appropriate$_2$ is a summons to appropriation$_3$ (propriation, enownment), and is inherently constitutive of a responsibility for grounding and maintaining the ontological dimension of openness into which we are by nature fatefully cast, and (iii) that, in the course of this threefold process of appropriation, new destiny-laden possibilities for remaking and redeeming history might emerge into a disclosive light.

Thus, I shall be arguing that, thanks to the three English meanings of "appropriation," "*Ereignis,*" understood not as event but as process, designates three essentially related moments, or phases, of appropriation: (i) "appropriation$_1$," as laying down a claim and accordingly summoning, (ii) "appropriation$_2$," as the process of taking up, taking over, and assuming responsibility for that claim, and finally, (iii) "appropriation$_3$," as the process of propriation, enowning, making one's own, entering into the process of coming to and becoming, with appropriate mindfulness, the human beings we essentially are.

But what *is* this claim of appropriation—(i) above—that we are called upon to appropriate in (ii) and (iii)? This question introduces one other strand in the argument I want to venture in this chapter. To approach this question, we need to understand that this process of appropriation—as in (ii) and (iii)—is called for by a claim on our responsibility, our enowning: called for by a claim, an appropriation—(i) above—that is constitutive *a priori* of our most fundamental bodily disposition. This disposition of our embodied nature makes a claim on us that is susceptible to being stirred and awakened by an ontologically significant event in the world.

It is crucial to bear in mind, in thinking about this disposition and its claim and summons, that the body involved in this disposition is not the encapsulated, substance-like body (*der abgekapsulte Leib*) of substance metaphysics, firmly positioned in some space–time location in a way that makes it little different from the tables and chairs and trees in our world—except for the fact that we living creatures are, somehow, substances mysteriously capable of self-movement (GA 7: 159/PLT 157).

In the second volume, we shall consider in some detail the implications of this appropriation for two of our perceptive modalities: our seeing and hearing. And we shall continue what we begin in this volume, exploring what this appropriation of perception purports for the possible transformation of our humanity and the destination (*Geschick*) of the world to which Heidegger believes we in the West must commit ourselves.

†

In a 1943 afterword to *What Is Metaphysics?*, Heidegger reflects on the ontological experience that set in motion the beginning of the discourse of metaphysics: the sheer facticity of the fact of being, the fact that there *are* beings instead of nothing—*daß* Seiendes *ist* (GA 9: 307, 310/PM 234, 236). In the course of this reflection, he takes us behind this experience to give thought to what makes this experience of being possible. Such deeper reflection is what he calls "originary thinking": a thinking so rigorously attuned to the experience that inaugurated metaphysics that it becomes, in effect, "the *echo* of being's favour [*Gunst*]" (ibid.). But what is the insight that makes such thinking "originary"? Of what is it an echo? I suggest that it is Heidegger's insight into the "forgotten" appropriation, a claim on our responsibility, not only operative in the phenomenology of ontological experience, wherein the issue is the very being of beings, but also operative, in fact—as we can discover if we are properly self-reflective—in the phenomenology of all our experience. But, where does the claim of appropriation come from? And how does it actually claim, call, and appropriate us? These questions lead us into the nature of our most fundamental disposition as embodied *Da-sein*—thrown-open beings.

†

In his *Critique of Pure Reason*, Kant characterizes the mysterious, philosophically unrecognized schematism of the imagination—its role in bringing together the experience of the senses and the faculty of understanding—as "an art hidden in the depths of the human soul [*eine verborgene Kunst in dem tiefen der menschlichen Seele*], whose real modes of activity nature is hardly likely ever to allow us to discover and to have open to our gaze."[4] In this chapter, I shall argue that this description also retrieves the most fundamental appropriating disposition of our bodily nature, illuminating in its hiddenness the operation that, in one of its uses, Heidegger's key word designates. Indeed, perhaps Heidegger had Kant's very words in mind when, in "The Way to Language" (1959), he said that the *Ereignis* is "the most inconspicuous of phenomena—indeed "the most inconspicuous of inconspicuous phenomena": "*[Das] Ereignis ist das Unscheinbarste des Unscheinbaren*" (GA 12: 247/OWL 128).

In this same text, "The Way to Language," Heidegger also described the *Ereignis* as "the most gentle of all laws" (GA 12: 248/OWL 128). How does this description figure in the explication of *Ereignis*? In this chapter,

I will explore the meaning and significance of this description, arguing for "dis-position" (with a hyphen that recognizes its dis-positioning, our thrown openness) as necessary for completing the phenomenological interpretation of *Ereignis*. That "dis-position" is crucial for understanding appropriation is something that, it seems, scholars have not appreciated; but only the dis-position of our bodily nature can explain Heidegger's extraordinary claim in terms of his project.[5] It is necessary to say here, though, that this dis-position, which Heidegger describes as our "most fundamental," is not at all an ordinary disposition—not like, say, being generous, being obstinate, being impatient, or being forgiving.[6] First of all, as "fundamental," it is ontological, not ontic. And second, it is another way of recognizing the structure of our *Befindlichkeit*, our thrown openness as *Da-sein*. As Heidegger observes in *Being and Time*: "The 'essence' of *Dasein* [human being] lies in its *existence* [*Existenz*]." That means that the characteristics of this being are not objectively present-at-hand "properties." Rather, they are in each case a possible way (*mögliche Weisen*) for it to *be* (GA 2: 42/BT 69). As fundamental dis-position, constitutive of our very existence as thrown-open beings, the *Ereignis* (*Ereignung*) is neither present-at-hand (*vorhanden*) nor ready-to-hand (*zuhanden*). It precedes and underlies these modalities of being: *vorausgeschickt*.

In contrast to these two modalities of being, the *Ereignung* is the most fundamental of dispositions, *structurally dis-positioning* our *Menschsein* at the deepest level of our existence—that is, as constitutive *a priori*, that is, prior to all experience, of the very possibility and potentiality of that existence, rendering us appropriated to *Da-sein*, *erlichtet*, opened-out and ex-posed in *Geworfenheit*, thrown openness. It is, moreover, the dimension embodying our *pre-ontological understanding of being*, a preconceptual, pre-liminary understanding that, until we "awaken" and recognize ourselves in our deepest, ownmost essence, our most fundamental disposition, only our embodiment bears and "knows." According to Thomas Sheeehan, Heidegger derived *Ereignis* from his translation of Aristotle's δύναμις (*dunamis*) as *Eignung*, referring to a coming-into-it-own (a coming-*ad-proprium*, i.e., being ap-propri-ated by and unto its *telos*). This derivation is significant for our understanding of Heidegger's key word, because it implies (i) that we need to think of *Ereignis* not only as a claim and summons but as a dis-position, a law of our human nature, and (ii) that we need to think of its actualization, its fulfilment, as engaging a process.

†

As should be apparent by now, *Ereignis* is a word that performs, in Heidegger's project, a number of different functions. Understanding *Ereignis* as *event* is certainly crucial for thinking not only about the ancient Greek inception of metaphysics and about the Western world that has developed in keeping with that metaphysics but also for thinking about ontologically significant events: perhaps uncanny epiphanies or strangely enchanting sounds, reminding us of the music of the celestial spheres, sounds seeming to come from nowhere, and suddenly audible in the midst of our own ordinary everyday life, when the mysteries of being suddenly claim our attention. Such moments might even provoke questions that would lead us to envision possibilities for another inception: a post-metaphysical way of thinking about, and experiencing, what it means to be, and, correspondingly, the making of a post-metaphysical world.

The early Greek philosophers—Heidegger concentrates on Parmenides and Heraclitus—manifestly experienced *ontological events*, events regarding being that seized their attention and appropriated them for an ontological dimension of thought, an unprecedented height of thought; but what they experienced did not draw them into the self-reflection of phenomenology. They were not ready for appropriation, the process of recognizing and enowning the full dimensionality of their role in the experience of being—although Parmenides did set in motion reflections on the "sameness" of mind and being that have not only influenced the entire history of metaphysics but even laid the groundwork for Husserl's phenomenological conception of intentionality. In "The Principle of Identity," Heidegger draws on Parmenides in order to revise, subtly but radically, Husserl's conception. Returning to Parmenides, he was inspired to rethink intentionality—the intentionality-relation between *Mensch* and *Sein*—in terms of a belonging-together—a *Zusammengehörigkeit*—in which he discerned something that Husserl missed: the operation of the claim of appropriation, beckoning us to hearken (GA 14: 51/OTB 42).

The historical significance of pre-Socratic thought cannot be underestimated. The move in their thought from experiencing entities in the world to contemplating their being would transform forever their way of experiencing what they encountered in their world. According to Heidegger, that moment in the archaic Greek world, that momentous event of thought, generating centuries of questions and arguments, was the very beginning of Western metaphysics. And it makes sense to regard that kind of experience, and the discourse of thinking it set in motion, as an event—indeed a historically *inceptive* event of ontological significance: an *Anfang*, not merely a beginning (*Beginn*), because of its continuing creative power, its power to continue originating, or generating, within the light of its purview, further ontological thought. As inceptual, such an event induces further thinking, and further questioning, in regard to the meaning of being: what it has meant, and what it currently means, for something—anything—to be. Hence, whereas mere beginnings happen in ordinary serial time (*Zeitlichkeit*), inceptive events happen in the deeper dimension of *Temporalität*, in which the past is not buried, finished, and gone forever in the linear succession of events, but is a living "future past," full of opportunities not taken but still available to contribute to the present in a way that could open it to a future that might otherwise not have been possible. This temporality resists submission to a diagram, although Heidegger made some awkward attempts.

Many centuries had to pass, though, before eventful moments of ontological significance could be experienced—and would be experienced—in the truth of their claim on our responsibility, namely, as appropriating. Parmenides and Heraclitus *experienced* the hermeneutics of being, its concealments and unconcealments; but they did not think of that hermeneutics in terms of the phenomenology of their appropriation in relation to it. The phenomenon of appropriation could come to light only *after* thinking had turned phenomenological. And so it seems that, in order to be able to think about appropriation, we first had to enter into the realm of subjectivity, going into its transcendental depths—and then had to find our way out of its metaphysics—as in Heidegger's phenomenology of thrown-open ex-istence.

†

Now, once we take *Ereignis* to concern our *appropriation*, as Heidegger's commentary on the cognate words *eignen* and *Eignung*, words the meaning of which is recessive within the *Ereignis*, indicates, then, I suggest, we cannot continue to think *only* in terms of some kind of event: not even an event of appropriation. Thinking of appropriation in that way makes it impossible to understand the phenomenology of its operation—how, even when *stirred and activated* by an event in the world that is taken to have ontological meaning, as it did for some of the early Greek philosophers, the appropriation *functions* as a claim and summons *intrinsic to, and issuing from,* our very nature as human beings, but also as a claim, a summons, that was in a certain sense "forgotten," and is consequently in need of a *process* akin to Platonic recollection: a process whereby the claim and summons—which have always already been operative, operative, we might say, *a priori*, despite their urgency and exigency, only as unrecognized, slumbering, forgotten potential, capability, disposition, and *Bereitschaft*—are finally "recollected," finally acknowledged, retrieved, understood, enowned, and enacted. Entering into the *Ereignis* is entering into something like a process of recollection, but it is much more than a mere retrieving, since it summons to a task of enownment and responsibility.

In *Time and Being*, Heidegger speaks of the need for a process of recollection [*Sicherinnern*], calling it an "awakening from the oblivion of being [*Erwachen aus der Seinsvergessenheit*]." It is, he argues:

> an awakening that must be understood as a recollection of something that has never been thought—but, on the other hand, as this awakening, not an extinguishing of the oblivion of being, but rather placing oneself in it and standing within it. Thus, the awakening from the oblivion of being to finally *experiencing* the oblivion of being—that is the awakening into appropriation. (GA 14:37–38/OTB 30)

In part, as the seminar on Heidegger's lecture noted, this "step back" into appropriation and recollection "would be a movement away from the openness of beings [*Offenbarkeit des Seienden*] toward the openness as such that remains concealed by manifest beings" (ibid.). Thus, a new and very different responsibility appears, namely, a responsibility for being itself, that is, for the very conditions that enable beings to be meaningfully present and absent in the fields of our perception.

In the final analysis, we must accordingly think of the *Ereignis* as necessarily involving *both* event and structure, both event and disposition, both event and potentiality, both event and process—two aspects, or dimensions, of one and the same dynamic phenomenon, in which the ontologically interpreted event, as something happening in the world that gets us thinking about the meaning of being, something laying claim to our responsibility for the meaning of being in the *Mensch-Sein* relation, something seizing and engaging our thought, perhaps blessedly, perhaps traumatically, draws us into a recollection (*Erinnerung*) of the "forgotten" *disposition potential* that constitutes the *essential structure* of appropriation, operating *leibhaft*, through our embodiment, as "the gentlest of all laws" (GA 12: 248/OWL 128). And this, in turn, calls for a process of enownment and enactment, actualizing the claim constitutive of the disposition potential. In the course of this process, a historically different, even revolutionary relation to being might be possible.

If we characterize this law of structure, this disposition of our bodily nature, as operative *a priori*, *vorausgeschickt*, we must understand that it is not the *a priori* in the metaphysics of German idealism: it is, first of all, constitutive of our embodiment, carried by its inherent structure; hence it is not an immutable essence but a structure that operates in lively interaction with the world, never complete, never final. What that law (*Ge-setz*) lays down (*setzt*) in our bodily nature is the dis-position to *Da-sein*, an embodied thrown openness (*Geworfen-werden*), a dispositioning claiming our appropriation. The *Verhaltenheit*—"restraint"—that characterizes this law is, says Heidegger, "the strongest and yet also most delicate [*zarteste*] preparedness [*Bereitschaft*]" of human existence for its appropriation [*Er-eignung*] to *Da-sein* (GA 65: 34/CP 29).

Interpreting *Ereignis* to mean "event" is unquestionably required by Heidegger's philosophy of history. However, it is not an ordinary event but an event the historical importance of which lies in the fact that it is an event that sets in motion a process of appropriation: the appropriation of the human being, "*das Er-eignis des Daseins*" (GA 94: 448). *Ereignis* thus engages much more than an event; it claims and summons us to *our enownment*, laying claim to our recognition and understanding of ourselves, questioning and challenging us, both individually and collectively, in the way we live our lives so that our responsibility for the historical meaning of being is actively engaged in the making of our world.

†

In his *L'Abécédaire*, Gilles Deleuze proposes that we think of *Ereignis* as designating an *event* in which we find a certain "liberation" in actualizing, or enacting, a potentiality constitutive of our historical existence.[7] This is helpful—as far as it goes. But it does not go deeply enough into the phenomenology of that process. We need to find ourselves in our *Befindlichkeit*, our situation as standing, thrown open, in our world. The *Ereignis* is our appropriation by a claim inherent in, and constitutive of, our most fundamental disposition, the grounding "law" of our nature, namely, to become, each of us, a site, a situating clearing, a *Da-sein*, a grounding for the laying out of open fields for the experiencing of what in any way presences. The *Ereignis* is the appropriating claim in a dynamic structure of great potentiality and capability—Aristotle would point to a δύναμις—inherent in our very nature as embodied beings, hence an existential structure always already operative in our lives, whether or not we are aware of it: a structure capable of undergoing *processes* in which that capability, that *Seinkönnen*, could be cultivated and developed. *Ereignis* thus designates a *claim* on our highest responsibility as human beings, a claim appropriating us for the potential that, in the form of the most fundamental disposition of our embodied nature, namely our essence as thrown openness, always already a clearing for world-disclosiveness, summons us to recognize, understand, appropriate, and enown its endowment, its dispensation, ceaselessly bringing it into actuality (Aristotle's *energeia*) through our greater mindfulness, our vigilant guardianship, and our assumption of responsibility for sustaining and enlightening the ontological character of the openness, the clearing to which that disposition has, simply by its facticity, already ventured and destined us.

We should accordingly understand that what Heidegger calls *Ereignis* involves a potential "sent" or "given" (*geschickt*) to us mortals by way of a fatefully dis-positioning disposition constitutive of our bodily (*leibhaft*) nature: this disposition, this potential, is an endowment, or dispensation, that shelters the existential claim and its demand. Although the claim has always (already) been operative in our everyday experience, and the summons has always (already) been calling us, we lapse early in our lives into an inveterate tendency to be unaware of its operation—and indeed to be lacking in any understanding of its meaning, its significance. Hence it requires our awakening to a recognition and understanding that eventuates in a process of individual enownment and practical enactment. Heidegger consequently hoped that somehow, in the course of our interactions, engagements with people, other animals, and the things appearing in our world, we might be *stirred* to this awakening and self-recognition, overcoming our "forgetfulness," our fateful lethargy.

So, *Ereignis* refers to the endowment, or dispensation, of a potential in which there are, so to speak, utopian intimations of a historically original process of transformation: the transformation of humanity (*Menschentum*) and world. *Such a dispensation is the granting of a possible historical destiny (Geschick) achievable, or approachable, only through our exercise of freedom.*

We are responsible for who we are and who we become—and that means, nurturing, cultivating, developing our given potential, transforming our capacities, our capabilities, including the prevailing character of our ways of seeing and hearing. We need to appropriate—that is, take over and take up, through a process of self-recognition, self-understanding, and enownment—the potential inherent in *Da-sein*, our thrown openness, our earth-cast nature, an appropriation appropriating—that is, claiming and summoning forth—our mindfulness as *Da-sein*, laying claim to our appropriation, our responsibility for actualizing the potential for self-development in our ways-of-being-the-clearing and in our ways of relating to the meaningful presence of things for which the clearing serves as ground and matrix.

†

Now, how should we understand Heidegger's assertion that *Ereignis* refers to a law? I suggest that *Ereignis* is a law because it is constitutive of our very nature as human beings: it is an existential *structure*—in fact, the most fundamental structure of our embodiment: the disposition in which, thrown open in and to the world, we human beings, in our embodiment, are claimed, summoned, and disposed to ourselves in the thrown openness of our existence. It helps to think in terms of the German word for "law," which is *Ge-setz*, referring to this dis-position as that which is laid down, *ge-setzt*, as our nature. I introduce the hyphen into "disposition" so that we keep in mind that it is intrinsically *dis-positioning*, *ent-setzend*, throwing us out of a set position, open to what is meaningful in the world outside ourselves. The hyphen thus represents our *Geworfenheit*. And it is "the most gentle of laws" because the disposition, bearing its claim, its appropriation, is not imposed from outside, but originates *within* us; and, when recognized, retrieved, and enowned, it develops and matures *within* us, gathering us into our very essence, operating as a claim and summons: a claim and a summons to take into our care and responsibility the openness of the clearing—the *Da-sein*—that we *are*, and into which we find ourselves cast, always playing, whether we like it or not, a certain role in the collective inheritance and destiny of history. Such is our *Befindlichkeit*: how we find ourselves inevitably situated.

Thus, inherent in this project is the envisioning of a singular responsibility in regard to our perceptual abilities. Moreover, this appropriation—this responsibility—is the precondition for any new ontological epoch, any new epoch in the paradigm of being, in which the meaning of being operative in the phenomenology of perception, our sense of what it means for anything to be encountered in the realm of the visible and the audible, would undergo a profound change. Perception, for Heidegger, is *Wächterschaft*: guardianship, a responsibility for vigilance, attentiveness, and reception—our ability to be appropriately responsive.

†

I now want briefly to give thought to Heidegger's 1925 *Prolegomena zur Geschichte des Zeitbegriffs*. In this early text, the philosopher discusses "the fundamental character (*Fundamentalcharakter*) of *Dasein* [the human being]": "*that it is in each case my 'always still to be*' [*daß es in meinem 'es je zu sein' ist*]."[8] This he also calls our "fundamental determination" or "fundamental disposition": *Fundamentalbestimmung*. And he explains this claim, arguing that

> *Dasein* is the being [*das Seiende*] that I myself in each case *always ever am* [*das ich je selbst bin*], in whose being I "take part" ["*beteiligt*"] as a being; a being that is ever in my own way to be it [*ein Seiendes, das ist, je meiner Weise es zu sein*]. This determination indicates the exceptional connection with being [*Seinsverhältnis*]." (Ibid.)

*Dasein* has a distinctive way of being (*Weise zu sein*): not at all like a thing, a *Was*. Its "way of being [*Seinsart*]—*to be it* [*es zu Sein*]—is in its essence and in each case *ever mine to be it* [*je meine es zu sein*], whether I explicitly know that or not, whether I have lost myself in my being or not. The fundamental character of the being of *Dasein* is from the beginning entirely to be grasped according to the determination [*erst in der Bestimmung gefaßt*]: *a being that is always in its particular temporality being-toward-its-own-being* [*ist im Jeweilig-es-zu-sein*]. With regard to the 'particular structure of temporality' ['*Jeweiligkeit*'], this 'actual temporality', this 'temporality of the moment' ['*je*', '*jeweilig*'] is constitutive [*konstitutiv*] for every ontological character [*Seinscharakter*] of this being, i.e., there is no *Dasein* at all that could be what it is, namely *Dasein*, without being, according to its meaning, temporal [*jeweiliges*] in this particular way."[9]

What I wish to call attention to in these textual passages is the structural character of the *Zu-sein*: I suggest that it bears on the structure of the *Ereignis* that figures in Heidegger's later thought, signifying our being always underway, our always being toward. I also want to call attention to the 1955 lecture "What Is Philosophy?" that was delivered in France. This text concerns a certain structural disposition: our *bestimmt-sein*, our *être disposé*. According to Heidegger:

> *Disposé* here literally [*wörtlich*] means: displaced, moved from its position [*auseinander-gesetzt*], brightened, cleared [*gelichtet*] and thereby transposed [*versetzt*] in its connections to what is. (GA 11: 21/WIP 77)

I would like the reader to notice the words *gesetzt* and *versetzt* in this passage, making a connection with the *Ge-setz* that is invoked in "The Way to Language" (1959) as characterizing the *Ereignis*. Nothing could be more unsettling and more dispositioning, however, than *Dasein*'s inherently "meta-phorical" bodily nature as thrown openness (*Geworfenheit*), our *Zu-Sein* as site of the clearing. And I shall argue that this thrown openness is, as William Richardson was the first to appreciate, a disposition—indeed, our *most fundamental* disposition, and that its openness inevitably dis-positions us, metaphors us, exposing us to situations and events in the world in ways that question and challenge us—not only with regard to our established sense of being, our sense of what is and what is not but also with regard to who we are, we, each of us a *Da-sein*, and who, in relation to our essence as *Zu-sein*, we want ourselves to be. In other words, events in the world can awaken and stir a claim and a summons, an appropriation (*Ereignis*), that is *already operative* within us, calling us to take into our care and responsibility the openness of the clearing as that which enables the conditions necessary for the meaningful experiencing of the world. (In the *Ereignis*, there is, so to speak, both a "subjective" factor and an "objective" factor.)

†

In *What Is Philosophy?* (1955), Heidegger gave thought to wonder and astonishment (*Erstaunen*) as "the ground of determination (disposition)," the "*Grund der Bestimmtheit* (disposition)," for metaphysical thought in ancient Greece.[10] *Erstaunen*, he suggests," is, as *pathos*, the *arkhé* of philosophy" (GA 11: 22/WIP 79, 81). "Thus," he argues, "*Erstaunen* is the disposition [*Disposition*] in which and for which the being of beings [i.e., the world-clearing] opens. *Erstaunen* is the attunement [*Stimmung*] within which, for the Greek philosophers, correspondence [*das Entsprechen*] to the being of beings was preserved [*gewährt war*]" (GA 11: 23/WIP 83–85). In other words, it was in the experiential event of wonder that the ancient Greek philosophers received being and were provoked and stirred to discover in thought the being of beings—concept of being itself. In this way, the experience of *Erstaunen*, an experience of *receiving* being, began the dialogue we call "metaphysics": "*So ist das Erstaunen die Disposition, in der und für die das Sein des Seienden sich öffnet*" (ibid.). "Astonishment [*Erstaunen*] is a disposition [*Disposition*] in which and for which the being of beings [i.e., the field of presencing, the clearing that enables beings to presence] opens." The Greek philosophers were, we might say, "appropriated" by the experience—called first of all to receive, and in receiving to give thought to being, being as such. But, Heidegger argues, they were unaware of this appropriation as such, unaware of this event (*Ereignis*) as something appropriating₁ (as *Er-eignung*)—as a claim and summons, appropriating them for self-questioning and ultimately, for appropriation₂ and appropriation₃ in the sense of enownment, coming into their essential nature. Our awareness of the appropriation in such experience is one of the things that separates us from those Greek philosophers of the ancient world. Our experience of appropriation is a *pathos*, an engaged passivity, a dis-position, a law of nature, the Greeks could not know.

Astonishment unquestionably was, and still can be, an experience of great historical significance, as, in its ontological resonance, it set metaphysical thinking in motion; however, it is crucial to understand that this experience, despite its metaphysical nature, *presupposes* our more fundamental disposition, namely the dis-position that throws us open into the world. Only because we are *already thrown-open*—dis-positioned—can we be disposed to be astonished, and consequently find ourselves astonished, by what we encounter—or find ourselves simply astonished by the sheer facticity of the world itself.

*Erstaunen* is a disposition, a capacity and capability for openness. One who is favored with having this disposition, this *Bereitschaft*—it is a contingency that one is so favored—is open to life, open to new experience, open to receiving, welcoming what comes. As this openness to experience, *Erstaunen* is indeed *pathos*, susceptibility, receptivity, indeed also a certain *sum-pathein*, essential for philosophizing, as Heidegger says. Nevertheless, *Erstaunen* is possible only because of our *Geworfenheit*. *Geworfenheit* is our *Befindlichkeit*, the ontological situation of openness, hence existence as exposure, in which we find ourselves. It is the deeper, underlying dimension of *Erstaunen*.

The *Ereignis* does indeed refer to our *Befindlichkeit*, in that our "situation" is such that we inevitably find ourselves *geworfen*, thrown open: dis-positioned in that sense, and open to experiencing wonder and astonishment. But this thrown openness is not only an event; it is existen*tial*, constitutive of the very structure of our existence. Not only an event, but rather a disposition of our nature, a disposition, however, that dis-positions us, positioning us in openness outside ourselves in the world. So *Befindlichkeit* and *Geworfenheit* characterize, or define, the *Ereignis* as appropriation. But "appropriation" means that something else, something more is involved, namely, our *proprium*: appropriation$_3$. This is because, in being thrown into the world "outside" ourselves, we find ourselves *thrown out* of our familiar, comfortable (sense of) identity, our established sense who we are. In question is a disposition, an appropriation, that refutes the Cartesian picture of the fixedly self-identical subject connected to an enclosed substance-like body. That, too, is what our *Geworfenheit*—and our *Befindlichkeit*—mean.

Consequently, *Ereignis* (*Ereignung*), together with the other terms in the constellation, that is, *Zueignen*, *Aneignen*, *Vereignen*, represents another way of thinking about *Jemeinigkeit* (my *es-zu-sein*), which, in his 1925 *History of the Concept of Time* (*Prolegomena zur Geschichte des Zeitbegriffs*, GA 20), Heidegger described as our *Fundamentalbestimmung*. But the importance of thinking in terms of an *Ereignis* is that it *carries forward* the individuality (*Jemeinigkeit*) discussed in *History of the Concept of Time* and *Sein und Zeit*, and, as such, it adds a dimension to *Geworfenheit*. We are not merely thrown open. That thrown openness engages us in a world that is *continually questioning and challenging us* to determine *who* we are! And as appropriated to the ontological dimension of the clearing, we are even challenged in regard to our openness. Hence, thrown openness claims us, summoning us to that determination: In *Geworfenheit*, we are *er-eignet.* The claim and summons appropriates us to *Jemeinigkeit* as being appropriated to be the clearing, that is, *Da-sein.* This appropriation to *Geworfenheit,* or rather, our *Geworfenwerden,* is an existential structure, our fundamental disposition, but one that inherently dis-positions us, and constantly summons and claims us in relation to our openness. Thus, *Ereignis* is another way of thinking about our *Jemeingikeit* in relation to that *Geworfenheit.*

Entering into the *Ereignis* (*Einkehr in das Ereignis*) is entering into our individual, personal, *existentiell* appropriation. The claim itself is a dis-positioning disposition, not an event. But our recognizing it, taking it up, and appropriating$_2$ it for a process of enownment (ap-propri-ation$_3$) *is* indeed an event: an event that engages us in a process. "Ereignis" signifies both an event and a disposition-in-process.

†

In his 1936 *Laufende Anmerkungen zu "Sein und Zeit"* (*Running Notes on "Being and Time"*), Heidegger asks us to ponder the origin of the situating "t/here" (the *Da* in *Da-sein*): whether it is already fully formed in the human essence or is instead a claim given as a historical task grounded in the appropriation (*Ereignis*) carried by our most fundamental disposition. For him, the *Da* is a "turning point in history itself": *t/here-ness* [*Da-heit*] essentially occurs only when we take over (appropriate$_2$) being-the-t/here, and in this leap, first create it. The leap from being merely a human *Dasein* into *Da-sein* is, he says, using italics for emphasis, "an *extraordinary moment of history*" (GA 82: 74). So, again, we must recognize that *Ereignis* serves two designations: it is at once event and process, at once (i) the happening of an *event* of appropriation$_1$, ultimately requiring the discontinuity of a leap into self-transformation, and (ii) appropriation$_2$ the *process* of recognizing, understanding, and enacting the developing of that appropriation, that is, actualizing the appropriated disposition of our nature that lays claim to us as human beings, summoning us to transformation—hence, eventually, appropriation$_3$. Thus, it is also both event and structure, event and law, potentiality and actuality.

†

*Pathos* is a crucial experience in and for philosophical thought because it draws conceptual thought out of its familiar realm, beyond what can be grasped in concepts that inherently introduce structures of separation and difference and cover over an earlier, more sympathetically attuned, more affectively formed experience of the world: a prereflective, preconceptual experience preceding the experience in which the polarity of subject and object, and ultimately the metaphysical projection of dualism, emerge and prevail. Neither the earlier nor the later experience is solely the truth. Each needs to be "adjusted" by considering what the other gives access to. Western metaphysics, entangled in conceptually formed dualisms, can learn from what *pathos* brings to light. *Pathos* is itself appropriating. However, even though *pathos*—as in the experience of astonishment and wonder—may lay claim to being a dimension in the phenomenology of the grounding disposition of philosophical thought in the Western world, it is not the most fundamental disposition. That title *must* be reserved for the *pathos* in the appropriation (*Ereignung*) by which we are claimed and to which we are summoned in consequence of the facticity that is our thrown openness, our dis-position to the clearing. For it is only because of that exposed condition that we can find ourselves—find our way *to* ourselves, experiencing our appropriation through the condition of being dis-posed—*pathos*. This *pathos* is what is engaged in the experiencing of our appropriation: our *Zugehören* and *Vereignet-sein* in relation to being (GA 14:51/OTB 42).

†

In his 1949 text, "The Turn," Heidegger deploys a metaphor—the image of an *Einblitz*—to characterize the phenomenology of the moment in which, as if by a flash of lightning, one suddenly finds oneself reminded of one's appropriation to *Da-sein*, hence to care for "the truth of being," that is, the matrix of relations in terms of which beings enter into meaningful presence:

> The in-flashing [*Einblitz*] is a disclosive event of appropriation [*Ereignis*] coming–to-pass within being itself [i.e., within the clearing]. This event [*Ereignis*] is a bringing-into-sight that appropriates [*eignende Eräugnis*, i.e., it is a powerful reminder that makes the individual aware of its appropriation to its *Da-sein*], bringing [it] into its own, its essential nature. (GA 11: 121/QCT 45)

This appropriated "essential nature" is the opening of a world that is the necessary condition for the possibility of meaningful encounters.

In his lecture "Time and Being" (1962), Heidegger argues that we should think the meaning of *Ereignis* from out of itself: "*Das Ereignis ereig-net.*"[11] Is this well-translated as "the event of being makes happen?" What this interpretive translation says is far from perspicuous; but I suspect that it perpetuates metaphysics. Perhaps a better translation would be "the event of being appropriates," meaning that our every encounter with something, our every experience—hearing a bird's song, hearing the bookshelf collapse, watching a hockey game, noticing the reflection of a tree in a puddle of rainwater—is one in which we are appropriated$_1$, called into question and summoned into self-awareness. These are "events of being": something meaningful is happening, something is meaningfully presencing in the world, and such events, like all that we experience, inherently generate questions regarding *what it is* that we are experiencing and *how* we are experiencing it. Consequently, every such "event of being" implicitly calls *us* into question—summons us to self-reflection, summons us to our *Ereignung*, our appropriation, our return to our proper essence. Who are we? So we might interpret that better translation to be saying that "being"—whatever is meaningfully presencing—is always an occasion, a situation, of provocation, asking us not only to respond in a fitting way to that presencing but also, properly and appropriately, to recognize, understand, and question *ourselves* in regard to that presencing: the experience of being is always a challenge, questioning who we are as individuals and as human beings and summoning us to enter into our ownmost nature, thrown-open, vulnerable. *Ereignis*, then, is not in the common sense designating an event, an occurrence, a happening, but, rather, it is the condition of possibility for questioning our relation to the meaning of being—the *Zusammengehören* of *Mensch* and *Sein*, the appropriation that underlies and makes possible any and every encounter with beings (GA 14: 24/OTB 19).

"*Das Ereignis ereignet.*" It would perhaps be helpful to read some of the text that surrounds Heidegger's almost impenetrably dense assertion:

> As we look through being itself, through time itself, and look into the destiny of being [*Geschick von Sein*] and the extending [*das Reichen*] of time-space, we have glimpsed what "appropriation" [*Ereignis*] means. But do we by this approach arrive at anything else than a mere thought-construct? Behind this suspicion there lurks the view that appropriation must after all "be" something [*das Ereignis müßte doch etwas Seiendes "sein"*]. However: appropriation neither *is*, nor *is* appropriation something *given* [*Das Ereignis ist weder, noch gibt es das Ereignis*]. To say the one or to say the other is equally a distortion of the matter, just as if we wanted to derive the source from the river.
>
> What remains to be said? Only this: appropriation appropriates [*Das Ereignis ereignet*]. Saying this, we say the Same in terms of the Same about the Same. To all appearances, this says nothing. It does indeed say nothing so long as we hear [*hören*] a mere sentence in what was said, and then expose that sentence to the cross-examination [*Verhör*] of logic. But what if we take what was said and adopt it unceasingly as the guide for our thinking, and consider that this Same is not even anything new, but rather the oldest of the old in Western thought: that ancient something

that conceals itself [*sich verbirgt*] in *a-letheia* [i.e., in forgetfulness of that which grounds the experience of truth]? (GA 14: 29/OTB 24)

It seems to me that the translation of the key phrase, interpreting it as "the event of being makes happen," gives us an interpretation that is not merely unnecessarily opaque, but it runs the risk of making *Sein* into a metaphysical source of agency. What I suggest Heidegger is saying here is: our encounter with beings in the world (people, other animals, things) is always an encounter in which their being meaningful provokes us to reflect upon ourselves, recognizing, understanding, and enowning ourselves. In other words, the experience with being—the being of beings— is always at least implicitly a challenge that calls for us to enter into our appropriation. That process of appropriation, recognizing, understanding, and enowning ourselves as *Da-sein* is what "the event of being"—every engagement with things in the world that gets us thinking about the conditions of meaningfulness—can "make happen." The provocation to take over, or appropriate, our essence typically comes *from* "being," that is, *from* what is happening in the world; however, what is happening in the world we are experiencing awakens and bestirs something *within* us, something that could in principle have arisen into awareness quite spontaneously, namely, from what Heidegger considers to be our "most fundamental disposition." That is because, even when unheard and unrecognized, our "most fundamental disposition" has nevertheless *always already* been summoning us to our appropriation in *Da-sein*—summoning us to recognize and understand our role in the phenomenology of meaningfulness, our role in the layout (in Greek: the *legein*) of the conditions according to which things can be meaningfully present in our world. If only we would silence the noise of the world and listen to the claim, hearing the call and its summons!

What the philosopher says next in that text is crucial: "The task of our thinking has been to trace being to appropriation, which is where it really comes from [*Sein . . . in sein Eigenes zu denken—aus dem Ereignis*]" (GA 14: 29/OTB 24).[12] In other words, *Ereignis* returns us from the lofty metaphysical way of thinking of being to the humbling phenomenology of our experiencing, summoning us thereby to understand and enown ourselves—our ownmost selves—*in our essential connection* (*Bezug*) to all that comes into meaningful presence in the interplay of concealment and unconcealment—an interplay that takes place in the clearing that is *Da-sein*.

†

In *Homo Sacer: Sovereignty and Bare Life*, Georgio Agamben nicely formulates the definition of "facticity" operative in Heidegger's thought: "Facticity does not mean simply being contingently in a certain way and in a certain situation, but rather means decisively assuming this way and this situation by which what was given must be transformed into a task."[13]

In this sense, we might be said to undergo, or suffer, our own facticity: We are thrown (*geworfen*), but also thereby sent (*geschickt*) into this world, sent to make our own way in it, and we consequently must, from out of the facticity of our thrownness, out of our being sent, project our own being—that is to say, realize the meaning that our own existence has for us. Only when we appropriate₂, that is, take over and take up, this facticity, this appropriation₁ (*Er-eignis*), this claim and calling, and are thus appropriated by it, are we authentically entering our appropriation₃, enowning and enacting, or taking upon ourselves, the meaning of our own (proper, *eigen*) existence. In *Hölderlin's Hymns: "Germanien" and "The Rhine"*, Heidegger says, in this regard:

> Only in such suffering can a destiny [*Schicksal*] take hold of us, a destiny that never simply lies present before us, but that is a sending [*Schickung*]—that is, it is sent to us [i.e., as our already given dis-position of nature]—and in such a way that it sends us toward [*entgegenschickt*] our vocation, granted that we ourselves truly send ourselves into it [i.e., enter into its appropriation: the *Einkehr in das Ereignis*] and know of that which is fittingly sent [*das Schickliche*], and, knowing it, will it. (GA 39: 175–76; 160 in the English translation)

Here we should recognize in the sending—in what sends us on our way—the gift of our nature, the destiny-bearing endowment that sets our dis-position. Here also we can discern some of the different ways that Heidegger deploys one of the two German words for *destiny*, the other being *Geschick*: very pliant words, compliant in generating a whole constellation of related words and meanings.

So, despite Heidegger's unequivocal repudiation, not only of the interpretation of *Ereignis* as an event in the common sense but also of the very idea of a history of being, the text we have just read seems to suggest the continuing importance for his project of a philosophy of history that requires *events*, especially in those contexts where he is thinking about the historical beginnings of metaphysics and events of self-recognition and self-understanding that might shape the future destiny of the Western world. In such contexts, his use seems to compel thinking of events in some recognizable sense.

†

Holding on, despite his scorching critique of our time, to a distinctive philosophy of history, a philosophical perspective that attempts to maintain a certain openness for the redeeming achievement of the destiny he considered proper to our humanity, Heidegger seems to have counted on the continuing possibility of ontological experiences—ontological events, events taken to concern being as such—for setting in motion what he imagined as "another [history-breaking, history-making] inception," profoundly shaping the course of Western civilization, at once reflecting its experience of being and nevertheless also reflecting upon it—deeply, critically.

It is not entirely clear what the possible future transformative events that Heidegger's use of the terms *Ereignis* and *Geschick* might involve, but it does seem that what he had in mind must be decisive history-making moments when the very meaning structure of an entire world order is compelled to undergo a radical change, a fundamental paradigm shift, not only in regard to knowledge, truth, and reality but also in regard to the character and very meaning of human existence. The interpretation I am inclined to favor is that that future possibility would crucially depend on the world-wide recognition by most individuals, as individuals, of our *appropriation*, hence *our responsibility* for being, that is, the ontological conditions necessary for a world of meaningful presence, with all that that purports both for the philosophical understanding of being and for a Western civilization that today, in the present epoch, is in thrall to the *Gestell*, the total imposition of reification, above all in regard to constant availability for use. This is a responsibility that extends to, and claims, the character of our receptive and responsive abilities in perception.

So, although Heidegger used the word *Ereignis* according to its customary meaning insofar as it is to mean "event," the events he actually designated with that word are not at all ordinary everyday events in ordinary serial time: as concerned with our understanding of the meaning of being, these events are distinctively ontological. Moreover, retrieving from the generative depths of the word *Ereignis* its semantic connection to *eigen* and *eignen*, referring to enowning, and also its connection to *Eräugnis*, meaning "bringing into view," or "rendering visible," he undertook to exploit the word's historically hidden *phenomenological* meaning. The term was given this other work to do: *Ereignis*, together with its constellation of associated words, would now also be used to designate our appropriation, a phenomenologically crucial *event*—and an ongoing, never-completed *process*, enowning, retrieving, and enacting, or activating, the potential in our most fundamental disposition, the *Da-sein* deeply structured into our bodily nature—as its most fundamental law. But in taking our thinking into appropriation, Heidegger was always seeking to *bring into view*—*eräugen*—a transformation in our way of being human, hence, too, our way of relating to our world. Behind this *Einkehr*, there was always, I believe, a certain philosophy of history guiding his project: an interpretation of history *keeping in view* the promising possibilities that could shape the destiny (*Geschick*) of mankind. And it all depends on our assumption of responsibilities both ontic and ontological: responsibilities engaging us in our ways of seeing and hearing.

†

In "Aletheia (Heraclitus, Fragment 16)," written in 1943, Heidegger states that "the event of clearing is the world [*Das Ereignis der Lichtung ist die Welt*]" (GA 7: 283/EGT 118). Given the double meaning of "*Ereignis*," as designating an event and designating appropriation, this sentence can mean both (i) that the event, or happening, of the clearing is (what opens) the (or a) world of meaning, and (ii) that the appropriation of the clearing (which is the appropriation of *Dasein* to *be* the clearing) is the opening of a meaningful world. I surmise that Heidegger wants us to think both (i) and (ii). In any case, the clearing *is* an event; but it is no ordinary event. Rather, it is an event that depends on and emerges from our thrown openness, the dis-position inherently appropriating us to *Da-sein*. Ontologically understood, then, the "world" is the appropriated, enowned, and properly grounded clearing. Unfolding this matter to make it more perspicuous phenomenologically, I suggest that we should say: *behind* the event, the taking place, of the clearing is the appropriation, the dis-position of *Dasein* that claims and appropriates it to *be* a clearing—a clearing that is the opening of the intelligibility conditions for a world of meaningfulness.

†

Ontological events, events that need to be recognized and understood as events of appropriation because they regard our *responsibility* in the meaning of being, are events belonging to the deeper dimension of temporality, and they have manifestly occurred in momentous history-breaking, history-making experiences with regard to the prevailing understanding of being and the nature of the relation of the human being to being—as in the experiences of being that stirred the earliest Greek philosophers, not only inaugurating thereby the discourse of metaphysics, the inception of philosophical thought but also contributing to the emergence and shaping of the world we know, the world that eventually developed and unfolded from, and around, that extraordinary experience.

However, according to Heidegger, such ontological experience does not happen only in momentous history-breaking, history-making moments, important though such moments are. Ontologically significant experience, exposing us to what *exceeds* our established sense of what it means for something to be, and causing us not only to *reflect* on the sense of being presupposed in our experience but moreover *to question ourselves* in regard to how we are *relating* to being (the being of beings)—that is something that can happen at any time and in any worldly encounter, any worldly engagement, even one that might otherwise have seemed very ordinary: losing our way in a forest, slipping on ice that looked like a puddle, breaking the handle of our hammer, discovering that what we thought was a duck is only a decoy. Experiencing such exposure—such *Ausgesetztheit*, a breakdown in expectations, a challenge, possibly traumatic, to our comfortably familiar way of relating to being and to our settled sense of being—is a potential inherent in *every* encounter, *every* engagement, that we human beings have with what-is in our world, although, as Heidegger complains, the summons to address that challenge seldom rises into reflective awareness and seldom is sufficiently unsettling to influence and alter the course of our history. We have many ways of defending against such unsettling, disquieting experience. Nevertheless, an ontologically appropriating event, laying claim to our response-ability, *can* catch our attention at any time— "whenever," as Richard Polt nicely articulates it, "our established sense of being is experienced as significantly challenged."[14] Although not necessarily history-breaking or history-making, the experience of an event exceeding and challenging the established sense of being can always serve to remind us of the unique phenomenological character of our connection to being: the bonding (*Bezug*) of a vibrantly oscillating intentionality, an interaction, a lively reciprocity, drawing *Mensch* and *Sein* into their belonging together. And it could engage us in the possible emergence of a new sense of being, something corresponding to a new sense of our ability to be receptive and responsive. Perception—as in seeing and hearing—belongs to a cultural history of significant changes. But perception depends on reception. So, the question is, are we prepared to take responsibility for our ability to be responsive?

In fact, although we typically do not realize it, *everything* we encounter in the world, whether in its presencing or in its absencing, faces us and addresses us with questions concerning the *character* of our relation to its being, calling upon us to be more aware, more thoughtfully engaged, and more fittingly, properly attuned and response-able. Thus, even the most ordinary encounter with other people, other animals, and the things of our world can potentially become the occasion, not only for an experience challenging some cherished belief, some reasonable expectation, some common assumption, or some tenacious prejudice, but also the occasion for an experience that in some way brings into question our ownmost being, the very character of our own existence, and thus even what it means to be a human being. This questioning of us, summoning and claiming us to get in touch with, and enact, the potential constitutive of our *proprium*, our being human, is what makes the ontological event an event *of ap-propriation*, laying claim to our response ability.

†

Understanding human existence calls for thinking in terms of events and structures. Thus, in the event, or rather the process, of appropriation, world *event* and *Dasein*'s existential *structure*, world *event* and *Dasein*'s existential *disposition*, function together, each drawing out the meaning, the ontological role, of the other: it is an *event* in the world that summons and activates the dispositional structure constitutive of our nature; but at the same time, and correspondingly, it is the responsiveness of the disposition, its *"Bereitschaft für die Er-eignung,"* that makes the event in the world an *occasion* for the *Übernahme*, the eventful *process* in which we undertake our appropriation, enowning and enacting the self-knowledge that our thrown-open nature demands of us. To exist is to be thrown into the questioning and learning that such exposure to openness inevitably occasions. The questioning of being is—intrinsically, necessarily—the corresponding questioning that draws us into our appropriation of ourselves. As Heidegger was already arguing in *Being and Time*: *"Übernahme der Geworfenheit bedeutet, das Dasein in dem, wie es je schon war, eigentlich sein"* (GA 2: 431/BT373). That is to say, the taking up, or appropriating, of our essential condition of thrownness means that *Da-sein* is truly living in and from that [given essential nature] which it *always already* was (GA 65: 322/CP 254).[15] "Always already was"—but also not fully recognizing, enowning, and enacting the given δύναμις, our given potential or capability of nature.

It is a question of *ontologically perceived events in the world*—events regarding the meaning of being—that stir and shake up the *a priori existential structure*, the fundamental disposition that, throwing us open into a clearing, sends us human beings on the way to our appropriation; it is a question of *ontologically perceived events in the world* that arouse us from our ontological slumber. Because of our fundamental disposition, we are not only inherently *ex-posed* to the questioning and challenging possible in events taken to concern being; we are also rendered especially *susceptible* to the appropriation, the claim on our capabilities, that such events call forth.

But what about the appropriation itself? It is the dynamic structure that, although not a teleologically fixed form totally unresponsive and immutable in its interactions within a world of contingent events, nevertheless lays the structural ground of our essential nature, the thrown openness that is *Da-sein*. However, as that to which we are summoned by this nature, appropriation, constitutive of our most fundamental disposition, requires a *process* in which it is recognized and understood as such, and in which it is accordingly taken up for enownment and practical enactment. Thus, it turns out that the "question of being" ultimately puts *our* being—*us*—in question. As the thrown-open beings we are, how are we going to comport ourselves in regard to being? Are we going to take responsibility for that ontological openness? Are we going to take it into our care, our *Wächterschaft*? That completes the phenomenological turn. And it explains why Heidegger eventually realized that, working with the *Ereignis*, his project no longer needed to work with the thought of *Sein*. And this meant a further—and decisive—sublation or surpassing (*Verwindung*) of metaphysics.

In fact, in the 1930s, Heidegger found that thinking by way of the *Ereignis* (*Ereignung*) not only made it possible for his project—the project as conceived in *Being and Time*—to proceed without further concentration on the question of being, but also made it possible, correspondingly, for his project to think differently about another matter crucial in that 1927 work, namely, our thrownness (*Geworfenheit*). Henceforth, this thrownness would be understood in terms of our appropriation. So, likewise, the task before us, which in *Being and Time*, is characterized as "*die Übernahme der Geworfenheit*" (GA 2: 431/BT 373)—the event, or process, that involves the taking over, or appropriating, of our essential condition of thrown openness—would henceforth be thought more deeply, because that thrown openness is our potential-for-being (*Seinskönnen*). Consequently, the task becomes the taking over of our having been appropriated: *die Übernahme der Er-eignung* (GA 65: 34/CP 29). As early as *Being and Time* (1927), we can see that Heidegger was already thinking, at least implicitly, in terms of the *Ereignis* (*Ereignung*), understanding it as appropriation (GA 2: 431/BT 373). And already, even then, he occasionally touched on what this means with regard to the character of our perception—seeing and hearing.

†

Heidegger's project tells us a story. From the moment when, at birth, we enter the shared world, we are sent—*geschickt*—on our way, sent on the journey of a lifetime. Sent with what destiny—*Geschick*—might hold before us and ahead of us. But we soon lose our way, and lose ourselves, in this bewildering world. This world is a theatre of distractions.

This makes it necessary that we find a way back to ourselves—if we are ever to discover, within ourselves, the way to appropriate and redeem the potential in the nature—the disposition—we were originally given. As Heidegger will say just a few years later in the texts published as *Contributions to Philosophy*: "The with-itself of the self [*Das Bei-sich des Selbst*] shows itself as the persistent insistence [*als Inständigkeit*] of the claim urging the taking over of our appropriation [*Übernahme der Er-eignung*, i.e., the taking over, or appropriating[1], of our appropriation[2] in awareness, recognition, understanding, enowning and enacting it]" (GA 65: 322/CP 254). By the way, we should note here that Heidegger uses *Ereignung* rather than *Ereignis*, fittingly suggesting that what is involved in this taking-over, this appropriation, is an ongoing *process* and not—or not only—an event, an episode. Heidegger himself implies this way of understanding appropriation because he speaks of "entering the appropriation" (*Einkehr in das Ereignis*) by taking a "step back" (*Schritt zurück*) and passing through "stages on a way back" (*Stationen auf einem Rückgang*) (GA 14: 38, 55/OTB 30, 45).

Who we are and who we are prepared to become influence the historical conditions necessary for the possibility of meaningful presencing, just as being—that which is necessary for meaningful presencing, given certain historical conditions—influences our appropriation to *Da-sein*. This "oscillation," an interactive back-and-forth dynamic—Heidegger will describe it, expressing his thought in words reminiscent of the Schellinginan spirit, as a *Gegenschwung*, a *schwingende Bereich* and a *schwebende Bau*—is what appropriation to our responsibility in the belonging-together of *Mensch* and *Sein* means as an event taking place in the clearing of a world.[16] The responsibility in this dynamics crucially involves our response ability for what we encounter, which always reflects back to us the way we are treating it, relating to it. Hence, as the philosopher observes, the belonging together (*Zusammen-gehörigkeit*) is a relational event in the world that always appropriates us, always questions and challenges us, engaging us in the dynamics of a two-way or reversible reflection, *wechselweise im Widerschein* (GA 11: 75/ID 69).[17]

In any case, the sheer *fact* of appropriation, the fact of its operation in all worldly encounters, even if, as typically happens, that operation is not recognized, encourages Heidegger to imagine the possibility of another ontological inception, another creative origin, and the emergence of another ontological paradigm of knowledge, truth and reality, not only in the context of philosophical thought but also in a world that has fallen into nihilism: a new way of living and a new way of understanding our mortal existence, dwelling on this earth under the great sky, a way grounded in our exposure to a radically new experience and understanding of being and our relation to being: "with the grounding [i.e., appropriation] of *Da-sein* [*Gründung des Da-seins*] every relation to being is transformed [*alles Verhältnis zum Seienden verwandelt*] and the truth of being [i.e., the clearing] is for the first time [*zuvor*] experienced" (GA 65: 322/CP 254). We are in fact always already grounded, in that, by the gift of nature, by the very nature of our existence, the existential structure of our most fundamental disposition, we find ourselves always already thrown open, *already Da-sein*, grounded in openness; but we are not yet *properly* grounded until that initial grounding with which we are sent out (*geschickt*) into the world has been acknowledged in self-awareness, recognized, understood, enowned, and more fully enacted or actualized. Thus, there are *two* "moments" (two appropriating events, two dimensions) in our grounding: the *existential* one that we are always already given—given however as *in need of* enowning and achievement and the one to which we are summoned by the disposition of our very nature to undertake as a personal *existentiell* task. As Heidegger explains, in entering into the "oscillation of appropriation" ("*Gegenschwung der Er-eignung*"), human *Dasein* "for the first time becomes itself" ("*erst selbst es selbst zu werden*"), that is, "the preserver of the thrown projection, the grounded one that grounds the ground" ("*der Wahrer des geworfenen Ent-wurfs, der gegründete Gründer des Grundes*") (GA 65: 239/CP 188–89). This taking up, or taking over (*Übernahme*) of that preliminary grounding—our natural endowment—is a crucial *event* (*Er-eignis*), a crucial stage, in the historically interminable self-transformative *process* of grounding our *Da-sein*, and it involves a certain assumption of responsibility for the *Wahrheit des Seyns*, the conditions of meaningful presencing—that is to say, for "that open realm [*jenes Offene*] to which and in which we humans [always already] belong as grounders and guardians [*Gründer und Wahrer*], since, from the very beginning, we have been appropriated [*er-eignet*]" (GA 65: 26/CP 22–23). But, as I shall argue, that existential appropriation, embodied in our nature, our disposition, as claim and summons (*Anspruch*) to enownment, is a gift-bearing task (*Auf-gabe*) that needs to be personally and individually (i.e., *existentielly*) appropriated. We shall return to the question of grounding.

The possibility of a comprehensive transformation of the civilization that now virtually holds sway over the entirety of this planet would presumably require, though, that we all undergo, as our own personal experience of being, something like that epiphany which must have stirred the ancient Greek philosophers: something exposing us to what exceeds and challenges in the most profound and even unsettling way the sense of being we had heretofore taken for granted in the course of our lives. Even in today's world, or perhaps especially in today's world, it seems unlikely that more than a few individuals, those committed to the deepest venture of thought, would find themselves thrown into the groundlessness of such experience. And what they might make of it would be, of course, a further question. But in every encounter with what it is given (*geschickt*) to us to experience, the *Es gibt* ("giving" "sending," making possible) of *Da-sein* opens up an entire field of possibilities within which, according to Heidegger, projections of destiny beckon. Our corresponding appropriation to *Da-sein*, our *proprium*, is, however, the precondition for the very possibility of any second, other inception. Destiny is not something fated; it comes only as something earned, something cherished and enowned in a commitment to freedom. Destiny is a question that lies in the appropriation of our potential-for-being. As Heidegger argues in his lecture on "The Principle of Identity" (1957), breaking the powerful "spell" of the *Gestell*, the imposition of total reification, is also a matter that depends on our appropriation, our assumption of responsibility:

> The belonging together of man and being in the manner of mutual challenge drives home to us with startling force that and how man is delivered over [*vereignet*] to the ownership of being and a connection with being is appropriate [*zugeeignet*] to the essence of man. (GA 11: 45/ID 36)

The lecture continues: "Within the *Ge-stell*, there prevails [*waltet*] a strange ownership and a strange appropriation [*ein seltsames Vereignen und Zueignen*]. We must therefore experience this owning [*dieses Eignen*], in which man and being are delivered over to one another [*einander ge-eignet sind*]. That is to say, we must enter into what we call the process of appropriation [*Ereignis*]" (GA 11: 45/ID 36). And before we can attain the power to bring about change, we must achieve a deep and thorough understanding of the ways in which we are subjected to the oppressive imperatives of the *Gestell*.

†

Drawing inspiration from the words of the Apostle Paul (2 *Corinthians* 12: 9–10), Walter Benjamin's "Theses in the Philosophy of History" (1940) invokes a "*weak* messianic power": "Like every generation that preceded us, we have been endowed with a *weak* messianic power, a power to which the past has a claim. That claim cannot be settled cheaply."[18] More on this messiancity in the chapter on *Das Geschick* (chapter 5). Despite the considerable differences between Heidegger and Benjamin, there are fascinating points of convergence and correspondence—such as their critiques of historicism, their repudiation of teleological determination, their conceptions of the relation between historical time and inceptual or revolutionary time, their metaphorical images to evoke a time of plight and danger and a time of rescue, and finally this notion of a messianic, or transformative power, which it might be fruitful to interpret, in the context of Heidegger's project, as operative in the individual's given potential-for-being (*Seinskönnen*), hence the "empowerment" in an orientation toward destiny, the fulfillment of our humanity, informing the *Er-eignung*, the claim of appropriation, as engaging our most fundamental disposition.

†

In "Time and Being" Heidegger says: "Without being, no being is capable of being as such. Accordingly, being can be considered as the highest, most significant event of all" (GA 14: 26/OTB 21). What he means is that, without the conditions that make meaningful presencing possible, there can be no beings, no entities. Those conditions are the conditions that the nature and character of our thrown-open experiencing lays out. Thus, what is ultimately significant in every encounter with being—with something that meaningfully presences in our world—is, for Heidegger, its being an event that appropriates human existence, *our* very being, laying claim to our responsibility in the inseparable interactive belonging together of *Mensch* and *Sein*, human being and being. Corresponding (co-responding) to that claim, that summons, getting in touch with its challenging questions concerning the essential character of our way of life, is what Heidegger calls "entering into appropriation": *"Das Einkehr in das Ereignis."*

We must take responsibility for our understanding of being, and that means taking responsibility for the character of our *relation* to the being (meaning) of the beings in our world. That assumption of responsibility, a responsibility bearing significant implications for our belonging to history— to heritage and destiny, is what Heidegger calls our "entering into appropriation." Thus, as he says in *The Event (Das Ereignis)*, reflections composed during the War years 1941–1942:

> We must learn to experience *das Ereignis* [the ontological event] as the appropriating; and we must first become mature enough for experience. Experience is never the bare sensory perception of objectively present things and facts. Experience is . . . belongingness to a past that is not yet past [*Zugehörigkeit in das Gewesende*]—hence it is steadfastness in keeping in mind [possibilities for] inceptuality [*Anfängnis*]. (GA 71: 183–84/E 156)

What this appropriation involves is the recognizing, understanding, enowning, and enacting of our appropriation, whereby we are turned, and in effect returned, to our ownmost nature, which is *Da-sein*—being (*-sein*) the place, site (the *Da-*) for the clearing that opens a historical world, determining what is possible in meaningful presencing.

In fact, there is always, inherent in our experience, a certain demanding responsibility, as Heidegger will argue with eloquence in so many of his writings, including the texts in the volume we are now reading. In another note in this same volume, Heidegger explains the need for such maturity:

> Metaphysical humanity exclusively knows beings in their beingness and cannot experience *beyng* (*Seyn*: another word for the clearing). . . . The task is to enter into the domain of disposition [*Stimmung*], where the word of beyng disposes comportment toward steadfastness in the preservation of the clearing of beyng [i.e., the clearing for the presencing of beings: the "of beyng" here is merely a way of indicating an ontological dimension of the matter]. (GA 71: 175/E 148–49)

"Yet all this," he observes, "remains concealed from metaphysical humanity, such that the relation of *beyng* to the human being is accessible only in the representation of the self-relating of the human being to *beings.*" Focused on beings, we miss and neglect the clearing (sometimes rendered as *Seyn* or *Seyn selbst*) that which, opened through the existential structure of the human being as thrown-open *Da-sein*, makes the presencing of things possible in the first place. The event that discloses to us our unique assignment (*Zu-eignung*) to *Da-seyn* (to being, as "grounders" of the place of the clearing) calls upon us to live on this earth in a way that is in keeping with its preservation—the "preservation of beyng" (ibid.). Taking the presencing of beings, hence the openness of the clearing, into our care, true to our essence as *Da-sein*. As he argues there:

> To remain steadfast [*Inständig bleiben*] in response [i.e., to the calling that reminds us of the interactive, reciprocal, *schwingende* nature of our relation to beyng] is the very essence of our historical responsibility [*das Wesen der geschichthaften Verantwortung*]. Thereby, human beings adhere to that wherein they are adopted [committed, assigned, engaged, *angeeignet*]. This adherence to the appropriated essence [*Dieses Innehalten des ereigneten Wesens*], taking on the role to which the very nature of our existence has assigned [and dis-posed us] is properness [*Eigentlichkeit*], i.e., authentically being a self [i.e., enownment, *das Selbstsein*]. Only in appropriated properness [*ereigneten Eigentlichkeit*], in the sense of the guarding and stewardship [*Behütung und Wächterschaft*] of the truth of

beyng [i.e., of the openness of the clearing] does the inaugural selfhood [*anfanghafte Selbstheit*] of historical mankind emerge [*entspringt*]. (GA 71: 156/E 134)[19]

Our future—our destiny—depends on our assuming responsibility for taking over, as our ownmost personal and historical project, the appropriating potential, namely our *Da-sein*, that we have been given by nature for our appropriation, our enowning. We need to be in essential correspondence [*Entsprechung;* the *homologein* in Heraclitus] to the claim [*Anspruch*] that every event of being makes on us. Although the ancient Greek tragedians and philosophers did not know about this appropriation as such, they would have approached an understanding of this responsibility for enownment in terms of self-knowledge, an *anagnorisis* (GA 65: 298/CP 235).

†

The *Einkehr* has two inseparable dimensions, or poles: in familiar traditional terms that ultimately must be renounced, it involves a "subjective" and an "objective" dimension or pole. The "subjective" is a personal, *existentiell* matter of self-awareness, self-recognition, self-understanding, self-enownment, and practical enactment. Although the original motivation and impetus for this "subjective" movement into appropriation can always to some extent come spontaneously from "within" us, there is *always* an "objective" pole or dimension operative in this movement. It would consequently be a grave mistake to think that the phenomenology of the *Einkehr* perpetuates the metaphysics of subjectivism: what it calls for is not a phenomenology of pure inwardness but rather a phenomenology of *dynamic interaction* between *Mensch* and *Welt*, the world of meaning we, in our appropriated thrown-openness, have cleared, and in which we find ourselves situated. Such a phenomenology is required, because everything that we encounter in the world "communicates" with us, responding to the character of our engagement in ways that question us, challenge us, summon us, and make claims and demands. Appropriation is a bipolar experience event, an *interaction*, taking place in the world, and in response to our worldly encounter with other people, other animals, and things; an experience event in which we find ourselves awakened to the claim and summons—and to the guardian response ability thereby entailed—that is already inherent in the deepest dimension of our embodied dis-position as beings who exist cast in world-openness. Of course, the *Einkehr can* certainly be felt to originate as a response to an urgent claim stirring and arising *within* ourselves; but in fact it always also emerges *from* our interactions with things in the world—and indeed mostly from such interactions, that is, in response to them. As the response (*Antwort*) appropriate to our responsibility (*Antwortlichkeit*). In fact, it is typically these interactions that provoke us to go into ourselves, remembering the appropriation claiming our deepest nature. The "Einkehr" is not reducible to an inner process.

This experience of personal appropriation is, however, not very common; moreover, the enownment and enactment (*Ereignung*) it can motivate is not ever assured persistence and endurance; nor can it ever be fully and finally achieved. The appropriation requires the continuing commitment of the community—all the more so, since the world that prevails (*waltet*) is extremely unsympathetic, indeed hostile, to the learning and nurturing of the response-ability that is required by the arrogation assigning ontological responsibility.

†

I hope it is evident by now that I am not proposing "dis-position" as a *translation* of *Ereignis* (*Ereignung*). "Dis-position" is an *interpretation* that tells us how *Ereignis* (*Ereignung*) should be understood; it tells us *how* the claim of appropriation *functions* in our lives. This claim should be understood as having the properties, the characteristics and function, of a disposition—a bodily carried, ongoing *a priori* (*vorausgeschickt*) disposition, a disposition that, when we become conscious of it, turns out to have been *always already* operative: *a priori* only in that distinctive sense (GA 65: 321–22/CP 254). However, I want further to suggest, using a hyphen, that its functioning manifests the sundered, stretched-out nature of our existence, an always becoming thrown openness, a *Geworfenheit*, that is our condition, our situation, our *Befindlichkeit*—the sundered, exposed, dispersed condition in which, as bodily beings, we find ourselves. I shall return to the significance of this hyphen in writing "dis-position"—and, too, for the same reason, in writing the word *Da-sein*. For now, let me simply observe that the *Ereignis* (*Ereignung*) is not only our *Geworfenheit*. The *Ereignis* (*Ereignung*) is also, as Heidegger repeatedly observes, a claim and a summons to *find ourselves* in the *enowning* of our true nature, including the retrieving of that initial embodiment of pre-ontological understanding belonging to infancy, and from which, in ontological "forgetfulness" (*Seinsvergessenheit*), we *first* separated without even knowing it as we entered into the ontic life of the human world. But if, in our maturity, we return to ourselves, we inevitably must separate from our familiar, comfortable (sense of) identity with an encapsulated, substance-like body. In the *Ereignis*, we are called upon by the very dis-position of our nature to come to, and enown with understanding, its ownmost embodied nature, thrown-open as *Da-sein*. This is our disposition, the nature of our appropriation. The gentlest law.

I take the appropriation (*Ereignung*) to come *from* the nature of our dis-position, that is, from "within" *Da-sein*. Fate has given us bodies that are appropriated to bear this dis-position, throwing us into the becoming of *Da-sein*, clearings for the truth of being. However, although the *stimulus* for *Ereignung* might come from *within*, coming in a claim, a calling, that the I alone can hear, we need to understand that this claim is *always stirred, always aroused, by the encounters, the provocations, that engage us in our sojourning through the world*. It is ultimately *always* what we experience *in the world* that summons our own slumbering dis-position to enown and enact our appropriation to the openness of *Da-sein*. However, coming into our own is indeed never fully achievable. It is ongoing "work" on ourselves: the *Menschen-wesen* is inevitably a *Menschen-werden*.

Who are we? It is estranging and unsettling when, in the self-reflective turn Heidegger calls an "*Einkehr in das Ereignis*," we begin to recognize and understand ourselves as *Da-sein*, as having always already been, without knowing it, appropriated in our very embodiment, thrown open to be, and be in, the clearing we always already have been.

What is given to us (*geschickt*) as the facticity of our nature is only given as a potential. We find ourselves endowed with a nature that importunes and summons us, laying claim to our reognition, understanding, and enowning. But we are always free to disregard and neglect that claim, that calling, letting it sleep in forgetfulness, and we are free to resist and deny it. So, what makes us listen to it and heed it? What brings us to resolute decision and steadfast commitment? The events and situations we find given in our world. All events and situations have ontological import; they are never merely ontical: they always involve a certain understanding of being, of what it means to be. If our nature were to be an essence (*Wesen*) as defined by metaphysics, it would be unchanging, untouched, and unmoved by events in our world. But according to the "essence" that Heidegger shows us, we are thrown open into a world, and our most fundamental disposition dis-poses us, dis-positions us, meaning that our very essence functions to unsettle us: it is always already taking us *out of ourselves* on the way to finding ourselves differently disposed. It is an essence that appropriates us to, and for, a challenging, unsettling openness (GA 65: 7–9, 25–27/CP 8–9, 22–23)[20] It makes us vulnerable. Our "nature" does not settle anything by itself, but on the contrary demands that we confront the contingencies of events in the world and decide how we want to live our lives. Appropriation is stirred and provoked by ontic life; but, as Heidegger argues in his *Contributions to Philosophy*, it inherently draws us into the ontological, the way we experience and interpret the meaning of being.

†

Something of the character of this thrown openness is nicely illuminated in Heidegger's "Building Dwelling Thinking" (1951), where, in the
course of phenomenological reflections on the relation of man and space,
Heidegger argues that "spaces open up by the fact that they are let into
the dwelling of man. To say that mortals *are* is to say that, *in dwelling*, they
persist through spaces by virtue of their stay among things and locations."
And, as he points out:

> Only because mortals by their very nature pervade and project through
> spaces are they able to go through spaces. But in going through spaces,
> we do not give up our standing in them. Rather, we always go through
> spaces in such a way that we already experience them by staying con-
> stantly with near and remote locations and things. When I go toward
> the door of the lecture hall, I am already there, and I could not go to
> it at all if I were not such that I am there as well as here. I am never
> here only, as this encapsulated body: rather, I am there, that is, I already
> pervade the room, and only thus can I go through it. (GA 7: 158–59/
> PLT 156–57)[21]

This is the phenomenology of our bodily dis-position: *Geworfen-sein:* our
*Da-sein.* It is manifestly not the substance body of metaphysics, not the
body of idealism—nor the body in the empiricism of Locke, Berkeley, and
Hume. The transformation in which the existence (*Dasein*) of the human
being (*Mensch*) becomes *Da-sein* (with the hyphen)—"*die Verwandlung des
Menschen in sein Da-sein*" (GA 9: 113/PM 89)—can be, as I have noted, dis-
turbingly estranging and unsettling [*verrückend*], as when we find ourselves
deprived of that "thin wall by which we are separated from the uncanniness
of our being": the "*dünne Wand, die gleichsam das Man von der Unheimlich-
keit seines Seins trennt.*"[22] But, the more we can recognize, understand, and
enown our thrown-open *Da-sein*, the less it remains an "*Ungewohntes,*" in
that it becomes truly lived in. "*Da-sein ist ein völlig Un-gewohntes, aller Ken-
ntnis vom Menschen weit vorausgeschickt*": *Da-sein* [i.e., our being, our existing,
as thrown openness] is something completely unaccustomed, unfamiliar,
not fully lived in, a nature given far ahead of all that is known about man
(GA 65: 312/CP 254). A nature we are given (*geschickt*), but it is not initially grounded, and not complete; nor is it preordained, a rigid, immutable,
impermeable, invulnerable essence unaffected by the vicissitudes of its situatedness in the interplay of time and space. As Heidegger already said very
clearly in *Being and Time*:

The "essence" of the human being [*Das "Wesen" des Daseins*] lies [*liegt*] in its existence [*Existenz*]. The distinguishing characteristics of this being are accordingly not the objectively present-at-hand "properties" [*vorhandene "Eigenschaften"*] of some entity present-at-hand, but rather in each case [*je*] possible ways for it to be and no more than that. (GA 2: 56–57/BT 67)

This makes what Heidegger means by "essence" fundamentally different from what Aristotle and the mediaeval philosophers meant by "essence." In the paragraph before this text, Heidegger says: "The 'essence' of this being lies in its '*Zu-sein*,'" substituting *Zu-sein* for *Existenz*, and explaining, in a footnote, that *Zu-sein* means that human existence, the human way of being, is intrinsically future-oriented, being-in-movement, always a being-toward, *unterwegs*, but without any teleological automatism driving it.

†

As we noted, in his *Contributions to Philosophy* (1936–1938), Heidegger describes the *Ereignis* in terms of a certain two-way interaction—a corresponding oscillation—structuring the relation between *Mensch* and *Seyn*:

Beyng [*Seyn*] requires man in order to happen essentially [*damit er wese*], and man belongs to beyng. . . . *This counterpoise of requiring and belonging* [*Dieser Gegenschwung des Brauchens und des Zugehörens*] constitutes beyng as *Ereignis*. (GA 65: 251/CP 198)[23]

Beyng, which the philosopher tells us names the clearing for the meaningful presencing of beings, both "needs and uses" (*braucht*) the *Da-sein* of the human being as its guardian and home. In turn, though, we cannot become *Da-sein* (sites of clearing for the presencing of beings) unless we are open so that *Sein* (*Seyn*) can take place. Thus, in the *Einkehr*, this dynamic, bpolar, reciprocating, *wechselweise* relation, joining and grounding *Sein* and *Mensch-sein* in the (being of the) *Da* (the site of a clearing), is more fittingly called a "bonding two-way pull" (*Bezug*) rather than a "relation" (*Verhältnis*), inasmuch as the latter term assumes that the connection is between two totally autonomous entities, and it also suggests a relation that is fixed rather than oscillating, dynamic, drawing-together.

Years later, in his 1957 lecture on "The Principle of Identity," Heidegger returned to this "*belonging*-together of man and being" (*das Zusammengehören von Mensch und Sein*), again revisioning Husserlian intentionality and interpreting it now in terms of an appropriation (GA 11: 45/ID 36):

The event in which the claim of appropriation operates is that realm of dynamic oscillating interaction [*der in sich schwingende Bereich*] through which man and being attain their nature [*Wesen*], each through the other, and achieve their ownmost essential truth [*ihr Wesendes gewinnen*], giving up those properties, those determinations, with which metaphysics had endowed them. (GA 11: 46/ID 37)

Moreover, in this interaction, there is, as we noted, "a distinctive enowning and a distinctive assignment and dedication" (*ein seltsames Vereignen und Zueignen*):

We must experience this reciprocal claiming, this enowning [*dieses Eignen*], in which man and being are delivered over to one another [*einander ge-eignet sind*]—which is to say, we must enter into what we call the claim of appropriation [*einzukehren in das, was wir das Ereignis nennen*]. (GA 11: 45/ID 36)

That claim constitutes our most fundamental disposition. The importance of the belonging-together, this reciprocal interaction, this *Schwingen* and *Schweben* in the *Bezug* that draws the two—*Mensch* and *Sein*—together, cannot be emphasized too strongly, because the phenomenology brings out the ontological responsibility—*the responsibility for being*—that appropriates our lives in the world. The word *Bezug* fits the vibrant, flowing interactive oscillation of this connection better than the word *Verhältnis*, which suggests a certain rigidity in the relation, keeping the two separated; hence it bears on the responsibility for being that the *Bezug* draws out of us. At stake is a responsibility that is very much a matter of our ability, as appropriated, to be appropriately responsive with regard to the phenomenon of being—that is to say, with regard to the being, the meaningful presencing, of beings. Perception, for Heidegger, is always a matter of responsibility.

This was already argued well in another text, one we considered in the preceding chapter (chapter 2). "On the Question of Being" (1955) not only supports this interpretation, but, going beyond the phenomenological analysis in earlier texts, it unequivocally brings out, without actually mentioning it, the claim of appropriation (*Er-eignis, Er-eignung*) that is inherently operative in the interaction of *Mensch* and *Sein*—operative, that is, in the relation that is really not a relation, because of the inseparable belonging-togetherness of *Mensch* and *Sein*:

Presencing ("being") [*Anwesen* ("Sein")], as presencing, is on each and every occasion [*je und je*] a presencing directed toward the human essence [i.e., *Da-sein*, our being situated here], insofar as presencing is a call [*Geheiß*] that, on each occasion [*jeweils*] calls upon the human essence [*des Menschenwesen ruft*]. The human essence as such is a hearing [*ist als solches hörend*], because the essence of human beings belongs to the calling of this call [*weil es ins rufende Geheiß ins An-wesen gehört*] in the approach of this presencing. (GA 9: 408–9/PM 308–9)

As I argued in the preceding chapter, every perceptual encounter addresses us, summons us, calls us, appropriating us for our appropriation as disposed in responsibility for the character of our role in the encounter. Every encounter summons us to awaken to our ontological responsibility in regard both to *what* is presencing in the encounter and *how* that which we encounter happens to be presencing. The call may be experienced as coming from what we encounter in the world; but in any event, because of the intertwining of the "subjective" and "objective" aspects of the situation, the call demands to be heard, and felt, to resonate "inside us" with the claim of appropriation that is constitutive of the disposition of our ownmost nature. The *Geheiß* comes from the appropriated disposition of our nature.

†

The "transformation" (*Verwandlung*) of Western mankind that Heidegger attempts to envision is, as he phrases it in his *Beiträge zur Philosophy* (*Contributions to Philosophy*), the "*Verrückung des Menschen in das Da-sein*" (GA 65: 356/CP 281). Heidegger thus characterizes as a *Verrückung* an unsettling and disquieting experience of recognizing and enowning ourselves as the *Da*-site of clearings. In the transformation this experience brings about, there is a major *Verrückung* in our situatedness in the midst of beings, our "*Stellung im Seienden*" (GA 65: 338/CP 268). This is not, however, as the common meaning of that word might suggest, a moment of madness; but it is certainly a dislodging or dis-positioning of our commonly assumed *position* (*Stellung*) of power among beings; and that certainly can be very unsettling, perhaps even traumatic (GA 65: 356/CP 281). So what is Heidegger using that word to say? I suggest that the *Ver-rückung*, understood as a dislodging or dis-positioning, is illuminated in the *Schritt zurück*, the step back, in which we "turn inward," so to speak, returning to our essential nature in order to retrieve, from our most fundamental disposition, some sense of our appropriation. That, according to the philosopher, is a "hermeneutical moment," the event in which, dislodged out of our inveterate fixety and opened up to new determinability, we get in touch with our heretofore hidden appropriation, our *Er-eignung*, an assignment and dedication (*Zueignung*) always already given in our bodily nature, that is, by way of our most fundamental disposition (GA 65: 26–27/CP 22–23).

†

Now, I have been arguing that it is necessary to recognize in Heidegger's discussions of the *Ereignis* as appropriation some crucial distinctions. Not only a distinction between the appropriation as event and appropriation as process but also a distinction between appropriation as event and appropriation as structure. With regard to the latter distinction, according to one interpretation, *Ereignis* as appropriation refers not to an *event* but to an existential *structure*: the structure, namely, that grounds *Da-sein*, and that, in his 1925 *Prolegomena to the History of the Concept of Time*, Heidegger characterized as our most fundamental disposition: our *Bestimmung* and *Seinsstruktur*, the "*Fundamentalcharakter des Daseins*" (GA 20: 205–10). That bodily disposition *calls for and structures* the process of appropriation. Some years later, in *Contributions to Philosophy*, a sustained meditation on appropriation as event and structure, Heidegger continued thinking about our *Grundstimmung*, declaring that "the basic disposition of the grounding is restraint [*Verhaltenheit*]" (GA 65: 34 and 52/CP 42).[24] And, explaining what this term meant for him, he said, in words that connect to his discussion of the most fundamental "law" determining our existence, our way-of-being:

> Restraint is the strongest and at the same time most delicate preparedness of *Dasein* for the appropriation, for being thrown into a genuine standing within the truth of the turning in the event [*Ereignis*]. (Ibid.)

We shall return to this question of "restraint," showing that, as the most fundamental structuring of *Da-sein*, our most fundamental disposition, appropriation operates, as Heidegger characterizes it, with the greatest restraint, indeed laying claim to our responsibility by way of "the gentlest" of laws. Although *a priori*, belonging to the corporeal nature we are given at birth, this *Grundstimmung* is not an absolutely fixed form but rather a *Sein-können*, a "*Bereitschaft für die Er-eignung*," a *capability* inherent in our being, an availability in regard to embracing and taking up our appropriation, our guardianship (GA 65: 34/CP 29). As disposition, therefore, it is unsettling, a *Verrückung*—a *dis-positioning* disposition. But it is also "steadfastness" (*Inständigkeit*) in "the *enduring* and the *enactment* of the truth of being [i.e., *Inständigkeit* in the *ereignete* clearing]" (GA 65: 33–34/CP 28). This is the meaning of the most fundamental disposition in which the "facticity" (*Faktizität*) of our nature has grounded us,[25] summoning us thereby to *take over* this grounding and continue redeeming its fulfillment. And it is in this way that the dis-position functions as restraint, as *Verhaltenheit*, "the strongest and at the same time most delicate preparedness of *Dasein* for the appropriation, for being thrown into a genuine standing within the truth of the turning in the event [i.e., within the truth of being]" (GA 65: 34/CP 29).

In *Being and Time*, facticity is already understood in terms of the thrown-open character of *Da-sein*. But it would not be long before Heidegger would think the facticity constitutive of *Da-sein*'s thrown openness as its most fundamental disposition, one that, in the grounding facticity of an *Er-eignung*, *appropriates Da-sein* to be the clearing, dispersed in its intentionality throughout the experiential field of meaning, dislodged in that way from ever having any fixed and firm position:

> The concept of facticity concerns the being-in-the-world of an entity "within the world" in such a way that this entity can understand itself as linked in its "destiny" to the being of the entities that it encounters within its own world. . . . With the facticity of *Dasein*, its being-in-the-world has in each case already [*je schon*] dispersed itself, or even split itself [*zerstreut oder gar zersplittert*], into particular ways [*in bestimmte Weisen*] of being-in-the-world." (GA 2: 75–76/BT 82–83)

This is *Dasein*'s most fundamental disposition, a dispositional structure that dis-positions it, grounds and appropriates it existentially to be, and be in, the clearing of its world in thrown openness. But that *existential* appropriation, as a structure, still needs to be, still calls for, being appropriated personally, propriated, grounded personally. That personal appropriation, taking up and enacting the disposition *existentielly*, is a *process*, a sequence of steps, engaging us in further grounding.

So, to answer a question that Richard Polt once asked me: What would completion, or rather continuation, of the grounding in our enactment of the *Ereignung* mean, or involve? I would answer this briefly by saying that it would mean, or involve, living a life in which some of the history-making possibilities implicit in our dis-position, our thrown openness, our being-a-clearing, are *manifestly* actualized. Living one's life, moreover, in a way that *makes manifest* the fact that grounding means one's life becomes hermeneutical, hence recollective as well as forward looking, retrieving what has already been granted—our "nature," our "essence"— for propriation, on-going living forward: *Zu-sein*. That also means that, in our thrown openness, we are grounded—situated—in a world of *interactive relationality*, such that, in enowning the *Bezug* connecting *Mensch* and *Sein*, the belonging togetherness in this *Bezug* is recognized and understood. And this means that we recognize and understand our role, our responsibility (response ability) in relation to being (i.e., in relation to the that-it-is, the what-it-is, and the how-it-is).

Thus, we can see that, and how, these two ways of thinking about appropriation, namely (i) as event and (ii) as appropriation, a dispositional structure in process, which some scholars believe to be in conflict, mutually exclusive, need instead to be, and indeed must be, bought into reciprocal support and reconciliation. Understood not only as an extremely significant ontological event but also as our *Grundstimmung*, appropriation, the disposition most fundamental in the structuring of *Da-sein*, a dis-positioning taking hold of us and throwing us open, is indeed a fateful, though not at all fated *Geschick*—the bestowing of an appropriated and appropriating disposition. But everything hangs on whether, and if so how, the appropriating, dis-positioning claim constitutive of our most fundamental disposition is retrieved and undergoes propriation, a process of enownment, actualizing its potential.

As the texts in his *Contributions to Philosophy* make unequivocally clear, it is crucial at least for Heidegger's philosophy of history that we think of this appropriation in terms that involve the idea of a *Geschick*—a *Geschick* in two senses: (i) as what we are *given* (*geschickt*) to appropriate and develop, namely the fundamental, dis-positioning disposition constitutive of, and appropriating, our *Wesen*, our endowed essential nature, as human beings, and (ii) the possible *destiny* (*Geschick*) that could be granted us—could be ours—insofar as we recognize, enown, enact, and develop the potential— the *Zu-sein*—given in that appropriating disposition. Of course, this destiny is given as a possibility only insofar as the process of appropriation engages the entire world.

†

In *Zum Ereignis-Denken*, thinking toward the *Ereignis*, Heidegger connects this key word, *Ereignis*, referring to our appropriation, and *Gedächtnis*, referring to our retrieving in memory: "The human being becomes *authentically* historical [*geschichtlich*] in the kind of remembering [*das Gedächtnis*] that happens in the event of appropriation": "Appropriation is the authentic form of remembering" (*Ereignis ist das eigentliche Gedächtnis*) (GA 73.1: 743 and 745). Why? What does he mean? I suggest that we begin with an interpretation of *Ge-dächtnis* as retrieving and gathering into mindfulness. What we need to understand is that this appropriation, this claim on us, this summons to propriation borne by our embodiment, has been, like a prelapsarian memory, "forgotten," and accordingly requires our going deeply into our ownmost, most truly essential nature, in order to get in touch with it, awaken it, and retrieve its *Aufgabe*, its given task. And because our condition of thrownness throws us into togetherness with the beings that belong in our world, we need to retrieve the *pathos* in our pre-conceptual, pre-ontological understanding of being—an understanding that we are given at birth and that our experiential bodies always still remember, even though "we" have forgotten and forsaken it in the course of leaving infancy and adapting to the exigencies of everyday ontic life. Recollecting this pre-ontological understanding of being is extremely important, because it connects us with the being of beings—the being of entities—at a level where *pathos*, our bodily felt sense of *Zusammengehörigkeit*, our belonging-together, reigns. *Gedächtnis* therefore "shelters" (*hütet*) our essential nature, the law of our appropriation: it is our *Hütte*. And it is out of this *Wohnung*, this dwelling, that ethical life develops (GA 73.1: 743–45). So I would rather express Heidegger's point this way: appropriation *requires* authentic recollection. Unfortunately, however, what Heidegger neglects here is the sheltering role of our embodiment. If our bodily nature did not *carry* the claim of appropriation as fundamental law of its disposition, there would be nothing for memory to shelter and retrieve.

In most other texts, Heidegger seems to prefer *Erinnerung* as the word for remembering and recollecting, with its emphasis on going *into* oneself, entering into a certain inwardness: namely, the inwardness, or *Er-innerung*, of our essence. In "Recollection in Metaphysics" (1941), Heidegger tells us that "recollection [*Erinnerung*] of the history of being in metaphysics" makes a "claim" (*Anspruch*) that calls for its appropriation: it "requires the courage [*Mut*]," he says, "for a response to the claim." And then he comments, bringing philosophical reflection on the history of being in the discourse of metaphysics down into personal experience:

> Recollection of the history of being entrusts historical humanity [*mutet dem geschichtlichen Menschentum zu*] with the task of becoming aware [*dessen inne zu werden*] that the essence of man is released [*eingelassen*] to the truth of being *before* any human dependency on powers and forces, predestinations and tasks. (GA 6.2: 482/EP 76)

This recollection is needed both (i) to retrieve our pre-reflective, pre-conceptual, pre-ontological relation to being, a relation sheltered in the nature of our most fundamental disposition, and (ii) to retrieve still available possibilities for heritage and destiny. I interpret this passage as calling for a personal, *existentiell* awareness and recollective retrieval of our *essence* as human beings—the "existenti*al* structure of human being in connection with being" (*die Fügung des Menschenwesens in den Bezug zum Sein*) that is always already operative structurally, hence *a priori*—in a historically defined sense of the *a priori* that recognizes its distinctive temporality and embodiment (GA 6. 2: 485/EP 78–79). And I take this awareness to be responsive to the claim constitutive of our fundamental, essential dis-position that being—that is, all that in any way *is*—holds us to in the experience of appropriation, namely, grounding the "truth of being," grounding the clearing, in all our interactions with worldly beings (GA 6. 2: 489/EP 82).[26]

My interpretation of Heidegger's invocations of memory in relation to our appropriation recognizes it as akin to, but also very different from, Plato's *anamnesis*. I suggest that, in the word *Er-innerung*, Heidegger hears a personal, *existentiell* movement of going *inward*, which is to say, going into oneself, to recognize oneself, enown oneself, and understand oneself. In brief, this remembering of what we have "forgotten," or rather, lost contact with, namely our ownmost nature or essence, is precisely the movement of propriation he calls "*Einkehr in das Ereignis.*" It is entering into a process in which we discover and learn about ourselves—ourselves in our belonging-together with being, that-which-is. In this *Einkehr*, we (i) enter into the event (*Ereignis*) in which we encounter the being of beings; and, in so doing, we (ii) enter into the nature of our experience, in order to appropriate ourselves, understanding and enowning our role and responsibility in this encounter. This second phase involves the *process* of entering into the *structure* of our appropriation (*Ereignis* in this other sense) and continuing its achievement in a process inseparable from the world in which we find ourselves. As Heidegger says, "The *Ereignis* [i.e., the event in which we encounter beings and become aware of experiencing their being] grants [*verleiht*] to mortals a return to sojourn [*Aufenthalt*] in their essential nature." And, drawing on the etymological connection between *Er-eignis* and *Er-äugen*, he explains: "*Das Ereignis ereignet in seinem Er-äugen des Menschenwesens die Sterblichen*": "In beholding human nature, appropriation makes mortals appropriate" (GA 12: 248–49/OWL 128–29). We are appropriated, claimed, called upon, to enter into the structure of our disposition and undertake a process of propriation, leading us into a life more appropriate to the character of our mortal nature, building on the earth, standing under the sky.

†

Now, as Heidegger told us in the Introduction to *Being and Time*, as his project involves understanding what, or who, we *already* are without knowing it, gaining an ontological understanding of ourselves requires entering *a hermeneutical circle* and retrieving a *pre-ontological* understanding of being—a pre-conceptual understanding, or experience—a kind of "anticipatory grasp," as the philosopher says—that we always inherently already possess, but with which, as we enter and become increasingly integrated into the life of the everyday ontic world we share with others, we lose contact, lapsing into "forgetfulness of being." (GA 65: 318/ CP 251).[27] Likewise, by nature, we are, each of us, *given* a fundamental dis-position, grounding us in a preliminary way in *Da-sein*. This *Da-sein* is the endowment of a bodily carried dis-position that claims and disposes us *a priori*, throwing us—*vorausgeschickt*—outside ourselves into the open-endedness of a destiny (*Geschick*) in the world. In its appropriation, *Da-sein* is, as essence, as *a priori*, disposed, *vorausgeschickt*; but, as Heidegger argues, this appropriation can go—and mostly does go—unrecognized, unacknowledged, a potential grounding that remains undeveloped or poorly developed.

But insofar as, on our own, we do not (sufficiently) experience and recognize ourselves as *Da-sein*, and consequently do not fully enown and enact this grounding of our existence in, and as, being-a-world-clearing, with all the responsibilities this entails, Heidegger argues that we need to heed the claim of appropriation and its summons and *enter* accordingly into the appropriation by way of a *hermeneutical retrieval* of this appropriation. We need to enter a hermeneutical circle in order to *continue* the grounding. This is the assumption (*Übernahme*) of a task that can never really be completed; and in fact, it is always vulnerable, precarious, and at any moment it can be brought into question, unsettled, even forgotten and lost. What was gained can always be lost. But unless we enter into a process of recollection, we will not be in touch with any sense of our historical existence—that historical opportunity which has been *vorausgeschickt* in virtue of the appropriation of our bodily dis-position in *Da-sein*. Destiny (*Geschick*) depends on our retrieving the historical meaning of our appropriation in a process of recollection: *Ereignung* in *Er-innerung*.

The *Ereignung* calls us to enter into a hermeneutic circle in this sense: We are always already grounded and appropriated, that is, claimed for, and summoned to, an authentic, enowned and fitting relation to being, but also, we are not yet *fully* appropriated, not yet *properly* grounded. Consequently, we need to "circle back" (or "step back") in a phenomenological process involving a certain *Er-innerung*, in order to retrieve and enown that relation of response-ability in the way we actually live our lives.

†

In explaining our appropriated but unrecognized nature, Heidegger's words suggest two early Greek adumbrations of the *Ereignen*: Parmenides' argument that mind (*nous, noein*) and being are "the same" and Heraclitus's argument urging us to learn the wisdom in gestures that correspond, in the *homologein*, to the law operating in the gathering layout of being—the *Legein* of the *Logos*. Thousands of years had to pass, though, before the appropriation they adumbrated could be recognized. And, as befits a thinking that is on the way to an originary experience, Heidegger's text, "The Way to Language," suggests a poetic characterization of this appropriation—one that supports my proposed interpretation of the claim of appropriation as constitutive of our most fundamental disposition:

> Appropriation grants to mortals their abode within their nature [*Das Ereignis verleiht den Sterblichen den Aufenthalt in ihrem Wesen*] . . . If we understand "law" as the gathering that lays down that which causes all beings to be present in their own, in what is appropriate for them, then appropriation is the plainest and gentlest of all laws [*dann ist das Ereignis das schlichteste und sanfteste aller Gesetze*, even more gentle than what Adalbert Stifter saw as the "gentle law." Appropriation, though, is not law in the sense of a norm that hangs over our heads somewhere; it is not an ordinance that orders and regulates a course of events: Appropriation is *the* law because it gathers mortals into the appropriateness of their nature and holds them there [*in das Ereignen zu ihrem Wesen versammelt und darin hält*]. (GA 12: 248–49/OWL 128–29)

This text, which it seems scholars have heretofore neglected to consider in thinking about appropriation, provides crucial and indeed decisive support for the interpretation I am proposing. As this law, appropriation is, I suggest, a disposition that "gently" lays claim *a priori* to our nature, a dis-position borne by us as embodied creatures and summoning us back to ourselves from our forgetfulness of being and our lostness in the world. Appropriation is a "gentle" law because it is not imposed from outside ourselves, but rather belongs to, comes from, and simply *is*, the dis-position of our ownmost nature: it is the law, borne by our embodiment, that "gathers mortals into the appropriateness [*das Ereignen*] of their nature and holds them there" (GA 12: 248/OWL 128). It is also "the nearest of the near," because it is constitutive of our very essence, our given bodily nature; but it is "the farthest of the far," because in today's world, it is neither widely recognized nor widely understood—and consequently not protected and maintained. Its summons to *Erinnerung* persists, though, even through our "forgetfulness," our *Seinsvergessenheit*.

†

Before we move on, I think it might be helpful to recapitulate very briefly at this point the principal elements in this exposition of Heidegger's key word. First, the three designations of *Ereignis* as appropriating *event*: (i) referring to the history-making event that set in motion the inception of Greek metaphysics, (ii) referring to the history-breaking and history-making event that might someday possibly set in motion another inception, and (iii) referring to an event that, like an epiphany, could happen at any time anywhere, in which, through an encounter with something in the world, the *being* of beings comes to light in our understanding. And second, taking advantage of the three different senses, or ways of using and meaning the English word "appropriate," we can articulate the three moments or phases of the *Ereignis*—or *Ereignung*—as *structured process* of appropriation. Heidegger's argument, through and through phenomenological, is that we human beings are appropriated (ver-*ereignet*) in three moments or phases: (i) in the first moment or phase, we are appropriated$_1$, that is, called upon, summoned, claimed, challenged, and engaged, (a) by an event in the world that is given ontological significance, and also, at the same time, (b) by our own disposition, a disposition structuring our embodied nature and bestirred, set in motion, by its exposure to that event; (ii) in the second moment or phase, we are appropriated (in sense one) to appropriate$_2$ (in the second sense), that is, take up, take over, and enown, this claim, this first-phase appropriation; and (iii) in the third moment or phase, we enter into appropriation$_3$, a project of *propriation, or enownment*, a *Sich-selbst-Haben* (a third sense of "appropriation"), becoming who we truly already are. Appropriation$_3$ is propriation, coming to one's *proprium*, one's ownmost nature. Such is our *Befindlichkeit*, how we find ourselves appropriated in our situatedness. And because we are, each one of us, called, appropriated, to become *Da-sein*, who we truly are is in large measure determined by the character of the way in which we take the things of the world, hence also the clearing itself, the very openness of the world, into our care. In this way, we are ultimately appropriated by no other "source" than the dis-position constitutive of our own, ownmost, innermost, deepest selves. This last point is of the greatest importance. As claim of appropriation, the *Ereignis* (*Ereignen*) is ultimately not something other than *Da-sein* itself. Although it will undoubtedly be aroused and stirred by something experienced in our interactions with the world, something that makes us ponder the meaning of being and stirs us to question our own being, it *originates* in our *experience* of the *Mensch-Sein* interaction that the dis-position of *Da-sein* structures: it is one's own *proprium*, one's own *Existenz* that is calling each of us—as Pindar, whom Heidegger quotes, so paradoxically said—to become what we already are.

Thus, borrowing a phrase from Samuel Beckett's essay on Proust, I suggest that entering the *Ereignis* begins "the transformation of a creature of surface into a creature of depth."[28]

†

Perhaps the sharpest, most unequivocal formulation of this understanding of *Ereignis* is to be found in a textual passage that we considered in the context of the chapter on being—and that we had reason to consider again, but from a different angle, in the context of the chapter on *Da-sein*:

> *Das Dasein* is the ever-individuated "it" [*das je vereinzelte "es"*] that gives [*das gibt*], that makes possible and *is* the t/here is [*das "es gibt,"* the that-there-is]. (*Zum Ereignis-Denken*, GA 73.1: 642)

This "individuation" is precisely *Dasein*'s enowning and enacting its appropriation—the phenomenology of its appropriation to a response-ability that makes the meaningful presencing of things possible. The human being is always already *verereignet*, always already bodily claimed, appropriated, and dis-positioned—called to take into our care the world we share with other beings, while also living, each one of us, in worlds of our own making. This, our *Sich-selbst-Haben*, is also what Heidegger calls our waking up to enter and stay in our appropriation: "*das Entwachen in das Einkehr in den Aufenthalt im Ereignis*" (GA 14: 63/OTB 53).[29]

This *event* of awakening from our ontological slumber to take over our appropriation, responding to the claim on our responsibility to which our disposition, our appropriation, ceaselessly summons us in a calling prompted and mediated by ontologically challenging *events* in the world, events perhaps destroying our heretofore secure sense of being, can happen at any time anywhere; and it could, in principle, be the personal experience of any human being—and indeed every human being. But this *Einkehr in das Ereignis*, the serious appropriation of such an experience, taking it up for further thoughtful engagement, requires a *process* that necessitates, in each instance, a personal *existentiell* commitment; it can only ever be a *freely undertaken* return, in self-reflection and self-recognition, to the appropriating dis-position that constitutes our essence as *Da-sein*.

Hence, recalling the *first* context for thinking of *Ereignis* as designating an *event*, namely, the experience of wonder that there is a cosmos instead of nothingness, and the *second* context, namely, the history-making inception of metaphysics emerging from that experience, we come to the *third* context for thinking of *Ereignis* as designating an event: (iii) the history-breaking, history-creating *event* that is merely a visionary possibility for some future time—the promise of an authentic destiny (*Geschick*) in the founding of a new world order, a new time–space: an inception, essentially expressed, in the *Contributions to Philosophy* (1936–1938), in the mood of the future subjunctive. Later, Heidegger will evoke this visionary possibility through the idea of the fourfold, gathering of earth and sky, mortals and gods.

It is doubtful, however, that such an *Einkehr* could ever be worldwide, or that even all the individuals of an entire nation or culture could ever enter more than occasionally into their existential dis-position, their essence as always-already-having-been-appropriated. Indeed, it is even doubtful, considering the nature of this dis-position and what it would require of historical conditions, that even one individual could ever *permanently* achieve this possibility; and it is also unlikely that, to transform an entire culture or nation, or the entire world, enough individuals could enter into their appropriation and thereby achieve the completion of its grounding. Such skepticism and pessimism can be unnecessarily self-defeating. But perhaps it could only be for us moderns, enduring a time of the most extreme ontological destitution, to undergo such dark reflexive moments, if it is true that, as Hölderlin observed, where there is the greatest danger, the greatest emergency, there is where the "saving power" also grows.

†

Thinking about the limits confronting appropriation as a history-making process, I suggest that it would have been much less confusing and misleading if Heidegger had consistently favored using the word *Er-eignung*, instead of *Ereignis*, to name what he wants to think of as appropriation, inasmuch as the first word intrinsically suggests, as the second word does not, something ongoing, never completed, and not belonging to the temporal succession of datable events: something, moreover, that, once we become aware of it, reveals itself as *to have been* always already operative—according to the phenomenology of all dispositions—and yet also always incomplete, never fully achieved, hence an ongoing process. That is to say, what he has in mind fits the logic, or grammar, of a *disposition-in-process* much better than it does the logic, or grammar, of *event*. Heidegger does sometimes speak of the *Er-eignung*, as when he invokes "*die Über-nahme der Er-eignung*"—but this word is not preferred with any consistency (GA 65: 322/CP 254). He also sometimes characterizes this appropriation using the words *An-eignung* (dedication, assignment, adoption) and *Zu-eignung* (arrogation, claim). Like *Er-eignung*, both of these words serve to define the concerns of the project far better than *Er-eignis*—and for the same reason. But in the context of Heidegger's philosophy of history, wherein it is a question of destiny, it is necessary, and makes sense, to think of *Ereignis* as an event. That is the word's principal service. However, instead of suggesting an *event* belonging to a moment of limited duration in time, Heidegger's words, cited above in his text on language (GA 12: 248–49/OWL 128–29) suggest the continuing of a *disposition*, a potential to be actualized, a potential extending over time, ongoingly dis-posing, summoning, calling, claiming, assigning, engaging, and committing: a process.

However, for the sake of illuminating the *event* that set in motion the beginning of metaphysics in the Western world and in contemplating the possibility of "another beginning," it is understandable that Heidegger retained the word *Ereignis*, with its sense of the historically eventful. He needed it to work in this way.

In fact, though, each and every experience, each and every encounter, each and every interaction, between human being and thing (*Seiendes*) qualifies as a phenomenological *event*—an *Ereignis*, moreover, that, whether recognized or not, bears a claim of appropriation—hence an *Ereignis* in this other sense. So what I think Heidegger needs to argue in this regard is that *every* event, relational, interactive, in which we encounter beings is *always* intrinsically an *event of appropriation*, always also an *Ereignis* in this other sense: always an *event* in and by which the inherent *dis-position* of the human being is solicited, summoned, called forth, and claimed—challenged to be and to enown the *Da* of, and for, world-openness; solicited to take appropriate responsibility for the fundamental phenomenology of that encounter. In other words: in every *event* of encounter, a *Da-sein*-appropriating response ability and *process* is summoned into emergence, awareness, and steadfast enactment. Whether recognized or not, this appropriation (as claim and process) is *inherent* in the very structure—the structuring phenomenology—of every perceptual event. That is what, in "The Principle of Identity," Heidegger's emphasis on the dynamic structure he exhibits as the belonging-together of *Mensch* and *Sein*, is implying.

This interpretation, I think, further brings out the conceptual logic of the *connection* between the term *Ereignis* as signifying an event and the term *Ereignis* (or, better, *Er-eignung*) as signifying *Dasein*'s appropriation, the claim and process inherent in the disposition always already operative, but needing to be recognized, "awakened" (*erwachen*) in, and by, every encounter between *Menschsein* and *Sein* (GA 14: 37–38, 63/OTB 30, 53).

We can see some of the complexity in this logic in a statement that Heidegger makes in his 1943 text "Aletheia (Heraklit, Fragment 16), in which he says: "*Das Ereignis der Lichtung ist die Welt*" (GA 7: 283/EGT 118). This can mean (i) that the *event, or happening* of the clearing is (what opens) a world of meaning, but it can also mean (ii) that the *appropriation* of the clearing, hence the appropriated clearing (i.e., the appropriation of *Dasein* to *be* the clearing, hence the claim on *Dasein* to become the clearing more vigilantly, more mindfully) is the opening of the intelligibility conditions for a world of meaningfulness. I think it means both. But we need to make this observation more perspicuous phenomenologically: *behind* the event, the taking place, of the clearing is the appropriation, a claim, embodied in the very structure of the dis-position of *Da-sein*, that appropriates it to *be* the clearing.

†

I have argued that we are *bodily appropriated* to our propriation, appropriated to appropriate and live up to—or say measure up to—the potential constitutive of the essence appropriate to our being human: *daseinsmäßig*. Do I now still need to add in emphatic terms that the dis-position that is the *embodiment* of this claim of appropriation must be understood in a way that constitutes the most radical departure from the mind–body dualism that has reigned not only in Cartesian metaphysics but also in various forms of empiricism? I suggest that the understanding of embodiment that Heidegger's concept of *Ereignis* calls for emerges with singular vividness in the phenomenology of some of Merleau-Ponty's late writings, writings strongly influenced, in fact, by his renewed reading of Heidegger's *Being and Time* and perhaps by his acquaintance with some other texts as well: writings in which the French philosopher subjects to challenge his earlier *Phenomenology of Perception*, noticing its vestiges of Cartesianism; writings in which he also takes over Heidegger's phenomenology for further development according to the exigencies of a capacity in perception that, in Heidegger's work, is for the first time radically opened up, both temporally and spatially in ways that I believe Merleau-Ponty did not recognize until that renewed reading late in his life.

†

The *Ereignis* forms in the embodiment of a disposition that calls for "poetizing," bringing forth authentic ex-istence in the founding (*Stiften*) of a locale (*Ortschaft*) for historical existence: a locale, in fact, where humans might "dwell poetically [*dichterisch*] upon the earth" (GA 7: 187–204/213–29). As Heidegger expressed this matter in 1936, writing about Hölderlin's poetic vocation: the *Ereignis* (*Ereignung*), understood as appropriating our existence "disposes over the highest possibility of being human" (GA 4: 38/ HP 56). A thought expressed in "The Question Concerning Technology" nicely connects this appropriation to learning a different way of seeing and hearing. The *Ereignis* (*Ereignung*) bestows and assigns this highest possibility first of all to our bodily nature—and that means it inscribes this assignment, this appropriation, in the dis-position of our perceptual abilities and responsibilities. But the claim needs, first of all, to be recognized and understood; and there is much in what we are "given," or "sent," in that embodiment that we need to recognize and learn:

> Wherever the human being opens his eyes and ears, unlocks his heart, and freely gives himself to meditating and striving, shaping and working, entreating and thanking, he finds himself already brought into the unconcealed. [*Wo immer der Mensch sein Auge und Ohr öffnet, sein Herz aufschließt, sich in das Sinnen und Trachten, Bilden und Werken, Bitten und Danken freigibt, findet er sich überall schon ins Unverborgene gebracht*]. The unconcealment of the latter has already happened [*hat sich schon ereignet*] whenever it calls the human being forth into the modes of revealing allotted to him. When the human being, in his way, from within unconcealment, reveals that which presences, he is only responding to the call of unconcealment, even when he contradicts it. (GA 7: 19/ QCT 18)

Notice, please, the attention Heidegger bestows on the appropriation of our response ability with regard to seeing and hearing. As process of unconcealment, stretching us open, the *Ereignis* is the dis-position of an appropriation (*Er-eignung*) that precedes and exceeds even our greatest capabilities. Hence Heidegger's task: a work that begins in reminding, retrieving in thought the most fundamental dimension of ourselves and attempting to bring us back, really for the first time, to ourselves—ourselves, that is, as *Da-sein* (GA 65: 33–35/CP 28–30). The *Ereignung* is a propriation that can bring us to a deeply satisfying "homecoming," as we return to dwell in our truest nature (GA 9: 337–38/PM 257).

†

In my interpretation, I accordingly try to stay close to what makes sense in phenomenological terms—the terms, namely, of our embodied experience. And in the context of this present project, that means interpreting matters in reference to the phenomenology of perception—as far as possible from the temptations of a metaphysics that, in Heidegger's view, can only lead us further into the emergency that threatens us in nihilism.

The appropriation operative in dis-posing us as *Da-sein* is what, to use Heidegger's own words, "makes possible the openness, the clearing [*er-gibt das Freie der Lichtung*], within which meaningful things—entities— can come securely into their truth [*anwähren*]" (GA 12: 247/OWL 127). However, "the truth of being," being itself, understood as *aletheia*, the field cleared and free for the interplay of concealment and unconcealment, becomes visible and audible only in the more poetizing moments of perception, a contemplative, acquiescent perception able to appreciate, in its eventfulness, the opening up of a world, bringing it forth out of concealment, and letting what is not now present, or not yet present, arrive for its time of disclosure.

Thought in terms of how the early Greek philosophers understood perception, the perception that we are taking to be addressing and claiming us is not only *aletheia*; it is also *physis* (the ever-emerging energies of nature), *moira* (fateful assigment, appropriate allottment), and *logos* (articulation). In perception, the *logos*—the meaning of being itself—is manifest in the gathering *layout* (*legein*) of a spatio temporal field: perception takes place (*sich ereignet*) in, and as, that *legein*. And, for the Greek philosophers, there was the greatest imaginable beauty in the experience of the truth of being. Their extant words attest to this beauty.

†

In Heidegger's reading of Parmenides, the saying that cognition (*noein*) and being are "the same" represents a very early intuition, perhaps the very first, of our ontological appropriation and its attendant responsibility.

This ontological responsibility, looking after being, emerges into the light when, following Heidegger's philological work, we discern the *eigen* and *eignen* in the word *Ereignis*: these words refer to what is one's own, what is ownmost. In the context of Heidegger's project, the word *Er-eignis* draws its meaning not only from *eignen/an-eignen* and from *eigen* (what is properly one's own) but also from *er-äugen,* (to place before the eyes, hence to show) (GA 14: 33–64/OTB 25–54).[30] When we "enter into the *Ereignis*," our life is brought, so to speak, before our own eyes: it is our very own nature—not some metaphysical agency or force—that appropriates us for the task of enownment. I interpret Heidegger's attention to this derivation of *er-eignen* from *er-äugen* to suggest also that seeing—and one might say perception—always involves our appropriation; and that means that what we see and hear always bespeaks a certain *claim* (*Anspruch*) on our seeing and hearing: a certain responsibility for our ability to be appropriately—ontologically—receptive and responsive.

Heidegger draws on this conjunction of meanings to make his "*Rückgang von Anwesen zum Ereignen*"—his return in thought from meaningful presencing back to the phenomenological conditions that make such presencing possible, namely, the appropriation of our existence to *Da-sein* (GA 14: 53–55/OTB 44–45).

In this phenomenology, there are—as in Husserl's version of the "reductions" that take us back from everyday experience (the "natural attitude") into phenomenology and then into his transcendental egology—certain "steps back," but returning, for Heidegger, is, by way of stages (*Stationen auf einem Rückgang*), into the *Ereignung*, our most fundamental disposition, not into a transcendental egology. This disposition is a dimension of our experience that is ordinarily hidden from us, though we cannot escape its dis-positioning, its throwing us open, its intrinsic ex-posure of our lives to what exceeds our present understanding, our present concepts, the sense of being we have taken for granted without recognizing the granting itself and as such (GA 12: 249n/OWL 129n).

That recognition matters, though, as Heidegger says in his commentary on Heraclitus, because it affects the quality of our mindfulness—and the character of our perception—as we go about our daily life:

> Mortals are irrevocably bound to the revealing-concealing gathering which lights everything present in its presencing. But they turn from the clearing, and turn only toward what is present, which is what immediately concerns them in their everyday commerce with each other. (GA 7: 287/EGT 122)

Heidegger's words here immediately translate into a summons to experience perception—seeing and hearing—differently, not in the way we habitually do.[31] His words also implicitly critique the entire history of Western metaphysics from Plato on.

†

To think further about this, I want to return one more time to Heidegger's discussion of *Ereignis* as appropriation in "The Principle of Identity." The discussion gets underway when, noting Parmenides' saying that *einai* (being) and *noein* (the human mind) are "the same," Heidegger argues that this "sameness" must not be confused with logical identity:

> *Er-eignis* is the realm of a vibrantly interactive reciprocity, a back-and-forth co-responding [*der in sich schwingende Bereich*], through which both human and being attain, through one another, their proper nature, each achieving its ownmost truth, its ownmost essence [*ihr Wesendes gewinnen*], by giving up those properties, those determinations, that metaphysics had attributed to them. (GA 11:46/ID 37)[32]

Now, according to Heidegger, because we human beings exist as inherently ek-static, by the very nature of our embodiment thrown open into the shared world, we are always already appropriated (*ereignet*), disposed, to be, each one of us, a clearing in that world, encountering other beings within our place, our sojourn (*Aufenthalt*), in that clearing. We are influenced and affected by what we see and hear. But, by the same token, *what* we see and hear is influenced, and may be determined by, the *way* we are seeing and hearing. The direction of the influence can be *reversed*, so that there can be a continuing back-and-forth. (Merleau-Ponty describes this reversibility in *The Visible and the Invisible*.)

Observing the organic unity of this dynamic interaction, *Mensch* and *Sein*, *nous* and *being*, Parmenides thinks of "sameness"—a "sameness" that is *outside* the law of identity. Heidegger recognizes and understands this interaction; however, what concerns him is something happening in the realm of the interaction that Parmenides could not see, namely, our appropriation. In existing, our being is always in question. And if we are responsible for who we are, and who we are is determined by our appropriation to be most properly the clearing, then that appropriation lays claim to our responsibility for the character of the ontological field of openness. Our responsibility for who we are cannot be separated from our responsibility in regard to the appropriated clearing: "The grounding of *Da-sein* transforms every relation to beings, and for the first time the truth of beyng [i.e., the clearing as field for the interplay of concealment and unconcealment] can be experienced" (GA 65: 322/CP 255).

Let us continue reading this brief but beautifully illuminating text. "When we understand mental activity to be the distinctive characteristic of man," he says, "we remind ourselves of a *belonging together* [*Zusammengehören*] that concerns man and being [*Mensch und Sein*]. Immediately [*Im Nu*], we find ourselves grappling with questions: What does "being" mean? Who, or what, is man? Everyone can see easily that . . . we lack the foundation [*der Boden*] for determining anything reliable about the *belonging together* [*Zusammengehören*] of man and being. But as long as we ask the question in this way, we are confined [*gebannt*] within the attempt to represent the 'togetherness' [*das Zusammen*] of man and being as a coordination [*Zuordnung*], and to establish and explain this coordination either in terms of man or in terms of being" (GA 11: 38–39/ID 30).

"How would it be," he asks, "if, instead of tenaciously representing merely a coordination [*Zusammenordnung*] of the two in order to produce their unity, we were for once to note whether and how a belonging to one another first of all is at stake in this 'together' [*ob und wie in diesem Zusammen vor allem ein Zu-einander-Gehören im Spiel ist*]?" This question, going beyond Husserl, stirs Heidegger to speculate about the possibility "that we might even catch sight [*erblicken*] of the belonging together of man and being, if only from afar, as already implicit, [hidden] in the traditional definitions of their essence" (GA 11: 39/ID 30–31). In other words, Heidegger is asking us to *retrieve* a sense of the prereflective, pre-conceptual belonging-together-in-unity that *underlies and precedes* what we *represent* today in metaphysical terms as a *connection* between the two: the belonging together of man and being that we have forgotten, even though, sublated, it remains operative and still to be retrieved; a connection that has become, in today's world, an opposition of subject and object. This is why Heidegger will prefer the word *Bezug*, suggesting the pull of a bonding, over *Verhältnis* in order to describe the structural "connection" in which *Mensch* and *Sein* come together. It should be noted here, however, that this belonging together in unity, though inspired by the "sameness" of mind and being that Parmenides argued for and also, I think, by Schelling, is nevertheless significantly different from the preconceptual unity of subject and object that Schelling explicates in his *System of Transcendental Idealism*. Schelling's unity is an "absolute identity" that is the metaphysical "ground of harmony between the subjective and the objective."[33] What I think Heidegger's exposition implies is rather much closer to the prepersonal, prereflective dimension in Merleau-Ponty's description of perception.

In any case, according to Heidegger, we tend not to realize in our everyday life that the question of who we are and the question of being are inseparably intertwined, and that that means that our responsibility for who we are, and who we need to become, is inseparable from our responsibility for the character of meaningful presence in "every relation to beings." That is what appropriation means in throwing us open, appropriating us to be the *Da*, the clearing.

Explaining how this might be so, Heidegger argues that, as a being, man obviously *belongs* to the realm of beings—"just like the stone, the tree, and the eagle." However,

> to belong still means here to be in the order of being [*eingeordnet in das Sein*]. But man's distinctive feature lies in this, that he, as the [only] being who can think, is open to being [*offen dem Sein*], face to face with being; thus man remains drawn to being and so answers to it [*auf das Sein bezogen bleibt und ihm so entspricht*]. Man *is* essentially [*eigentlich*] this relationship of responding to being [*dieser Bezug der Entsprechung*], and he is only this. This "only" does not mean a limitation, but rather an excess [*ein Übermaß*]. A belonging to being prevails [*waltet*] within man, a belonging [*Gehören*] that listens to being [*auf das Sein hört*] because it is appropriated to being [*weil es diesem übereignet ist*]. (GA 11: 39/ID 30–31)

Recognition of this "excess" in the *Mensch-Sein* correspondence (*Entsprech-ung*) is crucial; it means that there is never a strict logical identity between *Mensch* and *Sein*, *Mensch* and *Lichtung*: the dimensions of the clearing are not reducible to the finite reach of human intentionality, even though, as *Da-sein*, we human beings are thrown open in and by our *being-the-Da*, the opening of the clearing—and consequently must acquiesce to what exceeds our measure and nevertheless take on our ontological responsibility.

It is worth noting, in this regard, that, in his 1951 interpretation of Heraclitus's fragment B 50, Heidegger translated the key word *homologein* as *Entsprechung*. In Freeman's English translation of the Diels translation of the Greek, Heraclitus says: "When you have listened, not to me [i.e., my words, my *logoi*], but to the layout of the clearing (*Logos*) [i.e., being itself], it is wise to agree [*homologein*, i.e., to respond in correspondence] that all things are one."[34] This *homologein* concerns the relation between *Menschsein* and *Sein*, and it is urging us to listen not only to the philosopher's words but also to hearken, beyond the words, to being, their field of sounding, as that which makes possible and bespeaks the gathering of all beings in the language con-stitutive of our world. The point is that, in this singular relation, there is a belonging together (*Zugehörigkeit*) that *appropriates* us, calling us to a responsi-bility that corresponds, in the character of its responsiveness, in its hearkening, to that clearing that, as their condition of possibility, is silently resonating and echoing behind the audible and inaudible presencing of all beings.

And now, what remains to be said about being? Heidegger's medita-tion on the *Bezug* continues, illuminating the operation of the *Ereignis*, the appropriation:

> Let us think of being according to its original [phenomenological] meaning as presence [*Anwesen*]. Being is present to man [*west den Men-schen*] neither incidentally nor only on rare occasions. Being is present and abides [*west und währt*] only as it concerns man through the claim [*Anspruch*] that it makes on him. For it is man, open toward being [*offen für das Sein*], who alone lets being arrive and appear as presence [*läßt die-ses als Anwesen ankommen*]. Such becoming present [*An-wesen*] needs the openness of a clearing [*das Offene einer Lichtung*], and by this need [*dieses Brauchen*], it remains appropriated to human being [*dem Menschenwesen übereignet*]. (GA 11: 40/ID 31)

So, then:

> Man and being are appropriated to each other. They need and belong to each other. From this belonging to each other, which has not been

thought out more closely, man and being have first received those determinations of essence by which man and being are grasped metaphysically in philosophical thought. (Ibid.)

Consequently, Heidegger concludes that the only way we can begin to understand this belonging together, this two-way appropriation, would be "by moving away from the attitude of representational thinking" (GA 11: 41/ID 32):

> We stubbornly misunderstand this prevailing belonging together of man and being as long as we represent everything only in categories and mediations, be it with or without dialectic. Then we always find only [contingent and external] connections that are established either in terms of being or in terms of man, and that present the belonging together of man and being as [merely] an intertwining [*Verflechtung*]. (GA 11:40/ID 32)

What Heidegger means here, I suggest, is not to deny that the belonging together is an intertwining; rather, he should be understood to be arguing that it is *not only* an intertwining. To think of it as *merely* that is to miss the significance of the claim (*Anspruch, Aneignung*) on our responsibility, a responsibility for being, for what is, that is deeply constitutive of, and indeed intrinsic to, our *appropriation*, always already operating in the phenomenology of that intertwining. In our *Geworfenheit*, our thrownness, we are not merely thrown open; we are exposed to the claim on our ontological responsibility operative in the event of appropriation that takes place in connection with everything we encounter in the world.

I think Husserl would recognize in this belonging together a relation (*Verhältnis*) of intentionality. But Heidegger invests much more in this relation, making it a deep *Bezug*, a deep bond of belonging and appropriation, drawing *Mensch* and *Sein* together and constituting a *responsibility* for being, reminding us that *Menschsein* needs to propriate, that is, become *Da-sein*. In other words, much more is involved in the intertwining than the mere fact of the two-way, *wechselweise* phenomenological interrelation and interaction. Indeed, this appropriation draws us *beyond* the phenomenon itself into a recognition of the dimension of concealment, the inapparent that *exceeds* the reach of our resources of meaning.

Thus, Heidegger argues that, if we are ever to understand and break out of the dangerous conditions challenging and threatening our time, we need to recognize and understand, in the phenomenology of our relation to being, the nature of the appropriation to which we belong:

The *belonging*-together of man and being in the manner of mutual challenge [*wechselseitigen Herausforderung*] drives home to us with startling force that and how man is delivered over [*vereignet*] to the claim of being [i.e., delivered over to a singular responsibility for being] and how the way that being presences fits, or is appropriate to [*zugeeignet*], the essential nature of man. . . . We must experience this claim, this enowning [*Es gilt, dieses Eignen . . . zu erfahren*] in which man and being are delivered over to each other [*einander ge-eignet sind*]. That is, we must enter into what we call *the experience of appropriation*. . . . The term [*Ereignis*] no longer means what we would otherwise call a happening, an occurrence, an event. (GA 11: 45/ID 36)

Next, he points out a connection with vision that is certainly noteworthy: "The word *Ereignis* has been taken from ordinary speech. *Er-eignen* originally meant *er-äugen*, that is, look, see [*blicken*], catch sight of [*im Blicken zu sich rufen*], acquire, or lay claim to [*an-eignen*]" (Ibid.). In Heidegger's project, however, the word is being used, as he says, "as a *singulare tantum*" (ibid.). This semantic affiliation between *ereignen* and *eräugen* is not a merely quaint philological curiosity. It bears special significance in the context of Heidegger's project, because this project is indeed visionary: it envisions a profound transformation in the way we human beings experience ourselves and relate to the world—relate to the being of all the beings that figure in our world. But its envisioning is merely a glimpse, catching hints, signs, indications.

†

The phenomenological connection—the belonging together of *Menschsein* and *Sein*—that "The Principle of Identity" explicates in regard to the enactment of the *Ereignis* does not, however, get at the full significance of the phenomenology of the *Ereignis* brought to light in Heidegger's project. More is at stake than our relation to being.

Also at stake in the appropriation is, as I have argued, the question of our relation to ourselves: *our self-recognition and self-understanding* with regard to the very essence of our existence as human beings, namely, *our thrown openness*. What Heidegger wants to get at, thinking "the transcendental" in a radically new way, is our appropriation and arrogation (*Ereignung* and *Zueignung*) to *Da-sein*—what has been described in the summary of the seminar on Heidegger's lecture "Time and Being" as

the realm of projection for the determination of being [*der Entwurfbereich für die Bestimmung des Seins*], that is, of *presencing as such* [*des Anwesens als eines solchen*], caught sight of [i.e., becoming visible] from the opening-up of human being in its *Da-sein* [*aus der Lichtung des Da-seins*, i.e., from the standpoint of *Menschsein* as *Da-sein*, opening up a clearing for presencing]. (GA 14: 35/OTB 27)

The claim (*Aneignung*) on our ontological responsibility that is always already operative in the belonging together of *Menschsein* and *Sein* requires our self-recognition and self-understanding, steadfastness in taking on *Da-sein*'s role in the clearing. So Heidegger argues for that self-knowledge in "The Principle of Identity."

Appropriation is always already operative—both in presencing (*Anwesen*) and in the letting-presence (*das Anwesen-lassen*): operative no matter what it is that the historical conditions Heidegger calls *das Geschick* (*destiny*) might happen to "give" and "send" (GA 14: 25–27/OTB 20–21). Thus, as he says, always resorting to metaphors that can be very misleading: "The gift [or, more simply and neutrally, the *fact*] of presence is the property of the appropriation": "*Die Gabe von Anwesen ist Eigentum des Ereignens*" (GA 14: 27/OTB 22). In less metaphorical words, reflectively experiencing our appropriation to the clearing in self-recognition and self-knowledge makes the experience of presencing richer and more meaningful. It also makes us appreciate the importance of protecting and preserving it.

However, Heidegger's predilection for referring to perception as gift should not be construed to suggest that there is a powerful and benevolent being who bestows gifts. The giving of the given and the givenness of the given belong entirely within the world of perception. However, Heidegger's use of the word *Gabe* is his way of urging us to be mindful— *eingedenk*—in our experiencing. He asks: "Who are we?" This is a question about the human being. Here he articulates what the perceptual situation, namely the belonging-together of *Mensch* and *Sein*, means:

> Man, who is concerned with and approached by presence, who, through being approached, is himself present in his own way for all present and absent beings. . . . Man, standing within the approach of presence, but in such a way that he receives as a gift [*Gabe*] the presencing that there is [*es gibt*] by perceiving [*indem er vernimmt*] what appears in letting presence. If man were not the constant receiver of the gift given by that which enables presencing [i.e., by the clearing], or if that which is extended in the gift did not reach man, then not only would being remain concealed in the absence of this gift, not only closed off, but man would remain excluded from the realm of being. Man would not be man. (GA 14: 16/OTB 12)

The mundaneity of the so-called gift is the subject of further reflection a few pages later, where he says, using the word *Schicken* without any *necessary* implication of a force of destiny (*Geschick*): "the sending of being [*Schicken von Sein*] lies [*beruht*] in the extending, opening, and concealing of manifold forms of presence into the open realm of time-space" (GA 14: 25/OTB 20). It is here, in this, our engagement, our belonging, our bonding (*Verbundenheit*) in connection to what is given or sent into our field of experience, that we find ourselves claimed, summoned to our appropriation. And it is precisely here, in corresponding to that claim (*Anspruch*) that our responsibility arises:

> The quiet heart of the opening [*Das ruhige Herz der Lichtung*] is the place of stillness [*Ort der Stille*] from which alone the possibility of the belonging-together of being and thinking, that is, presencing and perceiving [*Anwesenheit und Vernehmen*], can arise at all. The possible claim [*Anspruch*] to a binding character or commitment of thinking [*Verbindlichkeit des Denkens*] is grounded in this bond [*Verbundenheit*]. (GA 14: 84/OTB 68)

In this chapter, I am accordingly arguing that the appropriation is a process that emerges from a claim inherent in the belonging together. Consequently, it is a claim that comes both from that which presences, namely an event of being, and, correspondingly, from us, that is, from the nature of our most fundamental bodily disposition, which bodily dis-positions us, throwing us open to being.

†

In his introduction to *Being and Time*, Heidegger attempts to draw our attention to what he calls our "pre-ontological understanding of being." He calls attention to this understanding not only in order to support his argument that we need to achieve a *properly ontological* understanding of being but also in order to get his project underway. That is because, in entering and growing up within the everyday world, we have had to relinquish, and hence lose contact with, that pre-ontological dimension of our experience. But *if* we could somehow break out of our inveterate everyday frame of mind and gain access to—gain contact with—that fundamental *pre-ontological* understanding, a *preconceptual* understanding constitutive of our very nature as bodily appropriated to a thrown openness in which we are always already interactively engaged with the *being* of beings, an understanding that as a gift of nature we have always already been given and continue to shelter, even when it is unrecognized, in the depths of our embodiment, *then* we might achieve some further measure of *ontological* understanding by retrieving and grounding for present living that earlier gift of nature, that earlier sense, or intimation, of being—the preconceptually lived experience of our belonging together in undifferentiated coherence with being. The clearing and what can appear, or be disclosed, in that clearing, always belong together: the character of the clearing affects the fate of what can appear in its matrix.

This task of grounding, he says, casts us into the hermeneutic circle. We cannot achieve that ontological understanding without first retrieving our pre-ontological sense and sensibility. We need insight, need therefore to circle back in recollection (*Er-innerung*), retrieving and enowning the response ability inherent in our relation to being in order to take a step forward in the way we actually live our lives.

However, in going back to retrieve the initial grounding in our appropriation for the sake of a genuinely personal appropriation, and a personally undertaken grounding, we are confronted with something abyssal: the being of the clearing, the truth of being, to which we are appropriated and dis-posed in thrown openness is a facticity behind which, as I noted, we learn we cannot go. There is an abyssal dimension that only our endeavors to ground the clearing we opened will reveal: we find ourselves compelled to confront the fact that there can be no intelligible explanation for existence, hence for the happening that is the clearing of a world. There is ultimately no answer to the question why. The abyss is the ultimate unknowability of the openness, the clearing. "This abyss," according to Heidegger, "is indeed a 'ground,' but one that 'grounds' only in the sense that it lets appropriation show through [*das tragende Durchragenlassen des Ereignisses*, i.e., as the real 'ground']" (GA 65: 380/CP 300). In its hiddenness, its groundlessness, "*die zögernde Versagung des Grundes*," "the abyss clears a space for the being of things [*die Wesung der Wahrheit*]." This withdrawing of an ultimate ground is, however, precisely what brings forth the time-space matrix of the clearing: "the happening of an openness for being." The abyss of unanswerability returns us to ourselves: the only answer to "why" abides in us. The text continues: "The hiddenness is like a hint [*ist der Wink*] in which the way we *are* the Open—as sustaining the clearing [*eben das Beständnis der lichtende Verbergung*]—is to be noticed [*erwunken*]. And what we catch sight of is, again, the dynamic connection between the 'call' to *Dasein* [to come forth as the Open] and our 'belonging' to it [*die Schwingung der Kehre zwischen Zuruf und Zugehörigkeit*]: Da-sein's being-appropriated, beyng itself [*die Er-eignung, das Seyn selbst*]" (GA 65: 381–82/CP 301).

†

We still need to give further consideration to appropriation in relation to the *grounding* of human life in the thrown openness—the dis-position— of *Da-sein*. As we noted earlier, in his *Contributions to Philosophy* (*Beiträge zur Philosophie: Vom Ereignis*), Heidegger succinctly explicates that relation and its great significance: "With the grounding of *Da-sein* [*Gründung des Da-seins*], every connection to beings is transformed [*ist alles Verhältnis zum Seiendem verwandelt*], and the truth of being [*die Wahrheit des Seins*, i.e., the clearing] is for the first time [*zuvor*] experienced" (GA 65: 322/CP 255). Indeed, he tells us that the word *Ereignis* is really to be thought as an *abbreviation* ("*in der Abkürzung*") for our propriation, "*das Ereignis der Dagründung*": "the grounding of the 't/here,' the *Da*" (GA 65: 247/CP 195). Hence it is a question of properly grounding our *Menschsein* in its dis-position as *Da-sein*, opening and sustaining the clearing—*Seyn selbst*, the *Lichtung*. "Grounding" here means not only recognizing and understanding but also putting that recognition and understanding into the way we relate to what presences in our experience. According to Heidegger:

> Initially, *Da-sein* stands in the grounding of the appropriation [*in der Gründung des Ereignisses*], creatively grounds [*ergründet*] the truth of *being* [i.e., the clearing], and does not pass from *beings* [*vom Seienden*] to their being. (GA 65: 322/CP 255)

As he so often does, in text after text, year after year, and perhaps most poignantly during the dark years 1936–1938, Heidegger reminds us, in his *Contributions*, that what is at stake in his project is nothing less than the earth and the sky—and our destiny as human beings:

> Who is the human being? The one needed by beyng [*Jener, der gebraucht wird vom Sein*] for the sake of withstanding the essential occurrence [*Wesung*] of the truth of being.
>     As so needed, however, humans "are" humans only inasmuch as they are grounded in *Da-sein*, that is, inasmuch as they themselves, by creating [*schaffend*], become the ones who ground *Da-sein*.
>     Yet beyng is also grasped here as making an appropriating claim [*Ereignis*]. Both belong [*gehört*] together: the grounding back [*Rückgründung*] into *Da-sein* and the truth of beyng [i.e., the clearing] as appropriating claim [*Ereignis*]. (GA 65: 318/CP 252)

In this "Rückgründung," we should recollect and return to the fundamental disposition that has always already laid claim to our nature, always already grounded it, in order to retrieve that appropriation and take it over for the *schaffenden* process of grounding. This personal, *existentiell* process of grounding, retrieving and taking over the fundamental, preliminary *existential* grounding, is accordingly the second "moment" in our propriation, grounding ourselves in and as *Da-sein*. Heidegger concludes this rumination with this unequivocal counsel:

> We grasp nothing of the direction of the questioning that is opened up here if we casually base ourselves on arbitrary ideas of the human being and of "beings as such" instead of putting into question at one stroke both the "human being" and "beyng" (not simply the being of the human being) and keeping them in question. (Ibid.)

As the question of grounding in regard to our appropriation concerns our retrieving and taking up—taking over—the dis-position of our nature, along with the distinctive guardian responsibilities for the ontological dimensionality of the clearing, the grounding of our appropriation necessarily involves a hermeneutical circle. This is indicated by what I take Heidegger to be arguing in his *Contributions to Philosophy*.

In this same volume, Heidegger offers a further explanation of what this becoming grounded in *Da-sein* means: "Only in the grounding of the appropriation [i.e., the *Er-gründung des Ereignisses* operative in our most fundamental dis-position] does the steadfastness of *Da-sein* succeed [*glückt die Inständigkeit des Da-seins*] in the modes of the sheltering of truth in beings [*Bergung der Wahrheit in das Seiende*] and on the path of that sheltering" (GA 65: 308/CP 244). This sheltering of the clearing is entirely our responsibility.

†

We need now to consider, if only very briefly, the historical significance of this grounding of appropriation for Heidegger's project, which at least in the years during which he was writing the thoughts in this volume was guided by a certain philosophy of history, albeit a point of view on the history of philosophy and the course of history in the Western world that is never fully acknowledged, articulated, and argued for:

> The essence of *Da-sein*, and thus the essence of the history grounded on *Da-sein*, is the sheltering of the truth of being, of the last god, in beings [*die Bergung der Wahrheit des Seins, des letzt Gottes, in das Seiende*]. (Ibid.)

I shall have more to say about "the last god" in chapter 5. Suffice it for now simply to say that I take it to be, among other things, his way of emphasizing that we must not foreclose the historical possibilities we inherit. Metaphorical invocations of gods often appear, as they do here, in Heidegger's awkward yet poetic efforts to envision a future in which he can invest his faith:

> Only one who grasps that man must ground his essence historically [*geschichtlich*] by grounding Da-sein [*die Gründung des Daseins*], [and that Da-sein] is nothing but dwelling in the time-space of that happening [*Anwohnerschaft im Zeitraum jenes Geschehens*] that takes place [*ereignet*] in the flight of the gods—only one who takes back into restraint [*in die Verhaltenheit zurücknimmt*] the dismay and joy of the appropriation [*des Ereignisses*] as the fundamental disposition [*als Grundstimmung*]—only that one is capable of having an intimation [*ahnen*] of the essence of being, and in terms of this understanding, preparing the truth for what will be true in the future [*für das künftige Wahre*]. (GA 65: 52/CP 42)

I take the "of" in the phrase "grounding of *Dasein*" to indicate both a subjective and objective genitive. The ambiguity of the preposition is in this instance useful. Human existence—*Dasein*—is indeed always *given* an existen*tial* grounding: it is always already grounded *a priori* in its essence, which is to-be-the-*Da*, that is, *Da-sein*. The *Ereignis*, understood as appropriation, throwing *Dasein* open, *is* (the insurmountable fact of) that existen*tial* grounding, inherently grounding the human being in openness, finitude, contingency, and incompleteness: as appropriated (*ereignet*) for its *Da*, the human *Dasein* is grounded, and the conditions for a world, a meaningful time-space leeway (*Spielraum*), begin to take place. However, this grounding is *not complete* until it has been personally taken over or taken up: not complete without *our* appropriated self-awareness and self-recognition and also not complete without our reception, understanding, enowning, and enactment of it. The existen*tial* structure of appropriation needs—claims, demands—that its fundamental grounding, the grounding that is given, given to be thought of, Heidegger says, as if it were a gift—must be personally achieved—by virtue of *Dasein*'s personal *Übernahme*, taking that grounding over for itself in a personal existen*tiell* commitment. That grounding takes place in our *Übernahme* of the disposition—namely, our "propriation" in what I have defined as the third sense of "appropriation."

This undertaking necessarily draws us into the reflexive circularity of the hermeneutical. The *structural* grounding (our disposition) we are given by nature is a claim and summons to appropriation that must still be *brought* to its grounding by processes of appropriation: *our* self-recognition, enowning, and enactment of our natural endowment. As the philosopher says, "in order to ground beings as a whole and as such [*das Seiende im Ganzen und als Solches*], but also to ground man in the midst [*inmitten*] of beings," the *structural* grounding we are given by nature—and as essence—must still be *given* its personal, *existentiell* propriation, grounding, securing the *Da* (GA 65: 8/CP 9). In grounding *beings*, we hermeneutically bring into view (*er-äugen*) the clearing *as* their condition of possibility, and we ground *ourselves* as the human beings we are by living—and *showing* in the way we live—our phenomenological role in regard to that clearing for beings. The grounding that our appropriation calls for ultimately means living one's life hermeneutically, that is, in a way that makes *manifest* that finite grounding and the life it calls for, retrieving and appropriating the conditions we have been granted in our *Zu-sein*, an ongoing living forward, always mindful, though, of the limits to our knowledge and power. This undertaking, attempting "*die Verwandlung des Menschen in sein Da-sein*" (GA 9: 113/PM 89), necessarily draws us into the reflexive circularity of the hermeneutical, a process of conversion, a περιαγωγή, of enowning and enactment, retrieving and enacting what has always already been *Da*, t/here.

†

This brings me to questions regarding Heidegger's invocations of "restraint" (*Verhaltenheit*) in his *Contributions to Philosophy* (GA 65: 322–23/ CP 254–56). What does *Verhaltenheit* mean as a characterization of appropriation that regards it as our *Grund-Stimmung*—"fundamental disposition," or "fundamental attunement"? Why does Heidegger describe *restraint* as "the grounding of the ground of *Dasein*, of the *Ereignis*"? Why call it the "*Bei-sich des Selbst*" and "the solitude of the great stillness in which the appropriation becomes truth"? Why and how does *Dasein* as appropriated *Augenblicksstätte* (site of the moment of vision) arise out of that "solitude"?

I suggest that Heidegger's discussion of "restraint," *Verhaltenheit*, bears on our entering into the appropriation, our "preparedness" for a revolutionary historical project, not only (i) because we must exercise restraint to avoid drawing into unconcealment the dimension that, in its concealment, withdrawing from our ken, surpasses and encompasses our world, or, in other words, because we must avoid reducing everything to what lies within the range of our cognitive and practical will to power but also (ii) because that process, our entering into the appropriation, cannot get underway so long as we are immersed in, and distracted by, the things of the world. We need to concentrate on the claim of appropriation that dis-positions us in our every relation to being and summons us to the enowning of our response ability in regard to the world, realm of meaning. We need to *hear* in contemplative quiescence the call—the *Geheiß*. The *halting* of our immersion, our distraction, returns us to ourselves—to "the solitude of the great stillness in which the appropriation becomes truth," but it returns us to ourselves in a way that *restrains* and *halts* our will to power, our will to dominate and control. *Verhaltenheit* is the restraint coming from a "law" (*Ge-setz*) of our own nature, a disposition that summons us to return to our *Aufenthalt*, which is the achievement of our *Ereignen*, the gentlest of laws, the "*sanfteste aller Gesetze*" (GA 12: 248/OWL 128). It is even, Heidegger says with emphasis, "*the* law," in that it "gathers mortals into propriation, the recognition and enowning [*Ereignen*] of their essence; and it keeps [*hält*] them there" (ibid.). Restraint, *Verhaltenheit*, is what makes possible our awareness and recognition of the summons to appropriation, the enowning of our response-ability—hence the call for our "*Übernahme der Geworfenheit*"—that is implicit in our every interaction with beings in the world (GA 2: 431/BT 373). And the *halting* of our immersion and distraction, all these forms of forgetfulness regarding being (*Seinsvergessenheit*), opens us once again—and yet also for the very first time—to the dimension that belongs to the "truth of being," the dimension of the interplay of concealment and unconcealment. "This restraint," Heidegger says, is a *disposition* that "disposes only as appropriated belonging to the truth of being" (GA 65: 35/CP 30). "Restraint is the ground of care" (GA 65: 35/CP 29).

†

As I have already suggested, our recognition, understanding, enownment, and practical enactment of the appropriation that lays claim to us, even claiming us and dis-positioning us bodily, bears on the historical beginning of metaphysics, namely in the form of a revolutionary break (*Verwindung*), winding down and overcoming, or rather sublating, that history not only in metaphysics but in the life of the *world* that metaphysics reflects: something we shall need to consider, though all too briefly, in the final chapters of this volume. But let me conclude this brief reference to a *Verwindung*, heralding the possibility of a fundamentally new inception, by quoting from the summary of a 1962 seminar on Heidegger's lecture on "Time and Being":

> Being—together with its epochal revelations [*Offenbarungen*]—is retained in the givenness of the conditions of possibility for the presencing of beings [*im Geschick einbehalten*], but as destiny [*als Geschick*] it is taken back into appropriation. (GA 14: 62/OTB 53)

In other words, structurally considered, being is retained as the clearing, but in manifesting the character of our destiny, it is brought back—by way of the phenomenological step back that returns us, from a concentration of thinking on being, to the question of our *Ereignung*—to our singular responsibility, as appropriated to *Da-sein*, for the safeguarding and sustaining of the clearing, that openness within which all that is in any way meaningful to us is brought into the light of presence—into a certain unconcealment, hence brought for a while into the fields of our response ability. Destiny is not a metaphysical agency; it lives only in our propriation and responsibility. And the phenomenology of appropriation illuminates the way to that responsibility.

†

In "Time and Being," Heidegger says, thinking toward that very prospect: "in being as presence, there is manifest the concern [*bekundet sich der Angang*] that engages us humans in such a way that, in perceiving and receiving it [*im Vernehmen und Übernehmen*], we attain the distinction of human being" (GA 14: 28/OTB 23). And he interprets this attainment in terms of the poetic way of living he calls "the fourfold." To live in this way is to see and hear all beings, all entities, all events, as gathering around themselves, each in its own way, the fourfold constellation, earth and sky, mortals and their "gods," the visionary embodiments of our most cherished values and ideals. In the report summarizing the seminar on this lecture, reference is made to Heidegger's earlier bold attempt, in "The Principle of Identity" (1957) to think being in terms of appropriation:

> What appropriation appropriates for propriation [*ereignet*], that is, brings into its own [*ins Eigene bringt*], [is] the belonging-together of being and man. In this belonging-together, what belongs together [*die Zusammengehörenden*] is no longer being and man, but rather—as the appropriated [*als Ereignete*]—mortals in the fourfold of world [*die Sterblichen im Geviert der Welt*]. (GA 14: 51/OTB 42)

Instead of *withdrawing* us from the world into transcendental subjectivity, the phenomenology of appropriation actually *returns* us to the world in all its meaningfulness—but only after having taken us, by certain "steps back," into the dis-position of an appropriation, a claim hidden within ourselves, unrecognized and unacknowledged, that summons us to the ontological response abilities constitutive of our highest responsibility.

†

Guiding our attention to an appropriation that bears the true nature of our relation to being, Heidegger attempted to free our understanding of being from its various representations in the history of metaphysics, where, even in Husserlian phenomenology, the influence of that history still held sway. But the dis-position of *Da-sein* cannot be understood without an understanding of human embodiment released at last from the metaphysical paradigm. Heidegger contributed to that release, that break, but he left that project glaringly incomplete, refraining from thinking beyond certain critical challenges to the Cartesian picture. This is a limitation, a shortcoming of great consequence in his phenomenology of perception because the work that the *Ereignis* performs in Heidegger's project, whether it is understood as history-making event or as process of appropriation, ultimately depends not only on our knowing ourselves and understanding our capacities but also on undertaking their cultivation. And if we interpret *Ereignis* to designate both history-making events and also our appropriation, this means working with the *embodied nature* of our *Da-sein*, working with the claim of appropriation that is borne by our embodiment in, and as, the most fundamental existential disposition with which we are endowed, taking on a responsibility urgently needed for responding to what threatens the ontological dimensionality of our world. If there were ever to be another ontological epoch in Western history, then the prevailing paradigm of knowledge, truth, and reality, the prevailing sense of what it means to be, would need to submit to a process of questioning grounded phenomenologically in the appropriation of perception—seeing and hearing. But in the consequential shift that Heidegger made, turning from the problematic of *Sein* to that of *Ereignis*, there is already an immensely valuable step, a necessary and urgent step, guiding us toward understanding what an epochal breakthrough, or *Verwindung*, demands of us.

The very first step is the engaging of our appropriation, a personal process of recollection (*Er-innerung*), going into ourselves and retrieving the disposition of our bodily nature that constitutes our thrown-open connection to being. Once the nature of this connection is recognized and understood, inceptual thinking can get underway. Such thinking concerns how we have conceptualized being in the history of metaphysics. Understanding the history of being is crucial, if we hope to break free of its sway. This understanding also involves *Erinnerung*; but in working with, and through, the history of being, it is rather a procedure that must attempt to disrupt the ordering of time we have imposed, taking for granted, as natural, its linearity and dimensionality. In "Recollection in Metaphysics (1941), Heidegger turns recollection, typically a conservative procedure, into a revolutionary, future-oriented project:

> Recollection in the history of being is a thinking ahead to the inception [*Anfang*] and belongs to being itself. Appropriation grants the time [*gewährt je die Frist*] from which history takes the granting [*Gewähr*] of an epoch [*Zeit*]. But that time-span [*Frist*], when being gives itself to openness, can never be found in historically calculated time or with its measures. The time-span [*gewährte Frist*] granted shows itself only to a reflection [*Besinnung*] that is already [*bereits*] able to get a certain felt sense [*ahnen*] of our role in the history of being, even if this succeeds only in the form of an essential need [*Not*] that soundlessly and without consequences [*laut- und folgenlos*] shakes [*erschüttert*] everything true and real to the very roots. (GA 6.2: 490/EP 83)

In "The End of Philosophy and the Task of Thinking" (1964), a later text, Heidegger continues the argument, observing that "our ecstatic sojourn [*Aufenthalt*] in the openness of presencing is turned only toward what is present and the existent presenting of what is present." Thus, he says, "presencing as such, and together with it, the opening granting it, remain unheeded" (GA 14: 87/OTB 71). Our restriction in the calculative order of time must be ended, opening up the past for our engagement and appropriation. Attempting to twist free of the dominion of time (*Zeitlichkeit*), which buries the past in pastness and loses thereby the *future past* with all its still unexplored possibilities, recollection could take us into the dimensions of temporality (*Temporalität*) that would enable us to retrieve those possibilities for our appropriation—and our responsibilities in regard to a future inception.

In lecture courses on Heraclitus given over the summers of 1943 and 1944, Heidegger asked us to consider these responsibilities: "Is inceptual thinking [*das anfängliche Denken*] metaphysics or preliminary to it, or does something entirely different occur [*ereignet*] within inceptual thinking?" (GA 55: 100/H 75). In presenting this question, Heidegger uses the verb *ereignen*, making it speak of what occurs within inceptual thinking. But that word, with its doubled meaning, is also serving to suggest that what must occur for thinking to become inceptual is a process of appropriation (*Er-eignen*). *Ereignis* as history-making (*geschichtlich*) event and *Ereignis* as process of appropriation come together in the forming of his question. Appropriation is necessary for the inceptual event. Its significance for inceptual thinking is that it is a process that deeply engages us in reflecting on the nature and character—and history—of our relation to being. Appropriation is a matter of destiny for our highest responsibilities.

## NOTES

1. Bernard-Henri Lévy, "We Are Not Born Human," "Opinion" section, *New York Times*, August 22, 2018. Lévy is strongly influenced by Heidegger as well as by Nietzsche: "Our humanity is a *process* that begins with negation. Being human means taking a *leap* out of the natural order. . . . This systematic denaturalization, this confidence that a piece of oneself can escape from the natural order of the world, is akin to a second birth. Nature is the first stage of humanity; but it can, under no circumstance, be its horizon. [So] there is also a third birth. To be human is to be part of another entity that we call society. [. . .] Man has never existed entirely on his own, with no attachment to a community of others. [. . .] *We are not born human; we become it. Humanity is not a form of being; it is a destiny.* It is not a steady state, delivered once and for all, but a *process.*" Italics added.

2. Also see "Aus einem Gespräch von der Sprache," GA 12: 127/OWL 39.

3. On the concept of *"Ereignis,"* see, among other scholarly commentaries and interpretations, William McNeill, "On the Essence and Concept of Ereignis," Supplement to the *Proceedings of the Fifty-First Annual Meeting of the Heidegger Circle* (March 2017), 24–34. I also note the contributions of Thomas Sheehan and Richard Polt, both of whom have developed significant interpretations of *"Ereignis."* I am greatly indebted to their work and the discussions we have had.

4. Immanuel Kant, *Kritik der reinen Vernunft*, Philosophische Bibliothek, Bd. 37, ed. Raymund Schmidt (Würzburg: Felix Meiner Verlag, 1956), A 141/B 180–81; *The Critique of Pure Reason*, trans. Norman Kemp Smith (London: Macmillan and Co., 1956), A 141/B 180–81.

5. I want to acknowledge the enormous, truly immeasurable indebtedness of the thinking attempted in this chapter to Richard Polt and Thomas Sheehan. Without the dialogue that I enjoyed with them both, a dialogue centered in part around certain disagreements I had with each of them, the interpretation and argument offered here would have been not merely far from sharp and clear but also far from comprehensive, and even farther from being as compelling as I fancy it is. Basically, I worked out my interpretation in the course of attempting to reconcile their seemingly irreconcilable positions regarding *Ereignis*.

6. Concerning "dispositions" (*Stimmungen*) in relation to *Ereignis*, appropriation in the history of beyng, see Heidegger, *Das Ereignis*, GA 71: 216–24; *The Event*, 186–92.

7. Gilles Deleuze, *L'Abécédaire* (Paris: Éditions Montparnasse, 2004).

8. Martin Heidegger, *Prolegomena zur Geschichte des Zeitbegriffs*, GA 20: 209. I am grateful to Thomas Sheehan for bringing this text to my attention. The argument I use it to make here is, however, my own.

9. GA 20: 206.

10. See the introduction to Heidegger, *What Is Philosophy?* by Jean T. Wilde and William Kluback, written for their English translation (Lanham: Rowman and Littlefield, 2003), 9–10.

11. Heidegger, "Zeit und Sein," GA 14: 29; *Zur Sache des Denkens*, 24; "Time and Being," in *On Time and Being*, 24. "*Das Ereignis ereignet*" and "*Die Welt weltet.*" I confess that, once upon a time, there was a moment when, lost in the labyrinth of interpretive possibilities, I was reminded of an invented word in Edward Lear's "The Owl and the Pussycat": "They dined on mince, and slices of quince,/Which they ate with a runcible spoon." Just what *is* a runcible spoon? Wittgenstein famously asserted that the meaning of a word is (in) its usage. How does this help us with Heidegger and Lear? At the end of the day, the accumulation of instances, read in their context, always does yield some intelligible patterns for Heidegger's words. But every assignment of meaning remains an interpretation subject to questioning: something like, or akin to, a hypothesis. Lear's word is nonsensical, but its sensible incarnation remains amusingly suggestive.

12. Also see GA 14: 49/OTB 40.

13. Giorgio Agamben, *Homo Sacer: Sovereignty and Bare Life*, trans. Daniel Heller-Roazen (Stanford, CA: Stanford University Press, 1998), 150f.

14. See Richard Polt, "Ereignis," in Hubert Dreyfus and Mark Wrathall, ed., *A Companion to Heidegger* (Oxford: Blackwell, 2005).

15. See *Beiträge zur Philosophie*, GA 65: 322; *Contributions to Philosophy*, 254: "The coming-to-itself of the self [*Das Bei-sich des Selbst*] shows itself in its relation to the persistence and steadfastness [*Inständigkeit*] of the claim urging the taking up [*Übernahme*] of our appropriation [*Er-eignung*]."

16. See Heidegger, "Der Satz der Identität," GA 11: 45–47; "The Principle of Identity," in *Identity and Difference*, 36–38 and see "Die Onto-theo-logische Verfassung der Metaphysik," GA 11: 75; "The Onto-Theo-logical Constitution of Metaphysics," *Identity and Difference*, 69, where Heidegger speaks of a "reciprocal reflection," a relation "*wechselweise im Widerschein.*" Also see his *Beiträge zur Philosophie*, GA 65: 239; *Contributions to Philosophy*, 188–89.

17. And see Heidegger, "Die Gefahr," *Bremer und Freiburger Vorträge*, GA 79: 64; "The Danger," *Bremen and Freiburg Lectures*, 60; "Der Satz der Identität," *Bremer und Freiburger Vorträge*, GA 79: 124–25; "The Principle of Identity," *Bremen and Freiburg Lectures*, 116–17.

18. Walter Benjamin, *Gesammelte Schriften* (Frankfurt am Main: Suhrkamp Verlag, 1974), I. 2: 694; "Theses in the Philosophy of History," in *Illuminations*, trans. Harry Zohn (New York: Schocken, 1969), 254.

19. And see GA 71: 154–78/133–150, regarding what Heidegger has to say in answer to the question "who is the human being?" In Merleau-Ponty's

phenomenology, this *schwingender Bezug* would be represented as intertwining and reversibility. See his work, *The Visible and the Invisible* (Evanston, IL: Northwestern University Press, 1968).

20. Also see *Anmerkungen A (1945–1946)*, GA 97: 195.

21. Committed to transcendental idealism, Husserl described this phenomenon of openness in more consciousness-related terminology as consisting of outward radiating beams of intentionality. In his *Phenomenology of Perception* (1945) arguing not only against subjective idealism, but against mechanistic physiology and intellectualistic psychology, Merleau-Ponty gives a description of our spatio temporal existence that fully supports Heidegger's account in "Building Dwelling Thinking," even emphasizing, as Heidegger does, the belonging together. He points out that each instant of a gesture or movement "embraces its whole span": the goal is already inscribed in the beginning. Thus, he says, "Insofar as I have a body through which I act in the world, space and time are not, for me, a collection of adjacent points nor are they a limitless number of relations synthesized by my consciousness and into which it draws my body. I am not *in* space and time [like a stone, tree, or house], nor do I merely *conceive* space and time; I *belong* to them, my body combines with them and includes them. The scope of this inclusion is the measure of that of my existence." Maurice, Merleau-Ponty, *Phénoménologie de la perception* (Paris: Librarie Gallimard, 1945), 164; *Phenomenology of Perception*, trans. Colin Smith (London: Routledge and Kegan Paul, 1962), 140. Also note this: "What counts for the orientation of the spectacle is not my body as it in fact is as a thing in objective space, but as a system of possible actions, a virtual body with its phenomenal 'place' defined by its task and situation. My body is wherever there is something to be done." Op.cit., 289 in the original French, 249–59 in the English translation.

22. For the first citation, see GA 2: 369/BT 323; for the second, GA 4: 87/ HP 112. Also see "Hölderlins Hymne "Der Ister," GA 53: 151. All my translations.

23. Also see GA 65: 17, 294, and 407; CP 16, 232, and 322–23.

24. For more on restraint (*Verhaltenheit*) and on *Stimmung*, the German translation of "disposition," see GA 65: 14–23, 33–36; CP 14–20, 28–30.

25. On "facticity," see *Sein und Zeit*, 56, GA 2: 75; *Being and Time*, 83. And see *Ontologie: Hermeneutik der Faktizität*, GA 63: 8; "*Facticity* is the term for the being-character of 'our' 'own' *Dasein*. More precisely, . . . *Dasein* is *there* for itself in the How of its 'ownmost' being." My translation.

26. "Die Erinnerung in die Metaphysik," *Nietzsche II*, GA 6. 2: 489; "Recollection in Metaphysics," in *The End of Philosophy and the Task of Thinking*, 82: "being claims the essential nature of human beings for grounding its truth in beings" (*das Sein zur Gründung seiner Wahrheit im Seienden das Menschenwesen in den Anspruch nimmt*).

27. Heidegger, *Beiträge zur Philosophie*, GA 65: 318; *Contributions to Philosophy*, 251: "*Da-sein*, grasped as the being of the human being, is (always) already grasped in advance. So the question of the truth of this anticipatory grasp remains the question of how human beings, in coming to be more eminently [who in essential

potential they already are], place themselves back into *Da-sein*, thereby [further achieving the] grounding [of] *Da-sein*. . . . This self-dis-positioning, however, is grounded in the appropriation."

28. Samuel Beckett, *Proust* and *Three Dialogues with Georges Duthuit* (London: John Calder Publishers, 1999), 50. In a philosophically wrought paradoxical way, Beckett's plays and short stories show something of this transformation. And see Heidegger's 1929 lecture, "Was ist Metaphysik?" *Wegmarken*, GA 9: 113; "What Is Metaphysics?" *Pathmarks*, 89.

29. Heidegger, "Protokoll zu einem Seminar," GA 14: 63. And see *Zur Sache des Denkens*, 57; "Summary of a Seminar," *On Time and Being*, 53. And on the awakening that involves the step back into appropriation, see GA 14: 38, which, in the English translation, appears in *On Time and Being*, 30 and in *Zur Sache des Denkens*, 32.

30. And see also "Der Satz der Identität," GA 11: 45–47. For the English, see *Identity and Difference*, the bilingual ed., 36–37. For more on *Ereignis* as the appropriation of *Dasein*'s thrown-open existence, see Thomas Sheehan, *Making Sense of Heidegger: A Paradigm Shift* (London and New York: Rowman & Littlefield, 2015), 133–85 and 231–47. Also see Richard Polt, *The Emergency of Being: On Heidegger's Contributions to Philosophy* (Ithaca, NY: Cornell University Press, 2006), esp. 23–213.

31. Heidegger, "Protokoll zu einem Seminar über den Vortrag 'Zeit und Sein'," GA 14: 63. Or see *Zur Sache des Denkens*, 57; "Summary of a Seminar on the Lecture 'Time and Being'," in *On Time and Being*, 53. Trans. altered.

32. And see a different version of the discussion on "Der Satz der Identität," in the 1957 "Grundsätze des Denkens," *Bremer und Freiburger Vorträge*, GA 79: 125–26; "Basic Principles of Thinking," *Bremen and Freiburg Lectures*, 118.

33. See Friedrich Wilhelm Joseph von Schelling, *System of Transcendental Idealism*, *Sämtliche Werke*, ed. Karl Friedrich August Schelling (Stuttgart-Augsberg: J. G. Cotta, 1856–1851), vol. III, 333–34.

34. Kathleen Freeman, trans., *Ancilla to the Pre-Socratic Philosophers* (Cambridge, MA: Harvard University Press, 1978), 28. And see Heidegger, "Logos (Heraclitus, Fragment B50), GA 7: 211–34/EGT, 59–78.

# 4

## *LICHTUNG*

### Living in the Clearing of Worlds

> As I sit by my window this summer afternoon, hawks are circling about my clearing.
>
> —Henry David Thoreau, *Walden*[1]

To introduce the key word on which we will now concentrate, I have gathered and arranged some translations of Heidegger's thoughts into this concise florilegium:

i. "The Origin of the Work of Art" (1935–1936): "In the midst of beings as a whole an open place occurs [*Inmitten des Seienden im Ganzen west eine offene Stelle*]. And it is right there that a clearing occurs [*Eine Lichtung ist*]." (GA 5: 39–40/PLT 53)

ii. *The Event* (1941–1942): "The appropriation of the t/here [*Das Da-ereignen*], the appropriative event of the clearing [*das Ereignis der Lichtung*], is Da-sein; and that is the essential occurrence [*die Wesung*] of the truth of beyng [*Wahrheit des Seyns*], i.e., beyng itself." (GA 71:140–41/E 120)

iii. *The Event* (1941–1942): "The appropriating [*Er-eignis*] . . . now means being steadfast in the clearing and its stewardship [*inständig in der Lichtung und ihrer Wächterschaft*]." (GA 71: 197/E 168)

iv. "The Origin of the Work of Art" (1935–1936): "That which is [*Das Seiende*] can only be, as a being [*als Seiendes*], if it stands within, and stands out within, what is lighted [*das Gelichtete*] in this clearing [*dieser Lichtung*]. Only this clearing [*Lichtung*] gives and guarantees [*schenkt und verbürgt*] to us human beings passage [*Durchgang*] to the beings [*Seienden*] that we ourselves are not, and access [*Zugang*] to the beings that we ourselves are. It is thanks to this clearing that beings are unconcealed [*unverborgen*], given, or sent, to us in various ways [*in wechselnden Maßen*]. A being can also be concealed, but it can show itself *as* concealed *only* in the realm [*Spielraum*] of what is lighted, the clearing." (GA 5: 39–40/PLT 53)

v.  "Letter on Humanism" (1946): "For us, 'world' does not at all signify beings [*ein Seiendes*], nor any realm of beings [*keinen Bereich von Seiendem*], but rather the openness of being [*die Offenheit des Seins*]. . . . 'World' is the clearing of being [*'Welt' ist die Lichtung des Seins*], into which we human beings [*der Mensch*] stand out on the basis of our thrownness, our essential nature [*aus seinem geworfenen Wesen her heraussteht*]. . . . Thought in terms of existence, 'world' is in a certain sense precisely 'the beyond' within existence. . . . The human being in its essence exists thrown into the openness of being, into the open region that first opens, or clears, the 'between' within which a relation of subject to object can 'be'." (GA 9: 350/PM 266)

vi. "Letter on Humanism" (1946): "The clearing grants nearness to being [*gewährt die Nahe zum Sein*]." (GA 9: 337/PM 257)

vii. "The Principle of Identity" (1957): "For it is man, open toward being, who alone lets being arrive as presence [*läßt dieses als An-wesen ankommen*]. Such becoming present [*An-wesen*] needs the openness of a clearing, and by this need remains delivered over [*übereignet*] to human being." (GA 11: 40/31)

In the texts gathered here, Heidegger explains the ontological clearing and its functioning: (i) In the midst of beings, a clearing happens, manifesting, the sheer presence of a human being in the world. (ii) Being situated as a site of clearing—being *Da*—is how human beings are present, how they exist and are manifest. The human being (*Mensch, Dasein*) is endowed with the nature of a fundamental disposition—a disposition carried by the body (*Leib*) we are—that claims and appropriates us to be thrown open, dis-positioned, forming the clearing that provides the ontological conditions according to which things (*das Seiende*) can be experienced in their presence and absence. (iii) This appropriated and appropriating dis-positioning, throwing the human being open, makes the human *Dasein* into a *Da-sein*, and its appropriation is a bodily carried (*leiblich*) disposition, bearing a claim that summons each *Da-sein* to be vigilant in safeguarding the ontological openness its presence intrinsically makes. In our bodily dis-position, we are appropriated, claimed, each of us, to be a vigilant protector (*Wächter*) of the clearing—"the truth of being." Can we, will we, safeguard the truth of being, "so that," as Heidegger says in his "Letter on Humanism," "beings might appear in the light of being as the beings they are" (GA 9: 330/PM 252)? (iv) Simply by existing, we are, each one of us a *Da-sein*, the taking place of an openness, a clearing for the coming of light; and it is that clearing that makes it possible for us to experience the presence and absence of things. (v) "World" gives us another way of thinking about the clearing: in the singular, it serves as a formal indication, designating the clearing, the openness; but it carries a different meaning, because "world" calls attention to a different set of properties, questions and concerns, enabling and encouraging us to reflect, for instance, on the changing interpretations of being in the different historical periods and epochs. Heidegger refers to the world as *Lichtung des Seins* and *Offenheit des Seins*. We must not be misled by the words *des Seins*. That phrase simply tells us that this clearing or openness is to be understood as referring to the phenomenology of the ontological dimension in which we, as *Da-sein*, live. *Sein* is not the name of a metaphysical agency, a hidden source of the clearing somehow independent of *Da-sein*. (vi) The clearing opens, and is, the field of experience—perception, cognition, imagination, memory, gesture—within which, and in terms of which, it is possible for us to encounter beings in their intelligibility and meaningfulness. Clearings open, and are, *worlds* of meaningfulness. (vii) The clearing, as that wherein beings come into modalities of presence (modalities of being), is identified with the openness of the human being (*Mensch*) appropriated and dis-posed to *Da-sein*.

†

"You have to get used to lighting up all your senses [*se encienden todos tus sentidos*] as soon as you set foot on the mountain." This is what a father says to his son in *No le temas a la montaña*, a short story by a documentary writer.[2] What he means, I think, Heidegger would immediately recognize as the father urging his son to keep open the *clearing* that his presence makes as he ventures from his village over the mountains to the school on the other side. The father conveys this counsel in terms of "lighting up," that is to say arousing, "setting on fire" the sentience in all his senses. It is a question of vigilance, alertness, attentiveness—aliveness, because the route to school—the only possible route—passes through a field of landmines. This intensity burns like a fire, lighting things up. (I will have more to say about this in relation to the "fire" in Heraclitus, *Fragment* 16.) But what, after all, is the clearing if not, precisely, the openness which that sentient aliveness makes? And expressed more "philosophically," the question is: what is the clearing, if not the given conditions of intelligibility and meaning, conditions themselves conditioned, forming and informing a world in terms of which *what is* and *what is not* can be given and received in the sentience of perception? But vigilance—attentiveness—affects those conditions, a mindfulness laying out a certain clearing in perception: a synesthetic field of meaning—a field of the visible and the invisible, a field of the audible and the inaudible, a world within the interplay (*Spielraum*) of which the presencing of entities becomes possible. "Lighting up" our senses, making them more alive, is making them *more open* to receive what it is that we find ourselves given through the "windows" of perception.

In dialogue with Heidegger, Eugen Fink, influenced by the philosopher, reflects on the fact that the human being is not only "a cleared being," *ein gelichtetes Wesen*, but also "a natural being": "A human," he says, "is predominantly a light kindler [*Licht Zündende*], he who is delivered over [*zugestellt*] to the nature of the light" (GA 15: 233/HS 144). This means that we are responsible for the lighting clearing: responsible as guardians of the clearing, because our very existence, our very presence, makes clearings, and we *belong* to their operation, although, being the mortal, finite creatures we are, we are endowed with only "a limited capacity for lighting and clearing" (GA 15: 226–27/HS 140).

†

Coming after the preceding chapters, which inevitably could not discuss their particular key word without reference to the clearing, only a few things regarding the opening of the clearing and its relation to appropriation remain to be discussed. The text recording the dialogue between Heidegger and Fink, and my brief comment on the father's counsel in the short story, suggests that one of the matters still in need of discussion concerns the relationship, in regard to what Heidegger calls *die Lichtung*, between the interpretation that translates it as "light" and the interpretation that translates it as "lighting," in the sense of opening and clearing. There are texts in which the philosopher supports the latter and unequivocally repudiates the interpretation that translates it as referring to any of the phenomenological modalities and configurations of light. According to Heidegger, the etymological origin of *Lichtung* indicates that, in its earliest usage, the word referred to a forest clearing, whether cleared by nature or cleared by a farmer or hunter. And yet, especially when thinking about the ancient Greek philosophies, his thought, early and late, is saturated by references to vision and vision-generated images and metaphors. And he makes unabashed use of texts in which phenomena of light, such as something gleaming and something brightly shining, are the center of attention. Moreover, even in setting out his own thinking, independent of the

Greeks, he at times uses unmistakable references to just such phenomena, using these references and metaphors in the very same way that the metaphysics he is contesting has used them in the past to represent truth, goodness, and beauty. Thus, for example, his thought of "the truth of being" still attributes to it a wondrous, radiant beauty.

So, what is the relation between (i) the phenomenon of light, *das Licht*, and (ii) the clearing, that Heidegger designates using the word *die Lichtung*, a word that some scholars, despite Heidegger's emphatic assertions, have translated as "lighting," instead of translating the German term by "clearing" or by "the open"? This translation—"lighting" —creates unnecessary confusion, but Heidegger's own thought, or his way of wording his thought, must bear some responsibility for the ambiguities. Heidegger adamantly insists that his term *Lichtung*, as in the phrase *die Lichtung des Seins*, does not mean "lighting": in fact, he argues that it does not refer at all to a phenomenon of light (GA 14: 79–83/OTB 64–67). However, there is a connection in German between *lichten* (to illuminate) and *leichten* (to make easy: lighten in that sense). And we know that, by reducing foliage, clearings do bring light; they enable light to enter into the forest. In any case, for Heidegger, a clearing is required to provide a time-space field in which something—anything at all—can appear: the clearing is an ontological dimension of openness in which something can show itself in its unconcealment. Thus, too, the clearing makes it possible for things to show up in the (metaphorical) "light" of our understanding of being. So the clearing (*Lichtung*) is that which *enables* the light (*Licht*) to enter; it is the condition that lets things be seen, visible, lit up, shining. If light is an ontical phenomenon, the clearing—or lighting in the sense of the clearing—is ontological: the necessary condition for the possibility of experiencing visible beings in their visibility and, too, invisible things in their invisibility. The clearing is lighting (*Lichtung*): light in its ontological or transcendental function, transcending its habitual, bodily sensed presence, yet not metaphysically transcendent. There is, however, an inherent connection between the clearing and the light: the clearing *is* a lighting; a lighting that is everywhere, coming from nowhere. But that lighting is only a *consequence* of the condition of openness made by the clearing. The lighting, in turn, grants visibility to things visible and invisibility to things invisible. *The Principle of Reason* maintains but connects the distinction between the clearing as lighting and the clearing as shining light: the clearing is twice described as shining (GA 10: 93/PR 63).

In "Aletheia (Heraclitus, Fragment 16)," Heidegger explains how the light and the lighting work together: "If we think of it [what Heraclitus called *pyr*, *das Weltfeuer*] as pure lighting [*das reine Lichtung*], this includes not only the brilliance [*die Helle*], but also the openness [*das Freie*], wherein everything, especially the reciprocally related [*das Gegenwendige*], comes into shining [*ins Scheinen kommt*]. Lighting [*Lichten*] is therefore more than mere illuminating [*Erhellen*], and it is also more than laying bare [*Freilegen*, i.e., unconcealing]. Lighting is the meditatively gathering bringing-before into the open [*Lichten ist das sinnend-versammelnde Vorbringen ins Freie*]. It is the granting of conditions favouring, or enabling, presencing [*Gewähren von Anwesen*]" (GA 7: 283/EGT 118).

Although Heidegger's primary concern is for the protection and preservation of the openness of the clearing, the ontological dimension of our experience, he does nevertheless give thought to the phenomenon of light itself, invoking in various contexts some of its many modalities: the shining, gleaming, glistening, and glowing of things; the presence of things radiant, luminous, dazzling; but also the concealments of darkness. For instance, in "Basic Principles of Thinking," he ventures a reflection on light and darkness as such without indicating that this light, or lighting, is the clearing: "The dark reigns distinct from the pitch-black as the mere and utter absence of light. The dark, however, is the secret of light. The dark keeps the light to itself. The latter belongs to the former. Thus the dark has its own limpidity [*seine eigene Lauterkeit*]" (GA 79: 93/BF 88).

†

There is, however, considerable ambivalence in his attitude toward these phenomena of light. When he is imagining the shining marble splendor of a Greek temple that the ancient Greek philosophers experienced in radiant sunshine, one senses his deep pleasure, but when he turns to contemplate the contemporary world, one finds that he sees only a shallow enchantment with what dazzles, a vain attraction to what shines, like the glittering of pyrite, the "false gold." And he laments observing a greedy pursuit of the colorful blinding people to "the truth of being." And whereas noting that metaphysics has long ascribed to the mind, and above all its ability to exercise reason, a "natural light," Heidegger unreservedly challenges the truth of this doctrine, not convinced by the metaphor that once defined rationalism and its later Enlightenment. And yet, it would not really be far-fetched to see in *Dasein's* appropriated *Erlichtet-sein*, in its appropriated role to be the opening of a clearing, the influence of an inspiration owed to that metaphor.

In *Being and Time*, Heidegger expressed hope that his critical enquiry into our experience of time and history might prepare for what he called "a moment of vision"—an *Augenblick*. And some years later, in "The

Turn," he described the history-making "turn" for which his thinking was attempting to prepare in the metaphor of a "lightning flash": it is that moment in which, suddenly, the ontological dimension of looking and seeing—*der Einblick des Seins*—would take hold of our vision, appropriating its nature and character. The invocation of this flashing *Einblick* is not, however, despite appearances, an invocation of being that anthropomorphically attributes a glance to being. Rather, it is a way of summoning human vision, our vision, to take responsibility for "the truth of being," opening our vision to its ontological dimension and sustaining that openness—*as if* our vision could be, or be like, a "glance of being." The added words *des Seins* merely bespeaks its ontological character.

†

Our sight—*das Ge-sicht*—gathers (expressed in the German prefix *Ge-*) and makes for itself a clearing (*Lichtung*) for light (*Licht*) to enter and pervade the openness of its visual time-space field (*Lichtraum*), letting things come into visibility in the interplay of concealment and unconcealment (GA 15: 226–27/HS 140). Similarly, our hearing—*das Ge-hör*—gathers and makes for itself a stillness, a field of silence, for sound to enter and pervade the openness of its time-space auditory field (*Raum der Laute*). Sight and hearing sojourn within, and pass through, the clearings and the silences—the worlds—that the sheer, ultimately unfathomable facticity of their existence makes. The opening of the openness, the lighting clearing, *precedes* [*geht voraus*] the light, making this familiar light possible; and likewise, an immeasurable silence, a clearing for sound and in sound, *precedes* the sounding and resounding of sounds and voices, making the sounding and echoing of things possible (GA 15: 231–32/HS 143).

In his texts on Heraclitus, Heidegger describes the *Logos* as the ontological layout that gathers, the primordial opening up and laying out of the conditions necessary for the possibility of articulation in all its manifestations, all its modalities: its ontological functioning is called, in Greek, *Legein*. Our seeing and hearing—modalities of perception—are modalities, or forms, of articulation (*logos*), and, as such, they clear and lay out (in their *legein*) fields of perception that gather beings into their openness (GA 7: 211–34/EGT 59–78; also see GA 55).

Why, then, does Heidegger nevertheless say that the "relation between the light and the lighting-clearing is difficult to grasp [*schwer zu fassen*]" (GA 15: 230/HS 142)? Perhaps the difficulty derives in large measure from the fact that, precisely because of this fundamental ontological precedence, the lighting up of the clearing is *taken for granted*, hence neglected, rather than *taken as [something] granted*. Consequently, the lighting clearing, though not entirely invisible, and not transcending the realm of the sensible, still remains for intrinsic causes mostly unnoticed, hence unprotected against reification; and the uncanny silence that enables meaningful sounds and voices to form in the auditory field, though not entirely inaudible, and not transcending the realm of the sensible, still remains mostly unheard and likewise unprotected from the *Ge-stell.*

We are as if obsessed with what is audible and visible, distracted by the things that we encounter within the world of the clearings. In our "distraction," the clearing that actually enables our encounters remains itself neglected: we are drawn away from it. But despite risking metaphysical or theological interpretation, Heidegger was occasionally tempted to describe this precedence as *vorausgeschickt,* "sent," or "given," in advance, as if it were something to be taken *as* "granted," *as* the *gift* of destiny—or rather, as the gift of a *potential* for the achievement of destiny—granted in a mysterious supersensible dispensation—a *Geschick.* Why he used words in a way that suggests theology I do not know.

†

In his 1946 "Letter on Humanism," Heidegger tells us that what he has all along been calling "being"—in, for instance, *Being and Time*—is actually to be understood as referring to the clearing, the open, as that which lays out the conditions that determine what it means for beings to be. But he then argues that "within the destiny of being in metaphysics the clearing first affords a view by which what is present comes into contact with [*be-rührt*] the human being, who is present to it, so that the human being can, in apprehending (*noein*) [*Vernehmen*], first touch [*rühren*] upon being" (GA 9: 332/PM 252–53). However, in our time, the time of the *Ge-stell,* imposing total reification to serve the nihilistic will to power, this view, this experience, is vulnerable to assault: "This view," he observes, "draws the perspect toward it. It abandons itself to such a perspective when apprehending has become a setting-forth-before-itself [*Vor-sich-Herstellen*] in the *perceptio* of the *res cogitans* taken as the *subjectum* of *certitudo*" (ibid.). The imposition today of totality threatens the ontological openness of the clearing. Our seeing and hearing are consequently under siege.

In his *Contributions to Philosophy,* Heidegger says that the clearing (*Lichtung*) is "the truth of beyng," meaning that the clearing makes meaningful experience possible—that is, it lays out the space-time conditions for our experiencing the presence and absence of beings (GA 65: 240/189). In his "Letter on Humanism," Heidegger reiterates this point: "Being is the clearing itself" (GA 9: 337/PM 256). He also says there that the human being is "claimed originarily" by and for this clearing—a description that

I interpret to mean that we are *appropriated* to *Da-sein*, being-the-here, a thrown-open situatedness—claimed in and by an *a priori* appropriation constitutive of our most fundamental bodily dis-position as *Da-sein*. Thus, as he explains, "Through this claim of beyng itself, [*Seyn selbst*], the human being is appointed as the steward of the truth of beyng." This means being human is to be "grounded in [its] *Da-sein*" (ibid.). Grounded in the world-clearing trajectories that we *are*—the world-clearing projects in which and as which we exist. We are stewards, guardians of the clearings, called to "ground" the clearings. That means we need to recognize, understand, enown, and safeguard the dimension of their ontological openness—and their countless vulnerabilities. However, even when engaged in grounding ourselves in opening and clearing, we must understand that our ability to ground is limited: the ground is ultimately abyssal—an *Ab-grund*.

†

In "Aletheia (Heraclitus, Fragment B 16)," a 1943 commentary on *aletheia*, "the truth of being" in the thinking of Heraclitus, Heidegger, fusing the light and its lighting clearing, laments our indifference, our neglect of the clearing, observing that "everyday opinion . . . does not see the quiet gleam (the gold) of the mystery that everlastingly shines in the simplicity of the clearing" (GA 7: 288/EGT 122–23). The "mystery," here, is really just the sheer fact of perception, for the clearing of which there can be no ultimate explanation. That ought to intrigue us, drawing thought into the phenomenology of the opening. The clearing, as opening a world that makes possible the meaningful presence and absence of things, is the truth (*Wahrheit*) of being—as Heidegger says, for instance, in *The Event*—in that it is the "*Ge-wahr der Wahrheit*": that which sustains and preserves the conditions of possibility for the truth of presencing: "The clearing is the essential occurrence of the open, and the open is the passageway for the departing and arriving of beings out of what is without any being [*Die Lichtung ist die Wesung des Offenen, das Offene ist der Durchlaß des Entgegen und Ankommen (Seienden) aus dem Seinlosen*]" (GA 71: 208/E178).

Heidegger reminds us of Heraclitus's Fragment 9: "Asses choose hay rather than gold." Are we like those animals? How otherwise, he asks, could we withdraw from (*entziehen*), and lose contact with, the *Ereignung*, the claim on our perceptual capabilities? How, Heidegger wonders, "could anyone *whose essence belongs to the clearing* ever withdraw from receiving and protecting the clearing [*sich dem Empfangen und Hüten der Lichtung entziehen*]" (GA 7: 288/EGT 122–23)? Insofar as there is an answer to this question, it lies in the *Ereignung*, our appropriation, the claim on our responsibility. The *Ereignung* constitutes—*is*—that very essence, with its long-hidden secret: "the golden gleam of the lighting's invisible shining [i.e., the opera-tion of the clearing] cannot be grasped [*läßt sich nicht greifen*], because it is not itself something belonging to the realm of grasping [*kein Greifendes*], but rather, it belongs to the pure event [*sondern das reine Ereignen ist*]." That is to say, it belongs to the "pure event" of opening that lies awaiting our recog-nition in the claim of appropriation (ibid.). We should notice that, although presumably referring to the clearing, Heidegger speaks of a "golden gleam" and an "invisible shining," phrases that would normally imply that this "lighting" refers to light. He presumably wanted the ambiguity to express the intimacy of the connection.

†

Even though every meaningful experience requires a clearing as con-text of intelligibility and meaningfulness, metaphysics has not given it the attention it needs. But in a poetic text written in memory of Erhart Kästner, Heidegger argues, thinking about the clearing, that, in living within the clearing, whether aware of it or not, we are encountering "the facticity of the inaccessible [*Gegenwart des Unzugangbaren*], into which, nevertheless, we mortals are from the very beginning [*anfänglich*] gathered and appropriated [*ge-eignet*]" (GA 13: 242). There is no way to explain why we are thrown-open to be clearings. Moreover, the clearings transcend their horizons. Thus, in regard to the clearing, metaphysics encounters the intrinsically inaccessible. This is troubling for metaphysics but not for genuine thinking.

Despite its crucial role in all modalities of experiencing, the clearing itself is neglected: (i) neglected since ancient times by almost everyone in their quotidian life, because human beings tend to be preoccupied with the things that are present in the world or absent from it, rather than with the clearing itself—that which "gives" or enables such presencing, and (ii) neglected by a metaphysics that is at once a critical reflection on this world and also, inevitably, an insufficiently critical reflection of it. Moreover, it cannot think outside the subject–object structure to contemplate that which underlies and grounds it, making it possible. However, because of the func-tion of the clearing and our role in it, we need to maintain and safeguard the openness of the clearing. Fortunately, this neglect is only a contingency, not necessary, not inevitable. And that is why Heidegger insists so vehemently on the need to overcome our neglect, our ignorance and indifference.

The "hiddenness" of the clearing is, however, deeper than mere ignorance, distraction and neglect would suggest. Even Parmenides and Heraclitus seem to have been aware of the clearing, the fact that all experi-ence takes place in terms of a clearing. They seem to have understood the hermeneutical nature of the clearing as that theater of experience in which there is an interplay of concealment and unconcealment, hence an intrinsic hiddenness. They seem to have understood, simply from meditative attention, that every clearing withdraws beyond the horizon, beyond our reach and range, into the depths of an impenetrable concealment. However, what these Greek philosophers did not know is (i) that what opens the clearing is *our appropriation* to the thrown-openness of *Da-sein*, and (ii) that this appropriation constitutes an ongoing responsibility. According to Heidegger, though, even we modern philosophical minds have not recognized and understood this, because we live today in a certain phenomenological alienation and estrangement from ourselves, a condition of at once the most extreme subjective narcissism and the most extreme objectivism. What has been most deeply hidden from us is not only the answer to why all our experiencing takes the structural configuration it does in order to be a context of meaningfulness: these are matters for which Heidegger says there is ultimately no possible explanation. What is most deeply hidden from us is the law of appropriation that claims our ownmost nature.

What is most deeply hidden from us is our own fated, appropriated role in the clearing. The intrinsic concealment of the clearing does not ever lift from our shoulders a responsibility for our ability to be fittingly responsive to what the clearing gives us to encounter—for instance, in seeing and hearing. And that responsibility is alone what finally matters.

In his "Letter on Humanism," Heidegger explains how his hermeneutical phenomenology of the clearing involves a sharp divergence from metaphysics: to be sure, he says, in metaphysical thinking, "every departure from beings and every return to them stands in the light of being [i.e. appears in the clearing]" (GA 9: 331/PM 252). However, metaphysics is not conceptually equipped to think the clearing as such: "metaphysics recognizes the clearing of being either solely as the view of what is present in 'outward appearance' (*idea*) or critically as what is seen in the perspective of categorial representation on the part of subjectivity. This means that the truth of being, as itself the clearing, remains concealed from metaphysics. . . . But the clearing itself is being. Within the destiny of being in metaphysics, the clearing first affords a view by which what is present comes into touch with the human being, who is present to it" (GA 9: 331/PM 252–53).

Metaphysics is a discourse about beings; despite its invocations of "being," it really is not able properly to recognize being itself, being as such, needing to reduce it to a singular being. So, it should not be surprising that, in their everyday life, very few people are mindful of the clearing, even though it is in its own discreet way ever present, necessarily contextualizing all ontic experience, which would be impossible without it.

"The human [*Mensch*] comes to presence [*west*] in such a way," says Heidegger, "that it is the *Da*, that is, the clearing of being" (GA 9: 325/ PM 248). And it is only because of this clearing, and within this clearing, that it is possible for things to appear in our world. Thus, as Heidegger says, reminding us of a position he had already formulated in *Being and Time*: "Only so long as *Dasein* is, is there [*gibt es*] being." And this, he explains, "means that being conveys itself [*übereignet sich*] to human beings only so long as the clearing of being happens [*sich ereignet*]" (GA 9: 336/PM 256).

The clearing is "the truth of being itself," because the *truth* of being is not correctness but rather what underlies it and makes it possible: *aletheia*, the clearing as that field, that dimension, wherein beings can come into presence in the interplay of concealment and unconcealment. The *Da* in *Da-sein* designates the essential *being* of the human as appropriated *to be* (*-sein*) the situating site (*Da-*) of an openness: an openness wherein things can be present for human beings and human beings can be present for themselves (ibid.). Heidegger describes this openness that the *Da-sein* (the being of the *Da*) clears and "breaks open" (*aufbricht*) as "a sphere of openness [*Sphäre von Offenbarkeit*]." And, expressing his phenomenological version of realism, he says that the presence of *Da-sein* is an eruption breaking open in the midst of the beings that are present in the world of its clearing: an "*aufbrechende Einbruch in das Seiende*."[3] As the breaking open of clearings, *Da-sein* is always a momentous event, an *Ereignis*—even when it is an event that, as such, goes unnoticed, neglected, and, in effect, "forgotten," as it is constitutive of our very nature as existing.

How could metaphysics have overlooked the clearing? After all, the clearing as context of meaningfulness, context of intelligibility, is necessarily presupposed by all experience. It is only because we are *always already* within a field, a world of meaningfulness, that we can encounter something meaningful. Yet metaphysics makes no effort to understand the clearing. That is because, instead of thinking phenomenologically, it persists in thinking abstractly: if the clearing is a necessary presupposition of all understanding, then any endeavor to understand the clearing must already presuppose the clearing. So, in the attempt to understand the clearing, metaphysics can discern only an infinite regress. Moreover, in the metaphysics of the "modern" world, only what is objective and measurable is recognized as reality. But the clearing resists objectification. The clearing is consequently not only neglected in everyday life, hence *contingently* hidden, in favor of what is present and absent within its matrix; it is also something that metaphysics is compelled to take, for *intrinsic reasons*, to be absolutely excluded from its system of knowledge.

But Heidegger argues that there is another explanation for the contingent neglect and hiddenness: we mortals are as if spellbound by the things that appear, so captivated that we neglect the functioning of the clearing as that which makes our experience possible. Commenting, in "Aletheia," on the textual fragments we have from the thinking of Heraclitus, Heidegger observes that

> mortals are irrevocably bound to the revealing-concealing gathering [i.e., the *Logos*, which, in its operation as *Legein*, Heidegger understands to be the same as the clearing] that lights [*lichtet*] everything present in its presencing [i.e., the clearing opens and clears a time-space for the light to shine on things, letting their presence be lit up]. But they [i.e., we mortals] turn [*kehren sich*] from the lighting, and turn only toward [*kehren sich nur an*] what is present, which is what immediately concerns them in their everyday commerce with each other. They believe that all this trafficking [*dieser Verkehr*] in what is present by itself creates for them a sufficient familiarity [*gemäße Vertrautheit*] with it. But it nonetheless remains foreign to them. For they have no inkling of what they have been entrusted [*zugetraut*] with: presencing [*Anwesen*], which in a lighting clearing first allows what is present to come to appearance [*zum Vorschein kommen*]. *Logos*, in whose illuminating clearing they come and go, remains concealed [*verborgen*] from them, and forgotten [*vergessen*]. (GA 7: 287–88/EGT 122)

The indictment continues:

> The more familiar to them everything knowable becomes, the more foreign it is to them—without their being able to know this. They would become aware [*aufmerksam*] of all this if only they would ask: how could anyone whose essence [is appropriated by and] belongs [*zugehört*] to the light-bringing clearing ever withdraw from receiving and protecting the clearing [*Empfangen und Hüten der Lichtung*]? How could they, without immediately discovering that the everyday can seem quite ordinary to them only because this ordinariness is guilty of forgetting [*das Vergessen*] what initially brings even the apparently self-evident into the light of what is present? (GA 7: 288/EGT 122)

Permit me to point out, once again, Heidegger's use of the word *vergessen*—referring, that is, to our "forgetting." We need to take it seriously, not only bearing, as it does, significant echoes of Plato's doctrine of *anamnesis*, although not at all involving metempsychosis, but rather indicating something of the utmost importance that we have neglected, failed to recognize and bring into consciousness. This "forgetting" also bears a sense that supports, and is correlatively supported by, the interpretation of the *Ereignis* (*Ereignung*) for which I have been arguing, namely, that, as appropriating claim, the *Ereignis* (*Ereignung*) constitutes our most fundamental *disposition*, a dimension of our embodied human nature, or essence, from which we have become estranged and with which we need to get in touch. What we have neglected—or say "forgotten"—is not only the clearing itself but also *ourselves*, our appropriated role and responsibility, inasmuch as we, in our *Da-sein*, *are* the clearing.

Another key word in this text would remind us of our "entrustment" in respect to the lighting, the clearing, as that which keeps and shelters all beings: we, we alone of all living beings, have been appropriated and entrusted (*zugetraut*) with presencing, hence necessarily also with the clearing that receives what presences. Our response abilities in perception are thus put in question. The other living beings—all the other animals—are also clearings. We human beings are not alone in this regard. However, we are the only beings capable of recognizing and understanding ourselves as clearings; hence we are the only beings who live as appropriated clearings, live, that is, with a responsibility that claims us for the clearings we inhabit and are.

In this connection, we should keep in mind the distinction between (a) the clearing as "existential," that is, as manifesting our essential bodily structure, the most fundamental disposition of our embodiment, the *Geworfenheit* (thrown-openness) of human being that is constitutive of our *Befindlichkeit* (situatedness) and (b) the clearing as a personal, individual *existentiell* way of living in the historical world, and, as Heidegger would hope, not only aware of our thrown openness but taking into our care its ontological dimension, maintaining its openness. What this distinction means is that in personal life, the *inherent disposition* of thrown world-openness is an appropriation, a claim, that can be not only unknown and unacknowledged; it can be known about and ignored, known about and neglected or even resisted and denied; or it can be known about and cultivated and shaped in many different ways and in many different configurations.

Maintaining the *ontological* dimension of openness is always desirable, in that it enables one to come near to experiencing things in their essential truth, as they "really" are. It is the most appropriate attitude for *initially* encountering whatever comes into the clearings that are constitutive of one's lifeworld. But, obviously, if what is coming into presence is threatening, hostile, and dangerous, then an attitude of *ontic* openness would not be wise. When Heidegger speaks of sustaining the openness of our thrownness—the openness of the clearing—he is referring *only* to an ontological attitude and not recommending any ontic attitude.

A similar point, *mutatis mutandis*, involves the imperative distinction between *Gelassenheit* (letting-be) as an ontological attitude and *Gelassenheit* as an ontic attitude. As an ontological attitude, *Gelassenheit* is an openness, a clearing, that enables one to get, as much as possible, a good, fitting sense of the situation one finds oneself in. But if, in the dimension of ontological *Gelassenheit*, one sees someone drowning in a lake or sees a stranger brandishing a knife and menacingly approaching a child, then adopting an *ontic* attitude of *Gelassenheit* would certainly not be right. Almost all the scholarship regarding *Gelassenheit* fails to make this crucial distinction. Heidegger himself fails to recognize it.

†

In "The Principle of Identity" (1957), Heidegger succinctly formulates the crucial role of the clearing in relation to perception (*Vernehmen*): "For it is man, open toward being, who alone lets being arrive as presence [*läßt dieses als An-wesen ankommen*]. Such becoming present [*An-wesen*] needs the openness of a clearing, and by this need remains delivered over [*übereignet*] to human being" (GA 11: 40/ID 31).

But the clearing, world in its openness, although *dependent* upon *Da-sein*, cannot be reduced to, hence cannot be *identical* to, the human being (*Dasein* without the hyphen): the dimensions of the clearing that our being, our existing, opens always extend beyond us or withdraw into the depths of concealment, intrinsically transcending the reach and range of the finite human being. Thus, for instance, when the sounds we hear fade away, they draw us into an abyss of silence far beyond the horizons of our capacity to hear. Heraclitus lucidly understood this in thinking and speaking about the *Logos*, whose sublime and terrifying sounding his words in Fragment B 50 evocatively echoed. The philosopher speaks of the *Logos* in an onomatopoeia in words that evoke in their sounding a roaring wind, a breath of cosmic dimensions (GA 7: 211–34/EGT: 59–78).

The argument regarding the relation between *Mensch* (i.e., human *Dasein*) and the clearing as "the truth of being" was already spelled out in Heidegger's 1949 "Introduction to *What Is Metaphysics?*":

> When "existence" is properly thought [*recht gedachten*], it is possible to think the "essence" [*Wesen*] of *Dasein*, in the openness of which being itself [*in dessen Offenheit des Seins selbst*, i.e., "the truth of being"] manifests and conceals itself, grants and withdraws [*sich bekundet und verbirgt, gewärt und entzieht*], without this truth of being [*Wahrheit des Seins*] ever getting exhausted [*erschöpft*] in, or by, *Dasein*—or indeed letting itself ever be posited as [strictly] at one [*sich in eins setzen läßt*] with *Dasein*, in

accordance with the [erroneous] metaphysical proposition that all objectivity as such is [reducible to] subjectivity. (GA 9: 373–74/PM 283)

The clearing *is* dependent on *Dasein* but not reducible to it. We need
to appreciate that the *Wesen* Heidegger invokes in this passage is not the
"essence" he inherited from metaphysics: it cannot be reified. *Wesen* is simply a formal indication, referring to the structure that happens to be constitutive of the way human existence *functions* (said in German: *west*) in the world.
To argue that, at a structural level, being itself—the clearing, the truth of
being—is "at one" (*in eins*) with *Dasein* does not in any way *reduce* its inherent openness, its dimensionality. Parmenides's dictum, that mind and being
are "the same," posits no strict logical identity and no reducibility of being:
it merely recognizes inseparability, a "belonging together" (GA 11: 38–47/
ID 29–38). We might recognize in his saying a certain precursor of the
phenomenological correlation, but it is archaic, an ancestor without all the
later metaphysical freight, a thought not yet caught within the subject-object
structure. It is impossible for the dimensions of the experiential field to be
totally unconcealed, reduced to and exhausted by our experiential reach as
human beings. As Heidegger states very plainly, distinguishing his thinking
from metaphysics, being itself—*Dasein*'s clearings—should not be treated as
having the character of objectivity; nor, however, are the clearings reducible
to subjectivity. Thus, why experience takes the form of clearings intrinsically
exceeds the grasp of our knowledge. The clearing—being itself—is an openness that always takes place in the midst of what remains withdrawn from
it in concealment. In fact, not even what appears, unconcealed, *within* the
clearing, ever lets itself be reduced to what is unconcealed. There is always
an excessive, situation-transcending "more-to-be-experienced." And this
"more" might turn out to shatter all our expectations—and thereby all that
we thought we knew. No entity can ever show itself in its totality.

†

In the *Zollikon* seminars and conversations with Medard Boss, Heidegger provides further illumination on the question of the *Mensch-Sein*
relation. To be sure, he says, the clearing is not possible without human
existence. Moreover, the human being *is* the guardian of the clearing (*der
Hüter der Lichtung, des Ereignisses*), sole guardian of the event that is "the
truth of being," but the human being "is not the clearing itself, not the
entire clearing; nor is he [*sic*] identical (*identisch*) with the whole clearing as
such" (ZSG: 223/ZSE 178). I *am* my essence but also *other* than my essence:
in some ways, more than it, in other ways less; but always other. Phenomenologically considered, I *am* the clearing, *am* the openness my presence has

opened and in which I stand. But the clearing, the opening, is not reducible to me, is not related to me in the strict sense of logical identity. And that is so, even when "the world" is understood to be "my world," "my own personal world" (my *Eigenwelt*): because even then, there is an openness, hence a dimensionality of concealment, an excess of meaning, over which I can have neither power nor knowledge.

The clearing transcends the human individual (*Mensch*), but does it also transcend *Da-sein*, the dis-positional structure itself? I suggest that even though *Da-sein* is the opening of a world-clearing, its structure, as openness, cannot *by itself* determine what takes place *within* that clearing. Consequently, I think we need to recognize that the dimensionality of the clearing not only transcends the reach of the human; it even *exceeds* its grounding in and by *Da-sein*. This is what our human existence as *Da-sein* means: exposure to what exceeds, what is beyond, what is other. Every clearing presupposes a clearing. But what grounds the latter? Only another clearing. This suggests that our lives are ultimately groundless, built hanging, as it were, over an abyss, always vulnerable to inherently unknowable situations, be they common and familiar, or strange and unprecedented, perhaps even apocalyptic catastrophes, radically traumatic events. This is what, invoking a God that Heidegger, however, would have refrained from introducing, Schelling would have called the "anarchy of the ground," the "incomprehensible base of reality in things"—"that which remains, never manifesting"—"*der nie aufgehende Rest.*"[4] The clearing is a structure that opens us to what exceeds the bounds of knowability within this structure. Thus, for Heidegger, *Da-sein* and *Sein* are, as Parmenides said, "the same," but they do not coincide: there is no logical identity.

†

In "On the Question Concerning the Determination of Thinking," a 1965 text, Heidegger attempts with exceptional care to clarify his statement in *Being and Time* (§28), where he said that the existence of the human being is, as such, the clearing: "*Das Dasein des Menschen ist selbst die Lichtung.*" *Dasein*, here, means the essence. But how should we understand this word *selbst*?

> *Dasein* [understood as appropriated, hence as *Da-sein*] is the clearing for presencing [*Anwesenheit*] itself but is certainly not [*durchaus nicht*] the clearing insofar as the clearing first *is Dasein* [*insofern die Lichtung erst das Dasein ist*], i.e., insofar as it grants *Dasein* as such [*d.h. es als ein solches gewährt*, thereby making it possible for *Dasein* to be, or ex-ist, in the first place]. The analytic of *Dasein* [in *Being and Time*] does not yet get at what is proper to the clearing [*gelangt noch nicht in das Eigene der Lichtung,*

i.e., does not get at the appropriation of *Dasein*] and in no way gets at the region [*Bereich*] to which the clearing for its part belongs [*zugehört*].[5]

A few years later, in the *Zollikon Seminars*, Heidegger argued that "*Da-sein*'s standing-in-openness [*Die Offenständigkeit des Da-seins*] 'is' the sustaining [*Ausstehen*] of the clearing. *Lichtung* and *Da-sein* have belonged together from the beginning [*im vorhinein*] and the determining unity of the togetherness is their *Ereignis* [appropriation]" (ZSG: 223/ZSE 178). Moreover, as he says in *Mindfulness*: "*Da-sein* is the historical ground, appropriated by the *Er-eignis*, of the clearing of being": "*Das Da-sein ist der aus dem Er-eignis ereignete geschichtliche Grund der Lichtung des Seyns*" (GA 66: 328/M 291). In neither of these statements, however, does the philosopher recognize a strict logical identity between *Da-sein* and *Lichtung*. The very notions of (i) sustaining the openness and (ii) historical grounding would seem to contradict such identity. *Da-sein* and "clearing" are indeed two names, two designations, for the same phenomenon; but they are not identical.

In his revised 1949 "Introduction" to *What Is Metaphysics?*, we find Heidegger already trying to resolve the unsettled questions his phenomenology raised with regard to the essence of *Dasein* in *Being and Time*: "In *Being and Time*, the term 'existence' is understood exclusively in reference to the being of the human being. But once 'existence' is understood correctly, the 'essence' of *Dasein* can be thought, in the openness of which being itself announces and also conceals itself, both granting itself and withdrawing itself; at the same time, this truthing of being [*Wahrheit des Seins*, i.e., the clearing for presencing in the interplay of concealment and unconcealment] *does not exhaust itself* in Dasein, *nor can it by any means simply be identified with it*, as in the metaphysical assertion that all objectivity is as such also subjectivity" (GA 9: 373–74/PM 283).

In this text, Heidegger defines what he means by "existence." That term names the *essence* (*Wesen*) of the human being (*Dasein*), namely *Da-sein*: "a way of being, specifically, the being of that being w*hich stands open* for the openness of being *in which it stands*" (GA 9: 374/PM 283–84. Italics added). Although the clearing—being itself—must be *identified* with *Da-sein* (the human essence, *Dasein* hyphenated) inasmuch as *Da-sein* is the situating *site* for the clearing, neither the *dimensionality* of the clearing nor its *historical form* can be reduced to individual human existence. Not even the latter, because *Da-sein* "merely" provides the essential, structurally necessary condition—the *Da* for the clearing to take place. In its ineluctable thrown-openness, the *Da* is the opening and clearing of a world; it lets the clearing happen as it must; but by itself, as such, the structural dis-position, namely, *Da-sein*, cannot fully determine the actual dimensionality and historical character of the clearing, which always remains beyond its powers of disclosedness, partially concealed; nor, *a fortiori*, can the open structure that is a *Da-sein* fully determine, by itself, what can appear within its clearing. We human beings, each a *Dasein*, exist in historical conditions beyond our control. And we know this phenomenologically.

The argument might be illuminated if we consider the figure–ground structure as it occurs in perception, where there is an organic, dynamic interaction between figure and ground. In the perceptual situation, the ground yields, both in the sense of giving over and in the sense of giving up: it gives, yields, or enables the emergence and saliency of a figure, while at the same time necessarily withdrawing from attention, yielding to the prominence of that figure. Even though the ground yields in both those ways, the intrinsically organic harmony of the whole is such that it necessarily "gives" or "sends" itself *together with* the figure. Of course, as the ground engaged in every perception is inherently an *openness*, it does not, and could not ever, "give" or "send" itself in totality. The ground always eludes totalization; in response to efforts to grasp or apprehend it in totality, the ground inherently withdraws in the formation of another, more inclusive ground, ultimately drawing us into an abyss. The logic of the ground is, in this way, ultimately abyssal. In its inherent openness, the clearing is not only irreducible to our human existence—*menschliches Dasein*; because of the dimension of concealment, it is not even reducible to the opened structure of clearing—the *erlichtetes Da-sein*—that appropriates human existence, throwing it open to be the clearing. Such is the phenomenological logic of the *Gestalt* in its historical reality.

†

In thinking with his key words, *Sein*, *Da-sein*, *Ereignis*, and *Lichtung*, Heidegger frequently invokes "world." What does he mean? In his 1946 "Letter on Humanism," written in response to the French philosopher Jean Beaufret, Heidegger explained, in what is perhaps his most lucid formulation, what he meant by "world," explicitly identifying it as a name for the opened clearing that, as appropriated, is *Da-sein*:

> "World" does not at all signify beings or any realm of beings, but only the openness of being [*"Welt" bedeutet nicht ein Seiendes und keinen Bereich von Seiendem, sondern die Offenheit des Seins*]. The human being is, and is human, in that he is the ex-isting one. He stands out in the openness of being. . . . "World" is the clearing of being [*"Welt" ist die Lichtung des Seins*], into which the human being stands out on the basis of his thrown essence. . . . Thought in terms of ex-istence [*Ek-sistenz*], "world" is

in a certain sense precisely "the beyond" [*das Jenseitige*] within ex-istence and for it. . . . The human being in his essence is ex-istent into the openness of being, into the open region that first clears [*lichtet*] the "between" within which a "relation" [*"Beziehung"*] of subject to object can "be." (GA 9: 350/PM 266)

"World" thus names that which makes it possible for us to experience the meaningful presence and absence of beings. Our very existence as human beings clears a world. Our commonly shared world is a clearing: a clearing with a long, intricately differentiated history. Each of us, as existing individuals, clears a world where we are, where we happen to be: our *Eigen-welt*, a unique perspective on the world that, in our *Mit-sein*, our being-with-others, we share and clear with others. We stand *in*, live *in*, the clearings, the worlds, our very existence intrinsically forms: we are not transcendental egos standing, existing, *outside* the worlds we open, as if these worlds, these clearings, were the *objects* that the transcendental ego produced for its beholding. Heidegger's use of the word *Inständigkeit* accordingly carries not only the sense of steadfastness, it also carries the sense of being situated, standing steadfastly *in* its world.

The world that is the structure of all these clearings is, as such, necessarily prior—structurally prior—to the subject-object relation. The subject–object relation, within which every individual *Dasein* becomes a "subject" and everything encountered becomes an "object," is a structure that emerges from, that is, out of, the belonging together of *Mensch* and *Sein* in the clearing of the world. According to Heidegger, it is a structure that emerged into experience and into its representation in metaphysical thought only in the modern world. It is distinctive of the character of our modern world.

In "The Danger," one of his 1949 Bremen lectures on "Insight into That Which Is," Heidegger says: "*Welt ereignet, es lichtend-wahrend, das Dingen des Dinges.*" That says: "The occurring of the world enables the thing to come into its own, protecting it by providing the clearing." Or perhaps: "World lets the thing be thing, protecting it in its clearing" (GA 79: 48/ BF 46). In other words, the world is to be understood as the open clearing, making possible the time–space interplay of concealment and unconcealment, the ontological dimension, within which things as things take place. But, according to Heidegger, there is a long history to be told about the emergence and predominance of this world order, epochs in the making.

†

Scholars will no doubt have noticed by now that, whereas Heidegger invariably speaks of the clearing, I often speak of clearings. This plural is not an insurrection against his singular. Heidegger tends to prefer thinking first and foremost in terms of formal indications—essential structures and functions. Formulated in the singular, the structure of this essence is brought to a certain admirable lucidity; but its phenomenological explication requires that thinking work with the plural, unfolding the richness about which the singular remains silent. There is not just *one* clearing. If, as Heidegger says, "world" is another way of referring to what he calls "the clearing," then we need to recognize that there are many worlds, many clearings: historical worlds past and present; cultural worlds; social worlds; imaginary worlds; and so many personal and private worlds, mine and yours. We might accordingly give thought to the world of Stone Age hunters; the world of medieval Dutch peasants; the world of the sixteenth-century Venetian cartographer; the world of plantation slaves in the American South; the world of movie stars; the world of tennis fans; the world of the emerging bourgeoisie in contemporary China; the world of the mid-twentieth-century suburban housewife in America; the world of the Gothic cathedral stone mason; the world of the ancient Greek shipbuilder. So many clearings, so many worlds.

We recognize in our historiography the succession of centuries, regarding them as a succession of worlds and worldviews. Heidegger thinks of *epochs* in the history of being, always remembering the hermeneutical truth that the Greek origin of that word conveys: every disclosing of the meaning of being—of what it means to "be"—emerges from a realm of concealment and unknowable possibilities, to which it remains inseparably bound. In the course of reflecting on the history of philosophy in the Western world and critically interpreting the modern world of the West in the light of his philosophy of history, Heidegger is unquestionably committed, despite his persistent use of *Lichtung* in the singular, to the recognition of a plurality of clearings—a plurality of worlds and historical epochs. Thus, in reading the history of Western philosophy, especially with regard to its representations of ontology, he recognizes and rigorously distinguishes unfolding conceptions among the Greeks, the Romans, the early Christians, the later medieval Christians, the early moderns, the later moderns, and his twentieth-century contemporaries. Likewise, the historical course of Western culture and civilization is subjected to a critical interpretation that represents this course in terms of historical periods and epochs: an evolution determined and marked above all by significant differences in the ways that being is concealed and unconcealed and culminating, in our own time, in the most extreme stage of nihilism—the nearly total reification and denial of being in a world that, formed in submission to the will to power, has virtually lost its needed dimension of concealment.

Even perception is thoroughly subject to historical influences, despite unchanging physiology. It is not only the common *understanding* of seeing and the nature of what is visible for seeing but the character of seeing itself, and the characteristics of what is visible, that undergo changes in the time from the world of pre-perspective medieval Italy to the world of late Renaissance Italy and from that world to the modern world, the world that we recognize as "true" to our own even in the late Cubist paintings by Pablo Picasso and the German Expressionism of Oscar Bluemner and Ernst Ludwig Kirchner. Hearing is also not the same in the Western world of today as it was even 300 years ago. The history of music abundantly confirms this fact: extreme musical dissonances and tonalities that were intolerable in Bach's world are in today's world received with praise when they appear in jazz and other contemporary forms of music. There was even a world of difference between the music of Bach and that of Mozart: a difference not merely of style but in their conceptions of musicality, a difference we can hear.

Crucial in the sharing of a world is language. In the sharing of a distinct language, or a distinct idiom or vocabulary, a distinct cultural world is shared. We human beings are the only beings endowed with a capacity for language. All the other animals, and of course plants, too, living without language as we know it, "are lodged in their respective environments, never freely inhabiting the clearing of being which alone is 'world'" (GA 9: 326/PM 248). The other, more developed animals live in habitats; but they are, Heidegger thinks, "world-poor," deprived of a world. They are not endowed with the ability to understand and question the world into which they find themselves cast.[6] The other animals do of course communicate among themselves and many communicate with human beings. But their means of communication are fundamentally different from human language.

Each of us has not only a private world of many modalities and dimensions but also a uniquely individual, personal perspective on the common world—or worlds—shared with others. And because we live with others in a shared world, it is possible for others to know and understand something about my private world far better than I can. So, even what might be called "my own little private world" exceeds and surpasses my knowledge and understanding. And when an individual dies, the private world of meaning that individual cleared, and the perspective that individual formed in regard to the world, or worlds, shared with others, will also pass away, never to emerge again. Worlds are opened, worlds are closed, each one with its distinctive representation of the meaning of being, clearing the way for our experience of the presencing of beings.

Remembering, and still mourning, the passing of his beloved aunt in a letter to George Sand, the incomparable artist Eugène Delacroix wrote: "Each of the beings necessary to our existence who disappears takes away with him a whole world of feelings that no other relationship can revive."[7] When we pass away, all the worlds of meaning our presence has opened perish, closing with us.

†

Unlike the other animals, we human beings are cast to live freely in this openness, this clearing—and we need to understand what this existence, this appropriation, means for the way we live our lives, because, although our nature is such that we all have a certain awareness of this openness, our understanding tends to be limited and misleading. We tend to go through life unmindful of the clearing and our role in its openness, attentive instead only to what the clearing gives us to encounter.

Now, when Heidegger says that we human beings "stand in the clearing," it is important to understand that, first and foremost, what is at stake is our standing in the *dis-position*, the essential structure that is our ownmost essential nature: "*das Innestehen des Menschen ins Da*" (ZSG: 221/ZSE 176). This "standing" is a question of our responsibility—our taking up of our appropriation. First of all, therefore, what is at stake is our "standing" *within ourselves*, that is, our standing or measuring up—*daseinsmäßig*—in regard to our essence, appropriation, not only our standing in the clearing, the world around us. If we are standing or staying in our essential nature as thrown open, then we are enowning and enacting the potential in our nature, our essential dis-position, thrown open to be the clearing, opening and grounding the world within which we are placing ourselves—opening a world-clearing within which we ourselves stand. Our appropriation to the clearing, the lighting, calls for steadfastness (*Inständigkeit*) in bearing responsibility for *maintaining* its openness—an openness that is our only possible hope for meeting the conditions necessary for the fulfillment of our destiny. So to stand in the clearing—our *Innestehen*—is to be steadfast in *taking responsibility* for its maintenance, its preservation. This is our *Ereignung*, our appropriation.

Let us recall what we discussed earlier in regard to "Aletheia (Heraclitus, Fragment 16)," written in 1943, where Heidegger remarks that "the event of clearing is the world [*Das Ereignis der Lichtung ist die Welt*]" (GA 7: 283/EGT 118). Given the double meaning of *Ereignis*, as event or as appropriation, this sentence can mean not only (i) that the event, or happening, of the clearing is (what opens) the (or a) world of meaning but also (ii) that the appropriation of the clearing (which is the appropriation of *Dasein* to *be* the clearing) is the opening of a meaningful world. The clearing *is* an event; but it is no ordinary event. Rather, it is not only the event constitutive of our very existence but also intrinsically an event that necessarily involves *our appropriation to Da-sein*. Ontologically understood, then, the "world" is the appropriated, enowned, and properly grounded clearing. Unfolding this matter to make it more perspicuous phenomenologically, I suggest that we should say: *behind* the event, the taking place, of the clearing is the appropriation, the dis-position of *Dasein* that claims and appropriates it to *be* the clearing that is the opening of the intelligibility conditions for a world of meaningfulness.

†

The concept of the clearing actually appears already in *Being and Time*. According to Heidegger, the clearing is constitutive of *Da-sein*. However,

> the light that constitutes this clearedness [*Gelichtetheit*] of *Dasein* is not something ontically present-at-hand [*vorhanden*] as a power or source for a radiant brightness occurring in the entity on occasion. That by which this entity [*Dasein*] is essentially cleared [*erlichtet*]—in other words, that which makes it [ontologically] both inherently "open" and inherently "bright"—is what we have defined as "care." (GA 2: 463–64/BT 401–2)

"In care," he says, "the full disclosedness of the "there" [the *Da*] is grounded":

> Only by this clearedness is any illuminating, any awareness, . . . made possible. We understand the light of this clearedness only if we are not seeking some power implanted in us and present-at-hand but are interrogating the whole constitution of *Dasein*'s being—namely *care*—and are interrogating it as to the unitary basis for its existential possibility. (Ibid.)

I suggest that we think of this caring, a crucial term in *Being and Time*, as a responsibility belonging to our appropriation—our *Er-eignung*. And what this appropriation demands of us is that we take into our care what it means to learn the ability to be appropriately responsive—for instance, in the character of our way of seeing and hearing.

In *Dasein*'s appropriation, Heidegger recognizes a certain ineluctable responsibility: *Da-sein* is the guardian of being, that is, vigilant protector of the ontological openness of the clearing (*Wächter der Offenheit des Seyns selbst*); and that means also that to be *Da-sein* is to be the preserver (*Bewahrer*) of the *truth* (*Wahrheit*) of being, preserver of the being of *beings* in regard to their concealment and unconcealment.[8] This is what ontological "care" ("Sorge") comes to mean. Many texts, texts written over the course of many years, support this understanding. In his "Letter on Humanism," Heidegger says: "As existing, the human being sustains *Da-sein* in that he takes the *Da*, [i.e., his opening of a site for] the clearing of being, into 'care.' [ . . . Thus the human being unfolds essentially in the thrownness of its being as a destinal sending [*Es west im Wurf des Seins als des schickend Geschicklichen*]" (GA 9: 327/PM 249). And as he explains in a letter to Roger Munier (July 31, 1969), summarizing his discussion of *Da-sein* in *Being and Time*: the point is to experience in *Da-sein* the sense that we, as human beings, are fully ourselves, the *Da*, that is, the situated, situating openness of being, insofar as we undertake to "preserve [*bewahren*] that openness and, in preserving it, unfold it [*entfalten*]" (GA 15: 145/FS 88).[9] Indeed, as Heidegger expresses this point, making a connection between words that, as it happens, is visible only in the German: "The opennness [*Offenständigkeit*] of *Da-sein* 'is' the bearing and enduring [*das Ausstehen*] of the clearing" (ZSG: 351/ZSE: 281).[10] We are appropriated, hence assigned and sent on our way, to be "steadfast in the clearing and in its stewardship" (GA 71: 197–99/E 168–69).

Thus, the *clearing* forms in the *Ereignis*, understood as our appropriated, appropriating dis-position to *Da-sein*. It is thus *Da-sein* as clearing that is the fundamental source of the "giving," or "sending"—the so-called *Schickung*—through which the presencing of beings happens. Heidegger's occasional use, in this context, of the nouns *Geschick* and *Schickung* as well as related verbs (especially *schicken* but also *schenken* and *geben* and the noun *Gabe*) can unfortunately lead to ontotheological misunderstandings. Granting us access to beings, the clearing, as Heidegger likes to say, "gives," "sends," or "dispatches" beings to us; but all that he means by these mischievous words is that the clearing makes it possible to experience things—experience things in meaningful ways. But, in a certain sense, the clearing itself is something "given" or "sent," in that, since our lives are conditioned by history, the clearings that are feasible for us are "dispensations" of being, fields of experience, shaped by the historical world and accordingly determining for a time the meaning of being—what, in the clearings of a particular epoch, can be intelligible and meaningful. Entities, of course, are never experienced outside, or apart from, the clearings or worlds from which they draw their meaning. Thus, the historical conditions that are involved in shaping the formation of *Da-sein*'s clearings are involved at the same time in determining the meaning of what can be "given" or "sent" in and through those same clearings. The essential point is simply, however, that our *Da-sein*—the human being (*Menschsein*) in its appropriation as appropriated—is nevertheless *responsible* for sustaining them in their ontological dimension and role.

"The Origin of the Work of Art" presents the relation between clearing and world this way: "This open [*Offene*] happens in the midst of beings. [In other words: An opening happens *whenever and wherever* there is a *Da-sein*.] To the open, there belongs a world and an earth. But the world is not simply the open that corresponds [*entspricht*] to the clearing; and the earth is not simply the closed [*das Verschlossene*] that corresponds to concealment [*Verbergung*]" (GA 5: 42/PLT 55). In the clearing, world and earth are in interaction: earth is the ground on which the world is built, and world is that within which the earth is given its meaning as grounding. Earth and world are in incessant, endless strife, the earth ever reclaiming for itself, reducing to earth, what the world builds upon it, whereas the world struggles with the earth, and against the earth, to make it serve human purposes. But it is only in the world that the earth receives meaning; and it is only in relation to the earth that we can fully understand not only the fragility and power of our world but also the frightening vulnerability of our grounding and building on the earth—and can harvest some meaning in our fated mortality.

†

Historical conditions operative in determining the ontological character of the clearings that *Da-sein* opens in the course of its existence affect in a multitude of ways the meaningful presence, or being, of all the beings that can be encountered in those particular clearings. The complex conditions involved in the clearings that *Da-sein* projects thereby determine, *by way of the clearing*, what things can appear meaningful within that clearing and how they can appear. At least in the 1930s and 1940s, Heidegger certainly seems to be proposing an onto-historical (*seinsgeschichtliche*) narrative about the Western world, identifying and marking the different historical phases, or epochs, in the unfolding of the different shapes and characteristics of the clearing itself as that which determines, for all recognized beings, the possible meanings of being.

In attempting to think critically about the fate of the question of being in metaphysics, Heidegger undertook an interpretation exposing the hidden logic in the historical unfolding of the discourse of metaphysics in the Western world. And this inevitably drew him into critical reflections on the historical unfolding of different worlds—or different epochs in the history of what we call the Western world. In Heidegger's thought, we can see a correspondence, a certain parallelism, between (i) the logic in the unfolding of the history of metaphysics as a discourse concerning being and (ii) the unfolding of different epochs in the history of the Western world. Thus, we find Heidegger reflecting not only on how, in its Roman inheritance, Greek metaphysics was fundamentally altered, but reflecting on a corresponding difference in the two worlds—in how Greek and Roman philosophers differently saw their respective worlds. Heidegger likewise proposes that we see an epochal change distinctive of the early and medieval Christian worlds and corresponding changes in the discourse of metaphysics belonging to those worlds. He also situates the metaphysics of Descartes and Leibniz in a certain world of culture and technology, and he reads Nietzsche in relation to developments in the modern world, simultaneously casting light on the philosopher's thought—nihilism and the death of God—and on the reification and denial of being in the distinctive world in which he lived. Consistent with Heidegger's unique interpretive narratives, we can discern other momentous events indicative of historical changes in the Western world, changes manifestly reflected in the course of Western metaphysics. And we can discern a distinctive world in the humanism of the Renaissance; different emphases, hence different worlds in the conceptions of Enlightenment that emerged in England, France, and Germany; and of course the character of a very different world in which we of today find ourselves living. Heidegger characterizes our contemporary world as totally dominated by the exigencies of "Machenschaft": machinery, technology, and the dehumanizing, reifying technocratic order it ruthlessly imposes. Different epochs, different worlds, different clearings—different understandings of being, of the truth of being, and of beings themselves: different paradigms of knowledge, truth, and reality.

Drawing on the Greek derivation of the word "epoch," Heidegger thinks of history in terms of a hermeneutic, *aletheic* logic of unconcealment and concealment: each historical epoch is an interpretive figure-ground *Gestalt* in which it is possible, retrospectively, to discern at least to some extent that, and how, a certain distinctively new understanding of being—of what it means, and could mean, for something to *be*—emerged into salience and predominance, paradigmatically organizing conditions of intelligibility and meaning, while earlier understandings and other understandings of being are in some way concealed, abandoned, suppressed, or sublated, left behind, forgotten.

Thus, in the history of painting—say, from the Byzantine period to the Italian Renaissance, we can discern very clearly the different epochal *Gestalten*: the striking fact of a comprehensible succession of ontological epochs, a narrative of historical succession that makes sense in regard to the way entities and their world were perceived and understood. In the Byzantine world order, the Christ was represented as all-seeing, beholding us and, in effect, holding us to account for ourselves, without our reciprocity, in the piercing gaze of His beholding; whereas, in the awakened humanism of the Italian Rinascimento, the power in the relation between the Christ and us mortals is reversed: asserting ourselves, we are in the position of the one who sees, holding the Christ in our beholding. This momentous historical development is discussed at greater length in my second volume.

†

Heidegger's thinking itself underwent significant changes over the course of his lifetime. Thus, in the Le Thor Seminar of 1969, he looked back on his ways of understanding the clearing phenomenologically: first, in an all-too-Husserlian way, he conceived his project in terms of the meaning of being; then, for a while misleadingly, as the truth of being (*die Wahrheit des Seins*); and finally, he turned from the question of being to the question of our appropriation to the clearing, conceiving the latter as the topology of being:

> With *Sein und Zeit*, the question concerning being receives an entirely other meaning. Here it appears as the question concerning being as being. It becomes thematic in *Sein und Zeit* under the name "the question concerning the meaning of being." (GA 15: 344/FS 47)

Later this formulation was given up in favor of "the question concerning the truth of being"— and finally in favor of "the question concerning the site or location of being [*Frage nach dem Ort oder Ortschaft des Seins*]"—a way of thinking about the clearing "from out of which the name 'topology of being' arose [*entsprang*]":

> Three words [*Drei Worte*], which, inasmuch as they succeed one another, at the same time indicate three steps along the way of thinking (*drei Schritte auf dem Weg des Denkens*]:
>     MEANING [*SINN*] – TRUTH [*WAHRHEIT*] – PLACE [*ORT*] (τόπος). (GA 15: 344/FS 47)

In this movement of thought, Heidegger corrected his misleading claims in regard to truth and completed his break with Husserlian subjectivism, while remaining committed to the discipline of phenomenology.

†

We bear some responsibility, not only for what comes to light, what appears in the clearing, and how it all appears, but also for the historical conditions and character of the clearing itself—that which makes possible or impossible, in their historicity, the appearing of beings in their presence or absence.

In this regard, I believe it is important to recognize that Heidegger is emphatic in arguing for the protection and preservation of concealment and darkness. In "The Age of the World Picture" (1938), he argues that we must take responsibility for "the 'happening' of unconcealment without falling into that presenting [*Vor-stellen*] of beings that forgets the simultaneous concealment of beings as a whole" (GA 5: 87/QCT 216). And in *The Event* (1941–1942), he says:

> The clearing is the essential occurrence of the open, and the open is the passage way [*Durchlaß*] of opposition and arrival (beings) out of what is beingless. The clearing can thus *seem* empty, if we forget that it illuminates and gives brightness [to the things that appear within its compass] and that the passageway as an enabling [*Lassen*] is . . . the protecting of the possibility of truth in the interplay of concealment and unconcealment [*Gewahr der Wahrheit*]. (GA 71: 208/E 178)

The clearing must not be thought hostile to concealment, hostile to darkness. In fact, as Heidegger argues in his commentary on Hölderlin's "Remembrance," the clearing is, as it must be, the guardian of truth, hence, too, of concealment. Indeed, it must be the guardian of darkness as much as it is the guardian of disclosure and light, if not even more so, as it is the darkness that allows the appearing to emerge from concealment, and it is the darkness that preserves the reality of the appearing in what is concealed (GA 4: 119/HP 141–42). And inasmuch as this question of concealment and unconcealment, darkness and light in relation to the clearing, is very much a matter of our rising up, as human beings, in the arrogance of a will to power, Schelling is perhaps once again one of Heidegger's deepest sources of inspiration, arguing: "In its genuine sense, the understanding is born from that which is without understanding. Without this preceding darkness, creatures have no reality; darkness is their necessary inheritance."[11] For Schelling, the raising into light of the deepest, darkest ground "occurs in none of the creatures visible to us other than man. In man there is the whole power of the dark principle and at the same time the whole strength of the light. In man there is the deepest abyss and the loftiest sky."[12] Although not willing to taking over the entire theological dimension of Schelling's metaphysics, Heidegger would nevertheless have liked this particular thought. So, as Heidegger remarks in that commentary on Hölderlin's poem, we human beings "must learn to acknowledge the dark as something unavoidable and keep at bay those prejudices [*Vorurteile*] that would destroy the lofty reign of the dark [*das hohe Walten des Dunklen*]" (GA 4: 119/HP 141–42). The dark reigns.

## NOTES

1. Henry David Thoreau, "Sounds," *Walden*, in *The Portable Thoreau*, ed. Carl Bode (New York: Viking Press, 1947), 366.

2. Dicxon Valderruten, *No le temas a la montaña* (Managua, Nicaragua: ANE Noruega, Edición del Centro Nicaragüense de Escritores, 2014), 52–53; *Don't You Fear the Mountain*, ch. 8, 47. In Spanish: "tenés que acostumbrarte a que cuando ponés un pie en la montaña se encienden todos tus sentidos."

3. Martin Heidegger, *Einleitung in die Philosophie*, GA 27:137.

4. See Friedrich Wilhelm Joseph von Schelling, *Philosophische Untersuchungen über das Wesen der menschlichen Freiheit und die damit zusammenhängenden Gegenstände*, *Sämtliche Werke*, ed. Karl Friedrich August Schelling (Stuttgart-Augsburg: J. G. Cotta, 1809), vol. 7, 359–60; *Philosophical Investigations into the Essence of Human Freedom*, trans. Jeff Love and Johannes Schmidt (Albany: State University of New York Press, 2006), 29; *Schelling: Of Human Freedom*, trans. James Gutmann (Chicago: Open Court Publishing Co., 1936), 33–34.

5. Heidegger, "Zur Frage nach der Bestimmung der Sache des Denkens," *Reden und andere Zeugnisse eines Lebensweges*, GA 16: 631.

6. For a lengthy set of reflections on the concept of world in relation to the being of human beings and the being of plants and animals, see Heidegger, *Die Grundbegriffe der Metaphysik. Welt—Endlichkeit—Einsamkeit*, GA 29/30; *The Fundamental Concepts of Metaphysics. World, Finitude, Solitude*, trans. William McNeill and Nicholas Walker (Bloomington: Indiana University Press, 1995).

7. Eugène Delacroix, *Selected Letters 1813–1863*, ed. and trans. Jean Stewart (Boston: Museum of Fine Art, 1970, 2001), 278. See Delacroix's 1835 painting of Madame Henri François Riesener.

8. Heidegger, "Beilage zu §41," *Grundfragen der Philosophie*, GA 45: 227; "Supplement to §41," *Fundamental Questions of Philosophy*. My translation. And see *Beiträge zur Philosophie*, GA 65:299; *Contributions to Philosophy*, 236, where Heidegger uses the phrase "Wächter der Wahrheit des Seyns," meaning "vigilant protector of the truth of being," where "truth of being" refers to the clearing.

9. Heidegger, *Vier Seminare. Le Thor 1966, 1968, 1949, Zähringen 1973*, GA 15: 145: *Es gilt, das Da-sein in dem Sinne zu erfahren, daß der Mensch das 'Da', d.h. die Offenheit des Seins für ihn, selbst ist, indem er es übernimmt, sie zu bewahren und bewahrend zu entfalten.*

10. Heidegger's letter to Medard Boss, dated September 24, 1967. Also see the "Einleitung zu 'Was ist Metaphysik?'," GA 9: 373–74; *Wegmarken*, 203; "Introduction"

to *What Is Metaphysics?*, 283–84: "What does 'existence' mean in *Being and Time?* The word names a way of being; specifically, the being of that being that stands open for the openness of being in which it stands in 'withstanding' it. This 'withstanding' is experienced under the name 'care.' Care is the ek-static essence of *Dasein.*" Here again Heidegger draws on a constellation of words related to standing and staying.

11. Schelling, *Philosophische Untersuchungen über das Wesen der menschlichen Freiheit und die damit zusammenhängenden Gegenstände, Sämtliche Werke,* ed. Karl Friedrich August Schelling (Stuttgart-Augsburg: J. G. Cotta, 1809), vol. 7, 360; *Philosophical Investigations into the Essence of Human Freedom,* trans. Jeff Love and Johannes Schmidt (Albany: State University of New York Press, 2006), 29; *Schelling: Of Human Freedom,* trans. James Gutmann (Chicago: Open Court Publishing Co., 1936), 33–34. And see, also Schelling's *Sämtliche Werke,* vol. 7, 362, 32 in the Love and Schmidt translation, and 38 in the older Gutmann translation.

12. Schelling, *Philosophische Untersuchungen über das Wesen der menschlichen Freiheit und die damit zusammenhängenden Gegenstände, Sämtliche Werke,* ed. Karl Friedrich August Schelling (Stuttgart-Augsburg: J. G. Cotta, 1809), vol. 7, 362; *Philosophical Investigations into the Essence of Human Freedom,* trans. Jeff Love and Johannes Schmidt (Albany: State University of New York Press, 2006), 32; *Schelling: Of Human Freedom,* trans. James Gutmann (Chicago: Open Court Publishing Co., 1936), 38.

# 5

## GESCHICK

## Toward Another Inception?

Where there is no vision, the people perish.

—Ralph Waldo Emerson, "The Method of Nature"[1]

History can sometimes seem to be a profound illusion, but if so, it is an illusion without which no insight into the essence of things would be possible.

—Gershom Scholem, *Briefe*[2]

In every epoch [*Epoche*], we must attempt anew to wrest [*von neuem . . . abzugewinnen*] the tradition we take over [*die Überlieferung*] from a conformism that is about to overpower it [*überwältigen*].

—Walter Benjamin, "Theses on the Philosophy of History"[3]

History is the transporting of a people [*die Entrückung eines Volkes*] into its appointed task [*in sein Aufgegebenes*] as entrance into that people's endowment [*als Einrückung in sein Mitgegebenes*].

—Heidegger, "The Origin of the Work of Art"
(GA 5: 65/PLT 17)

Our vigilance and guardianship [*Wächterschaft*] of the truth of being [the openness of the clearing that makes presencing possible in the interplay of concealment and unconcealment] is the ground for another history.

—Heidegger, *Contributions to Philosophy*
(GA 65: 240–41/CP 190)

221

> Is inceptual thinking metaphysics or preliminary to it, or does
> something entirely different occur [*ereignet*] within inceptual
> thinking?
>
> —Heidegger, *Heraclitus* (GA 55: 100/H 75)

Time and history are of immeasurable importance in Heidegger's great project. Introducing time into metaphysics, Heidegger deconstructed the illusion of constant and immutable presence that, from Plato to Nietzsche's contemporaries, had taken possession of European philosophical thought. Arguing, in *Being and Time*, for the distinction between straightforward serial time (*Zeitlichkeit*), time that can be calculated, and the underlying phenomenological dimensions of ek-static temporality (*Temporalität*),[4] and later, in texts wherein he attempted to understand the historical significance of the pre-Socratic Greek philosophers, arguing for the distinction between a historical beginning (*Beginn*) and a historical inception (*Anfang*), Heidegger challenged in the deepest and most unsettling way our prevailing experience of time and history: our negation of the past, reduction of the present, and abdication of responsibility for a redeeming vision of the future.

Even before *Being and Time* (1927), he was already arguing for the importance of thinking about history for the sake of the future. Living our historicality authentically should mean finding in the past possibilities for constructing a fitting future out of the present. Here is a passage from a 1924 lecture on "The Concept of Time." Concentrating on Dilthey, it is the first draft of what would become his 1927 book:

> The possibility of gaining access to history is based on the possibility of being futural [*zukünftig*], according to which what matters each time is a present that *understands* itself. . . . The riddle of history lies in what it means to *be* historical, or *live* historically [*Das Rätsel der Geschichte liegt in dem, was es heißt, geschichtlich zu sein*]. (GA 64: 123/CT 20)

This retrieving of the past for the sake of the future constitutes a task for the present that Heidegger thinks needs to be guided by the concept of *Geschick*. Thus, as he says in "The Anaximander Fragment" (1946):

> Little depends on what we represent and portray of the past; but much depends on the way we are mindful of what is destined [*des Geschicklichen eingedenk sind*]. (GA 5: 338/EGT 27)

This passage is one of the few times when he uses the archaic-sounding expression *eingedenk sein*. We need to be mindful of what as yet unrecognized, unexplored potentialities for the future there might be even now in that which has been (*das Gewesene*), the still living past that we have been given to receive and appropriate. But what exactly does it mean to "live historically"? In the 1920s, 1930s, and 1940s, Heidegger manifestly struggled with this question, formulating it as a question to work through in the philosophical context he opens for thought. In a way, as he understood, it is not a question for which there could ever be one final comprehensive answer.

In this chapter, we will concentrate on matters pertaining to history—in particular, the philosopher's thoughts regarding "the history of being" and its *Geschick*. Although "Geschick" is a key word in Heidegger's project, a considerable number of the contexts in which the word is used render its meaning extremely unstable and problematic. This chapter will attempt to untangle the knots and resolve the ambiguities—or try, at the very least, to bring the nature of these interpretive problems into sharper relief.

In *Being and Time* (1927), what Heidegger means by *Geschick* (in the sense of "destiny") is quite clear. It refers to a community's assumption of responsibility for the futurity of its heritage, sustaining the vitality of this heritage by renewing in remembrance and critical thought an experience of its bearing on the present. Somewhat later, namely, in the 1930s and early 1940s, the word's sense of destiny in his writings takes on the ideological character of German nationalism, a nationalism strongly brewed in centuries of ethnic and cultural superstition, prejudice, and animosity. But, by the late 1930s, it seems that Heidegger began to question what he wanted his use of "destiny" to say. Consequently, in texts belonging to the last years of the Second World War and the years in its wake, it becomes increasingly difficult to determine what content we should attribute to his invocations of destiny, even when we connect it to the idea of inception: the beginning of another paradigm of knowledge, truth, and reality in philosophical thought—and also, presumably, a correspondingly fundamental change in the organization and character of the life prevailing throughout the Western world. Moreover, in the post-War years, the word *Geschick* appears to take on an entirely different sense and reference, serving instead the phenomenology of *Da-sein* as clearing—although, as I shall argue, destiny is still very much at stake in this phenomenology (see, e.g., GA 14: 22/OTB 16–17). Indeed, even after the abuse of the concept in National Socialism and the Holocaust it enjoined, Heidegger's project never unequivocally abandoned the thought of destiny. However, he came around to realizing that the redeeming of a destiny is not something that can be achieved within historical time experienced in the way we habitually tend to do, namely, as a linear, one-dimensional series of encapsulated moments.

During the 1930s and the early 1940s, there is also a "history of being" freighting the philosopher's thought. Emphatically denied the familiar sense of history, this concept, possibly irremediably ambiguous and confused, defies easy interpretation, remaining elusive and indeed of questionable coherence—until, so it seems, the philosopher, repudiating it with exceptional vehemence, ceased to find it necessary or even useful.

†

In my judgment, one of Heidegger's greatest and most enduring contributions is his deep and fairly comprehensive interpretive meta-narrative regarding the history of Western philosophy, which, at least for a long time, he considered, by way of an original and insightful critique, to be a tragic but not at all inevitable history of decline: a *Verfallsgeschichte*. Behind this project of his there was always (i) a certain *philosophy of history*, a certain distinctive way of thinking about history, namely in terms of the potential in the past we inherit for achieving the great "destiny" that he thinks we should take to be summoning us, and (ii) a certain *history of philosophy*, or rather, more specifically, an original critical interpretation, or reading, of the history of metaphysics, showing its historical pattern in a logic of reductionism, reification, and totalization—hence, a history of decline, not only in the discourse of metaphysics but also in the Western world that it both critically reflects upon and—nevertheless—cannot avoid reflecting and repeating.

Heidegger's meta-narrative regarding history is thus always two-pronged: at once (i) a critique, a critical analysis and diagnosis, of a Western world that, together with its metaphysics, is perilously "out of joint" but also (ii) a poetic envisioning of an alternative future world the potential for which, conceived as "destiny," depends on our individual and collective assumption of responsibility for its appropriation and actualization.

†

In the course of his lifetime, Heidegger rigorously interrogated an impressive number of the greatest philosophical texts, spanning the history of philosophy in the Western world from the earliest pre-Socratic philosophers to Nietzsche. He certainly did not do justice to Spinoza, the greatest of Jewish philosophers, mostly neglecting his contribution, although not, I think, because of any prejudice, but rather because connecting his own thought to Spinoza's system, discerning the conflicts and affinities, and drawing material from it for use in his own project would have required a considerable stretch, with no obvious benefits (see, e.g., his invariably brief references to Spinoza in his lectures on Schelling's *Treatise on the Essence of Human Freedom*, GA 42). For Schelling, however, Spinoza was an extremely important thinker.

I will argue that we cannot understand Heidegger's project, which involves his interpretation of the history of philosophy, nor grasp its full significance, unless we recognize that behind it, though never sufficiently acknowledged, defined, and argued, there is an original philosophy of history, not only (i) constituting a singular *perspective* from which to interpret both the modern world we live in and the metaphysical discourses that belong to this world but also (ii) making possible a compelling critique of these discourses, and consequently (iii) laying the groundwork for a new paradigm of knowledge, truth, and reality, together with a new envisioning of life on this planet. While reading the historical texts in metaphysics, he always kept in mind the *world* that corresponds to these texts, because he understood that philosophy is not only a reflection on the world but inevitably also, no matter how original and critical, a reflection of it. Thus, in forming a critique of the one, he was always able to venture a corresponding critique of the other. And in these critiques, he always sought to discern possibilities for something better.

†

Heidegger manifestly loved and enjoyed the pre-Socratics, especially Anaximander, Parmenides, and Heraclitus, reflecting with insight on what their thinking brought to light, setting in motion the beginning of a philosophical discourse in the Western world. According to Heidegger's historical-ontological narrative, the "first inception" in philosophical thought commenced in the world of ancient Greece, when it occurred to the earliest philosophers—thinkers such as Anaximander, Heraclitus, and Parmenides—to ask the question of being. They were the first to elevate their thought above the tumult of the world to think being as such. But they did not make the phenomenological turn, reflexively questioning and understanding their own position in relation to this unconcealment of being: they did not reflect on being in terms of the phenomenology of their appropriation. Their profound reflections on being underwent a momentous change beginning with Plato, whose thought, as Heidegger interpreted it, produced the metaphysics that has culminated today in a pervasive nihilism, realizing the immanent but concealed potential in that first inception, the essence of which has become increasingly manifest only in the modern epoch—let us say with the beginning of large-scale industrialization and the creation of new institutions for the functioning of capitalism.

Singularly revealing was what he learned as he sought to understand, with as much scholarly rigor as possible, what these earliest philosophers of the Western world were thinking with their key words—for instance, *nous, logos, nomos, physis, aletheia, diké, moira, aitia, eidos, techné*—and pondered how, in the course of their adventures through history, these words could have been made to bring forth such different conceptual descendants.

According to Heidegger, the discourse that the early Greek philosophers set in motion was not merely a beginning (*Beginn*), the first in a straightforward succession of different derivative, more or less coherent contributions; it was, rather, an inception (*Anfang*), a beginning that originated and inaugurated something profoundly new—a beginning, moreover, that has continued to generate original thought, as Heidegger's own thought demonstrates. Thus, whereas a *beginning* is a point in time that passes away into an irretrievable past, an *inception* is a beginning that continues, like a freshwater spring, to generate new historical forms of life: it becomes a past that refuses to be buried; it is a past that belongs to the future, a past with claims on the future, pressing toward it. Therein it is full of promise, bearing a message of hope for those capable of recognizing and interpreting it.

However, this hope for the future is struggling today to survive. Heidegger's history of philosophy, in particular, his history of metaphysics, is a compelling reflection on the danger increasingly threatening the Western world. In this narrative, Heidegger connects (i) his critique of the great philosophical texts of the past to (ii) a critique, strongly influenced by Nietszche, in which he reads the neglect and denial of being in the history of philosophy in correlation to the history of a world in decline, a pattern of ever-increasing conceptual closure, reducing and reifying the ontological dimensionality of things, reducing and reifying the being of beings, and being itself, even to the point of regarding what is named "being" to be nothing, nothing at all—idle chatter. Thus, he exhibits consequential *correlations* between the nihilism he sees in metaphysics and the devastation of nihilism that he sees increasingly pervasive in Western culture and Western life.

A consequence of the neglect or outright denial of being, a strange "forgetfulness," is that, in the historical transmission of interpretations of being within the discourse of metaphysics (the discourse of ontology) in the Western world, all the original core concepts in Greek thought—*nous, logos, nomos, physis, aletheia, diké, aitia, eidos, techné,* and so on—have undergone, as early as their Roman appropriation in translation, devastating changes: an increasing reification, a certain narrowing, delimiting, hardening, and closing off in regard to their ontological dimensionality, their wonderfully rich poetic, metaphorical resonances and shadings of meaning, deep, complex, and intricate. *Nous* has been reduced to neurophysiology; *logos* has been reduced to standardized logical notation and logistics; *nomos*, originally divinely ordained law, remembered in poetic song according to the oral tradition of transmission, has been reduced to the institutional rule of unequivocal written law; *physis* has been reduced to the measurably physical; *aletheia*, the ground of truth, where an interplay of concealments and unconcealments occurs, has been reduced to truth as correctness; *diké* has been reduced to a justice of calculation; *aitia* has been reduced to physical causation; *eidos* has been reduced to a fixed essence detached from interactions with the world; and *techné* has been reduced to mechanical technique.

†

Heidegger's critique of philosophical discourse sensibly leads him into a corresponding critique of the modern world—everyday life in all its habitual everydayness. In keeping with this project, *Being and Time* condemns the ontological "forgetfulness" that his phenomenology shows to be at work even in the realm of perception—at work, for instance, in all our seeing and all our hearing. These demonstrations also reveal how, in consequence, the beings that we encounter in our seeing and hearing— and indeed, therefore, the world itself, as field or dimension within which these sensible, perceptible beings appear before us—are affected by such ontological "forgetfulness," such oblivion or reduction of their ontological dimension.

Thus, in *Being and Time*, Heidegger's thought was already moving outside the texts of philosophical discourse, outside a history of the generation and transmission of concepts, to render, by way of phenomenological description, what amounts to a scathingly critical judgment regarding the ontologically "forgetful" character of our habitual quotidian interactions with things, with beings, in the realm of perception: part of a more extensive critique of the modern world, a world suffering, he says, under the nihilism that has taken hold in the empty triumph of our will to power.

As Nietzsche argued and logical positivism subsequently confirmed when it denied values and ideals—the realm of merely subjective fictions— any relation to truth and even to meaningfulness, such nihilism turns everything into a subjective value and then further reduces such value to nothing. Suggesting that, in its rise to power, the modern ego-logical subject, bent on a destructive course of technological and technocratic mastery and domination, must for purposes of control subject to objectification the being of everything in the world, and ultimately reduce the world itself, including its horizons of possibility, to an objective totality, Heidegger follows Nietzsche in foreseeing the danger of a time of ultimate nihilism, when this willful egoism and anthropocentric power, in a final, desperate act of freedom, having nothing left to turn against and reduce except itself, subjects even itself to objectification and empties itself of all interiority, all inner life—including all capacity for critical thought. The ultimate destitution. For, in order to dominate, hence objectify, the realm of nature, the ego-logical subject ultimately had to dominate, hence objectify, hence sacrifice, even its own inner nature, its own inner life. Our inner life must conform now to the exigencies of our commercial systems and technologies. Too much important communication gets reduced to tweets. Mutual liberty is sold in an advertisement for insurance.

In consequence, paradoxically and ironically, the ego's imposition of this paradigmatic objectivism, which is necessary for the sake of the most absolute ego-logical sovereignty, and which logical positivism turned into unquestionable dogma, ends up denying the subject its very subjectivity— its inner nature, rendering it hollow, empty of meaning, empty of truth. This diremption, emptying our interior life, hence damaging our capacity for critical thought and judgment, is what Adorno and Horkheimer diagnosed in their work on the "dialectic of Enlightenment."[5] Furthermore, the misguided individualism this modern subject has prized has increasingly lost its way—lost itself—capitulating to the overwhelming pressures for operational conformism, standardization, and predictability that *Machenschaft* totality requires. This leaves such remnants of individuality as these pressures have failed to control or vanquish to suffer irremediably on account of the diminished field for freedom and their diminished capacity for freedom.[6] What remains of the individualism that once could proudly proclaim its virtues and achievements is now a ruthless pursuit of self-interest.

And time and history also suffer reification and reduction, increasingly made to serve the exigencies of advanced capitalism and its technological systems. The institutions of this technocracy take control of time, and they threaten to make history into a means of domination.

As Heidegger represents this nihilism in its ever-increasing totalizing triumph, it compels the subjective life of the spirit to submit to ever more demanding conditions of reification, standardization, and quantification; it subjects humanity to the most dangerous forces of technology, all the machinery (*Machenschaft*) of late capitalism, operating in the service of reckless military ventures and the commercial interests of the rich and the powerful. We are living, he says, in a world in which the quantitative objectivity that rules in the prevailing paradigm of knowledge, truth, and reality suppresses the immeasurable *aletheic* ground of truth, robbing us of ways to ground claims to rationality and validity. We are living in a time of the most extreme crisis: a time of emergency. But like Hölderlin and Nietzsche before him, he believed that such times are also times when something really new and great, something even perhaps unimaginable, might emerge from the failures, the ruins, the destitution, and danger of the present.

†

Behind these endeavors to imagine and think beyond the present into a new and radically different future—writing here, for the moment, as if, with a new inception, it would still even make sense to invoke a "future," insofar as that would presuppose the continuation of the same type of temporal order (*Zeitlichkeit*) we have been inhabiting since the beginning of recorded time—there stands a certain philosophy of history. But Heidegger leaves in considerable obscurity what this philosophy of history is—and how we might contribute to, and thus prepare for, another future, another *Geschick*, a new constellation of historical conditions, enabling the "new beginning" or "new inception" that he invokes. Would this *Geschick* involve a supervenient apocalyptic disruption, an external breakdown, catastrophic or felicitous, in the historical continuum, or instead only an internally unfolding transition, a slow transformation that would take place by gradual evolution or historical revolution *within* the overall continuity of history?

In a comment addressed to me on this matter, Richard Polt argued for an interpretation I find compelling, namely, that there are passages in the *Black Notebooks* where Heidegger suggests or implies that what the extremity of our time needs is a felicitous catastrophe—precisely what he imagined Hitler's National Socialism to represent. However, observing the Nazi movement from such a standpoint, Heidegger understood and acknowledged that this movement would not itself be the new inception but only rather its harbinger, its necessary, and necessarily violent groundwork.

Heidegger offers few specific, concrete clues regarding what he calls, thinking toward the future, "the other beginning." When he opined, in a late interview for *Der Spiegel*,[7] that "only a god could save us," the philosophy of history implicit in that remark suggests that the kind of transformation he is contemplating must involve a *Geschick* of supervenient intervention—a *theologoumenon*. Whether this represents his most deeply thoughtful judgment is not something we can easily ascertain. But it is possible, considering the context in which he was conveying his thought, that he was merely expressing himself in a looser, more vernacular, demotic way, saying (i) that he hoped we could be rescued from the nihilism of our time and (ii) that he does not have much of a clue as to how we might actually be rescued and saved.

Perhaps the frequently awkward, tortured grammar and word formations of the War years and the years in their immediate wake show us how terribly difficult it must have been for Heidegger to break out of the metaphysical framework, theologically generated and politically warped, in which his thinking was formed. The writings of his later years, simpler, more serene, more poetic, bear much less evidence—fewer traces—of that struggle and torment. But the challenge in overcoming the weight of history remains. Heidegger's philosophy of history represents his attempt to contemplate and address that challenge.

†

Heidegger was convinced that a fundamental transformation, including our sensibility and perception, is desperately needed today. But he was under no illusions regarding the magnitude of the difficulty involved even in demonstrating this need in a compelling way. If the desolation of the earth—its ever-extending *Verwüstung*—is not seen, despite its visibility; if the deadness of the silence in forests that songbirds used to enchant is not heard; if we no longer miss the visibility of the stars at night because of all the electric lights here on earth; and if the threats to our shared humanity are not felt, then what transformation, and what renewing inception, interrupting history to begin a time of true enlightenment, could still—for us and even more, for those coming after—be possible? Although looking and seeing, listening and hearing are "natural" events, not things we normally have to will, if we are to develop our ontological potential, there are fundamental things we still need to *learn* in our seeing and hearing.[8]

Heidegger's critique of the predominant character of perception, of the seeing and hearing reigning in our time, a character implying a growing catastrophic danger for our future, is inseparably intertwined with a much larger critique of the modern world and with a critique of philosophical thought, grounded in a reading of the *history* of the philosophical treatment of the question of being.[9] This reading of the history of philosophy, itself grounded in a philosophy of history that makes the question of being, and, later, the question of our appropriation, historically decisive, is perhaps Heidegger's most original, most radical, and most significant contribution—not only to philosophical discourse but, more generally, to critical reflection on our world, our time, our experience. Paramount in this broader critique are the themes of our estrangement from our ownmost potential as individual selves; the rise to power of the ego-logical subject; the pervasive domination of calculative, instrumental rationality and its industries and technologies; the breakup of community life and the uprootedness of people as a consequence of political corruption, poverty, civil wars, and genocides; the increasing expansion of the totalized economy of global capitalism; and our alienation from nature, abusing its hospitality in a devastating mechanization, plunder and commodification of its bounty.

†

Reading the story that Heidegger tells about the principal concepts of philosophical thought, tracing their history from the pre-Socratics down to our time, it is difficult to deny what has happened. In keeping with the reductions and reifications that Heidegger's conceptual genealogies bring to light, there has indeed been a decline in the critical powers of reason: its ability to posit and judge ends is increasingly reduced to a use of rationality exclusively occupied with instrumentalities, ways, and means— *Machenschaft*. And what about us? According to Heidegger's narrative, we are losing our humanity: increasingly, we are not people, not persons, not truly individuated individuals, reduced, now, to being nothing but subjects in a world of objects. And in fact, we are even losing our subjectivity, our inner life, in a world where only what is fully visible and accessible to all, the objective, the quantifiable, the finitely measurable, counts as reality. We are also losing our familiar world of things, as they are captured by our economy and turned into commodities, mere objects of use and profit. These reductions that philosophical thought reflects—of people to subjects, subjects to numbers, and things to objects—should make clear the whole point of Heidegger's strange "obsession" with the question of being—the *being* of beings, the way things now *are*. His conviction seems to be that, by attending to the *being* of beings, and to the opening clearing, the necessary conditions behind presencing that is being itself, we could perhaps at least avoid the temptation to *abuse* the beings in our world, imposing rigidly designated identities, supporting harmful categorizations, and recognizing value only in what can be of use and profit. Accomplishing that would be a good beginning—and a promising reception of the *Geschick* that we find ourselves "given" or "sent" (*geschickt*) in and through the clearing. And, drawing on the double meaning of *geschickt*, referring to something "sent" and something "skillful," we could describe the *character* of this "promising reception" in the fields of our perception as constituting the innermost essence of "skillfulness" (see GA 8: 17–19, 26–28/WCT: 14–16, 23–25). Unfolding the implications of Heidegger's thought, we need to keep in mind this inner connection between destiny and the ontological character of perception.

†

In his writings on technology, Heidegger compellingly argues that the historically formed conditions of the world determine (*schicken*, "send," "give") the modes of revealing—modes of presencing—that are possible:

they determine (i) what beings can appear in the clearing, the world, and (ii) how they can appear. In speaking of historically formed conditions determining what is possible, Heidegger often uses the metaphysically mischievous word *Geschick*, needlessly making the *givenness* of the conditions that we are *given* to live with seem to be "sent," "allotted," and "assigned" by some metaphysically otherworldly agency, even though that is unquestionably contrary to his intention. The invocations of *Geschick* are, I believe, an endeavor to get at the *ontological dimension* of everyday life and, moreover, to understand how historical changes in everyday life are, and might be, related to changes in the operative meaning of being—that in terms of which things are experienced and understood to be what they are and the way they are. Unfortunately, that key word creates unnecessary problems for his project.

But, as I shall argue, the reformulating of the "question of being" in terms of the *Ereignung*, hence as a question for our personal and collective responsibility as the appropriated guardians of the clearing, is of the greatest consequence in this regard, because, even more than the question of being, the question of our appropriation to ground the clearing in our care and responsibility summons us to open our eyes and ears to an encounter with unforeseeable possibilities of history-making significance breaking into the world from a sonorous and visionary dimension beyond the limits presently conditioning the character of our sensory experience. Within Heidegger's project, *Geschick*, too, eventually gets reformulated in terms of the *Ereignung*, although perhaps still leaving intact the more elusive idea of *Geschick* as destiny. See, for example, the lecture on "Time and Being" (GA 14: 24–30/OTB 19–24).

†

It would be reasonable to consider Heidegger's history of philosophy, in particular his history of the treatment of being in metaphysics, as an attempt to draw critical attention to the dangers into which we are falling and instruct us regarding what we have lost and what we have gained on the way to our present epochal phase of modernity. Heidegger did not return to the dawn of philosophical thought because his thinking had succumbed to nostalgic romanticism, nor because he wanted a reactionary regression to the past, but because he believed that we can *learn* from that past, retrieving its forgotten or abandoned treasures for the sake of a future in which a new, more ontologically attuned modality of perception would be able to emerge: a perception more attentive to the being, that is, the *essential nature* of the beings that figure in its world, mindful therefore also of the way beings actually presence, namely as concealed even in unconcealment.

He cast his gaze back into the past only in order to envision intimations on the horizon of something radically different—another *Ursprung*, another inception. The attention he lavished on the ancient Greeks came from a well-reasoned conviction that we can learn from them: not only to avoid repeating old mistakes but to appreciate that there might be alternatives to inherited thought. If what now feels inevitable and perduring was in the past, at least once, quite otherwise, then what now prevails could in future be otherwise.

As individuals and communities, we always find ourselves living in historical situations not entirely of our own making, nor fitting to our satisfaction our intentions and expectations, our ideals and hopes. But it is always possible to exercise such limited freedom as we have to make something of our own out of those situations in their obdurate ineluctable givenness. And if we can do that freely and with a sense of purpose, undertaking to realize significant ideals, then it may be argued that we are shaping our destiny (*Geschick*) in history (*Geschichte*), making the *Es gibt*, the undeniable *givens* of our historical situation (the *Geschick* in the sense of what we are *given*, or *sent*, to work with), into our *Geschick* (in the sense of our destiny). Thus, whereas in the time of fate (in my preferred translation of *Schicksal*), everything is determined and freedom is absolutely impossible, in the time of destiny, it is a question of the sagacious use of our finite freedom in struggling with the givenness of the world-clearing we are in for the sake of possibilities making a different, more desirable future.

We should remember, here, that, despite Heidegger's attraction to Greek tragedy, he rejected the view that, like puppets or actors in a play, we human beings are subject to determinism—the law of fate. He gives no encouragement to fatalism. For Heidegger, when "history" is properly understood and practiced, it shows the way to freedom.

Of course, we cannot by an act of sheer will choose our ontology—the conditions that determine the modality in which presencing can take place, opening up a world—the way we can choose a trail for hiking or choose a vocation for which we have discovered a distinctive aptitude; but we are not like the characters played on a chess board, moved as if by the hand of an invisible, transcendent god or demon, an immutable law of nature, the secretive manipulations of capital, or some metaphysical force to which we must helplessly submit: we are participants in the way worldly beings presence, participants too in the very emergence and sway of being itself. The character—*ethos*—of our engagement is crucial. Whereas fate is the past sealing us in the most absolute unfreedom, destiny is a future that belongs to the appropriated, hence responsible, assumption of freedom.

The well-established distinction between *Schicksal* and *Geschick* that I want to retain, following the common understanding of these words, cuts across the distinction that Heidegger makes in *Being and Time*, wherein *Schicksal* refers to the freely chosen life of the *individual* and *Geschick* refers to the freely chosen mission of the *community*. Heidegger's way of defining these terms is contrary to our common intuitions and indeed contrary to the common understanding of the logic, or grammar, of these concepts. For him, *both* terms signify the free appropriation of a heritage, recognizing in what that heritage is handing down its possibilities of meaning for the present and the future (GA 2: 507/BT 435). Thus, Heidegger does not think of *Schicksal* as an external imposition; nor does he regard it as some unavoidable future. It does not, for him, mean "fate." On the contrary, in his use, both terms essentially involve our capacity, as individuals and as belonging to a particular community or society, to exercise a limited freedom within given historical conditions. Thus he holds that only the "fateful" *Dasein*, finite and mortal, resolute in its intention, and only the *geschicklich* community or society, struggling to make its own the conditions it has inherited, can be authentic, resisting the pressures of prevailing historical formations of meaning. What rules the use of both these terms in *Being and Time* is the question of freedom or determinism, not only whether the subject is the individual or the community. However, if we follow common usage, wherever there is freedom, there is the possibility of destiny (*Geschick*), a destiny worthy of our humanity; and wherever there is no freedom, there indeed is fate (*Schicksal*). In any case, Heidegger's history of metaphysics is unequivocally, unambiguously motivated by a philosophy of history that projects this destiny of freedom.

So, the "tragic" history Heidegger laments and documents is not inevitable—is not a fate. Thus, in his dialogue on *Gelassenheit*, Heidegger has the scientist character say that the subject–object relation is not something we must regard as eternal, necessary, and inevitable: it is plainly "only a historical variation [*nur eine geschichtliche Abwandlung*] of the relation of the human being to the thing, insofar as things can become objects" (GA 77: 140/CPC 91). And the same holds true of the human being: both in life and in philosophical representations at least since the time of Descartes, the historical human being has been increasingly reduced in its being to the condition of an ego-subject, and, even worse, in fact, the inner life of the human being has been increasingly threatened by its emptiness and worthlessness, hollowed out as objectivity becomes the paradigm of reality for the will to power. But if we could gain an understanding of this experience of inner destitution, then the exercise of our freedom, limited though it is, could perhaps still save us from the ontological danger that continues to threaten our world.

A fearlessly lucid understanding of the human condition, considering the being of things beyond their objectification and considering the human beyond essence and its reification, could profoundly affect our situation. It is in this spirit that Heidegger will get us thinking critically about the essence of technology and the technologization of our lifeworld and get us thinking critically about our relation to the earth and the sky. These ventures into thinking about our lifeworld give another dimension of meaning to the more strictly conceptual analyses worked out in the context of his history of philosophy.

Something analogous might be said about the virtues of reading the philosophers, historians, and writers of the past. Learning about a past in which things were experienced differently can be surprisingly useful in getting us out of our "captivity in that-which-is," as Heidegger phrases it in his study on "The Origin of the Work of Art." Heidegger's return to the pre-Socratics is pedagogic strategy. He knew perfectly well that we cannot live our lives like pre-Socratic Greeks. Nor did he want us to. Besides, if I might borrow a congenial trope from Bernard of Chartres, I suggest that, although the archaic Greek philosophers were certainly giants, we of today nevertheless have the possibility of seeing and hearing more, or better, than they could, because we are sitting on their shoulders. Heidegger offers an important example of our advantage when he argues that, whereas the Greeks possessed the word *aletheia*, they were not at that time able to experience—as we, coming much later, have been compelled in our misfortune to experience—the *betrayal* of truth that reduces it to correctness by denying the more fundamental ontological dimension of concealment and unconcealment. Their wonderful word bears for us moderns a crucial dimension of meaning that the ancients could not have known: we can now think concealment as such, unconcealment as such—but only because we are suffering a terrible loss, a real deprivation, a closure of dimensionality that they, in their moment of philosophical innocence, were never compelled to feel. There is a certain tragic sense always haunting the knowledge we have so proudly gained.

†

Although claiming to represent an ontologically grounded enquiry, Heidegger's *Seinsgeschichte*—what I take to be his history of philosophical interpretations of the meaning of being—can never be other than speculative and hypothetical. To propose interpretations of history based on the thoughts of a philosopher about the shared "essence" or "spirit" of an age, or about the prevailing ontology of an epoch in the history of being, can only be speculative and hypothetical. After all, can the philosopher—be it Heraclitus, Plato, or Fichte—even represent the truth, *die Wahrheit des Seins*, of his own time? Even somewhat more modest onto-historical claims, such as the representation of the ontology implicitly operative in the particular nation or culture the philosopher lives in, cannot be freed from epistemological skepticism. For that matter, can Heraclitus represent the *Weltanschauung* of the stone mason? Can Plato represent that of the illiterate farmer in the countryside far from Athens? Can Fichte represent the understanding of being that his own servants might have?

Each world-clearing, and each epoch in the history of the paradigmatic meaning of being, has its own historically situated, individually appropriated time and shape. How exactly are the different world-clearings and epochs connected? Heidegger leaves us with many questions—and even some puzzles.

†

The distinction Heidegger makes, in reading the Greeks, between a mere beginning and a genuine inception is a distinction that we can fully understand only in the context of his philosophy of history. Heidegger does not read the history of philosophy from a neutral point of view; he reads the history of philosophy from the original and critical perspective of a certain philosophy of history—a philosophy, namely, that is oriented toward a future world defined by a sense of destiny that would engage us in endeavors to redeem the great potential—in ourselves, in our forms of community, and in the realm of nature—that we human beings have been *given* (*geschickt*) to care for. This is the key to making sense of his project as a whole.

According to Heidegger, the beginning (*Beginn*) of the history of metaphysics—which, as we noted, is not the same as the originary inception (*Anfang*) of the history of *being*, took place and was set in motion when, for the first time, the Greek philosophers lifted their eyes above the worldly things that had bound their attention and found themselves struck, as if by a bolt of lightning, by an uncanny question: What is being? Thinking beyond the beings they encountered in their visible world, they suddenly found themselves thinking about what it means for these beings to be. In this way, being manifested and showed itself to mortals in an event (an *Ereignis*) that, experienced in wonder and awe, gave rise to metaphysical speculation. That speculative thinking was the moment in ancient, pre-Socratic Greece that Heidegger honours as the originary *inception* (*Anfang*) of metaphysics: an *event* of great historical significance.

This event (*Ereignis*), in which being seized attention and showed itself as such, was, in effect, the first summons (*Anruf*), the first claim (*Anspruch*), the *first phase* in the appropriation of Greek thought. In this first phase, however, the appropriation, namely, the participation of the philosophers in the experience, remained hidden, unrecognized as such. It is only in a second phase, a self-reflective phase that only came to light through Heidegger's own struggle to think that event in both phenomenological and ontological-historical terms, that the *appropriation* (*Er-eignung*) inherent in the event was properly recognized and understood. The second phase requires our recognizing and understanding the summons, the claim implicit *in* that event as *our* distinctive (*eigene*) appropriation (*Er-eignung*), making each of us, individually and collectively, responsible, as *Da-sein*, for the openness and character of the clearings, the worlds, within which beings come into presence, being either present or absent.

What Heidegger calls "the other beginning" (*Anfang*) would thus be an *inception* that commenced with an authentic event of appropriation: the recollecting and retrieving of a deeper, hermeneutically hidden *sense* of the event, namely, recognizing and understanding the experience of being *as* appropriation, *as* an *event* in which being as such showed itself, namely, in and through *Da-sein's appropriation* to serve as guardian and grounder of the truth of being, being itself—that is, to *be* the opened clearing (*ereignete Lichtung*), that which makes possible the presencing of beings (*das Anwesen der Seienden*).

The early Greek inception involved an understanding of the event— the sublime and awesome experience of being—in which being showed itself as such, but its appropriation was not available to the early Greek philosophers. Their reflection on being did not draw them into reflexive subjectivity. The "other beginning" is called *Anfang* because, for the very first time, being would be *properly grounded* in the phenomenology of a recognition of our *Ereignung*: our appropriation, our belonging, in relation to being. For the first time, there would be an experience of the way being emerges for us as meaning. And so, for the first time, being would be *grounded* in the phenomenology of *Dasein's* appropriated opening of the clearing; and, as such, this second beginning would actually be in an ontological or transcendental sense "earlier" than the actual, ontically "factical" Greek beginning, belonging as it would to an entirely other temporal order: not merely the ontical *Zeitlichkeit* of typical historical events, occurring in an irreversible, one-dimensional order of Nows, but the structurally originary life of *Temporalität*, in which the claim and summons of appropriation abides in the *ek-static form* of the more fundamental dimensionality of time, no longer what can be pictured by an arrow, suggesting an irreversible linear series of now times. In "Time and Being," Heidegger describes this fundamental dimension of time, and its importance for history and destiny, in terms of human existence (*Da-sein*) as time–space clearing:

> The dimensionality [of human ex-istence] consists in a reaching out that opens up, in which what approaches from the future brings about, or consummates what has been, and what has been brings about, or prepares for futural approaching, and the two-way interactive connection between them brings about the opening up of openness. (GA 14: 19/OTB 14–15)

The eventful recovery of this phenomenological origin of time and history in the ek-static temporality claiming our appropriation opens up for faith and hope the possibility of *another* inception, a *future* inception: this one, however, were it to happen, would belong to a future coming *after* our present epoch—after the nihilistic epoch of the *Ge-stell*, that is, after our current historical situation has been overcome, more or less completing the unfolding of epochs belonging to the first inception—the one that began in the discourse of metaphysics belonging to the world of ancient Greece. Appropriation is consequently the very first step toward another inception. But the Greek philosophers were not able to make that step, since, as history has demonstrated, it would have required their passing into and through subjectivity. Appropriation requires of us that we go into subjectivity and out beyond it—out of the subject–object structure, beginning the process of taking on responsibility for the very *being* of beings.

In this regard, I submit that what Heidegger has to say about life in the epoch of the *Ge-stell*—our time, our world, our *Geschick*—makes a compelling argument for the proposition that we are in a time of crisis and emergency, and that reflection on the closure (*epokhê*) that, in the time of the *Ge-stell*, is threatening our world desperately needs not only the ontologically grounded historical narratives Heidegger provides but also a rich phenomenological interpretation in terms of our capacity for perception. Venturing a contribution to the latter is the singular motive behind the project of this volume and the volume that will follow. But this project really cannot be understood unless it is contextualized in terms of Heidegger's intertwining of a meta-narrative history of philosophy and a guiding philosophy of history.

†

In the years following the publication of *Being and Time* (1927), Heidegger's extremely ambitious project involved an attempt to weave together three "theaters" of history in regard to what he conceived as the manifestation of being (*Offenbarung des Seins*): (i) the *historical lifeworld* of Western mankind, (ii) the "logic" at work in the history of the concepts fundamental for philosophical thought—a history exhibiting, from the time of the early Greek philosophers into the time of Nietzsche, the conceptual transformations taking place in the Western discourse of metaphysics, and (iii) the history of being (*Seinsgeschichte*), eventually recognized, I think, as an unnecessarily grandiose way of thinking about (ii), the historicity of the meaning of being—as this meaning shows its character, its essence, in the beings that appear in the various epochs of its "dispensations" (*Schickungen*), its various formations (*Prägungen*). Although Heidegger abandoned (iii), he was not satisfied with (ii), important though it is, because it neglects the role of appropriation in the unfolding history of the concept of being.

Moreover, even when Heidegger's history of metaphysics seems to be merely following (ii), that is, the logic of concept formation (e.g., from *aletheia* in Heraclitus, where it means unconcealment, to Plato, where it is reduced to correctness, or from the *logos* in Heraclitus to a system of logic in Leibniz, where it is reduced to reason), it is still very much in the service of a distinctive philosophy of history—a narrative, that is, in the *Temporalität* of which inheritance and destiny, a still unrecognized, unfulfilled *past*, a *present* suffering dangerous decline, and a possible *future* of redeeming achievement, are thought together, intertwined in a critical way. The fundamental connection between Heidegger's history of philosophy and his philosophy of history has so far not, I believe, been sufficiently recognized and clarified. The key to this connection is, of course, our appropriation in terms of the dimension of *Temporalität*.

Here is how he formulated the project in *What Is Called Thinking?* (1952). We can see very clearly that, at this time, he was still searching for a way to think the difference between a mere beginning and an "inception," recognizing the greatness of the inception that the Greeks accomplished while also recognizing the emergent need for another inception, a possibility requiring, to begin with, an enowned, hence authentic belonging to history, in which the assumption of responsibility for the meaning of being would necessarily play a decisive role:

> Western thought begins with an omission, perhaps even a failure. So it seems, as long as we regard oblivion as only a deficiency, something negative. Besides, we do not get on the right course here if we pass over an essential distinction. The beginning [*Beginn*] of Western thought is not the same as its origin [*Anfang*]. The beginning is rather the veil that conceals the origin—indeed an unavoidable veil. If that is the situation,

then oblivion shows itself in a different light. The origin keeps itself concealed [*verbirgt sich*] in the beginning. (GA 8: 156/WCT 152)

In his history of philosophy, Heidegger argues that this origin—which will turn out to lie in the *Ereignis*, the appropriation of *Dasein*—was *already* operative, albeit in concealment, even *within* the thinking that we attribute to the earliest Greek philosophers. And it has remained concealed within that thinking which we call "the (first) beginning." In fact, Heidegger argues, it has also remained in concealment within all the philosophical thought derived and unfolded from that very beginning. Thus, as Heidegger was already thinking in writing *The Phenomenology of Religious Life* (1920–1921) and never ceased to believe:

> [The task is] to gain a genuine and originary relationship to history that is explicable in terms of our own historical situation and facticity [*aus unserer eigenen geschichtlichen Situation und Faktizität*]. History exists only from out of a present. (GA 60: 124–25/PRL 89)

But years later, in his *Contributions to Philosophy* (1936–1938), Heidegger made a startling declaration: "Mankind has never yet been [authentically] historical" (GA 65: 492/CP 387). What did Heidegger mean by "being historical," or "living historically"? What exactly is an authentic and originary relation to history? Why did he insist, paradoxically, that we in the Western world have not yet—not ever—been authentically, truly historical? What is he criticizing and lamenting? What is he urging?

Actually, he is not only lamenting our historicity in its common sense. What concerns him first and foremost is an ontological matter: that we have never yet situated ourselves *properly* (*eigentlich*) in relation to the "history of being"—never recognized the fact that being, that is the meaning of being, *has* a history, and never yet connected our existence and world to *that* history in an *essential, intrinsic* way, awakening to the truth of our *belonging* to that history, recognizing ourselves *in* that very history, and thoughtfully *taking responsibility* for appropriating it. A few years later, this point is supported by his perplexing claim, no less paradoxical, in "Recollection in Metaphysics" (1941) that "the history of being"

> is neither the history of the human being and of a humanity [*eines Menschentums*], nor the history of the human relation [*des menschlichen Bezugs*] to beings and to being. The history of being is just being itself [*des Seins selbst*], and *only* this [*und nur dieses*]. (GA 6.2: 489/EP 82)

"However," he adds,

> Since being claims human being [*das Menschenwesen in den Anspruch nimmt*] for grounding its truth in beings [*zur Gründung seiner Wahrheit im Seienden*], man is drawn [*einbezogen*] into the history of being, but always only with regard to the manner in which he takes his essence from the relation of being to himself [*aus dem Bezug des Seins zu ihm*] and, in accordance with this relation [*gemäß diesem Bezug*], takes over his essence [*übernimmt*], loses it, neglects it, gives it up, grounds it, or squanders it.

Thus, even though the history of being is not, as such, a history *of* the human being, and also not, as such, of the human *relation* to being and to beings, Heidegger nevertheless *does* want us to understand that, if the meaning and significance of this history is to show itself, it needs to be thought *in relation to us human beings*—but only, Heidegger says there, as a matter that concerns the very *essence* of the human, "which is appropriated and determined by the claim of being," and not merely with regard to historical facts in the ontical world, the contingencies of our "existence, actions, and accomplishments within the world": the typical concerns of historiographical narratives. Once we recognize and understand the implications of the fact that the meaning of being has a history, it becomes possible for us to begin taking responsibility for this history and its future in an exercise of our situated, finite freedom. We shall return to this question of responsibility, which Heidegger in fact had already raised in earlier texts (1938–1940), published under the title *The History of Beyng* (GA 69: 93/HB 79).

†

So, as noted, Heidegger was deeply distressed by our failure to be genuinely historical. And he understood that he needed to take us in an existentially meaningful way into the history of philosophy in order to argue for and show the enowning of responsibility hidden behind the Greek beginning. This demanded a work of *recollection* very different from the ordinary process of memory. And it drew his thinking into the ontological dimension of temporality (*Temporalität*) underlying the ontical order of serial time (*Zeitlichkeit*): a dimension in which past and future, inheritance and destiny, are vitally present *as* absent—absent as having-been and yet-to-come—in every present moment.

Hoping to "overcome" our failing in regard to history, Heidegger endeavored to gather us into a process of recollection, an *Erinnerung* through which we might return from our lostness in the world to find and recover *ourselves* in relation to an authentic historicity. And yet, in *Country Path Conversations*, Heidegger's warden summons us to find our "release from history"—a *"Befreiung von der Geschichte"* (GA 77: 184/CP 120). Despite appearances, there is really no contradiction between these two propositions, once they are sufficiently understood. On the contrary, they are actually compatible and mutually supportive. We need, first of all, to get free of a serial *conception* of history that recognizes only *die Vergangenheit*, what is past and gone forever, history dead and buried, so that we might begin to retrieve *das Gewesene*, that which has been, namely, a past that was offered, but never taken up: possibilities unrecognized, opportunities missed, a past available for retrieval in the present for the sake of a more promising future. We need to retrieve and work our way through our individual and collective roles and responsibilities—the phenomenology of our appropriation—in the making and interpreting of history, if we are ever to wrest free of a history that continues to lead us into nihilism. And we need to retrieve and work through the history of metaphysics if philosophical thought is ever to get free of that deadening history. In order to become truly historical in Heidegger's sense, we need, as he contends in *Mindfulness*, to become mindful of the "truth of beyng," for *"Da-sein* is the historical ground of the clearing" (GA 66: 300, 328/M 268, 291).

He also recognized that there are other metaphysical assumptions and concepts into which we have become bound and from which we need to be freed. What does this "getting free" involve? In a text called "Die Überwindung der Metaphysik," it might seem as though, influenced by Nietzsche, he is suggesting an "overcoming." But that is not actually his position. In the course of developing his critique of metaphysics, Heidegger makes a distinction between *Überwindung* ("overcoming") and *Verwindung* ("sublation," moving past while retaining) arguing that metaphysics needs to be properly appropriated and rededicated—*not* abandoned, *not* overcome, but rather returned to the phenomenology of its living source.[10] This, he thinks, is the only way for philosophical thought to move past the metaphysical paradigm of our epoch and "begin" again.

Heidegger understood that we cannot overcome metaphysics by abandonment, as if we could simply erase and forget the fact that we inherited the questioning and thinking it represents; he understood that we need instead to return to its living source, retrieving something of the ontological experience—the experience of being—that *originally motivated* metaphysical thought, in order to see if we can discover a way to venture another beginning, developing new concepts, and a new paradigm, *from* the givens of our inheritance. That is what I believe is at stake in Heidegger's insistence on the *Einkehr in das Ereignis*, our entering into the phenomenology of our appropriation. What he hoped to see emerge from this undertaking, this hermeneutical "recollection," would be something more faithful to what that tradition was actually attempting to understand—something more faithful, and perhaps more deeply disclosive, than it itself was able to be. Above all, more faithful by virtue of recognizing the ontological importance of temporality, hence, also, the bearing of historicity on our understanding of what it means for something to be.

In *The Event*, he explains that "*Da-sein* is the appropriated time-space [*der ereignete Zeit-Raum*], the hearth place [*die Herd-Stätte*] of recollection. At this hearth, inceptuality is a potential that glows in concealment [*An diesem Herd glüht die Anfängnis*]" (GA 71: 222/E 190). In an authentic belonging to history, the "historical ground" of inceptuality is *our* responsibility. And this means, as he says in "The Origin of the Work of Art," that we need to struggle for release, for freedom, from a history that repeats itself, a continuum perpetuating our "captivity in the realm of what-is" (GA 5: 55/ PLT 67). Consequently, we need to ground our historical existence—and the "*geschickhafte* character" of being itself—by understanding the essence of our role in the conditions that make meaningful being possible, and by accordingly taking on the responsibility inherent in the claim on our appropriation. That, I submit, is how Heidegger thinks we might become *authentically* historical, and perhaps even prepare the ground for another ontological inception, another paradigm of knowledge, truth and reality, an experience of being worthy of our inheritance of the first inception, the gift we received from the earliest Greek philosophers.

That gift did not remain confined to philosophical discourse. It made its way, little by little, mostly unrecognized as such, into our Western lifeworld, ceaselessly undergoing changes in interaction with changing historical conditions.

†

For Heidegger, we are still living, to borrow Hölderlin's phrase, "*in dürftiger Zeit*"—indeed, in a time of even greater danger: an uncanny danger and emergency. This conviction lies at the very heart of Heidegger's philosophy of history and consequently underlies his conception of authentic history, whether this be the history of Western philosophy or the history of the Western lifeworld. So, the philosopher's preponderant concern is that, unless we understand what an *authentic* relation to history is and put that understanding into practice, we cannot be expected to make historical life meaningful, nor engage with it in critical thought, hence in a way that would make it possible to redeem the possibility of realizing our destiny. This redeeming is a possibility that the loss of historical memory and the corruption of historical responsibility have betrayed, making it exceedingly difficult to get our grounding in the ontological, hence outside the chain of events—the *Geschehnisse*—determining our modern form of historical life so that we might free ourselves thereby for the projection of a different future.

In "The Turn" (1949), Heidegger once again argued, as he had already in *Being and Time* (1927), against the prevailing historiographical conception of history and, correspondingly, for an understanding of history grounded in his visionary and revolutionary—that is to say, transformation-oriented—philosophy of history, a philosophy oriented by a certain conception of destiny as that possibility for us to take up and fulfill which comes to us hidden in what we encounter in and through the clearing that, as *Da-sein*, we essentially *are*:

> We are still too easily inclined, because accustomed to conceive that which, deeply understood, pertains to destiny [*das Geschickliche*] in terms of what happens [*aus dem Geschehen*] and to represent this as a course of historiologically determinable incidents [*einem Ablauf von historisch feststellbaren Begebenheiten vorzustellen*]. (GA 79: 68–69/BF 65, QCT 38)

"We locate [*stellen*] history," he says, "in the realm of what occurs [*in den Bereich des Geschehens*], instead of thinking history in accordance with its essential provenance [*Wesensherkunft*] in terms of destiny [*aus dem Geschick*]" (GA 79: 68–69/BF 65, QCT 38).

Thus, *das Geschick* is never determined by something historical [*das Geschichtliche*], and especially not by the historiologically conceived occurrence [*historisch vorgestellte Geschehen*], but rather, on the contrary, every time what occurs is already something pertaining to the destiny of beyng in what is granted [*sondern jedesmal ist das Geschehen schon das Geschickliche eines Geschickes des Seyns*]" (GA 79: 69–70/BF 65–66, QCT 39). This point is emphatically recapitulated near the end of the text. Here, Heidegger gives voice to his lament. Philosophical thought has failed so far to "bring us into the proper relation to destining." Our relation to history must be grounded—and history must be thought philosophically—*in the light of destiny*. "No merely historiological representation of history as occurrence [*kein historisches Vorstellen der Geschichte als Geschehen*] brings us into the fitting relation to destiny [*bringt in den schicklichen Bezug zum Geschick*]" (GA 79: 76/BF 72, QCT 48). Nevertheless, he acknowledges that destiny is something that is hidden (*verschleiert*), in that it has to be retrieved from the possibilities for the future that we recognize in the facticity we are given (GA 11: 122/BF 71, QCT 47). The retrieving presumably involves the exercise of freedom and judgment; and this calls for interpretations of historical events. We can retrieve destiny only entering *Temporalität*.

We need to think history *"aus dem Geschick des Seins."* What does this imperative relation to destiny purport? And how is it connected to the history of being? Is it even certain that this phrase, *"aus dem Geschick,"* must (always) be interpreted as "in terms of destiny" or "from the perspective of destiny"? As we shall discuss, there are other, later texts in which this rendering seems to be challenged: it remains fitting, but it needs to be accompanied by a phenomenological interpretation, working out the meaning of *Geschick* in terms of our appropriation in time. From what Heidegger tells us, we know that, and why, the so-called *history of being* is not ordinary history. But what this ontological history *is* remains stubbornly obscure. Above all, perhaps, why an engagement with destiny is necessary for the history of being. "Destiny," he explains, continuing this thought, with its sharp distinction between (i) normal historical narrative and (ii) what he is undertaking, "is essentially [i.e., is an ontological possibility that comes in] the destiny-bearing givenness of being [*Geschick ist wesenhaft Geschick des Seins*], so much so, that being, in giving itself, each time presences as a *Geschick* [*und je als ein Geschick west*] and accordingly transforms itself in terms of this givenness [*und demgemäß sich geschicklich wandelt*]" (GA 79: 69/ BF 65, QCT 38)—certainly a very obscure explanation.

As in all the translations I am using, these translations of *Geschick* are interpretations—hypotheses and, sometimes, unfortunately, only guesses. In the case of *Geschick*, they are all exceptionally problematic, in that it does not always seem right to translate this key word as "destiny." In Heidegger's contexts, the word is frequently ambiguous. But what would seem right—what would make sense—is not always apparent. The point Heidegger seems to be making in this passage is that destiny is the interpretation of a possibility for the transformation of history that comes, hidden and unbidden, into the world of our experience—with and in what type of being that world lets presence. In other words, it is in what we understand, or interpret, our situation to be *giving* us to contend with—*das Schicken*—that possibilities in regard to the history of being might appear for the achievement of our (supposedly) proper historical destiny (*Geschick*). But we must bear in mind, here, that the clearing that we *are* as *Da-sein*, and therewith the destiny that is given as possibility for the exercise of our freedom, will always be historically conditioned, as we are thrown open to live within those conditions as we encounter them. However, according to Heidegger, the traditional practice of history as we know it will never be able, by itself, to recognize that possibility of destiny in its way of understanding the events we are given to live with. In its accounting of what takes place, historiography neglects to think the ontological dimension of history and consequently obscures that interpretation, that recognition, of promise and destiny. And, insofar as historical events are determined by an ontological regime that the very assumption of destiny challenges, historical conditions will resist the recognition of destiny and, together with it, its possibility of a second ontological inception, a fundamentally new ontological formation of being.

†

At stake in such an approach to history is always a question of who "we" are—who "we" are as a nation; or who "we" are as a particular community; or who "we" are as cosmopolitan citizens of the world—or who "we" are simply as human beings. In *Being and Time*, the "we" refers to the German people, in whose historical heritage the gift of a promising destiny is supposed to be found. In the years after the War and the Holocaust, the "we" seems to refer to "us" as human beings. And the meaning of "destiny" in Heidegger's thought seems to follow, and correspond to, that significant shift. However, struggling to rescue the reputation of the *Geschick*, his key word, in the wake of its catastrophic misadventures during the madness of National Socialism, Heidegger quietly brought the question of destiny into the phenomenology of historical life, taking it away from political ideology, metaphysics, and theology. But in order to do this, he had to create for the word a dual meaning. Unfortunately, this gave the word a confusing ambiguity that required many more words for him to elucidate and resolve.

In the course of considering Heidegger's complaints about our relation to history, we have had to think in terms of his numerous invocations of the *Geschick*. But both the sense and the substance that these invocations involve are elusive. We can say with confidence, however, that Heidegger is not rehabilitating a teleology; nor, therefore, is he arguing for an eschatology. But we must explore further what we are to make of the philosopher's use of this cryptic and elusive word, *Geschick*.

†

Before directly confronting the questions raised by the word *Geschick*, we should perhaps resume pondering the questions surrounding Heidegger's "history of being"—his *Seinsgeschichte*. During the 1930s, and even into the early 1940s, this idea of a history of being seized his attention, taking possession of his thought. What sense can be made of it? What use does it serve? We know that, in his contributions to the history of philosophy, Heidegger carefully follows the logic in the unfolding histories of the fundamental concepts in metaphysics, beginning of course with "being." The task involves not merely exhibiting their factual transformations but also exposing the hidden logic—the essential character and ontological significance—of these conceptual changes. We may debate his historical facts and his interpretations regarding what these changes mean; but in any case, we must agree that the project itself, reminiscent to some extent of Husserl's *Sinnesgenesis* ("genesis of sense"), makes good sound sense and contributes significant illuminations. However, Heidegger seems to insist that his *Seinsgeschichte* is manifestly not this. That is to say, as he conceives it, it is *not*—or not only—an endeavor to show how, down through the epochs, from the time of the discourse of the earliest Greek philosophers, the grammar of "being" and, connected to it, the concept of "being"—hence what it means to be—have undergone important changes. After all, the logic of those discursive conceptual changes can be exhibited without any reference whatsoever to destiny—the *Geschick*. So, what distinguishes his *Seinsgeschichte*, his "history of being," from a narrative such as we find in Husserl, exhibiting the logic of conceptual changes, for example with regard to the concept of being, or with regard to the grammar of "to be"?

Heidegger's meta-narrative history certainly includes texts that may be read as such straightforwardly historical narrative, documenting and interpreting how the *concept* of "being" has figured and unfolded in philosophical discourse from its beginning in the thought of the earliest Greek philosophers to its inheritance and transmission in Heidegger's immediate predecessors. Although Heidegger does not at all deny the usefulness of historically ordered presentations of the logic of concept formation with regard to epistemology and ontology—for instance, Hussserl's project of providing the *Sinnesgenesis* for the conceptual formations operating in physics, he does criticize contributions to the history of philosophy that concentrate *exclusively* on this logic (GA 2: 496/BT 427). And, too, he rejects the ego-logical idealism in Husserl's "transcendental constitution" of sense. But, committed as he is to a phenomenology of existence, he does at least always insist (i) that philosophical thought must be recognized as historical and (ii) that the history of philosophy—above all, a history of ontology and epistemology—cannot be told without reference to *Dasein*'s existence.

This eventually brought him around to drawing out another sense of *Geschick*, referring in a general way to *das Schicken*, the phenomenology of the "sending," or "giving" and "givenness," that takes place in all experience—that is to say, in and through the structure of *Da-sein*'s clearing.

Struggling with a semantic problem that he calls "treacherous," *verfänglich* (GA 14: 26/OTB 21), and that does not exist for philosophers thinking in English, a problem unique to the German language, namely the double meaning of *Es gibt*, which can mean both "There is" and "It gives"

(GA 14: 23–24/OTB 17–19), Heidegger introduces the other meaning for *Geschick*:

> There is a growing danger that, when we speak of the "It" (*Es*), we arbitrarily posit an independent power which is supposed to bring about [*bewerkstelligen*] all giving of being and of time [*alles Geben von Sein und von Zeit*]. (GA 14: 22/OTB 16–17)

However, he argues, we can escape this danger "if only we look ahead [*aus der Vorsicht*] toward being as presence [*auf das Sein als Anwesenheit*] and toward time as the realm of a clearing [*als den Bereich des Reichens des Lichtung*] where, within its extensive range, a manifold presencing takes place and unfolds." And he concludes this thought by unequivocally recognizing and introducing a distinction between destiny and the givenness of what is given in experience, locating destiny in what is "sent" or "given" according to the interpretation of our experience. Destiny is the availability, or givenness, of a possibility to be achieved—located nowhere but right in what we interpret the historical circumstances to have given us to retrieve from our experience. But destiny is available only in *Temporalität*:

> The giving in "It gives being" (*Das Geben im "Es gibt Sein"*) proved to be a sending and a destiny of presence [*zeigte sich als Schicken und als Geschick von Anwesenheit*] in its epochal transmutations. (Ibid.)

"We need," he argues, further illuminating the distinction he is making, "simply to think the 'It' in regard to the kind of giving that belongs to it: giving [*das Geben*] as destiny [*Geschick*], giving as an opening up that reaches out [*das Geben als lichtendes Reichen*]. Both belong together, inasmuch as the former, destiny [*das Geschick*], lies [*beruht*] in the latter, the clearing in its extending and opening up" (GA 14: 24/OTB 19). And, as regards the "It" that gives time and gives being, he says that that giving (i.e., of beings in presence) takes place through our appropriation, which "opens and preserves" (GA 14: 24, 25–26/OTB 19, 20).

And, as he points out: "The giving in 'It gives time' proves to be an extending, opening up the four-dimensional realm" (GA 14: 22/OTB 17). This deep ek-static temporality is what makes it possible for the *Schicken* to bear, hidden within what it brings into our field of presence, the potential for an achievement of destiny—*das Geschick*. Thus, as he says: "Appropriating [*Das Ereignis*] has the peculiar property of bringing human beings into their own as the beings who perceive being by standing within [*innesteht*] true time" (GA 14: 28/OTB 23).

He also observes that "the sending in the destiny of being [*das Schicken im Geschick des Seins*] has been characterized as a giving [*ein Geben*] in which the sending source [*das Schickende selbst*] keeps itself back [*an sich hält*] and, in that way, withdraws from unconcealment [*sich der Entbergung entzieht*]" (GA 14: 27/OTB 22). This dynamic should be very familiar, recognized as characteristic of the vitality operative in the figure–ground structuring of perception—and indeed, of all our experience. The clearing that makes perceiving and presencing possible withdraws, or recedes, letting what presences come forth and draw our attention to itself.

Once the *Geschick* is also to be understood simply as *das Schicken*, that is, as the "sending" and what is "sent," taking place in and through the clearing—understood, thus, as what comes our way to be encountered, then we must recognize, bringing the *two senses* of *Geschick* together, that *all* experience can be considered destiny bearing: *all* the experience we are "sent" or "given" to encounter in life *can* be appropriated in a way that would bear on the question of our responsibility for a destiny befitting our ideal sense of humanity. Hence, as Heidegger will come around to saying: "Destiny" (*Geschick*) is what emerges from our appropriation (*Ereignen*) in the course of experiencing what comes our way—*das Schicken*—to be encountered: "*Das Schicken ist aus dem Ereignen*" (GA 15: 367/FS, 61). We should recognize in this thought a breakthrough of the greatest possible significance for the philosopher's project. More on this point soon.

†

However, even when Heidegger's contributions to the history of metaphysics present the history of being in terms of *Dasein*'s activities, our practical life in the world, the historical time (*Zeitlichkeit*) in this first kind of narrative construction will be linear, sequential, and irreversible. Hence the past will accordingly be regarded as irrevocably past. Some of Heidegger's texts provide a history of concepts in this sense; and although one might fault his history for its selectivity, incompleteness, inaccuracies of interpretation, and inadequacies in argumentation, the meta-narrative that these texts on the unfolding of ontological concepts offer is still insightful, illuminating, and, on the whole, I think, quite compelling. However, this order of time did not permit Heidegger's project to address the question of destiny; nor could it permit thinking to explore the possibility of another inception.

According to documentary narrative, a meta-narrative cast within the order of linear time, the history of metaphysics in the Western world began when the early Greek philosophers, suddenly struck by the sheer wonder, the sheer facticity of being, were drawn to reflect upon this disclosive event (*Ereignis*), this ontological experience, the fact that there is (*es gibt*) being, an extraordinary, uncanny "moment of vision." And this reflection brought them to attempt explaining the world with which they were familiar by reference to its invisible logic, or law, a metaphysical dimension of sublime order.

The ancient Greek interpretations of being and beings that opened the beginning of the discourse of metaphysics in the Western world are taken, in Heidegger's history of philosophy, to represent not only the reflective experience of the philosophers but also the experience, such as it was, of their cultural world in its time. But the world of those Greek thinkers perished long ago, passing as it did so through enormous changes; and in the course of time these changes in the world, affecting the way the presencing of beings could be received as given—that is, received in its givenness, found their way into the metaphysical interpretations of later philosophical thought. Consequently, Heidegger's history of metaphysics recognizes, as symbolic formal indications of their time, *distinctly different epochs*, formed at critical junctures, sometimes disruptive and unsettling, in the reception and interpretation, hence in the corresponding givenness, of the singular phenomenon of ontological disclosure: epochs that, however, different, are still, all of them, essentially derived under the influence, the regime, of the first, originary self-disclosing event of being—the phenomenology of the hermeneutics of being—that provoked the inception of the history of metaphysics in ancient Greece.

Each epoch is intrinsically defined by what it reveals and what it conceals. That is to say, each epoch represents a span of historical time in which only certain kinds of being could come into unconcealment, appearing only in certain ways, and with only certain properties. Hence, the course of this history is marked by different hermeneutical epochs of ontological interpretation, bringing forth, within *the one and only* regime of ontological disclosure that we know, different paradigms of being and beingness in the representation of knowledge, truth, and reality. In Heidegger's historical narrative, these epochs, epochs both in the lifeworld and in the corresponding philosophical representations, unfold *as if* derived from an origin (*Ur-sprung*) the destiny of which is already implicit in the very beginning—but only as a *contingent* possibility, not only requiring recognition and understanding but also, of course, requiring enactment. But Heidegger would not be telling this story if he did not have faith in our *freedom* to interrupt the course of that derivation, that *Herkunft*. It should not be surprising, therefore, that *Überlieferung*, referring in its customary translation to a transmission, assumes the sense, in Heidegger's thought, of liberation. There is no teleology determining the course of the ontological epochs. There is only a history of contingencies and emergencies in relation to the grammar and meaning of being.

In the course of a recent email conversation, Richard Polt commented:

> At crucial junctures, who we are can come into question, so that we are thrust into a condition in which the sense of things as a whole becomes an urgent issue for us; our inherited interpretations might then be transformed into a new destiny.

As some of Heidegger's writings show, the history of metaphysics is a project that can get us rewardingly reflecting on the profoundly disruptive, even violent and traumatic changes in the experience and meaning of the being of beings that took place, as the Byzantine Christian world emerged from the pagan world of the Roman Empire; reflecting on the unsettling changes that occurred as the spirit of the Renaissance, with its relativizing infinity of perspectives, emerged from—and destroyed—the oppressively closed, yet in some ways more disorderly coherence of the medieval world; and reflecting on the unnerving transformations taking place today, in the epoch of *Machenschaft*, when machinery and mechanization, computer and internet technologies are imposing their requirements of total uniformity and standardization, determining the character of our encounters, not only with nature and things but even with people.

In each of these distinctive historical epochs, all of them unfolding *within* the ontological regime of concealment and unconcealment that began in ancient Greece and still prevails today as our world falls ever more deeply into the nihilism implicit within it, profound and often traumatic changes in the experience of the being of beings (*Seinsverständnis*), and of the source or essence of meaningfulness (*Bedeutsamkeit*) took place—both in the quotidian lives of the people and in the philosophical texts attempting to represent, in the language of concepts, our more deeply reflective, and often heatedly debated understanding of these matters.

And as philosophical thought is not only a reflection *on* the world, but inevitably also a reflection *of* it, this ontologically oriented history that Heidegger tells would increasingly become, in his hands as in Nietzsche's, a powerful critical rumination on the modern experience of the lifeworld, tracing the shapes of existential experience—the character of lifeworld experience—that, he thinks, we might usefully regard as corresponding to the conceptual transformations that emerge into view in his straightforwardly historical survey of the logic of concepts unfolding in metaphysics.

The principal critical point shaping this history meta-narrative is Heidegger's demonstration that all the major philosophical constructions or systems he examined neglect to address the concealment and negation of being. But if the world in which we are now living is a world suffering under the ever-increasing imposition of nihilism, it becomes urgently important to understand the root causes of this nihilism, causes operating not only in the realm of philosophical thought but also in the Western lifeworld. Heidegger's history of philosophy, concentrating, as at one time he believed it must, on the history of the concealments and unconcealments of being, therefore undertakes to rethink this history and narrate it in a way that, considered from the viewpoint of a philosophy of history, is able to bring to light what needs to be engaged, namely the *Ereignung* of *Dasein* and the *Geschick* in the clearing. Bearing this understanding in mind, another interpretive undertaking, another narrative, suggests itself, namely, a narrative concerned with the question of yet another inceptual beginning—a second beginning for historical life, unfolding very differently the meaning of being.

The significance of Heidegger's critical narrative concerning the history of metaphysics is that: (i) it shows us as fact that there have been *many* different kinds of experiences and representations; hence (ii) it frees us thereby from the assumption that beings have always and everywhere been experienced in just the way that we relate to them here and now; and consequently (iii) it shows us a field of different possibilities, in relation to which, released from our "enchantment" with things and our "captivity in the present" (*Befangenheit im Seienden*), we might learn, for the sake of a very different future, a new, very different way of relating to the openness of being (*zur Offenheit des Seins*), hence a very different way of encountering the beings that figure in our world (GA 5: 55/PLT 67). Heidegger's history-tracing meta-narrative, focusing our attention on the various representations of being, and showing the difference between past and present, encourages a critique of the present for the sake of a possible future transformation.

†

But if Heidegger's "history of being" is not a meta-narrative in this more or less familiar sense, a narrative exhibiting the history of changes in the concept of being, then what exactly is it? It seems that Heidegger himself struggled with this question, eventually—sometime in 1947 or 1948—confiding his suspicion to his private journal, the so-called *Black Notebooks*, that this "history" he was attempting to think is really nothing but "*eine Verlegenheit und ein Euphemismus*": an "embarrassment"—by which I think he just meant that it is something causing him unnecessary difficulties—and a "euphemism"—by which I think he just meant that, if it simply follows the logic of transformation in the concept of "being" in the context of a history of the fundamental concepts of Western metaphysics, then it is unnecessarily pretentious and grandiose.[11] So, again, if not this, then what is it about? The answer, I think, is that it is instead about the *Geschick*—something that no other history of philosophy ever properly thought about. Clearly, insofar as it is about the *Geschick* of being, this "history of being" is not, in the common understanding of "history," a meta-narrative about the history of concepts.

The vehemence of Heidegger's eventual repudiation of the *Seinsgeschichte* project does seem to indicate, however, a desire to distance himself from the terminology of the reigning ideology, registering his contempt for the kind of misguided chatter he was hearing at that time—namely, the 1930s and War years—among German historians and philosophers. Although, in *Being and Time*, Heidegger asserts that what philosophical thought most needs to reflect upon is the question of being, that work is, in his own words, a phenomenologically grounded "analytic of *Dasein*." In other words, it approaches the question of being in terms of, or from the position of, *Dasein*. However, in the 1930s and early 1940s, the years belonging, in Germany, to National Socialism, Heidegger's thought got very much caught up—briefly entangled, one might say—in reflections on what he called "the history of being," a narrative essentially oriented by the idea of destiny not easily disconnected from the ideology of German nationalism nor freed from the very theological metaphysics he was struggling to overcome.

How, in the 1930s and early 1940s, at such a politically troubled time, could Heidegger use a cluster of words—*Geschick*, *Schicken*, *Schickungen*—so weighted with associations that reverberate in their attunement with National Socialism and its ideology? Was he hoping, perhaps, to take that constellation of words back from the Nazis, to steal it, thereby depriving them of their means of communication and giving the words a new, liberated meaning? Maybe, but if so, that intention was ill conceived! In the privacy of his *Black Notebooks* (1938–1939) he acknowledged his egregious error:

> Thinking purely "metaphysically" (that is, in terms of the history of being), I took National Socialism in the years 1930 to 1934 to be the possibility of a transition to another beginning, and that is simply the interpretation I gave it.[12]

This acknowledgment, expressed without any sense of remorse, leaves much to be desired. Besides noticing a certain evasion of critical reflection, a reluctance even to explain himself, and also its belligerent defensiveness, we should notice that this remark is nevertheless a repudiation of National Socialism, and also, perhaps, a crucial step away from what he termed "the history of being"—a project serving a certain philosophy of history. Indeed, as I just discussed, one of his private notes from the late 1940s indicates that, even regarding the very meaning of *Seinsgeschick*, Heidegger seems to have been ambivalent and conflicted.[13]

But, once he understood the full significance of the *Ereignis*, then, without entirely ceasing to think in terms of being, the history of being, and the ontological-historical sense of destiny, he shifted emphasis, concentrating once again on the *phenomenology* of *Dasein*, explicating the implications of that phenomenology for the historical overcoming of the *Gestell* that holds our epoch in its terrifying power. In the time of the *Gestell*, being as such is denied. And, what is even worse, our responsibility for that nihilism is not recognized. That could, and might, seal our destiny—taking us ever closer to a terrible *Geschick*.

In the 1930s, but also the early 1940s, when, to some considerable extent, Heidegger let himself be caught up in the extreme madness of his grandiose vision for Germany and the Western world, imagining that it would lead into a new era, he declared, as we noted, that human life has "never yet" been historical (GA 65: 492/CP 387). What he meant by this shocking thought is that, although we humans have of course been "historical" according to the *common* understanding of that term, collecting and recollecting events in their chronology, we have not yet been "historical" in the sense he regarded as crucial, namely, by contemplating historical events from the perspective—the *Augenblicksstätte*—of a philosophy of history in which the sense of being at stake in those events is subjected to the most courageous questioning in regard to the heritage they grant us and the destiny our "skillful" (*geschicklich*) reception of that heritage might make possible for us. This means entering originary temporality.

Unfortunately, his meta-narrative reading of the history of being never entirely freed itself from all *seinsgeschichtliche* phantasmagoria, a philosophy of history seeming at times, despite the most adamant denials, to be indebted to an apocalyptic ideology and eschatology, and all too near, when invoking being, to positing the secret operation of a godlike agency. Some philosophers find such a reading of "being" to be appealing. This glorification of being, however, is an interpretation I think he vehemently wanted us to avoid. It is obviously incompatible with the "free relation" that his critique of the *Gestell* argued for—incompatible with his insistence that, despite the powerful dominion of the *Gestell*, despite its attempt to achieve totality, our surviving under the conditions imposed by the *Gestell* is not—or not yet—our doom, not—or not yet—our fate. Critical thinking is still possible; freedom is still feasible. Heidegger's phenomenological exposition of an "originary temporality" should be understood in this light as a crucial reminder of our freedom from the tyranny of the present.

†

Ultimately, though, Heidegger's history of metaphysics is much more than a critique. It is a thinking oriented by the *Geschick* as a question of destiny. His history seems to invite, and even to encourage, reading it as a meta-narrative indicating the possibility of a worldly, secular, earth-bound "redemption," telling the history of philosophy in the light of a philosophy of history grounded in human freedom—a finite freedom inseparable from its situation, to be sure, but understood as the assumption of our ontological appropriation and our consequent responsibility to protect the ontological dimension of the world of our experience: "*die Bergung der Wahrheit des Seins*" (GA 65: 35/CP 29). This involves our "release into freedom for the openness of the clearing": "*Die Befreiung in die Freiheit für die Wahrheit des Seins*" (GA 69: 24/HB 22). In this meta-narrative, the "redemption" in question, coming *after* the "death" of God—and indeed after the time of religion and theologies—calls for another beginning for philosophical thought, another ontological regime, another paradigm of knowledge, truth and reality, reflecting in the realm of thought a significant transformation of the human being in relation to the way the being of beings has been understood and experienced. And, presumably, this philosophical revolution would accompany in reflection corresponding changes in the world and the lives it makes possible.

†

According to Heidegger's meta-narrative, metaphysical thought began in the West when the early Greek philosophers—the ones Heidegger favors are Anaximander, Parmenides, and Heraclitus—sought to understand the being of their world. Going in thought beyond entities to understand them as a whole and as such, Heraclitus called what was engaging his thought using the word *physis*, a word that seems, once upon a time, to have communicated the awe in his sense of being, observing the visible-invisible nature of this world as a dynamic, growing, ever-emerging, ever-changing, ever-concealing *cosmos*—an abiding order of radiant splendor and immeasurable energy.[14] Other words, naming the same, that is being, but contemplating different aspects of its meaning, were *aletheia, logos, nomos, diké,* and *moira.* But despite their words, these Greeks, and the philosophers who followed, never gave thought to what made being itself possible: their thought remained bound to entities and their ways of presencing, leaving unrecognized and unthought the clearing, the openness as that within which all things must appear—and, equally unrecognized and unthought, our role in sustaining the conditions necessary for being. That enowning, that process of appropriation (*Er-eignung*), however, as I think Heidegger would argue, would be absolutely crucial in any preparation for "another inception," another paradigm in philosophical thought. Destiny, as Heidegger will eventually say, is *"aus dem Ereignen"* (GA 15: 367/FS, 61): it depends on, and emerges from, our engagement with the world in the process of appropriation—*Da-sein*, appropriated to the *Lichtung*.

†

Although Heidegger greatly admired the Greek philosophers and learned much from them, he concluded that the presuppositions constitutive of their metaphysical thought must be challenged, and he accordingly undertook to think outside of, or beyond, the history of metaphysics. Once freed from all the old metaphysical assumptions, we might perhaps, he thought, begin to hear the words of the pre-Socratics in a new way (GA 55: 175–77). What his thinking uncovered and retrieved was a hidden or rather unrecognized *phenomenological* dimension already implicit in the early Greek beginning: our appropriation as *Da-sein*. Conceivably, that could be the basis for another inception—or it could at least set in motion a significant challenge to the ontology that rules our present epoch.

As Heidegger points out in his *Contributions to Philosophy: From the Event* (1936–1938), to think our appropriation and "enter" into it is to achieve an understanding not only of the nature of our existence as *Da-sein* but also of our role in the history and future of being:

> *Da-sein*, in the sense of the other beginning that asks about the truth of beyng, . . . is not some characteristic of the human being, as if this name that extended to all beings were now simply restricted, as it were, to the role of designating the presence of human beings. (GA 65: 297/CP 234)

"Nevertheless," he adds,

> *Da-sein* and human being are essentially related, inasmuch as *Da-sein* signifies the ground of the possibility of future human being, and humans *are* futural by accepting to be properly situated historically, understanding their historical role as stewards of the truth [the aletheic, hermeneutical manifestation] of beyng. This stewardship is indicated by the term "care." 'Ground of possibility" is still a metaphysical expression, but it is to be thought here in terms of our steadfast *belongingness* [of being and the human being as *Da-sein*]. (Ibid.)

When thought in terms of the other inception, taking over as a task of responsibility what in our essence we already are, namely *Da-sein*, is something we absolutely need still to attain. And, as we know: "*Da-sein* is the steadfast sustaining of the clearing [*Das Da-sein* [*ist*] *die inständige Ertragsamkeit der Lichtung*]" (GA 65: 298/CP 235). This therefore is a stewardship, a preserving and protecting, "carried out by human beings who understand, in self-knowledge, that they are appropriated to being" (ibid.). That means recognizing, understanding, and enowning our appropriation, our responsibility for the being of beings—beginning, I would suggest, with the disclosive nature of perception.

The argument in his *Contributions to Philosophy* also appears in the texts published as *The History of Beyng* (1938–1940). But we should note that, even as Heidegger invokes the role—and the stewardship responsibility—of *Dasein*, his thinking at this time, in a Germany already ruled by the Nazis, was still under the sway of a philosophy of history constructed around the destinal idea of the history of being. However, the history that Heidegger is calling for, he says there, is

> the history of beyng, and therefore the history of the *truth* of being (i.e., the open clearing as the space-time interplay of concealment and unconcealment), and therefore the history of the *grounding* of truth, and therefore history as *Da-sein*; and thus it is only because *Da-sein* is instantiated [i.e., fully becomes itself] through the guardianship [*Wächterschaft*] of a given humankind that the human being can be [authentically] historical. This historicality unfolds in an essential way only in the belonging [*Zugehörigkeit*] of the human being to the truth of beyng [i.e., only in our guardianship, our protection of the interplay of concealment and unconcealment that the world-clearing of our time makes possible]. (GA 69: 93/HB 79)

For those who understood it, this argument for *Wächterschaft* defied and resisted the ideology of National Socialism; it also challenged the tyrannical rule (*Herrschaft*) that had taken over the developed world at that time: what he will call the epoch of the *Gestell*. So, contrary to the idea of destiny in National Socialism, Heidegger's conception of authentic ontological history and destiny is the opening up of history to "the essential manifesting [*Wesung*] of the truth of being." We should understand this as saying that it is a history formed by appropriation and memory (*Er-eignung* and *Erinnerung*): history, therefore, as "the eventful appropriation of the clearing" (GA 69: 101/HB 85). However, "because humankind has not yet at all been appropriated into *Da-sein*, i.e., *Lichtung*, and indeed because the abandonment of being reigns within beings, it must be recognized that this humankind is as yet *without history*, and for this very reason is merely 'historiographical' through and through" (GA 69: 94–96/HB 80–81). Without history—hence also without destiny, without a future befitting our humanity. Although not the toys of fate, we are still not exercising our true freedom. Free, authentic resolve (*Entscheidung*), obedient to our appropriation and mindful of our situatedness and finitude, is what makes the difference between fate and destiny.

The beginning of this authentic historicity requires our appropriation. We need to shift attention from the ontic (that which is presencing) to the truly ontological (presencing itself, and what makes that presencing possible), and from there return to ourselves, recognizing ourselves in the clearings our existence as *Da-sein* makes. Hence, as Heidegger remarks in a 1969 seminar at Le Thor, authentic historicity requires a "step back" to experience our appropriation, our role, our responsibility, in the *Es gibt* or *Es läßt*, that is, the clearing that he calls, in that seminar "the event [*Ereignis*] of being as [the necessary] condition [and essential element] for the arrival of beings" (GA 15: 362–67/FS 58–61).

†

We now will read a sequence of texts belonging to the late 1940s and extending into the last years of the 1960s. What I hope this interpretive reading shows is Heidegger's gradual recognition of the ultimate significance of the *Ereignung* for our understanding of the *Geschick* and our recognition of the potential for another epoch to emerge from, or erupt out of, the paradigm of being currently prevailing in this epoch. Here, in brief, is a summary, bringing to the fore the unfolding structural threads of the argument, which culminates in Heidegger's returning of the *Geschick*—the *Seinsgeschick*—to the phenomenology of the *Ereignung*. Drawing it back, where it belongs, into this phenomenology, he finally released the key word from its captivity in metaphysics and theology, where it had served for too long a history of violence. Following the summary, I will propose lengthier arguments.

(i) First, Heidegger's "Letter on Humanism," composed in 1946, after the War was finally over, in response to questions from the French philosopher Jean Beaufret, wherein Heidegger states in no unequivocal terms that, properly understood, the *Geschick* "occurs (*ereignet sich*) as the clearing of being (*als die Lichtung des Seins*), as which it is (*als welche es ist*)" (GA 9: 337/PM 257). This is an extremely important formulation because it suggests that the key word bears a *second* meaning besides signifying destiny, namely, the "sending" and "giving"—the *Geschick* of beings—that takes place in and as the clearing. In other words, the *Geschick* is the "sending" of beings that "gives" them their presence in the clearing. This second meaning would not in any way necessarily preclude the first meaning, which is destiny. Thus, what is "sent" and "given" (in the second sense of *Geschick*) might *also* carry a possibility bearing on our destiny. (ii) Second, *The Turn* (1949), wherein Heidegger argues that history must be understood "*aus der Geschick.*" Presumably, this means "in terms of, or in relation to, destiny." (iii) Third, "The Question Concerning Technology" (1955), wherein Heidegger argues for an authentic, truly free relation to the essence of history, history understood, therefore, from the perspective of "destiny" ("*als ein geschickliches*"). (iv) Fourth, *The Principle of Reason* (1956–1957), wherein Heidegger explicitly confirms that, for him, in the "history of being," being comes to light in the hermeneutics of its various epochal formations (*Schick-ungen*); and, in that explication, he brings the *Geschick* "back home," out of the reach of a grandiose metaphysics and into the humble phenomenology of *Da-sein* and its clearings. (v) Fifth, the 1957 lecture on "The Principle of Identity," wherein Heidegger brings being into the *Ereignis*, the process of appropriation, asserting that "being itself does belong to us and depend on us [*gehört zu uns*]; for only through us [*nur bei uns*] can it be itself [*kann es als Sein wesen*], i.e., come to meaningful presence [*an-wesen*]" (GA 11: 41/ ID 32–33). (vi) Sixth, "The Onto-Theo-Logical Constitution of Metaphysics" (1956–1957), where, in reflecting on Hegel, Heidegger introduces the thought of epochs unfolding in a *Lichtungsgeschichte*. Thus, his *Seinsgeschichte* is now recognized as a *Lichtungsgeschichte*. That is significant, because it suggests how we should think about the *Geschick*. (vii) Seventh, the 1962 lecture on "Time and Being," read together with the "Summary" (*Proto-koll*) of a seminar on that lecture, wherein Heidegger explicates the bonding (*Bezug*) that is the drawing together and belonging together of *Mensch* and *Sein* in terms of appropriation, giving *Ereignis*, the ordinary word for "event"—a *Geschehnis* or *Vorkommnis*—a totally new, and decisively significant meaning (GA 11: 45/ID 36). (viii) And eighth, the 1969 seminar in Le Thor, wherein Heidegger makes two gigantic and consequential moves: *first*, Heidegger speaks of the *Geschick* in a way that suggests the *second* sense of this key word, namely, as denoting the sending or giving of being in and through the clearing; and *second*, the *Geschick* (in both senses, albeit differently) is returned to appropriation. So, we know that the *Schicken*, as he argues, is "*aus dem Ereignung.*" But if the *Geschick* is identified with that which "sends" into meaningful presence, then it is the "*ereignete Lichtung.*"

This ends my summary. A longer exposition now follows.

†

i.   In his 1946 "Letter on Humanism," wherein Heidegger proposes a critique of humanism and ventures to suggest another humanism more befitting who we are in our essence as human beings, the philosopher unequivocally identifies the *Geschick* with the ontological functioning of the clearing. However, it is not entirely manifest whether that key word is (a) to be understood as invoking a destiny, describing how it occurs (*sich ereignet*), or whether it is (b) to be understood—either also or instead—as referring to the ontological role of the clearing as the *Geschick*, that which "gives," "sending"—enabling—beings into meaningful presence. This ambiguity, or confusion, will eventually get resolved. But in this text, it remains a still unrecognized problem. In any case, this text shifts our attention away from any metaphysically conceived *Geschick*: what matters is something *strictly* phenomenological. Whether and how what is "given" in this givenness of experience brings us closer to a recognition and understanding of our *destiny* is another matter. But whatever we are given (sent, granted) to experience in the clearing that our existence has opened *can* always be taken up as a question regarding destiny—the meaning and mission of our humanity.

What I am suggesting is that, in a passage from this letter, Heidegger seems to use the key word *Geschick* in *two* distinctly different ways, suggesting two distinctly different, though intertwined, senses. In one of those uses, the word seems, unquestionably, to signify destiny, as it commonly does. But there also are uses—contexts—where it seems that it must carry a distinctly different meaning, although one *still connected* to the issue of destiny. In each instance here, the key word compels us to decide its meaning, whether it be an invocation of destiny or a reference to the functioning of the clearing as *Da-sein*'s *Es gibt*, that which admits beings into their experiential givenness, their form of presence within the time-space field:

> Assuming that in the future we human beings will be able to think the truth of being [i.e., the clearing as time-space field for presencing in the interplay of concealment and unconcealment], we will think it in terms of ex-istence. The human being stands ex-istingly in the *Geschick* of being. The ex-istence of the human being is historical as such, but not only or primarily because so much happens to the human being and to things human in the course of time. Rather, because it must think the ex-istence of *Da-sein*, the thinking of *Being and Time* is essentially concerned that the *historicity* of *Dasein* be experienced. (GA 9: 336–37/PM 256–57)

In the interpretation of this passage, it does seem right to translate the word *Geschick* by "destiny," although what "standing in the destiny of being" is supposed to mean is not easily determined. However, in this sentence, the key word could also be translated, by way of interpretation, as "clearing," so that Heidegger would simply be saying that the human being stands existing in the historicity of the clearing of being, or in the midst of what is historically given (*geschickt, gegeben*) in and through the clearing. We stand in the midst of what the clearing "sends" and "grants." No direct invocation of destiny at all.

In any case, an interpretation that avoids the worst metaphysical projections might be that it is a question of living one's life mindful of the fact that we must bear responsibility for the historical meaning of being: we must protect the very being of beings from the forces of nihilism; and this means that the "destiny" of being itself—its historical future—depends on our commitment.

In this passage, the two meanings for the word *Geschick* seem equally compelling. There are other passages, however, where it seems more problematic to assume that *Geschick* only means destiny. But what the word does mean is not easy to determine. The text of the letter continues, using the word in a way that strongly suggests the other meaning I am proposing:

> But does not *Being and Time* say that where the "t/here is/it gives" [the *Es gibt*, i.e., *Dasein*-as-clearing] comes to language, "Only so long as *Dasein* is, is there [*gibt es*] being"? To be sure. It means that, only so long as the clearing of being occurs and propriates [*nur solange die Lichtung des Seins sich ereignet*, i.e., only as long as the ontological dimension of the clearing is brought into awareness, recognized, understood, enowned, and enacted, as such], does the truth of being properly convey itself to human being [*übereignet sich Sein zum Menschen*]. But the fact that the *Da*, the clearing as the truth of being itself [*Daß aber das Da, die Lichtung als Wahrheit des Seins selbst*], takes place and propriates [*sich ereignet*] is the givenness (dispensation) of being itself [*ist die Schickung des Seins selbst*]. This is the *Geschick* of the clearing [*Dieses ist das Geschick der Lichtung*]. (GA 9: 336/PM 256)

How should we translate the last sentence? What does "*Geschick der Lichtung*" mean? It is perhaps Heidegger's clearest, most unequivocal recognition of the fact that, in his project, the word *Geschick*, normally thought to signify destiny, has this other more fundamental, more phenomenological meaning. The presencing of being is the dispensation—the *Geschick*— of the clearing: it is what the clearing "sends" and "gives," what it makes possible. It is also true, however, that destiny can only manifest in and through what we are "given" or "sent" in our experience: the *Geschick* as destiny is intrinsically dependent on the *Geschick* as what occurs (*ereignet*), "sent" or "given" in the world of our experience.

We should also ponder the grammatical ambiguity in the phrase "*Geschick der Lichtung.*" The phrase seems to solicit a double reading. To be sure, one possibility is a reference to what the clearing might become, or could become, in the future: the "sending" of the clearing into its future, hence the "destiny" of the clearing. But there is another possibility for the phrase, namely, that the *Geschick* (i.e., history and destiny) belongs to, and belongs in, the clearing. The *Geschick* is indeed about destiny; but it is about the destiny that is sent by, and coming by way of, the clearing. It is a destiny that informs the clearing in its different historically constituted and conditioned structurations, deeply affecting the character of its "sending" and "giving"—and correspondingly affecting, by way of its various *Schick-ungen*, what formations of being, or what ontological commitments, the clearing can make possible. In the context of Heidegger's project, the possibility of destiny (*Geschick*) is something granted, hidden, in the sending, coming and givenness (*Schickung*) of beings. For Heidegger, it is through the interpretation of what we are "sent," what we are *given* to experience in the clearing, that a vision of the way to redeeming the claim in our destiny might emerge.

So, must we assume that Heidegger's paragraph is necessarily about destiny? Might it perhaps simply concern the *clearing* as that which lets-presence—in other words, as that which sends, gives, enables, and makes possible the givenness, the facticity, of beings? This, the *Geschick* in its various configurations (*Schickungen*), is the function of the clearing. Invoking the *Geschick* of the clearing would thus be a way to recognize the fact that it is *in and through the clearing* that beings can come into modalities of meaningful presence. So *Geschick* would simply refer to the *function* of the clearing: the fact that the clearing "sends" beings into meaningful presence; or "gives" beings meaningful presence; or "lets" beings come into presence.

I suggest that there are, in fact, four possible interpretations of the phrase "*Geschick der Lichtung.*" All four make perfectly good sense. And they are compatible with one another. All four could be true. Nevertheless, it is important that we differentiate them and do so as incisively as possible:

1. The phrase invokes destiny and refers to the possible future, or destiny, of the clearing in its historically interpreted role.
2. The phrase invokes destiny and says that destiny belongs in, and to, the clearing. "Destiny" is an interpretation of what occurs— what takes place—in the world of *Da-sein*'s clearing. So, if and

when the possibility of our historical destiny is fulfilled and its promise is redeemed, that is something that would take place in and through the clearing, under its auspices.

3.  The phrase does *not necessarily* refer to destiny, but either instead, or also, to the *clearing* as the time–space field of the *Geschick*, that is, as that which, in the openness of its dimensions, makes possible ("gives," "sends") the presencing of beings. In other words, the *Geschick* refers to the role of the *clearing* as that in and through which the presencing ("sending," "giving") of beings occurs. And as I noted earlier in the summary, this connection makes sense, because the *Schicken* is said to be *"aus dem Ereignen."* That is precisely what must also be said of the clearing—*die ereignete Lichtung*: "Destiny propriates as [i.e., in its actualization and fulfillment, destiny must operate as, must become] the clearing of being—which it is. The clearing grants nearness to being. In this nearness, in the clearing of the *Da*, the human being dwells as the existing one. [*Dieses Geschick ereignet sich als die Lichtung des Seins, als welche es ist. Sie gewährt die Nähe zum Sein. In dieser Nähe, in der Lichtung des 'Da,' wohnt der Mensch als der Ek-sistierende*]." And, Heidegger adds, we are unfortunately, even today, still—not yet— "able properly to experience and take over this dwelling" (GA 9: 337/PM: 257).

4.  The phrase does *not necessarily* refer to destiny, but either instead, or also, to the *clearing* as itself *geschickt*, shaped and conditioned by the historical situations in which we, as *Da-sein*, find ourselves cast. In other words, *Geschick*, here, refers to the phenomenological fact that the clearing that we *are* is always *experienced* as conditioned, subject to the *Geschick*, the facticity—the reality—of the situation we are "given" or "sent." The clearing is thus always a particular, historically situating *"Schickung."* The *Geschick*, in this sense, refers to the fact that the clearing always takes place in relation to the "giving" or "sending" of the world-historical conditions involved in determining the character of the clearing, that is, determining the conditions necessary for a *Da-sein's* making presencing, meaningful appearing, at all possible.

In the second textual fragment, as well as in other texts, Heidegger brings *Geschick* as destiny into association with a semantically related constellation of words, words that could be suggesting the other meaning, notably: *schicken, zuschicken, Schickung, Es gibt, geben, Gabe, schenken*. With these words, and others in or around the constellation (e.g., *gewähren*), it seems that the philosopher is drawing us into a dimension of phenomenology that enables us to think of destiny—"the destiny of being"—as referring to the possibilities for the achievement of a redeemed world that are carried, hidden, within what, in the world of our clearing, we are given, or granted, to experience. We do know, from singularly important texts, that it is the clearing that makes the meaningful experiencing of beings possible: in other words, staying with Heidegger, we might say that it is the clearing that sends, gives, grants, enables, and lets-take-place the presencing, or being, of beings; so we might conclude from this fact that, in making presencing possible, the clearing is also that *in and through which* the possibilities that might be granted us for achieving our destiny would come—come to light. Thus, "*Geschick der Lichtung*" might with equal reason be interpreted as referring to the sending *of* the clearing, that is, *by* the clearing, *in and through* the clearing: the fact that the clearing is what "sends," "gives," lets-presence, and makes possible. The only problem with this is that it does not accord with our ordinary everyday experience, in which what we encounter in our field of experience does not normally "come" or "emerge" or "appear"; nor is it experienced as something "sent" or "given," as if a gift. Instead, things are typically experienced in the sheer facticity, or givenness, of a naïve realism, presented as simply "being here." But this, of course, speaks precisely to the heart of Heidegger's lament about the way we contemporaries are living our lives. Even our experience in perception has suffered distortion and impoverishment. Failing to experience the role of the clearing and failing to interrogate our historical experience in regard to its bearing on the question of our destiny, has serious consequences.

If, in our time, the rule of the *Gestell*, the imposition of total reification, is determining our *Geschick*, our given historical reality and destiny, and indeed the character of all our experience, then this would indeed submit the clearing itself, which Heidegger often calls "the truth of being," to the rule of the *Gestell,* with all the conditions it imposes.

†

ii.   "The Turn" (1949). The "Letter on Humanism" makes a contribution of great significance, bringing the *Geschick* into our thinking of the clearing. However, the ambiguity in the interpretation of *Geschick* that we find in the "Letter" persists in this later text. Let us recall that, in "The Turn," Heidegger asserts: "We tend to locate history in the realm of happening, instead of thinking history in accordance with its essential origin [*Wesensherkunft*] from out of the *Geschick* [*aus dem Geschick*]" (GA 11: 115/GA 79: 69/38). Is it absolutely necessary to read this as "from out of destining"? Could we read the key word, together with its relatives, *schicken* and *Schickung*, as referring instead, or also, to the function of the clearing—as in what, in "The Onto-Theo-Logical Constitution of Metaphysics," Heidegger calls a *Lichtungsgeschichte*? (see GA 11: 60/ID 51). If so, then the critical point Heidegger is arguing would be that, fatalistically, we tend to locate the events of history in a realm of happening—agencies and forces—causes over which we have no control, instead of recognizing our role and responsibility for the interpretation of these events: they need to be recognized and understood as *"Wesensweise des Seins"* (GA 11: 115–16/ GA 79: 68–69/QCT 37–38), modes of coming to presence" that take place within the theaters of our clearing; they belong in, and to, the paradigm of a historical world that we have wrought. "Destiny" unquestionably haunts this text from beginning to end; but the possibility of an alternative, hence double reading—a phenomenological reading concerning the role of the clearing, hence farther from metaphysics—remains for our reading throughout the paragraph. According to this other rendering, what is destining (*das Geschickliche im Geschick*) in the *Geschick*—in what we have been "given" or "sent"—would be a singular, uncanny characteristic we *freely attribute* to what presences, a possibility to be brought forth by interpreting what is given (*die Begebenheiten*), what comes or is sent (*geschickt*), in and through the situations of the world we have cleared and brought to light. Indeed, although authentic history must be, for Heidegger, *"aus dem Geschick,"* we shall learn, in the Le Thor Seminar (1969) two decades later, that the *Geschick*, as that which names the clearing as "sending," "giving," and enabling meaningful presencing, is to be understood as *"aus dem Ereignen."* In its *Wesensherkunft*, the *Geschick* must itself be traced back— back to its phenomenology in the clearing, the appropriation of *Da-sein*. We must accordingly return authentic history—and its sense as destiny—to our appropriation, no longer either (a) neglecting the possibilities that the inheritance of history offers for the shaping of our future in attunement to what would correspond to our shared sense of destiny or (b) surrendering the future in that inheritance to the irrational forces so frequently attributed to destiny.

†

iii.  In "The Question Concerning Technology" (1955), Heidegger offers what could be considered a definition of *Geschick*, although it might better be regarded only as an illuminating perspective from which to think about the meaning of that key word: "We shall call *Geschick* that sending-that-gathers [*jenes versammelnde Schicken*] which first brings human beings upon a way of unconcealment [*auf einen Weg des Entbergens bringt*]" (GA 7: 25/ QCT 24). Are we justified in translating the word *Geschick* in this sentence as "destining"? Not, I think, necessarily. This "sending-that-gathers" could nicely describe the clearing, leaving the question of destiny unresolved. Be this as it may, I would like, in this chapter, to lay down a few *Stolpersteine*—a few stumbling blocks—on our way to the invoking of destiny. It is, after all, a word haunted by horrible histories, not to be used lightly or loosely.

Reading destiny in Heidegger's words, we have him arguing that it is "from out of this destining, or out of a sense of destiny [*von hier aus*], that the essence of all genuine history [*Geschichte*] is to be determined." Thus:

> History is neither simply the object of written chronicle [*Historie*] nor simply the fulfillment of human activity [*der Vollzug menschlichen Tuns*]. That activity first becomes genuinely historical [*geschichtlich*] when understood as something that concerns destiny [*als ein geschickliches*]. (Ibid.)

So, what is genuinely historical is to be understood "henceforth" as "*aus dem Geschick.*" Genuine history inherits the past as a vital question about our way into the future. In this inheritance, we are given an opportunity to confront a question of destiny calling upon our freedom. History in its customary sense, in contrast, captures the past as a totally reified object. Thus, in an important way, it denies us our freedom. What Heidegger calls the *Gestell* characterizes our epoch as one in which being undergoes the nullifying imposition of total reification. But it is, he says, just like every other modality, or way, of disclosing, "an ordaining of destining" — "*eine Schickung des Geschickes*" (GA 7: 25 ff./QCT 24 ff). In this context and phrasing, it does seem fitting to think of the word *Geschick* as invoking destiny. Destiny (*Geschick*) comes, is given, within and through the clearing, in many different ways and forms (*Schickungen*). However, the modality of what is given today is different from all the earlier modalities of the given in Western history, because what is now given assaults and hides the clearing—that openness wherein unconcealment, presencing, comes to pass. Our greatest historical task, therefore, is to use our freedom thoughtfully, to protect and preserve the openness—*das Freie*, the clearing itself, *as* "realm of destiny" ("*Bereich des Geschickes*"). Or should we perhaps rather say, acknowledging the possibility of double meaning in the key word: we need to protect and preserve *the clearing* as the realm in which we experience what is given—what *es gibt*—from an interpretive perspective that enables us to contemplate the question of our shared destiny?

In any case, whenever possible, I think we should consider substituting "the situation we find ourselves given" for the metaphysically, theologically freighted word and its constellation of relatives. Why must history be judged by the inherently problematic idea of destiny, rather than—let us say—by measuring up to our ethical and moral ideals? After all, it is possible to think about a future world in which the promise in human nature and the ideals we profess to cherish would be substantially redeemed without *necessarily* invoking the idea of destiny. Heidegger, though, must have believed, at least for quite a few years, that this idea represented a necessary standpoint and perspective, without which we would be hopelessly reduced to the empiricism of the present. In fact, the idea of historical destiny seems to have survived his eventual abandonment of the *Seinsgeschichte*.

However, interpreting and translating *Geschick* as referring always to "destiny" is problematic, even if we have a conception that is clearly defined and free of dangerous ideology, metaphysics, and theology. Even in this text, a certain ambiguity persists. "Destiny" is always a possible translation. But sometimes, the word could instead, or also, refer to the role of the clearing as that which "sends" beings into presence, that is, makes their presencing, their givenness, possible—a sense of *Geschick* that might, or might not, bear on destining. The doubled meaning of *Geschick*—as "the destining of destiny," but also as the disclosing that comes to pass in and through the clearing, namely by way of its "sending," "giving," "letting," or "making-possible"—shows up, for example, when he says: (a) "Enframing [*Das Gestell*] comes to pass [*ereignet*] as a *Geschick* [structuring] of disclosing [*des Entbergens*]" and (b) "Enframing is a *Geschick* [a way of structuring what comes into presence in the clearing] that gathers everything together into a disclosing [*Entbergung*] that challenges forth. Challenging is anything but a granting [*Herausfordern ist alles andere, nur kein Gewähren*]. Or so it seems, so long as we do not notice that the challenging-forth into the ordering of the real as standing-reserve [*das Bestellen des Wirklichen als Bestand*] still remains a *Schicken* [a structuring of the clearing] that *sends* man upon a way of revealing [*auf einen Weg des Entbergens bringt*]" (GA 7: 32/ QCT 31). In each instance, as my bracketed translations suggest, the word "*Geschick*" can be an invocation of destiny, or it can be simply a way of referring to what is occurring *in and through* the clearing; or even, perhaps, as referring to the taking place, or the historically conditioned "sending" or "giving," of the clearing itself: a *Schickung* or *Schicken* of the clearing in the objective genitive sense. In any case, we need to recognize that every clearing is itself a *Schickung*, a field of experience, a matrix, formed, as if "sent," or "given," in the conditions of the historical world into which *Da-sein* finds itself thrown: a field of experience, moreover, that "sends" beings into their meaningful presence, a field that "gives" them such presence. Thus, we need to consider an alternative interpretation—not "destiny," or not only "destiny," but rather, or also, what, in its coming into presence or in its being received into presence, bears the possibility of destiny, when the philosopher asks us to consider: "If this *Geschick*, as enframing [having the character of *das Gestell*], is the extreme danger, not only for the coming to presence of human beings, but for all disclosing as such, should this *Schicken* [i.e., this historically particular manifestation of the *Geschick* that is involved in the formation of the clearing] still be called a granting [*ein Gewähren*]? Yes, most emphatically, if in this *Geschick* [i.e., this historically distinctive type of structuring of the clearing], the saving power is said to grow" (GA 7: 33/QCT 31–32). A huge "if"!

By the time he gave the lecture series on *The Principle of Reason* (1955–1956), we can see that Heidegger had achieved a much clearer and firmer understanding of what he had wanted both words, *Geschick* and *Seinsgeschichte*, to say.

†

iv.  *The Principle of Reason* (1956–1957). By the mid-1950s, Heidegger more explicitly recognized that his project required, and in fact was using without sufficient acknowledgment, a second, different but phenomenologically related sense of *Geschick*. This recognition, appearing in *The Principle of Reason*, finally resolved the ambiguity and confusion that, in texts from the earlier years, had troubled his discussions of the *Geschick* and the history of being:

> When we use the word *Geschick* in connection with being, we mean that being is granted to us in a clearing [*daß Sein sich uns zuspricht und sich lichtet*], and that the clearing makes room for the time-space interplay, within which beings can appear [*und lichtend den Zeit-Raum-Spiel einräumt, worin Seiendes erscheinen kann*]. In relation to the *Geschick* of being, the history of being is not thought of in terms of a happening characterized by passing away and process. Rather, the essence of history is determined on the basis of the *Geschick* of being, of being as *Geschick*, of what as such proffers itself to us in withdrawing [*sich uns zuschickt indem es uns entzieht*]. . . . The term "*Geschick* of being" is not an answer but a question, among others the question of the essence of history. . . . At first, the *Geschick*-character of being can appear quite strange to us. . . . However, if there is some truth in saying that being always proffers itself to us even in its withdrawing [. . .], then it follows that "being" means something different from "being" as it occurs in the various epochs of its *Geschick*. (GA 10: 91/PR 62)

The *Geschick*, here, refers both to the granting and the "making room." And it can refer both to (a) the beings that come into meaningful presence for us, as what the clearing "sends" and "gives" and also, it seems, to (b) the clearing itself, as what "makes room," what "furnishes," what proffers in withdrawing, yielding in both senses, "sending" and "giving" beings into meaningful presence while itself yielding and withdrawing from our attention. The "being" that proffers and withdraws is precisely the clearing—it is that which makes the presencing of beings possible: It is the fourth sense of "being," as discussed in my chapter on being. But "being" as it occurs in the various epochs is being in the first and third senses, namely, as what it means for something to *be* in regard to what is presencing. Moreover, because all beings that enter our fields of experience, even hallucinations and mirages, both give themselves and withhold themselves, *Geschick* and *Schickung* can also refer to the presencing of all beings—the fact that all beings are *geschickt*, "sent" and "given." Thus, Heidegger would be invoking the entire *phenomenology* of the *Geschick*, the so-called "dispensation," namely, (α) the *ontological dimension* of the beings that, in the various epochs belonging to the history of being, are "sent" or "given" in and through the clearings—and also (β) all the different ways, or modalities, in which, in the course of Western history, beings are, and have been, "given," or "sent," in and through the clearings, that is, the different experiences of what it means to be, characterized in relation to different epochs in the history of being. The first use, (α), refers to beings; second use, (β), refers to the clearing, being itself.

In the lectures belonging to *The Principle of Reason*, the "*Geschichte des Seins*" is said to concern the "*geschickhafter Charakter des Seins*" (GA 10: 91/PR 62), namely, the character of being in regard to its "dispensation," that is, the phenomenology of its way of "giving itself," "sending itself," "presenting itself" to us. So it turns out that what matters is, first and foremost, the *phenomenology* of the *Geschick*: , that is, what matters first and foremost is not *Geschick* in the sense of "historical destiny" but rather the *phenomenology* of presencing, that is, (a) the fact that something meaningful is being given or sent (*geschickt*) into our experience and (b) the ontological character and dimensionality of that givenness—the "*geschickhafter Charakter des Seins*." The question of destiny would consequently arise, if at all, only at a later stage of enquiry, when the concern really is about the history of being as a meta-narrative interpreting the hermeneutical character—the interplay of unconcealment and concealment, proffering and withdrawing—of the historical succession of different paradigms of being.

Immediately preceding the textual passage that we have just read, Heidegger makes an observation of the utmost significance, challenging, as it does, the enthusiasm that some scholars (still) have for interpreting and translating every invocation of *Geschick* as signifying "destiny":

We usually understand *Geschick* as being that which has been determined and imposed through fate [*Schicksal*]: a sorrowful, evil, or fortunate *Geschick*. This meaning, however, is actually a derivative one. For *schicken* ["sending"] originally denoted "preparing," "ordering," "bringing each thing to that place where it properly [i.e., appropriately] belongs." Consequently, it also meant "furnishing" [*einräumen*] and "admitting" [*einweisen*]. Hence it can mean "to appoint" [*beschicken*] a house or a room, "keeping it in good order," "straightened up and tidied." (GA 10: 90/PR 61)

This interpretation of *Geschick* is exciting, because instead of reiterating the idea of destiny, what it leads us into is the phenomenology of the clearing: the clearing as time-space *einräumen*. Of all the explanations Heidegger provided for *Geschick*, this is, I submit, his single most important statement. It completely sweeps away all the onto-theological, metaphysical interpretations, assigning that key word to the work of the clearing. In keeping with this rendering of *Geschick*, Heidegger explains the structural role and character of the clearing—*Lichtung*—in the phenomenology of our experience:

That [namely, *Sein selbst*, one of Heidegger's ways of referencing the clearing] wherethrough all that which comes to presence on its own emerges and comes to presence never lies over against us as do the particular beings that are present here and there. Being itself [*Sein selbst*, i.e., the clearing] is thus in no way as immediately familiar and manifest to us [*vertraut und offenkundig*] as are particular beings [*wie das jeweilig Seiende*], yet it is not as though *being* keeps itself completely concealed. If this were to happen, then even beings could never lie over against us and be familiar to us. Indeed being [i.e., the clearing] must of itself shine and clear, shine and clear already in advance, so that particular beings can appear. If being [i.e., the clearing] were not to shine, not to clear, then there would be no region [*Gegend*] within which an "over-against [*ein Gegenüber*, i.e, an ob-ject] could settle. (GA 10: 93/PR 63)

We should notice here, first of all, how the meaning of *Lichtung* oscillates, swinging easily between meaning light and meaning the lighting, or clearing: The clearing does shine and let shine. The clearing is that which "sends" or "gives" beings: it is that which makes presencing possible. It opens and "furnishes" its clearing with what appears within its embrace. Destiny is not immediately invoked. If we heed what is indicated and implied in these passages, then we need to interrogate with a measure of skepticism all the translations that interpret *Geschick* and the constellation of related words in terms of destiny and its coming, sending, giving, and granting. It is possible that, in the 1930s, Heidegger's thinking, at times insufficiently self-critical, was captivated by the vision of a great new destiny for the Western world, but that, by the early 1940s, Heidegger was no longer under the spell of this vision and was reappropriating and rededicating *Geschick* and its constellation of words, giving them a new, equally difficult assignment, namely, to guide our attention into the *phenomenology* of experience: experience understood in the light of the *Ereignung* and for the sake of breaking the hold of the *Gestell*. This is an assignment that would dedicate the *Geschick* to the redeeming of a very different mission and destiny. But this would depend, ultimately, on thinking the *Geschick* phenomenologically, in its more fundamental meaning.

†

v. "The Principle of Identity" (1957). In this text, Heidegger reflects on the meaning and significance of Parmenides' claim that being and perceiving or thinking are the same. Taking this claim to mean the essential belonging together [*Zusammengehören*] of man and being [*Mensch und Sein*], he argues that, in this relationship [i.e., *Bezug der Entsprechung*], the two "are appropriated to one another":

> A belonging to being prevails within the human being [*Im Menschen waltet ein Gehören zum Sein*], a belonging that listens to being because it is appropriated [*übereignet*] to being. And being? Let us think being according to its original meaning, as presence [*Anwesen*]. Being is present [*west*] and abides [*währt*] only as it concerns [*an-geht*] us through the claim [*Anspruch*] it makes on us. For it is us human beings, open toward being, who alone let being arrive as presence. Such becoming present needs the openness of a clearing [*das Offene einer Lichtung*], and by this need remains appropriated [*übereignet*] to human being. (GA 11: 38–40/ OTB 30–31)

Although, in this lecture, there is no invocation of the *Geschick*, Heidegger does make a connection between (a) the character of our historical situation, which today is threatened by the total imposition of reification that he calls the *Gestell* and (b) the reflections in this passage on the essential nature of our relation to being (GA 11: 44ff/OTB 35ff). Thus, it is clear that he recognized and understood the relevance, hence the implications, of what he was arguing in this text for the interpretation and critique of our moment in history—and that means also for the interpretation and critique of our engagement with the question of *Geschick*. The *Seinsgeschick* belongs to the belonging together of *Mensch* and *Sein*. Once *being* is to be understood in terms of our appropriation, and finally, indeed, absorbed into it, then it is just the smallest of steps in thought to recognizing that, after its errant sojourn in the precincts of onto-theology, the *Geschick des Seins*—the *Seinsgeschick*—must likewise be returned to appropriation. Destiny is neither something objectively given nor something merely subjectively projected; rather, it is a possibility we discern and appropriate, interpreting the historical meaning of the situations we find "given" or "sent" (*geschickt*) in the world of our clearing. And in the context of history, the *Geschick* thus belongs as a "future past" to our *appropriation*, our enowning of the historical background of the situation in which we happen to be living.

†

vi. "The Onto-Theo-Logical Constitution of Metaphysics," Heidegger's 1957 lecture on Hegel, is also pertinent here. It was written around the same time as *The Principle of Reason* and "The Principle of Identity." In this short text, Heidegger still wanted to recognized the importance of contemplating the meaning and significance of being in terms of a certain ontological recollection oriented toward "the entire history and destiny of being"—"*das ganze Geschick des Seins*." However, as we can learn from this text, he continued his struggle to free this process of recollection from metaphysics:

> The little word "is," which speaks everywhere in our language and tells of being even where it does not appear expressly, contains the whole history and destiny of being. (GA 11: 79/ID 73)

Is he really still concerned with destiny, solely with destiny—or is he instead thinking about the different historical ways or forms—the various *Schickungen*—in which, over the centuries, over the epochs, being has been experienced in the beings we have encountered? If the latter, then "destiny"—*Geschick*—would more specifically be the word for the still unknown futural possibilities for being that might emerge.

Significantly introducing the clearing into the argument, Heidegger notes that "discourse about being and beings can never be pinned down to *one* epoch in the history of the clearings for being [*Lichtungsgeschichte von Sein*]" (GA 11: 60/ID 51). In keeping with this conception of a history and destiny of being, *The Principle of Reason*, an earlier text (1955–1956), undertook to clarify what he was understanding to be the "*geschickhafte* character of being," that is the conviction that what the Western world has implicitly understood by "being" has a history and therefore a destiny, such that it would make perfectly reasonable sense to contemplate what "a history of being" involves (GA 10: 91/PR 62). But an even sharper elucidation emerges in "The Onto-Theo-Logical Constitution of Meta-physics," where, arguing that it is not possible to represent being as the "general characteristic" of particular beings, Heidegger goes on to observe that we *can* identify the general characteristics of being that hold sway over particular epochs. In other words, we *can* characterize particular paradigm formations of being as predominating in one or another historical period:

> There is being [*Es gibt Sein*] only in this or that particular historical char-acter [*nur je und je in dieser und jener geschicklichen Prägung*]: *physis, logos, hen, idea, energeia,* substantiality, objectivity, subjectivity, the will, the will to power, the will to will. But these historic forms cannot be found in rows, like apples, pears, peaches, lined up on the counter of historic representational thinking. (GA 11: 73/ID 66)

In his reflections on Hegel, Heidegger invokes the *Geschick*, not primarily to speak of destiny but rather as a way of referring to the fact that the being of beings always figures in particular, historically shaped forms of clearing, particular, historically shaped matrices of conditions:

> Being gives itself only in the light [*nur in dem Lichte*] that cleared itself [*gelichtet*] in Hegel's thinking. That is to say, the manner in which it [*es*], being, gives itself [*sich gibt*], [i.e., the manner in which beings can come into, or be without, meaningful presence] is determined by the way it figures in the clearing [*aus der Weise, wie es sich lichtet*]. (GA 11: 73/ID 67)

The meaning of "being" depends on the historical conditions laid down by and for particular historical clearings—particular epochs in the history of the world. This is how, in the final analysis, Heidegger wants "the history of being" to be understood. It not only makes sense; it guides and strength-ens his idea of destiny, returning it to our responsibility. But this explica-tion of being also fits in with a very different interpretation of *Geschick*, namely, an interpretation that returns it—together with its constellation of words—to the phenomenology of the clearing and, thereby, to a history of the unfolding of the clearing as a structure conditioning the presencing of beings: a *Lichtungsgeschichte*. The temptations of metaphysics are finally almost overcome, as the *Geschick* and its various historical *Schickungen* are taken back into phenomenology. In the context of phenomenology, however, Heidegger's reliance on the constellation of words that *Geschick* governs—for instance, *schicken, schenken, geben*—is problematic, because there is no source, no agency involved: beings simply are present in the clearing. Thus, if we are inclined to continue saying that the clearing *gives* or *sends* or *grants* what we encounter in the clearing, or claim that the things we encounter are *given*, *sent*, or *granted*, then we must be alert to the misleading implications that might be drawn.

†

vii. In the lecture "Time and Being" (1962), given about five years after *The Principle of Reason*, Heidegger was still ruminating on the idea of a history of being, attempting to defend an interpretation that would be free of problematic metaphysics:

> The development of the abundance of transformations of being looks at first like a history of being. But being does not have a history in the way in which a city or a people have their history. What is history-like in the history of being is obviously determined by the way in which being takes place and by this alone. After what has just been explained, this means [that the history of being concerns] the different ways in which there is being [*es gibt Sein*]. (GA 14: 11–12/OTB 8)

Heidegger's phrase, "different ways in which there is being" draws our attention to the appearing of beings—but in regard to an essential paradigmatic unity and coherence. This statement turns our thinking back from *being*, the realm of metaphysics, to *beings* in the phenomenology of our history-making role as *Da-sein*, appropriated to be the clearing in the openness of which *beings* are given the possibility of meaningful presence and absence, always appearing in the hermeneutical interplay of concealment and unconcealment. And the "history of being," as defined here, is no longer an oddity, an unfamiliar way of contemplating the changes through which what it means to be has passed. It is an attempt to recognize the different ontological forms or configurations (*Gestalten, Prägungen*) in which *beings* (plural) have been experienced. This concerns the *Geschick*: not in the sense of destiny but in the sense that refers to the "giving" or "sending" of beings. The history of being must accordingly be concerned with the different historical formations of the clearing and consequently the different ways in which, considering the given historical conditions affecting the clearing, it would be possible for beings to presence meaningfully. Thus, emphasizing the *Es gibt*, Heidegger states that

> the history of being means the *Geschick* of being in the sendings [*Schickungen*], in which both the sending [*das Schicken*] and the it-which-sends-forth [*das Es, das schickt*] hold back in their disclosure [*Bekundung*]. To hold back or withdraw [*An sich halten*] is, in Greek, *epokhé*. Hence we

may speak of *epochs* in the destiny of being [or the historical forms of givenness, in terms of which beings have been experienced]. (GA 14: 13/OTB 9)

In other words, we need to recognize that there are *epochs* in the hermeneutics of the clearing, *epochs* in the history of being, the different meanings of which unfold in a history formed by an interplay of concealment and unconcealment. We must bear in mind that "epoch" derives from the Greek word for restraint, limitation, withdrawing. This passage is also important, however, in laying out the *other* meaning of *Geschick*: not meaning destiny but rather the phenomenology of the clearing: its functioning as the field in which presencing and absencing take place: what Heidegger articulates in terms of "sending" and "sent": it is the clearing that is the *Geschick*, the dynamic structure of "sending" and "giving." And the countless different "sendings" and "givings"—what happens, or takes place, in the clearing, are accordingly called *Schickungen*.

Unfortunately, he continued in this lecture to resort to words (such as *schicken, Geschick, Schickungen, die Gabe,* and *das Geben* as well as phrases that are troublesome even in German but irremediably problematic in English, such as *Es gibt,* that encourage interpretations that run the risk of maintaining an ontotheological metaphysics). Thus, in explaining "epoch," he says:

> "Epoch" does not mean here a span of time in occurrence, but rather the fundamental [hermeneutical] characteristic of sending [*den Grundzug des Schickens*], the actual holding-back of itself [*An-sich-halten*] in favor of the discernability of the given [*zugunsten der Vernehmbarkeit der Gabe*], that is, of being with regard to the grounding of beings. (Ibid.)

But, strictly speaking, nothing is being "sent," there are no "sendings," there is no "sender," there is no "giving," and there is no "gift"—or would Heidegger really want to suggest the secret operation of some *theologoumenon*? I would like to suggest that the "giving," or "sending," and the "holding-back" should best be thought in terms of, or on the model of, a figure–ground *Gestalt*—completely free, therefore, of all metaphysical freight.

In its *Anwesen-lassen*, the clearing-*Geschick* proffers and itself withdraws—just as in the formation of the figure/ground *Gestalt* that occurs in the vitality of perception, in which the ground withdraws and recedes, while a figure emerges into salience, claiming most of the attention (GA 14: 46/OTB 37). In other words, the *epokhé* that makes sense of the history of being is the figure-ground *Gestalt* of perception writ large. This holding back—*Verhaltenheit*—is not only historically conditioned or determined; it is also determined by the hermeneutical nature of all human experience, such that, in perception, memory, imagination, and other modes of cognition, the *Gestalt* that forms is always structured by the withdrawing or holding back of the ground in favor of the figure that draws and holds our attention. This fundamental dynamic, constitutive of the clearing, is nicely described in "Time and Being," but in terms that can make the humble phenomenology difficult to recognize:

> A giving [*Ein Geben*] that gives only its gift [*seine Gabe*], but in the giving holds itself back and withdraws, such a giving we call sending [*das Schicken*]. According to the meaning of the giving that is to be thought in this way, being—that which is given [*das es gibt*]—is what is sent [*das Geschickte, sent by the clearing*]. Each of its [historically significant] transformations [*Wandlungen*] remains destined in this manner [*dergestalt geschickt*]. What is "historical" [*Das Geschichtliche*] in the history of being is determined by what is sent forth [i.e., given the possibility of presencing] bearing promising possibilities for the discernment and appropriation of our destiny [*aus dem Geschickhaften eines Schickens*]. (GA 14: 12–13/OTB 8–9)

Later in this lecture, Heidegger asks "who are we?" And he follows this with thoughts that provide some further clarity regarding the *Geben* and its *Gabe*—the giving and the given—words best understood without imagining anything celebratory. The words and phrasing are strange; but what he has to say essentially describes the phenomenology of every perceptual situation, even the most ordinary. Despite the strangeness, the text has a clarity that would otherwise be difficult to achieve:

> We remain cautious in our answer. For it might be that that which distinguishes the human as human [*den Menschen als Menschen*] is determined precisely by what we must think about here: we human beings, who are concerned with and approached by presence [*von Anwesenheit Angegangene*], and who, through being thus approached, are ourselves present in our own way for all present and absent beings. (GA 14: 16/OTB 12)

We human beings stand within the approach of presence, but in such a way that we receive, as a gift, the presencing, the "It gives" [*dies jedoch so, daß er das Anwesen, das "Es gibt," als Gabe empfängt*], by perceiving what appears in letting-presence [*indem er vernimmt, was im Anwesenlassen erscheint*]. If the human being were not the constant receiver of the gift [*der stete Empfänger der Gabe*] given by the "It-gives-presence" [*aus dem "Es gibt Anwesenheit"*], if that which is extended in the gift did not reach us, then not only would being remain concealed in the absence of this gift, not only closed off, but we would remain excluded from the expansive realm of that which is [*ausgeschlossen aus der Reichweite des "Es gibt Sein"*]. We would not be human (GA 14: 16–17/OTB 12).

It is necessary to recognize that, for Heidegger, the *Geschick*, understood as the way to the redeeming of historical destiny, can be found right here, in the more "humble" sense of *Geschick* that is understood as referring simply to what is "given," or "sent," in and through the clearings of perception. I suggest that it might be for this reason that Heidegger's invocations of "the gift" should not be dismissed as merely rhetorical embellishment. But are all the things we encounter in our world gifts? Are all events to be received as gifts? A troubling question.

†

In the summary of the seminar that followed Heidegger's 1962 lecture on "Time and Being," it is reported that the philosopher began by observing that neither being nor time *is*. And this brought him to the "It gives":

> The 'It gives' ['Es gibt'] was discussed first with regard to giving [*im Hinblick auf das Geben*], then with regard to the *It* that gives [*auf das Es, das gibt*]. And the *It* was interpreted as appropriation [*das Ereignis*]. More succinctly formulated: The lecture goes from *Being and Time* past what is peculiar to 'Time and Being' to the It that gives, and from this to appropriation [*von diesem zum Ereignis*]. (GA 14: 35/OTB 27)[15]

This is a movement in reflection that, I submit, unequivocally brings to the fore the phenomenology that accounts for the more down-to-earth sense of *Geschick*. Thus, just as Heidegger argued that *being* is to be thought phenomenologically "*aus dem Ereignis*" (GA 14: 29/OTB 40), so he might also have argued here, astutely, as later he actually did, that the *Geschick* (the *Schicken*, or the *Schickungen*) should likewise be thought phenomenologically —"*aus dem Ereignis*." And that, of course, returns us to *Da-sein* as the appropriated clearing. The point is that our appropriation—for "the role of human being in the opening out of the clearing for being" ("*die Rolle des Menschenwesens für die Lichtung des Seins*")—is *behind* the phenomenology of the *Es gibt*, the "sending" or "giving" by the clearing: behind it, not only in the sense of accounting for it, but also behind it in being typically neglected, even denied, both in everyday life and in the historical discourse of metaphysics: sending and withholding (GA 14: 36/OTB 28).

Being gives itself and withholds itself. "Oblivion [*Vergessenheit*]," says Heidegger, "essentially belongs to it" (GA 14: 37/OTB 29). But there is also a forgetfulness of being that is contingent, not intrinsic; and that is the habitual forgetfulness that Heidegger's work summons us to overcome. In recollecting our role in the clearing, Heidegger hopes to return us to ourselves. Because, in the course of that return, we can reappropriate the *Geschick* as that hidden *possibility* of destiny that comes to us, "given," or "sent," in and through the clearing, but needing interpretive insight and perseverance even for its recognition.

†

There is a surprising development in Heidegger's thinking to be found in the summary of this seminar. It recapitulates, and then develops, what was argued in (v) "The Principle of Identity":

> If the appropriation [*das Ereignis*] is not a new formation of being in the history of being [*nicht eine neue seinsgeschichtliche Prägung des Seins*], but instead [*umgekehrt*] being belongs [*gehört*] to the appropriating and is reabsorbed [*zurückgenommen*] in it (in whatever manner), then the history of being [*Seinsgeschichte*] is at an end [*zu Ende*] for thinking in terms of appropriation, that is, for the thinking which enters into the process of appropriation [*einkehrt in das Ereignis*]—in the sense that being, which lies in the sending [*das im Geschick beruht*], is no longer what is specifically and properly [*eigens*] to be thought. Thinking then stands in and before that [*Jenem*, i.e., the clearing] which has sent forth the various forms of epochal being [*die verschiedenen Gestalten des epochalen Seins zugeschickt hat*]. However, what as event of appropriation sends, or makes possible, namely the different forms of being [*das Schickende als das Ereignis*, that is, more precisely, *Da-sein*'s field of clearing, its *ereignete Lichtung*], is itself unhistorical [*ungeschichtlich*], or more precisely without destiny [*geschicklos*]. (GA 14: 49–50/OTB 40–41)

There are, in this textual passage, two decisively significant developments in Heidegger's thinking. First of all, *Geschick* is made to take on a second meaning: besides meaning "destiny," as it does at the end of the last sentence, it is now made to designate that—namely, "*das Geschick* as *das Schickende*"—which "sends," "gives," or "grants" (makes possible) the experiencing (meaningful presencing) of beings. And that refers us to the clearing, that is, *Da-sein* in its appropriated function as the clearing. Second, being, hence also the history of being and the *Geschick* (historical destiny) it might bear, are now to be reabsorbed, or taken back, into the process of appropriation by which we human beings find ourselves *dis-posed* to exist as the opening of clearings—as *Da-sein*. The history of being thus becomes the history of the clearing, the *Lichtungsgeschichte*, as Heidegger, writing about Hegel, says in "The Onto-Theo-Logical Conceptualization of Metaphysics"

(GA 11: 60/ID 51). And as such, the history becomes a narrative delineating, and making sense of, the various historical epochs, defined in relation to the historical conditions involved in shaping the time-space fields, that is, the clearings, within the dimensions of which the presencing of beings can take place. Hence too, it becomes a narrative disclosing the "logic"—the sense—operative in the historical unfolding of paradigms in ontology, following the beings themselves in regard to (a) what beings can appear, (b) in what ways they can appear, and (c) with what characteristics they can appear: in sum, what it means to be. Moreover, in this seminar, Heidegger invokes the process of appropriation and illuminates as never before the role of *Da-sein* in the *Geschick* constitutive of this history of being. *Geschick*, here, is an abbreviation for (1) the "sendings" that, in the givenness of their various *Schickungen*, or *Prägungen*, their various historical configurations, occur in and through the clearings and (2) the possibilities for redeeming the summons to destiny that are given—Heidegger likes to say "sent," *geschickt*—in and through the situations and events taking place in the clearings. But all this is "unhistorical" in the sense that it is not to be comprehended in terms of the one-dimensional, linear temporality that serves the purposes of history as commonly conceived and narrated.

†

viii. Seminar in Le Thor, 1969. By the late 1950s, Heidegger unequivocally believed that genuine historicality, hence the achievement of our essence, our "proper," or "appropriate" destiny as human beings, decisively depends on our appropriation, that is, our self-recognition, self-understanding, and the actualization of our *potential* as human beings: "*Das Schicken ist aus dem Ereignen*" (GA 15: 367/FS 61). Not the reverse, which would perhaps suggest the operation of an absolutely transcendent metaphysical agency—a certain metaphysical determinism. No, his dictum clearly favors the *Ereignung* as that which, appropriating human existence for clearings, would make the achievement of historical destiny possible. So we see that, in the years after the War and the Holocaust, Heidegger seems to have returned to the sanity of the phenomenological approach.

In this 1969 Seminar in Le Thor, the phenomenology is given further illumination. Here, finally, Heidegger is able to resolve his struggles with the conception of the history of being and its *Geschick* that he began to work out in the 1930s. Here, finally, it is given the most explicit, most unequivocal resolution, grounded in the phenomenology of appropriation, bringing out our role, our corresponding (*entsprechende*) responsibility, in the history of the meaning of being. He came around to the startling realization that, once we deeply and properly understand the phenomenology of the appropriation of human existence to *Da-sein*, and understand the clearing that opens in *Da-sein* as that which enables—"sends," "gives"—the presencing of beings, then there is no more need to invoke being; all the work that had been attributed to *Sein* could actually be handled by the phenomenology of presencing:

> When we emphasize the letting [*Lassen*] in letting-presence, then there is no more need for the word being. [*Wenn die Betonung lautet Anwesen lassen, ist sogar für den Namen Sein kein Raum mehr.*] (GA 15: 365/FS 60)

Consequently, "it is a matter here of understanding that the deepest meaning of being is letting [*Lassen*]. Letting the being be [*Das Seiende sein-lassen*]. This is the non-causal meaning of 'letting' in 'Time and Being'." This represents a momentous turn in Heidegger's thinking. With the recognition of the *Er-eignung*, taking a "step back" from metaphysics to the phenomenology of the *Es gibt* or the *Es läßt*, that is the clearing that *Da-sein* opens as "that which lets beings presence" (GA 15: 362–67/FS 58–61), his thinking was able to retrieve, in *Dasein*'s "*Ereignung*," *Da-sein*'s appropriation to the clearing, the *phenomenological origin* that was *hidden* behind the Greek's beginning (GA 15: 367/FS 61). Properly considered, there is actually no more need for thinking about "being" as such—"*sogar für den Namen 'Sein' kein Raum mehr*" (GA 15: 365/FS 60), because, in Heidegger's extremely condensed formulation, "being" simply concerns, or lies in, the *Geschick*, the time–space fields of the clearing as sending or giving, or making possible, the presencing of beings: "*Sein, das im Geschick beruht*" (GA 14:49–50/OTB 40–41). But destiny also concerns, or lies in, that sending or giving of the clearing. In Heidegger's sentence, "*Geschick*" does not in the first instance refer to destiny, but rather to a "sending" and to what is being "sent" in the "sending," or "*Geschick*," that is taking place in and through the clearing. But the interpretation of being is of course fundamental in the determination of destiny. Destiny is a possibility to be discerned in what is being sent or given. So, being *does* lie in destiny (*im Geschick beruht*): Heidegger is telling us that he remained deeply concerned about the destiny of being. However, insofar as "being" concerns the destiny-bearing sending or giving, what we need to concentrate on is, rather, the appropriated *clearing* that makes possible such "sending" or "giving" ("*Geschick*," or "*Schickung*," first of all, in that less lofty sense). And this insight, in turn, is what enabled Heidegger to venture a bold reinterpretation of the history of being—and the constellation of irremediably metaphysical notions it required—as cornerstone of his narrative in regard to the history of philosophy.

What "sends"—makes possible (*möglich*)—all the historical forms of the clearing, that is, all forms of "epochal being," is to be found in the historical conditions of the appropriation (*Ereignis*) of *Da-sein*'s existence. Heidegger describes the various historical formations (*Gestalten*) in which the world-clearings are "given" or "sent" (*gegeben, geschickt*) as "epochal" (withholding), not only because (a) in each epoch, the predominant meaning of being that constitutes that epoch's disclosure of being inherently conceals, or perhaps suppresses, other possible understandings, but also because (b) these unconcealments of being conceal, hence withhold, the *Geschick*, the *Es* that *gibt*, that "gives" or "sends" them: we can speculate, but we do not fully know, and cannot ever completely know, why it is that we find ourselves given a certain *Geschick*, a certain clearing, or world order, to live in. Or, phrased in another way, we do not fully know, cannot fully know, why it happens that we are living in the particular world-clearings of meaningfulness that we find ourselves living in, nor can we completely know how each one of these world-clearings emerges with its correspondingly distinctive ontological configurations, possibilities for being. Consequently, once one recognizes and understands *Da-sein*'s appropriation, entering into it, standing in, and before it, then *Sein*, which concerns the destiny-bearing *Geschick*, that is, the "sending" or "giving" of the clearing, is "no longer what is properly [*eigens*] to be thought." Finally, moreover, hardly a surprise, although a conclusion of the utmost significance:

> In the event of appropriation [*Ereignis*], the history of being [*Geschichte des Seins*] does not so much arrive at its end [*ihr Ende gelangt*], as that [at last] it now shows itself [in its truth, its use] *as* history of being. There is no epoch of events *inherently* bearing destiny [*Es gibt keine geschickliche Epoche des Ereignisses*]. Rather, what grants destiny is, conversely, what comes from our own process of appropriation [*Das Schicken ist aus dem Ereignen*]. (GA 15: 366–67/FS 61)

In reflecting on this text, we should remember, first of all, that, in "The Turn," Heidegger said: "We locate [*stellen*] history in the realm of what occurs [*in den Bereich des Geschehens*], instead of [properly] thinking history in accordance with its essential provenance [*Wesensherkunft*] in terms of destiny [*aus dem Geschick*]" (GA 79: 68–69/BF 65, QCT 38). So, in a genuine relation to history, history is to be understood in terms of, or from the perspective of, the *Geschick*—*aus dem Geschick*. But now, here, Heidegger wants the *Geschick*, and *Sein* itself, to be understood in terms of, or from the standpoint of, the *Ereignen*: in other words, "*aus dem Er-eignen*." And in this regard, we should notice that Heidegger says *Ereignen*, not *Ereignis*. I interpret this to be his way of emphasizing that what is involved is not an event but rather a process: the process, namely, in which we "enown" the essence of our existence as *Da-sein* and take guardian responsibility for the ontological dimensionality of the clearings we are. *Das Geschick*, in Heidegger's new sense of the word, refers to the coming-into-presence of what comes into presence—what is "sent" or "given"—in and through the clearings our existence makes by virtue of our appropriation. But thereby, the word also refers, in its common meaning, which is of course *destiny*, to what comes, what emerges, *from* our *interpretation* of the situations and events we are given (*geschickt*) to live in, and *from* what, in taking on our historical responsibility and using our freedom, we are able to make of those situations and events, redeeming our potential as human beings and redeeming the promise in the world we have made, so that, in building a truly humane world, we might become worthy of the "gift" we have been granted. Destiny depends entirely on what we make of all that we have been given.

In "The Ister," one of his river poems, Hölderlin says: "long have we sought the fitting."

> *lange haben*
> *Das Schickliche wir gesucht*[16]

It is a question of attempting with appropriate skillfulness—*Schicklichkeit*—to learn *das Schickliche* in seeing and hearing, learn a way of keeping the world we share with others open and welcoming, as befits our humanity. This is the meaning of Heidegger's thought that "*das Schicken ist aus dem Ereignen*" (GA 15: 366–67/FS 61). For a shamefully long time, ideologies of "destiny" have kept this meaning concealed, supporting colonialism, wars, and genocides.

†

As our destiny, the *Geschick* is an *Augenblicksstätte*, a possibility that emerges into view *at a particular moment in historical time* and *from out of our appropriation* in relation to the *Geschick* as (i.e., in the sense of) dispensation—as *Schickung*, what is granted and sent to us in and through the clearing. In the givenness of every clearing, every historical *Geschick*, there is implicit an existential calling, a persistent, *a priori* claim on the appropriation of our lives, both as individuals and as collectivities: an *Anruf*, an *Anspruch des Seins*. The *Geschick* is a twofold dispensation, a twofold *Gabe*, at once (a) a dispensation, a givenness (an *Es gibt*) that must ultimately be accepted as what we have been given, that is, as determining the historical character of the clearing itself, but also, thereby, as making possible certain modes of revealing, certain ways for things to be, certain formations of character in the presencing of what presences (*das Anwesen des Anwesenden, das Anwesen des Seienden*) and, correspondingly, excluding or concealing other modes, other formations; and yet also, (b) within that very dispensation, within the historical bounds of that very givenness, indeed precisely because of its exclusions and concealments, it is our given historical situation, our circumstances, our world, all that is happening at the present time within the ontological epoch of the *Ge-stell*—but viewed *from the promising standpoint of the Geschick as destiny*, as our projection of the future possibilities, perhaps still unrecognized, or still concealed, for appropriating and actualizing, *through the exercise of our freedom*, the ownmost, most essential meaningfulness of our historical existence in relation to being—what it means to be.

Whether this could ever be a project achieved for an entire epoch, an entire civilization, or even an entire nation, is, however, eminently questionable. But perhaps certain individuals might, in the creative conduct of their own lives, achieve something consequential in this regard, not only to some exceptional extent breaking free of the prevailing paradigm but even venturing the projection of a relation to being that adumbrates another epochal paradigm. But such destiny-bearing freedom is never a permanent achievement. It can vanish, or be vanquished, in a flash. Although we human beings are indeed free and able, in different ways and to different degrees, to influence and shape the different conditions and formations of being, there are always many other factors involved, factors such as geological events, climate, and genetics, over which, at least at the present time, we have at best very limited dominion. At the present time, we can only adapt to the givenness—the "sending"—of those factors. But even adaptation involves the exercising of freedom. There are many different ways of adapting to what we are given to cope with. And this freedom is well-served if the adaptation is undertaken in accordance with our powers of reason.

†

If, as Thomas Sheeehan has argued, Heidegger derived his technical term "*Ereignis*" from his translation of Aristotle's δύναμις as "*Eignung*," referring to a coming-into-it-own (a coming-*ad-proprium*, i.e., being appropriated by and unto its *telos*), then we need to recognize the connection between our "*Ereignung*" and the notion of "*Geschick*": not only the "*Geschick*" as destiny, but, more fundamentally, the "*Geschick*" as the clearing, that in and through which beings are "sent" into presence. I am arguing that Heidegger's ultimate thinking brings us to the position that the *Geschick* in both its senses (i.e., as referring to a "sending" or "giving" and as referring to destiny) is to be understood as "*aus dem Ereignen*." That appropriation makes both clearing and destiny always a question of our responsibility.

Heidegger's thought seems to be that it is inherent in the very nature of human existence—what I argue is a temporal, bodily carried *a priori*—that it claims and summons us to its fulfillment. This requires that we freely and resolutely take up and take over our having been appropriated (*ereignet*) as finite open clearing. But whether and how individuals might undertake this work is not at all predetermined. And that means that, while we can perhaps at least imagine what it might be like for some individuals occasionally to achieve their appropriation, it is difficult to believe that any *Volk*, any entire nation, civilization, or epoch could ever fully and forever achieve its *Geschick* in the sense of a historical destiny.

We find ourselves thrown into historically shaped situations—indeed a world—not entirely of our own making, but we can exercise such finite freedom as we have to make the world meet the needs and promise constitutive of that sense of humanity toward which, and with which, for thousands of years, Western civilization has painfully struggled. In the ontological *Geschick*, there is a certain ineluctable *givenness* to acknowledge and respond to. The *Geschick* is the historically formed world-clearing that we are *given*, or sent, such that, with whatever capabilities we mortals happen to carry into our thrownness, we are sent on our way, sent to thrive or to perish, sojourning in that world-clearing. However, bearing our "calling," our *Ereignung*, into the historical world, into the particular finite world we have been given (*geschickt*) to live in, we can always, in the exercise of our finite freedom, attempt to make that world our own, perhaps making it "erlichtet" according to our image, our idea, of the good.

The two senses of "*Geschick*," the common meaning and the singular phenomenological one that Heidegger wrests free from the word, thus work together—because both have a role in returning us to our appropriation, hence to our highest historical responsibility, our *Wächterschaft*, protecting, for the sake of the truth of beings, the ontological dimensionality of experience—that which he calls "being." Therein lies "the quiet force of the possible"—"*die stille Kraft des Mögliches*" (GA 2: 520/BT 446).

†

But how could we experience our world in its essential historicality so that it might *disclose* "the quiet force of the possible"? All of Heidegger's project of thought is implicit in this question.

However, Heidegger did not always think of the new, other beginning as a "quiet force." In fact, in his *Contributions to Philosophy*, he was tempted to suggest that it might require something more apocalyptic: "Only through great breakdowns and upheavals of beings" (GA 65: 241/CP 190). And he explained this vision, saying: "The essence [of *beyng*] cannot be exhibited like something present at hand (*vorhanden*); we must await its happening from out of the depth of its essential element [*Wesung*] as if we were preparing for a shock [*ein Stoß*]."[17] It is this kind of rhetoric that unfortunately encourages interpreting Heidegger's invocations of *Ereignis* as suggesting that the other beginning would inevitably happen in, and as, a supervenient apocalyptic event: a *Geschick* in that onto-theological, destiny-laden sense. Insofar as there really is this implication, we should, I think, unequivocally resist it. As I hope this chapter will have convincingly argued, a more temperate, more benign interpretation of *Ereignis*, *Geschick*, and thus "the other beginning," is feasible. And indeed, Heidegger's thinking, from the late forties on, shows us how, imagining a world of poetic building and dwelling, a world in which the fourfold gathers around all things, all beings.

†

If all the different paradigms of knowledge, truth, and reality that, epoch after epoch, have speculatively interpreted the history of being in the Western discourse of metaphysics from the time of their beginning in Greece, and that constitute, in Heidegger's synoptic narrative, a single, coherent, unified ontological regime, are to be overcome or surpassed in another future inception, inaugurating another historical succession, then Heidegger is suggesting that the event that would ignite this inception would again be an extraordinary, unforeseeable experience, another appropriating *event*, bringing forth a very different, presently unimaginable manifestation of being, irreducible to whatever it means to us now, that would set in motion the beginning of another regime of ontology, another paradigm of knowledge, truth, and reality. In this connection, Richard Polt insightfully comments:

> An inception is always infinitely unsettling—an abyssal ground (Abgrund). It literally takes place, or seizes time-space in founding a momentous site (*Augenblicksstätte*). In this way, the inception is the basis for a way of dealing with and representing beings; but it cannot itself be represented, reproduced, or explained, for it inevitably withdraws. We can, at best, experience the movement of its withdrawal, and in this way combat our oblivion of it. Normally, however, we have fallen into manipulating and representing beings—a tempting behavior that tries to compensate for our willing oblivion of the inception through a willful exploitation of resources.[18]

Needless to say, this exploitation can ultimately lead us only into the most desperate destitution.

†

As the ancient civilizations went through what we think of as "progress," and the modern world passed into, and through, technological, industrial, and economic revolutions and, too, the ensuing stages of social and political modernization, the technological, mechanistic cast of mind that made our modern world possible, a cast of mind functioning in terms of an instrumentalized, means-centered, quantitatively oriented rationality emerged, unrecognized, in the philosophical concepts that were used to translate the ancient philosophical words and their successors. As Heidegger has pointed out, in each of the moments of revolution that, from ancient times to our own time, have shaken the very foundations of the world and its mentality, these concepts have undergone the most profound recasting. In fact, even the Roman translations of the philosophical Greek words already recast their meaning, completely suppressing their originary poetic spirit, their metaphorics, their sublime dimensionality. The Roman world into which the Greek words were translated was a greatly different world, not at all like the Greek: it was truly a rationalized empire, unified by military force and sustained by local governments under the command of a centrally organized administration. Reading the Roman translations of Greek philosophy, Heidegger was convinced that immeasurably precious qualities and dimensions of meaning were lost. Lost, above all, was the Greek's sublime vision of the effulgence of being— φύσις. And the medieval world of Christianity, which to a considerable extent drew its metaphysics and ontology, its paradigm of knowledge, truth, and reality, from its conflicts and reconciliations with the Roman worldview as well as with an Aristotelian metaphysics read in the filtered light of early Christian experience, theologically transformed but still perpetuated the failure to recognize appropriately the ontological claim that speaks for the presencing of being itself. Subsequent epochs of concealment and unconcealment in the history of the hermeneutics of being—the Renaissance, the Baroque, the early modernity of the late sixteenth century, the industrial revolution beginning in the seventeenth century, the advanced modernity of the eighteenth-century Enlightenment, and finally our own much later modernity—continued this failure, in consequence of which the experience and sense of being as such continued to suffer, unnoticed, even greater reductionism, even greater suppression and concealment, eventually leaving the world to endure the conditions imposed by nihilism and its *Ge-stell*.

Moreover, instead of serving as a source of critique, a source of independent, critical thought, philosophical reflection had unwittingly become part of the problem, complicit in that nihilism, confirming and accepting developments in the lifeworld that mirrored or reflected its own "forgetfulness," its own negligence of that dimension of the experience of things—namely, their very being—that, according to the pre-Socratic philosophers, so intensely provoked and stirred them to gaze at the world and listen to its sounds and voices in wonder, enchantment, and awe. In today's world, that sublime early Greek experience of being amounts to nothing. As it is not something that can be objectified, grasped and validated in an operational concept, held in the grip of totalizing power, the mystery and wonder of being has been reduced to nothingness and the being of beings has been rendered bereft of meaning and value. But ironically, precisely in its nothingness, "being" represents the most absolute challenge to the domination and violence in all reification, all totalizing power. That, in fact, is its immeasurably fateful importance.

Hoping, no doubt, to defeat fatalism by giving our contemporary world some sense of an alternative, some sense of future-subjunctive possibility, and showing that a thoughtfully critical reading of the history of metaphysics suggests the possibility of a relation to being very different from the relation that prevails at present, Heidegger struggled to retrieve traces of what historical transmission (*Überlieferung*) had left buried, understanding the reception and taking over (*Übernahme*) of that transmission to offer an opportunity for liberation: release from the tyranny of what is, making it possible to bring to light the concealed treasures of what has been [*verborgene Schätze des Gewesenen*] (GA 10: 153/PR 102). Heidegger wanted us to understand "*Überlieferung*" as a transmission that *can be* ontologically liberating insofar as it breaks away from the procedures of historiography, for which the past is simply irretrievably past. Thus he took a "step back," first of all, from thinking about entities (*Seiende*) to thinking about being as such (*Sein selbst*), the phenomenology and hermeneutics of presencing; and secondly, he took a "step back," returning in thought to the ancient past of our Western civilization. The return to the past was not taken in nostalgia, in a futile and misguided longing for a return to the past. Nor were they attempts to repeat and reinstate the past—the Greek beginning. They were, on the contrary, his way of clearing an opening into the future of possibilities— his way of showing that what might seem inevitable is actually, as historical recollection can show, not so. If he could demonstrate that, in the past, relations to the presencing of being—thus, too, philosophical attitudes in regard to the meaning of being—have been *otherwise*, that would suggest that there might be a way out of the nihilism that prevails at present.

That way out, however, could not be by some further enactment of the will to power, because it is that very will to power which, for Heidegger, has played a major role in our nihilism—the reduction of being to

the subjectivity of meaning, anthropocentric power, and finally to nothingness. But, although recourse to our will to power cannot rescue us from this
plight, this destitution of spirit, Heidegger will ultimately leave unresolved
and open the possibility of an extraordinary future crisis, an emergency
leading us to force a break in the historical continuum and to prepare for
the emergence, from *within* the oppressive conditions of the present historical world, of another inception, or at least a profoundly different epoch, in
relation to the history of being.

Might it be possible for the being of beings to presence otherwise than
as either practical-pragmatic or deliberative-theoretical? Might we someday
find ourselves released from a presencing of beings that is, in Heidegger's
terminology, either (a) practical availability, that is, being ready-to-hand
(*Zuhandensein*), or else (b) the more contemplative, more detached, more
abstract modality, being present-at-hand (*Vorhandensein*)? It is of course
impossible for Heidegger to answer such a question; but his thinking
encourages us to imagine that possibility. That encouragement of our
poetic imagination, coming from the vision defining his philosophy of history, is what makes his meta-narrative reading of the history of philosophy
so important—and so timely.

†

Reflecting, in his *Überlegungen XII–XV* (1939–1941) on the question of another inception for both philosophical thought and our world,
Heidegger wrote down this thought: "In the first inception, being comes
into the essentiality of its presence [*west*] as emergence [*Aufgang*] (*Physis*);
in the other inception, however, being would come into the essentiality of its presence as appropriation [*Ereignis*]. Stated succinctly: '*Aufgang,
Machenschaft, und Ereignis sind die Geschichte des Seins*' (*Überlegungen XII–XV*,
GA 96: 157). In other words, the essence of the first inception is the emergence of being as *physis*; after that time of origination come various epochs
exhibiting the ways in which the being of beings has been experienced and
understood, culminating in an epoch determined by the total technologization of our contemporary world, in which being is increasingly reduced
to total reification. Consequently, if there is ever to be another inception,
it would have to emerge from a *third* phase in the history of being: the
process of our awakening and appropriation. This is not likely to happen
without geo political conflicts and violent struggles for the political control
of capitalism.

For Heidegger, the possibility of another inception within philosophical thought depends on a process of recollection (*Erinnerung*) that would
pass through unfolding epochs in the history of philosophy in order to

retrieve, as originary, the phenomenological *ground* of the very possibility of the beginning. It is in this sense that Heidegger's history of philosophy is not only oriented by a philosophy of history but is critically thought out *for the sake of* recovering the *Er-eignung*, our destined appropriation, the *phenomenological* origin that philosophy—metaphysics in particular—has for too long buried in forgetfulness. And it is only with the recovery of our *Er-eignung* that another history—another beginning and another end—would become possible.

As regards the transformation of the lifeworld outside philosophical thought, Heidegger's project assumes that, if there were ever to be another inception, a different ontological paradigm no longer operative within the historical regime of a way of life that leads us ever deeper into nihilism, then it would depend on preparations involving the appropriation and transformation of our perceptual life, which is at present under the sway of the *Ge-stell*. The beginning of that "other beginning" is the *Ereignung*, which claims us for our self-recognition and enownment as *Da-sein*, the "hearth" (*Herd-Stätte*) of a recollection in which we finally recognize and understand the nature of our appropriation—and its corresponding response ability. "What is to be recollected," Heidegger says, "is nothing past [*kein Vergangenes*]; instead it is the essential occurrence of what is still coming [*das Wesende des Kommens*]—being itself in its truth [*das Sein selbst in seiner Wahrheit*]" (GA 71: 57, 222/E 46, 190). But in this "still coming," there is a relation that does essentially involve the past: a belonging to what is still summoning us, the potential from a past that was given, but still, even today, has not yet been fully recognized—and received: *das Gewesene*.

In *The Event* (1941–1942), Heidegger argues that the phenomenology of the appropriation of *Dasein* can be retrieved from what lies hidden, implicit in the Greek inception: by "entering into our appropriation, it is possible, he believed, to overcome "the concealed ineffability of the first beginning" (GA 71: 58/E 55). Getting at this appropriation of *Da-sein* is, he says, a hermeneutical work of memory, recollection, delving into the first beginning, that is, the beginning in pre-Socratic thought, in order to retrieve from within the textual indications of that experience its immanent potential as anticipation of the other beginning: "onto-historical thinking is recollection going into the first inception as the way into the other": "*Das seynsgeschichtliches Denken ist Erinnerung in den ersten Anfang als in den anderen.*"[19] Moreover, only by retrieving the appropriation implicit but unrecognized in the thinking that inaugurated the Greek beginning can the truly originary moment in that first inception be taken up as preparatory for the originating of the "other" beginning: "*In der Vorsicht des vorbereitenden anfänglichen Denkens kann aber der anfangende Anfang erst nur der 'andere' Anfang zum ersten genannt werden.*"[20] In other words, there is an origin for the inception even "earlier" than the Greek; it abides, however, not in the "externality" of history, but in our appropriation, that is to say, in the phenomenology of the disposition that, as an *a priori* assignment given by nature to each individual, bears the *Ereignung*—claim of appropriation—that calls us to enown and mindfully enact *Da-sein*. This "other beginning," projection of a vision, a hope, originating in the phenomenology of an *Ereignung* unrecognized in the early Greek experience yet immanent within it and awaiting the time of its recognition, recollection, and retrieval, already stirs, as Heidegger would eventually be able to tell us, in the *a priori* nature of the *Er-eignung* of *Dasein*, hidden in the very depths of the soul. In our awakening to this process of appropriation, history would finally come alive; and the past, liberated from the serial order of time we impose, would become a creative source of meaning for our lives.

†

In "The Turning" (1946), Heidegger invokes the lightning-like glance of being—the "*Blick des Seins*" (GA 11: 120–24/QTC 45–49, BF 69–73). Is this anthropomorphism? Yes. It is interpreting the *Geschick des Seins* in a way that is intended to remind us of our *Ereignung*, our appropriation to ontological responsibility. Is it anthropocentrism? No! Absolutely not! It is, on the contrary, radically decentering. And it is, of course, metaphoric. There is, after all, no such creature as being; being has no eyes to see with. The grammar of "*des Seins*" should not mislead us into positing being as a metaphysical subject, the agency behind the looking: those two words function more like an adjective, evoking an ontologically attuned way of seeing. Designed to make us reflect critically on our own ways of seeing, Heidegger's prosopopoeia sets up an analogy that challenges us to make our seeing into an ontological organ, corresponding to the way that we might imagine how being itself would see—if, defying common sense, its logic, its grammar, it were to be a human character capable of seeing. It is thus merely a rhetorical figure intended to urge us to bear in mind, when we are looking and seeing, that we should not neglect the ontological dimension of things, in the phenomenology of which *Mensch* and *Sein* belong inseparably together—in our guardianship. His metaphorical figure is also a strategy for bringing up to date the Heraclitean notion of the *homologein*, a *correspondence* requiring that we abandon our habitual, ontologically forgetful way of listening and learn the hearkening informed by ontological understanding that Heraclitus is recommending.

†

In one of his fictional *Conversations on a Country Path about Thinking* (1946), Heidegger addressed the question of our *waiting* for the coming of another inception—or at least another epoch in the meaning of being:

> If you consider that in *Logos*, as the gathering toward the originally all-unifying One, something like vigilant attentiveness [*Achtsamkeit*] prevails [*waltet*], and you begin to ask yourself whether such attentiveness is not in fact the same as the sustained waiting [*stete Warten*] for that which we named the pure coming [*das reine Kommen*], then perhaps one day you will suspect [*ahnen*] that, even in the earlier conception [*Wesensbestimmung*], the essence of the human as the being who is capable of waiting [*als das Wartende*] was experienced [*erfahren wird*]. (GA 77: 225/CPC 146)

This waiting for what might come, however, is not passive, not lazy, not doing nothing; nor can it be an attempt to force and impose that event by acts of will. The "waiting" in question, the "waiting" at stake, must be a composed vigilance of the spirit, a preparation in mindfulness, open to seeing, listening, learning, in which, individually and together, we work on ourselves, steadfastly and quietly—what Plato named *epimeleia tes psyches*. This is the *Er-eignung*, caring for what is fundamental and yet unfulfilled in our historical existence. It is a waiting that is not waiting. It is a waiting with steadfast forbearance.[21]

It is significant that, as early as *Mindfulness* (1938–1939), Heidegger was already arguing that "the process of appropriation [*Er-eignung*] 'occurs', and truly [*wesenhaft*] becomes *history*, when it is the grounding of the clearing in the *Da-sein* of man" (GA 66: 308/M 274). This point is made even more forcefully at a later point in this text: "*Da-sein* is the historical ground of the clearing of beyng—a ground that occurs [*er-eignet*] through our appropriation [*Er-eignis*]" (GA 66: 328/M 291). It is in this context that Heidegger can assert that it is when appropriation, that is, the claim on the role and responsibility of the human being in making and maintaining the conditions necessary for the presencing of beings, is finally recognized and understood that there is for the first time the beginning of an *authentic* relation to history—hence to our role in the originating of being in history. And it is by virtue of that appropriation (*Er-eignung*) and responsibility that history can become "originary history"—"*ursprüngliche Geschichte*," history still capable, springlike, of generating an upsurge of new formations, new *Gestalten*, new *Schickungen*—maybe even another epoch, or another inception—in regard to the meaning of being in our lives (GA 65: 32/CP 27–28).

Heidegger consequently emphasizes that the ontological perspective inherently calls into question our readiness or willingness to be *appropriately responsive* in our perceptivity. What we behold or attend to in hearing is always a claim on our responsibility, a claim on the exercise of our freedom. Thus, contrary to what some readers have believed, misreading his invocations of destiny, Heidegger not only rejected fatalism; he consistently sought to indicate "*Denkwege,*" paths that thought might take by free resolve, confronting the nihilism that increasingly rules our world, taking possession, now, and ever more surreptitiously, subtly disguised in the very language of spirit.

What the *Geschick* means in its phenomenological, more fundamental sense is simply our *facticity*, the givenness of what we are given (*geschickt*) to experience in our shared world; and what, in this regard, its givenness demands of us is our *Wächterschaft*, our guardianship, our cosmopolitan responsibility as human beings to protect and take care of the *ontological dimension* of the clearing, the ontological dimension of the facticity we are *given (geschickt)*, the situations in which we find ourselves thrown. And it would be in the *Schicken,* in what is given in that dimension of things, that we, in virtue of our humanity, might find the hidden *Denkweg* to our proper historical *Geschick* in the more common sense of destiny. In our time, I suggest, what summons us first and foremost in the way of our destiny is the task of protecting and maintaining, against the imposition of totality, the openness of the clearing to the dimension of concealment, the dimension of our world in which all that is withdrawn from presence abides.

†

Despite its problems, Heidegger's meta-narrative, his so-called "history of being," is guided by the light from a weak ray of hope, keeping us alert, for the sake of another possible inception, to hints of alterity, fragments and shards in historical events and situations that question and challenge the established paradigm of being, shattering the tyranny of our grammar and granting us a glimpse, perhaps, of being otherwise: being that is neither *Zuhandsein* nor *Vorhansdensein*. In "Imagining History," Tilottama Rajan nicely condenses what is at stake, not only in Heidegger's philosophy of history, with its distinctive ontological concerns, but also in the projects of other philosophical minds equally inspired by the hope of ending the old historical order and making way for a new beginning:

> At issue . . . is history as our own unassimilable alterity, our difference
> from the directions in which "history" is pushing us . . . a different

conception of history—one where historical thinking is the dimension
in which thought becomes responsible to what is other, lost, uncon-
scious, or potential, yet to be.[22]

What future might we then venture to hope for? In his introduction to the
First Book of *The Ages of the World* (the 1815 version), Friedrich Schelling
expressed his hopes for a glorious future time in which "there would no
longer be a distinction between the world of thought and the world of
actuality."[23] But we of today, he says, are without any compelling vision
that would enable us to gather into a unified, comprehensive, systematic
narrative, as the ancient seers once attempted, "what was, what is, and what
will be." The time of such a transition, or revolution, has not yet come:
"It is still a time of struggle. . . . We cannot be narrators, only explorers."

†

On the last page of "Overcoming Metaphysics," we see Heidegger
situating his critique of metaphysics in the context of his philosophy of history, connecting this overcoming or sublation (*Überwindung* or *Verwindung*)
to an argument that suggests, or hints at, a narrative presenting the perspective of redemption:

> No transformation [*Kein Wandel*] comes without anticipatory escort
> [*vorausweisendes Geleit*]. But how does such escort come near unless there
> is an appropriation that opens and lights the way [*wenn nicht das Ereignis
> sich lichtet*] and, calling, needing, envisions [*er-äugnet*] human being, that
> is, glimpses [*er-blickt*] the human and, in that glimpse [*im Er-blicken*],
> brings mortals to the path of genuine thinking, poetizing building. (GA
> 7: 98/EP 110)

What transformation, redeeming our humanity, does Heidegger have in
mind? I suggest that the nearest he comes to envisioning what that transformation involves is to be found in the texts of his later years, in which
he describes a world lived in keeping with the idea of the fourfold—*das
Geviert*, gathering together earth and sky, mortals and their "gods," the
embodiments of our ideals, principles, and values. In representing our
relation to the realm of nature (earth and sky), the perspective of this
vision is appealing; but it is strikingly silent regarding how mortals would
be gathered together in their *Mitsein*. And it tells us nothing about the
"anticipatory escort" as such—his figure, I take it, for the perspective of the
messianic—although, crucially and decisively, it makes the "escort" depend
on the event of our appropriation, hence on our assumption of responsibility. This suggests, I think, that what Heidegger is calling "the anticipatory

escort" need not be interpreted as designating some singularly charismatic human being; rather, it might better be taken to refer to the existence of all the spiritually edifying *teachings* guiding us toward the redeeming of our moral condition and the world through which we pass.

On the last page of his *Minima Moralia*, in an aphorism no doubt intended to bear an eschatological meaning, Theodor Adorno acknowledges that, inspiring and guiding his relentlessly critical observations and reflections on the character of ethical life in today's world, there is a certain philosophy of history, a narrative concerned with the redemption of our world:

> The only philosophy which can responsibly be practised in the face of despair is the attempt to contemplate all things as they would present themselves from the standpoint of redemption [*vom Standpunkt der Erlö-sung*]. Knowledge has no light [*Erkenntnis hat kein Licht*] but that shed on the world by redemption. . . . Perspectives must be constructed that displace and estrange [*versetzt, verfremdet*] the world, revealing it to be, with its rifts and crevices [*Risse und Schründe offenbart*], as indigent and distorted as it will appear one day in the messianic light [*im messianischen Lichte*]. To gain such perspectives without velleity or violence [*ohne Willkür und Gewalt*], entirely from felt contact [*aus der Fühlung*] with its objects—this alone is the task of thought.[24]

However, he adds, warning against finding utopian wish-fulfillment in idealism:

> The more passionately [*Je leidenschaftlicher*] thought denies [*abdichtet*] its conditionality for the sake of the unconditional, the more unconsciously, and so calamitously, it is delivered up to the world. It must even comprehend its own impossibility only for the sake of the possible. But beside the demand thus placed on thought, the question of the reality or unreality of redemption hardly matters [*fast gleichgültig*]. (Ibid.)

What matters, in the end—*zum Ende*—is whether, and how, this fictional standpoint of redemption can enable us to undertake the needed transformation of our lifeworld. There is, in this regard, an affinity with Heidegger's vision of the fourfold.

In giving thought to history from this standpoint, both philosophers, each of course in his own way, find it useful to invoke the fiction of the messianic. According to Jewish theology, the Messiah—or, as I would prefer to say, messianicity—has not yet come. We are awaiting "his" arriving. We are living in a time of anticipation and hope. According to Christian theology, the Messiah already came, embodied in Jesus Christ. But, as Christian history acknowledges, Christ was not recognized. He was crucified, having failed to transform and redeem the world—although he left with us a sublime teaching and a presence that bears extraordinary redemptive power.

In *Parables and Paradoxes*, a collection of writings, Franz Kafka opined that, as he put it: "The Messiah will come only when he is no longer necessary; he will come only on the day after his arrival; he will come, not on the last day, but on the day after."[25] What might this ironic and paradoxical claim be telling us? Essential to the coming of the Messiah is his recognizability. Without that recognition, it is as if he had not come at all. But recognition of the messianic is possible only among those who have already undertaken redeeming transformation and are already living in the light of messianicity. Thus, ironically, the Messiah will come only when no longer necessary. And he will be recognized as *having already* come only on the day *after* the messianic transformation of the world. The point is that redemption is entirely up to us. However, with every achievement, the day of redemption withdraws farther into the distant future, because, as the poet Dante understood, the more we learn on the path of redemption, the more we become sensitively attuned, recognizing in ourselves and in our world forms of cruelty, violence, and inhumanity that still require transformation.[26]

Thus, I would like to add, grateful for Benjamin's retrieval of Kafka: There is "an infinite amount of hope—but not for us."[27] It is in this hope, however, that redemption lies. But this is a hope that cannot be just for ourselves. It must be a hope redeeming our humanity: hope, therefore, for the sake of the other.

Heidegger's words are fitting here: "*Das Schicken ist aus dem Ereignen.*" What is destined is what emerges from the process of our appropriation— hence, it can come only from our assumption of responsibility, a responsibility that needs to be at work even in our most commonplace perception, as our ability to be appropriately receptive and responsive to the ontological dimensionality of what is given. *As if* the given were always—even when beyond our comprehension—a gift.

†

In "Dawn of Being,"[28] one of Heidegger's *Thought-Poems* (*Gedachtes*, GA 81), there is an illuminating recapitulation of his history of being, a narrative survey that takes us on a journey in thought that goes from the momentous event in which the Greek philosophers' experience of being began, thereby setting in motion the discourse of metaphysics, traversing epochs of history to arrive in our own time, finding us not only undergoing a nihilistic estrangement from being—that is to say, from the claim that being makes on our response-ability in recognizing, understanding, enowning, and enacting our appropriation—but yet also exposed to bright, enlightening possibilities, events in which a new sense of being might emerge, exceeding our prevailing understanding and bearing the promise of another beginning, another destiny. I offer here not a translation, but rather an interpretive paraphrase, calling attention to the role of perception. This paraphrase is in prose form but with the structure of Heidegger's lines of versification approximated. I give the last words to Heidegger, who, for the sake of another *Geschick*, invokes here the sublime poesy manifest in "the dawn of being":

"The Dawn of Being"

While called to being, hidden from the very first, | then released into the hesitant, stammering beginning | by an event of appropriation, a claim | long unrecognized by themselves, | and hidden from within their very freedom, | the ancient Greeks, even when finally almost able to contemplate, daringly, | the clearing, with its concealed dispossession in appropriation, | find themselves abandoned to their solitary destiny: | freed in their ascent into the metaphysical, yet exceptionally shy | in the harvesting, the gathering of all light | in the invisible providence of dispensation, | thus first to be enlightened by an appearance of light. | Glimpsed in that light, the gathering that takes place in perceiving | was able to grow into looking | for the sake of truly seeing, whereby it became possible | to choose the most faithful meaning for the eye; | and ever since, the world appears as it does, | a world construed from the viewpoint of visual presence: it is.

So the future history of being was decided, | coming into appearance | shining unnoticed among unreflected lights. | According to the measure of shining self-showing, | cognition becomes genuine perception, | a looking that gives entitlement to appearance, | setting it forth in the keeping | of steadfast presence, | having forgotten its origins | in the thinking of the early poetry | hidden in the poesy of beyng; | so the future itself in its own truth | has henceforth been veiled, a denial of itself, | close only in an estranged intimacy, | surprising distances in nameless futile beckonings, | in its own separation from awareness, | returning back to a once pure deferred dispossession. | Perhaps this light, even though not | the illumination of the poetics | of appropriation, | will become the dawn | still hidden—what is to be cared for | in that freedom, | which is not yet the openness that is the redeeming truth | of being (see "The Enowning Claim).

In the context of his major work on Nietzsche, Heidegger said: "Being is the promise of itself" (*Sein ist das Versprechen seiner Selbst*) (GA 6.2: 362–69/N4: 226).

# NOTES

1. Ralph Waldo Emerson, "The Method of Nature," Essays and Lectures, ed. Joel Port (New York: Library of America, 1983), 115.

2. Gershom Scholem, Briefe (München: Beck Verlag, 1994), vol. I, 471ff. My translation.

3. Walter Benjamin, "Über den Begriff der Geschichte," Gesammelte Schriften (Frankfurt am Main: Suhrkamp, 1974, 1991), vol. I.2, 695; "Theses on the Philosophy of History," Illuminations, trans. Harry Zohn (New York: Schocken, 1969), My translation.

4. Also see GA 14:20/OTB 15.

5. See Theodor W. Adorno and Max Horkheimer, The Dialectic of Enlightenment, trans. Edmund Jephcott (Stanford, CA: Stanford University Press, 2002).

6. See Herbert Marcuse, One-Dimensional Man (Boston: Beacon Press,) and Theodor W. Adorno, Negative Dialectics, trans. E. B. Ashton (New York: Continuum, 1973).

7. The interview with Der Spiegel took place on September 23, 1966, and was published by the magazine on May 31, 1976. See "Nur noch ein Gott kann uns retten," Der Spiegel, Nr. 23 (Mai, 1976): 193–219; Reden und andere Zeugnisse eines Lebensweges, 1910–1976, GA 16: 671. Trans. by W. Richardson as "Only a God Can Save Us" in Thomas Sheehan, ed., Heidegger: The Man and the Thinker (1981), 45–67.

8. See Rainer Maria Rilke, The Notebooks of Malte Laurids Brigge: "I am learning to see. I don't know why it is, but everything penetrates more deeply into me and does not stop at the place where, until now, it always used to finish. I have an inner self of which I was ignorant." (New York: W. W. Norton, 1949), 14–15. Also, see The Letters of Rainer Maria Rilke 1910–1926, ed. and trans. Jane B. Greene and M. D. Herter Norton (New York: W. W. Norton, 1947), 139–40, where, in a letter to Princess Maria von Thurn and Taxis-Hohenlohe (August 1915), the poet writes of imagining human eyes more seeing, ears more receptive, and the other senses too more sensitive. And see W. G. Sebald, "Aufzeichnungen aus Korsica," second version, in Ulrich von Bülow, Heike Gfrereis, and Ellen Strittmatter, ed., Wandernde Schatten. W. G. Sebalds Unterwelt (Marbach am Neckar: Marbacher Katalog, Literaturmuseum der Moderne, Deutsche Schillergesellschaft, 2008), 208. Almost certainly writing with Rilke in mind, Sebald observes, with characteristic skepticism, irony, and despair: "The eye learns to look away from that the sight of which causes it pain; indeed, perhaps it learns to love the world even in its becoming ever more graphite-gray, just as the families of miners have learned to love their familiar valleys, where there is nothing but coal, stone and dust, and where their children merrily go sledding on the cinder waste dumps." Similarly, the ear learns to tune out whatever is disagreeable, whatever importunes and interrupts and distracts—or makes an unwelcome claim on our time, our attention, our moral feelings, our life.

9. See especially, in this regard, some recent works by Heidegger scholars. Since extensive bibliographies are already available, I shall mention here (in no particular order) only a few of the books that have been particularly useful in their bearing on my thinking: Richard Polt, *The Emergency of Being: On Heidegger's "Contributions to Philosophy"* (Ithaca, NY: Cornell University Press, 2006); Daniel O. Dahlstrom, *Heidegger's Concept of Truth* (Cambridge: Cambridge University Press, 2000); Gregory Fried, *Heidegger's Polemos: From Being to Politics* (New Haven, CT: Yale University Press, 2000); David Wood, *Thinking after Heidegger* (Cambridge: Polity, 2002); Richard Capobianco, *Engaging Heidegger* (Toronto: University of Toronto Press, 2010); Charles Scott, Susan Schoenbohm, Daniela Vallega-Neu, and Alejandro Vallega, eds., *Companion to Heidegger's "Contributions to Philosophy"* (Bloomington: Indiana University Press, 2001); Hubert Dreyfus and Mark Wrathall, eds., *A Companion to Heidegger* (Oxford: Blackwell, 2005); David F. Krell, *Architecture: Ecstasies of Space, Time, and the Human Body* (Albany: State University of New York Press, 1997), *Daimon Life: Heidegger and Life-Philosophy* (Bloomington: Indiana University Press, 1992), *Intimations of Mortality: Time, Truth, and Finitude in Heidegger's Thinking of Being* (University Park: Pennsylvania State University, 1986), *Of Memory, Reminiscence, and Writing: On the Verge* (Bloomington: Indiana University Press, 1990), and *The Tragic Absolute: German Idealism and the Languishing of God* (Bloomington: Indiana University Press, 2005); Dennis J. Schmidt, *On Germans and Other Greeks: Tragedy and Ethical Life* (Bloomington: Indiana University Press, 2001) and *Ubiquity of the Finite: Hegel, Heidegger, and the Entitlements of Philosophy* (Cambridge, MA: MIT Press, 1988); Jean-Luc Marion, *Reduction and Givenness: Investigations of Husserl, Heidegger, and Phenomenology*, trans. Thomas A. Carlson (Evanston, IL: Northwestern University Press, 1998) and *In Excess: Studies of Saturated Phenomena*, trans. Robyn Horner and Vincent Berraud (New York: Fordham University Press, 2002); and of course John Sallis, *Delimitations: Phenomenology and the End of Metaphysics* (Bloomington: Indiana University Press, 1986); *Echoes: After Heidegger* (Bloomington: Indiana University Press, 1990); *Force of Imagination: The Sense of the Elemental* (Bloomington: Indiana University Press, 2000); and *Logic of Imagination: The Expanse of the Elemental* (Bloomington: Indiana University Press, 2012).

10. See "Zur Seinsfrage" (1955), GA 9: 411–16; "On the Question of Being," PM, 311–14. "Erinnerung an der Metaphysik" (1941) is to be found in GA 6.2: 481–90/EP 75–83 and "Überwindung der Metaphysik" (1936–37) in GA 7: 68–98/ EP 84–110.

11. Martin Heidegger, *Anmerkungen I–IV (Schwarze Hefte 1942–1948)*, GA 97: 382. (More precisely, see *Anmerkung* IV, 1947–1948).

12. Heidegger, *Überlegungen VII–XII (Schwarze Hefte, 1938–1939)*, GA 95: 408.

13. See Heidegger, *Anmerkungen I–IV (Schwarze Hefte)*, GA 97: 382. (See *Anmerkung* IV, 1947–1948).

14. See "Being at the Beginning: Heidegger's Interpretation of Heraclitus," the admirable essay by Daniel Dahlstrom, in Dahlstrom, ed., *Interpreting Heidegger: Critical Essays* (Cambridge: Cambridge University Press, 2011), 135–55.

15. And see *Zum Ereignis-Denken*, GA 73, 1: 642: "*das Dasein ist das je vereinzelte 'es', das gibt; das ermöglicht und ist das 'es gibt.'*"

16. Friedrich Hölderlin, "Der Ister," *Sämtliche Werke* (Berlin and Darmstadt: Der Tempel Verlag, 1962), 347.

17. Regarding "dispositions," and, in particular, the one he calls "basic," see GA 65: 21–23, 395–96/CP 18–20, 313–14. And see also GA: 71: 215–23/E 185–92. According to Heidegger's account, the "basic dispositions" constitutive of the history of being are: at first, wonder, then astonishment, but then shock (at the realization of what is required of us for the transition to another beginning), and finally, thankfulness for being granted the possibility of another beginning. As Walter Benjamin pointed out, historical shock was a major theme in the nineteenth-century poetry of Charles Baudelaire. Benjamin's historical narrative, like Heidegger's, is guided by a distinctively original *philosophy* of history. And, like Heidegger, Benjamin regarded his historical narrative as a mode of recollection capable of bearing promising possibilities for the "redemption" of humanity.

18. See Richard Polt, "Traumatic Ontology," forthcoming in *Being Shaken: Ontology and the Event*, ed. Michael Marder and Santiago Zabala (New York: Palgrave Macmillan, 2014).

19. *Über den Anfang*, GA 70: 93–96, 105, 140ff. But see especially op. cit., 141.

20. *Über den Anfang*, GA 70: 19.

21. On the question of waiting, see my discussion of Siegfried Kracauer in *Gestures of Ethical Life: Reading Hölderlin's Question of Measure after Heidegger* (Stanford, CA: Stanford University Press, 2005), 169–75.

22. Tilottama Rajan, "Imagining History," *PMLA* 118, no. 3 (2003): 428, 433.

23. Friedrich W. J. Schelling, *Die Weltalter, Schellings Sämtliche Werke*, ed. Karl Friedrich August Schelling (Stuttgart-Augsburg: J. G. Cotta, 1861), vol. VIII, 206; *The Ages of the World*, trans. Jason M. Wirth (New York: SUNY Press, 2000), xl.

24. Theodor W. Adorno, *Minima Moralia: Reflexionen aus dem beschädigten Leben* (Frankfurt am Main: Suhrkamp Verlag, 1951, 1969), 333–34; *Minima Moralia: Reflections from Damaged Life*, trans. E. F. N. Jephcott (London and New York: NLB, 1974; Verso,1978), 247.

25. *Franz Kafka: Parables and Paradoxes*, ed. Nahum Glatzer, trans. Clement Greenberg (New York: Schocken, 1946), 80ff.

26. Dante, *The Inferno*. Trans. Robert Hollander and Jane Hollander (New York: Doubleday Random House, 2000), Canto VI: 107–108, 110: "*quanto la cosa è più perfetta, | più senta il bene, e così la doglienza*": "the more perfect a thing becomes, the more it is cognizant of the good, and for precisely that reason, it suffers [in its absence]." My paraphrase.

27. See Walter Benjamin, "Franz Kafka: Zur zehnten Wiederkehr seines Todestages," *Gesammelte Schriften*, II. 2, 414; "Franz Kafka: On the Tenth Anniversary of His Death," *Illuminations*, trans. Harry Zohn (New York: Schocken, 1969), 116.

28. See "Die Frühe des Seyns," in *Gedachtes*, GA 81: 68–69. Despite the challenge, an admirable English translation—by Eoghan Walls—of a selection of the *Gedachtes* is forthcoming. I have seen the translation and have drawn rich understanding from it, but my paraphrase suggests an interpretation that diverges from his translation in a number of ways.

# INDEX

# ABOUT THE AUTHOR

**David Kleinberg-Levin** is professor emeritus in the Department of Philosophy at Northwestern University. He holds a bachelor's degree from Harvard and a PhD from Columbia University. He is the author of *The Body's Recollection of Being* (1985), *The Opening of Vision* (1988), *The Listening Self* (1989), *The Philosopher's Gaze* (1999), *Gestures of Ethical Life: Reading Hölderlin's Question of Measure After Heidegger* (2005), *Before the Voice of Reason: Echoes of Responsibility in Merleau-Ponty's Ecology and Levinas's Ethics* (2008), *Redeeming Words and the Promise of Happiness: A Critical Theory Approach to Wallace Stevens and Vladimir Nabokov* (2012), *Redeeming Words: Language and the Promise of Happiness in the Stories of Döblin and Sebald* (2013), and *Beckett's Words: The Promise of Happiness in a Time of Mourning* (2015).